# ANYTHING FOR A VOTE

# ANYTHING
## FOR A
# VOTE

DIRTY TRICKS, CHEAP SHOTS, AND
OCTOBER SURPRISES IN
U.S. PRESIDENTIAL CAMPAIGNS

## JOSEPH CUMMINS

QUIRK BOOKS
PHILADELPHIA

Library of Congress Cataloging in Publication Number: 2015941308
ISBN: 978-1-59474-832-5

Printed in the United States of America
Typeset in Brothers, Knockout and Baskerville
Cover designed by Doogie Horner and Timothy O'Donnell
Interior designed by Timothy O'Donnell
Illustrations by Eugene Smith
Cover photos courtesy of AP Images
Production management by John J. McGurk

Quirk Books
215 Church Street
Philadelphia, PA 19106
quirkbooks.com

10   9   8   7   6   5   4   3   2

**FOR DEDE AND CARSON,
WHO GET MY VOTE EVERY TIME**

# CONTENTS

# INTRODUCTION

*"What do men gain by elective governments, if fools and knaves
have the same chance to obtain the highest office, as honest men?"*
—NOAH WEBSTER TO THOMAS JEFFERSON, 1801

The idea for this book was born shortly after the 2004 presidential election. In that contentious contest, Democratic candidate and war hero John Kerry was vilified as a coward by an organization called the Swift Boat Veterans for Truth, while incumbent president George W. Bush was rumored to be such a dunce that he had to be wired to a transmitter to participate in a public debate.

During election postmortems, I listened as pundits moaned about how sleazy the campaign had become, how candidates had stooped to new lows of dirty tricks and polarizing discourse. Yet it seemed that I'd heard this same tune played after every presidential contest I'd lived through. So I asked myself, are things really getting worse? Have presidential campaigns truly turned more vicious?

After a year and a half spent researching and writing *Anything for a Vote: Dirty Tricks, Cheap Shots, and October Surprises In U.S. Presidential Campaigns*, I can happily answer that question with a resounding No. Presidential elections haven't gotten worse—they're just as dirty now as they've always been. Democracy has never been for the faint of heart. Every dirty election in current times can easily be matched by one further back in history. What party stole a close presidential election from the Democrats in Florida? The Republicans in 1876, during the Hayes–Tilden face-off. Which presidential candidate kept company with a "smoking bimbo" and was rumored to have sired a love child? That would be Warren Harding in 1920. What president bugged his opponent's headquarters? Why Richard Nixon, of course—but also Lyndon Johnson, whose 1964 campaign against

9

Barry Goldwater is one of the dirtiest on record.

Probably the only clean election in American history was the first one, in 1789, in which George Washington ran unopposed. By the next ballot, in 1792, the nation's first political parties had begun to form. Four years later, the two rivals were going at it full force . . . and they haven't stopped since.

During the past 200-plus years of Americans voting for their presidents, much has changed. In the beginning, the framers of the Constitution dictated there would be no direct popular vote; instead, the president was chosen by electors appointed by state legislatures. Each elector could cast two votes for president: the top vote-getter became president, the runner-up vice president. This made it possible for a president to have a vice president from a different party, as happened in 1796, when Thomas Jefferson became John Adams's White House partner. (For a contemporary reference, imagine George W. Bush with John Kerry as his veep and you'll have some idea of the trouble this caused.)

In 1824, however, Americans began electing their president by popular vote, and over the next century, presidential electioneering became the country's favorite spectator sport. Nineteenth-century customs dictated that candidates maintain a dignified public silence during the campaign, but that didn't stop members of both parties from fighting like pigs over truffles. Huge rallies were held in candidates' honor, and newspapers—usually aligned with a political party, a practice that ended only in the mid-twentieth century—hurled lavish insults at the presidential hopefuls. (You haven't lived until you've been trashed by a nineteenth-century tabloid.) Voter turnout was extraordinary—consistently in the high seventieth percentile. Note that today, depending on which statistics you believe, it ranges from 49 to 55 percent.

As I wrote this book, many people (hidden agendas gleaming in their eyes) asked me which party had resorted to the dirtiest tricks. Depends on the situation, I would usually reply. Frankly, they've both acted pretty badly at different times throughout the nation's history.

But in general, my research suggested that parties with the strongest ideologies—be they Democratic or Republican—tend to wage the nastiest battles. If you sincerely believe that you have a better candidate and a superior life philosophy, you're more willing to pull out all the stops to ensure your party wins.

And dirty tricks do influence the outcome of presidential elections. In some of the ugliest elections of all time—from the Jefferson–Adams bloodbath of 1800 through the Hoover–Smith smearfest of 1928 to the Bush–Gore millennial madness—the party responsible for the dirtiest tricks usually won.

If all that sounds pretty grim, cheer up. Without smears, innuendo, and thievery tainting our electoral system, what would we have to connect us to our quickly vanishing past? Believe me: you could take any Whig or Federalist of yore, plunk him down in a modern presidential campaign, and—once accustomed to the 24-hour cable news channels and social media—he'd be up and shrieking with the best of us.

We're Americans, after all. A nice, dirty election runs in our blood.

SLEAZE-O-METER

1789

★

GEORGE
# WASHINGTON

VS.

# HIMSELF

★

"WELCOME, MIGHTY CHIEF! ONCE MORE/
WELCOME TO THIS MIGHTY SHORE/NOW NO MERCENARY FOE/
AIMS AT THEE THE FATAL BLOW!"
—Ode to George Washington performed by thirteen girls (one for each
of the new states) as Washington journeyed to his first inauguration

In the very beginning—before primaries, the blogosphere, Twitter, Super PACs, and spin control—electing a president was a clean, sober, and dignified affair.

Before the first presidential election in 1789, Alexander Hamilton envisioned future candidates as men "most likely to possess the information and discernment requisite to such complicated investigations." Those who chose such men would, by definition, also be men of high seriousness and probity, the kind of men who might pick a pastor for a church or select the head of a new university.

And the first time, that's pretty much how it worked out.

## THE CAMPAIGN (SUCH AS IT WAS)

In 1789 America was like a newborn babe, and because its birth pains included a bloody and divisive war, a calming paternal figure was needed. The only one who really fit the bill was Commander-in-Chief George Washington, who even back then was being called the father of his country.

Washington was not happy about his role as the anointed one. He was a genuinely reluctant leader who, at age fifty-six, thought he was too far past his prime to undertake such a challenge. As he told his future secretary of war, Henry Knox: "My movement to the chair of Government will be accompanied by feelings not unlike those of a culprit who is going to the place of his execution."

But Washington had presided over the Constitutional Convention, which met in Philadelphia in 1787 to create a coherent democratic governing system. His friends Alexander Hamilton and James Madison convinced him that America needed his presence—if only to make sure that the gains of the Revolutionary War did not disappear in factional infighting between states' rights advocates and those who favored a strong central government.

Never mind that the general had some decidedly undemocratic ways, such as his habit of referring to himself in the third person like an eighteenth-century Julius Caesar, his dislike of shaking hands (he preferred bowing), and his ownership of slaves. Washington was the chosen man.

The first presidential election in American history was also the quickest. There was no popular vote (one would not be held until 1824); rather, following rules set down in the newly ratified Constitution, each state appointed presidential electors in January 1789. Except New York, which failed to appoint its allotted eight electors by the deadline and so sat out the first election. With the first Electoral College thus established, electors cast two votes for two people—a point that became extremely controversial in early American history. The man who received the most votes would be president; the man with the second-most amount would be vice president.

The only hint of skullduggery came from the crafty Alexander Hamilton. He urged electors to "waste" their second votes on candidates not even in the running to ensure that his rival John Adams—patriot and framer of the Declaration of Independence—would have no chance of becoming president.

## THE WINNER: GEORGE WASHINGTON

Hamilton's strategy was quite unnecessary, for Washington had everything sewn up from the beginning and walked away with all sixty-nine electoral votes. All Hamilton really accomplished was to royally tick off John Adams; he would later complain about the "scurvy manner" in which he had been made vice president.

These grumblings foreshadowed things to come—but for the

time being, all was wonderful. Washington made his triumphal entry into New York City, the nation's temporary capital, on April 30, 1789. Thousands of spectators thronged the road that led from Mount Vernon, cheering and tossing flowers. The first president was ferried across the Hudson River on an enormous barge manned by thirteen white-smocked sailors; the barge was surrounded by a veritable flotilla of ships, filled to the gunwales with celebrants who sang Washington's praises to the spring skies.

In more ways than one, the election of 1789 was the smoothest sailing an American presidential candidate would ever have.

★★★

**Of Course, the Sailing Wasn't Completely Smooth** The acerbic John Adams did claim that the only reason Washington was chosen for everything was that he was taller than anyone else in the room.

SLEAZE-O-METER

1792

GEORGE
# WASHINGTON

VS.

# HIMSELF
(AGAIN)

"DAMN 'EM, DAMN 'EM, DAMN 'EM. YOU SEE—
AN ELECTIVE GOVERNMENT WON'T DO!"
—John Adams

I n 1792 things got just a little worse. Being the first president meant that George Washington had a lot of ceremonial stuff to figure out—for example, what he should be called ("Mr. President" was finally settled on, although John Adams grumbled that the term recalled such commoners as "presidents of fire companies and clubs"). But much more substantial fare was on the presidential menu, including the ever-delicate matter of relations with Great Britain and how the administration should react to the French Revolution (Washington was all for it until the Terror brought up the fearful specter of mob rule)

As father of the nation, Washington also had to deal with quarreling kids. The children in this case were cabinet members Alexander Hamilton and Thomas Jefferson, and their dispute helped create something the framers of the Constitution hadn't quite bargained for: America's first political parties.

Hamilton, despite (or because of) his impoverished origins, had no great trust in "common" people. He believed in a strong firm-handed central government and, as secretary of treasury under Washington, created a federal bank and sponsored measures that helped rich merchants, bankers, and manufacturers living in the cities of the Northeast. People who shared Hamilton's views came to be called Federalists.

Secretary of State Jefferson, although a landed aristocrat by birth, believed in the power of the people—with the people preferably being farmers in an idealized agrarian society. He thought that Hamilton's form of government meant too much power vested in too few hands. Those who agreed with Jefferson's views called themselves Republicans.

## THE CAMPAIGN

With his first term nearing completion, Washington wanted nothing more than to return to his home at Mount Vernon to spend his remaining years in bucolic retreat with his wife, Martha. But the country was starting to fracture, so he decided to run one more time, as a unifying figure.

Fifteen states participated in the 1792 election, compared with only ten in 1789. North Carolina and Rhode Island had ratified the Constitution; New York, which had abstained from the first election, now added its vote; and two new states joined the Union: Vermont and Kentucky.

Since Washington was considered a shoo-in, the only remaining question was whether the Federalist vice president John Adams would win a second term. Republican congressmen from five states convened in the fall and proposed Governor George Clinton of New York as their veep candidate. Federalists perceived this candidacy as such a threat that even Alexander Hamilton, Adams's own sworn enemy, saw fit to coach the vice president in spin control, advising Adams to tone down some of his more inflammatory Federalist pronouncements. For instance, Adams had written that the country would be a better place if ruled by "the rich [and] well-born." Perhaps an honest pronouncement, but terrible PR.

## THE WINNER: GEORGE WASHINGTON (AGAIN)

No one was surprised when all 132 electors gave their first vote for Washington. Adams received 77 votes to Clinton's 50. The former considered this turnout a sign of disrespect, and so the stage was set for the first truly contested presidential election in American history.

★★★

**If You Can't Beat 'Em, Libel 'Em** Alexander Hamilton and his pal John Fenno, editor of the *Gazette of the United States*, took aim at Thomas Jefferson and Republican supporters like James Madison at every opportunity. They claimed that Jefferson (whom Hamilton was fond of addressing in print as "Generalissimo") was a man of "profound ambition and violent passions" who would do anything to be president. Jefferson responded by funding a rag called the *National Gazette*, in whose pages James Madison wrote nineteen articles hoping to fan anti-Federalist flames. Hamilton's adherents, Madison said, were "monied men of influence." He told his readers that, under Hamilton's plan, citizens "should think of nothing but obedience, leaving the care of their liberties to their wiser rulers."

**The Voice of Grog** These days, presidential candidates go on television and urge citizens, in soberest of tones, to do their civic duty and vote. In 1792 candidates had a different idea: get voters hammered on your tab and of course they'll vote for you. The *Gazette of the United States* reported that "a bystander, observing the particular situation of a great number of electors, who had been regaled at the expense of one of the candidates, remarked . . . that the Voice of the People was the Voice of Grog."

SLEAZE-O-METER

1796

JOHN
# ADAMS
FEDERALIST

VS.

THOMAS
# JEFFERSON
REPUBLICAN

"[I PRAY] THAT YOUR ADMINISTRATION MAY BE FILLED
WITH GLORY AND HAPPINESS."
—Thomas Jefferson, in an unsent letter to John Adams

No man can be president for long without becoming, as John Adams so nicely put it, "the Butt of Party Malevolence," and George Washington was no exception. During his last term of office, Washington often wished he were back home with Martha, swilling madeira on the front porch. Every day brought a new headache. When a few farmers in western Pennsylvania refused to pay an excise tax on homemade spirits, Washington put down the so-called Whiskey Rebellion with what freedom-loving early Americans thought was excessive force. Predictably, perhaps, Republicans began calling our first president a tyrant and a dictator.

Then there was the touchy issue of relations with Great Britain. American sympathies with France—then at war with Britain— caused friction in London, and it seemed inevitable that hostilities between the former mother country and the colonies would again arise. Washington dispatched Chief Justice John Jay to London to hammer out a treaty, and Jay returned with a document that, though not perfect, gave America peace with Great Britain. Washington signed it and Republicans howled, calling it a cop-out to Federalist "monarchist" tendencies and a supposed desire to return America to England.

Throughout his career, Washington benefited from a superb sense of timing, and 1796 was no exception. That winter he began to hint about his plan to leave office; earlier, on September 19, he had published his "Farewell Address," in which he warned against divisive political parties. All to no avail—as soon as the farewell was released, hungry politicians began scheming to fill Washington's shoes. One such politician—Thomas Jefferson—couldn't resist a parting shot at his old boss and revolutionary comrade: "The president is fortunate to get off just as the bubble is bursting, leaving others to hold the bag."

It's nice to know that even the author of the Declaration of Independence occasionally fell prey to mixed metaphors.

## THE CANDIDATES

**FEDERALIST: JOHN ADAMS** John Adams was a two-term vice president and getting on in years (he would turn sixty-one during the campaign). His acerbic personality won him admirers and enemies in equal measure. While pretending he was planning to leave public life—he liked to discourse on the "foul fiend" of electoral degeneracy—Adams in fact craved being president. "Hi! Ho! Oh, Dear!" he gaily started off one letter to his wife, Abigail, when it became apparent that Washington would not seek a third term.

**REPUBLICAN: THOMAS JEFFERSON** Jefferson had retired from his position as secretary of state in 1793 to return to Monticello and attend to his affairs (including the one he had with Sally Hemings, the enslaved woman who bore several children by him). As 1796 approached, he still maintained that life in politics—what was even then being called the "game"—was "a useless waste of time." But it was clear to everyone where his ambitions lay.

## THE CAMPAIGN

The ten weeks after the publication of Washington's farewell address were filled with feverish activity and loud proclamations by both parties—except their candidates. Following what would be the custom for the next century, both men maintained an aloof and dignified public silence.

A good deal of campaigning was under way, but no official manner of picking candidates had yet been established. The Constitution was silent on the issue, and the first national nominating convention was more than thirty years away. Until that time, prominent members of each party decided the candidates and then tried to convince their members to follow suit, with varying degrees of success. Since the parties, too, were barely formed, party discipline was a joke: electors often voted based on local enmity, personal friendship, or mere whimsy. In this election, nearly 40 percent of the 138 electors voted for candidates outside their own parties or for candidates not even on the ballot!

What the parties lacked in organization, they made up for in character assassination. For anyone who loves the democratic process, it's reassuring to see how immediately and viciously the politicians in early America launched malicious attacks via handbills, pamphlets, and articles. In the Republican newspaper *Aurora*, for example, editor Benjamin Franklin Bache (grandson of Benjamin Franklin) went for the throat—er, tummy—referring to chubby Adams's "sesquipedality of belly." Bache also warned that Adams was "champion of kings, ranks, and titles." Not to be outdone, Federalists cited Jefferson for his supposed "atheistic" tendencies and his love of the French Revolution, especially the bloody mob. Jefferson's Republican followers became "cut-throats who walk in rags and sleep amidst filth and vermin."

Meanwhile, in the first examples of balancing a national ticket through judicious selection of a vice-presidential candidate, Federalists nominated southern diplomat Thomas Pinckney to offset New Englander Adams, while Republicans paired the Virginian Jefferson with Aaron Burr, an up-and-coming New York lawyer and early Tammany operative.

As usual, Alexander Hamilton acted the spoiler. Taking advantage once again of what was rapidly being acknowledged as a defect in the Constitution—that electors voted for two candidates—he urged certain Federalist voters to withhold their votes for Adams and vote only for Pinckney. If his plan had succeeded, Pinckney (whom

Hamilton rightly considered far easier to manipulate than Adams) would have become president, with Hamilton acting as the power behind the throne.

## THE WINNER: JOHN ADAMS

Electors cast ballots in their respective state capitals on the first Wednesday in December. At this time in American history, an odd law stipulated that ballots could not be opened until the second Wednesday in February, when both houses of Congress were in session. It seemed like weeks of rumor and wild speculation would ensue—but by mid-December the cat was out of the bag and everyone knew that Adams had squeaked into the presidency, 71 votes to Jefferson's 68. He was president, indeed, but the wisdom of the framers of the Constitution had ensured that he had a member of the opposition party as his vice president. Over the next four years, there would be nothing but trouble.

★★★

**Francomaniac vs. the Angloman** In charges that foreshadowed the "egghead" slurs launched at future presidential candidates such as Adlai Stevenson and Eugene McCarthy, Federalists painted Jefferson as a "philosopher" and "visionary." Jefferson, one writer harrumphed, was "fit to be professor in a college . . . but certainly not first magistrate of a great nation." Just to make sure people got the point, Jefferson was also called an anarchist and a Francomaniac. Adams had his own share of detractors and bizarre nicknames, including "Monoman" and "Angloman." The Republican-leaning *Boston Chronicle* wrote quite seriously that if Adams were elected, hereditary succession would be foisted upon America in the form of his son John Quincy. With Jefferson, the paper added, who needed to worry? Even if he had hidden monarchist intentions, the man had only daughters.

SLEAZE-O-METER

1800

★ THOMAS
# JEFFERSON
REPUBLICAN

## VS.

JOHN
# ADAMS
FEDERALIST
★

"THE REPUBLIC IS SAFE. . . . THE [FEDERALIST] PARTY
IS IN RAGE AND DESPAIR."
—John Dawson, Republican congressman, Virginia

**B**y 1800 the American population had increased to 5.3 million, Washington, D.C., had replaced Philadelphia as the new "Federal City," and a mellow dude named John Chapman (a.k.a. Johnny Appleseed) was dispensing wisdom as well as gardening tips throughout the Ohio Territory.

And in a harbinger of things to come, America had its first presidential free-for-all—the first election in which, at the end of the day, bodies lay strewn everywhere. Forget Bush vs. Gore, forget Nixon vs. Kennedy, forget most of the other really nasty national elections you've experienced in your lifetime. The 1800 contest between John Adams and Thomas Jefferson can be ranked as one of the top five dirtiest elections of all time, and all for two reasons:

One: It is hard to think of two parties in the history of American politics who hated and vilified each other more than Adams's Federalists and Jefferson's Republicans.

Two: For the first and last time in American history, a president was running against his own vice president.

What a way to start a century.

## THE CANDIDATES

**FEDERALIST: JOHN ADAMS** The chief foreign policy issue of Adams's presidency was America's relationship with France. Since the French and British were at war and America had signed the Jay Treaty with Britain, the new French Republic declared that any American trade with Great Britain was an act of war. French seamen soon began boarding American ships and seizing goods. When Adams tried to raise money for a larger navy to counter the threat, he was attacked by the Republicans for being a warmonger. When he attempted negotiations with France, Hamilton's gang called him an appeaser. He just couldn't win.

Another factor in the 1800 campaign was the Alien and Sedition Acts, steered through Congress by the Federalists during the height of war fever. Under the Sedition Act, anyone who criticized or sought to undermine the U.S. government or the president could be fined or thrown in jail, and many were. Republicans reviled the law as a violation of Constitutional rights. People weren't even safe in the neighborhood bar. One tavern patron in New Jersey was arrested and fined for drunkenly noting that the president had, to put it indelicately, a big ass.

Despite Federalist reservations about Adams (reservations may be too mild a word—one prominent Federalist prayed openly that the president suffer a carriage accident), he was the only candidate they had. For his vice-presidential running mate, the party picked General Charles Cotesworth Pinckney, brother of Adams's 1796 veep nominee, a seasoned diplomat, and southern ticket balancer.

**REPUBLICAN: THOMAS JEFFERSON** Thomas Jefferson had spent most of the four years of his vice presidency adroitly maintaining a safe distance between him and his boss, John Adams. As a result, almost nothing that Adams was associated with—including the Sedition Act, which Jefferson had done little to keep from passage in Congress—rubbed off on his V.P., who was in a strong position to run. For his vice-presidential candidate, the Republicans once again picked Aaron Burr, whose star had continued to rise since the '96 election.

## THE CAMPAIGN

What a difference four years can make. The 1796 presidential campaigns had begun roughly a hundred days before the election. By 1800 the parties were launching attacks a full year before votes were cast.

The first strike against Adams came from Jefferson, who secretly hired a writer named James Callender to assail the president in print. Callender—the kind of hack one imagines skulking in the back of foul taverns, cackling as he scratches away with his quill—set to work with a vengeance. Adams, he wrote, was "a repulsive pedant," a "gross hypocrite," and "a hideous hermaphroditical character which has neither the force and firmness of a man, nor the gentleness and sensibility of a woman." Not surprisingly, Callender was jailed for nine months under the Sedition Act, giving the Republicans a convenient martyr.

The Federalists fired back, spreading rumors that Jefferson had swindled his legal clients, that he was a godless atheist from whom one had to hide one's Bibles, that he had been a coward during the Revolutionary War, and that he slept with slaves while at home in Monticello. A few mischievous Federalists even circulated a story that Jefferson was dead, knowing full well that it was a slave at Monticello by the same name who had died.

The savage sallies increased, and by fall both parties had reached a fever pitch of character assassination. The Republicans, in particular, discovered the power of the press—their attacks ran in single-page circulars, newspapers, and pamphlets as long as fifty pages. In one of the first attempts at true national organization, Jefferson's party set up committees of correspondence responsible for producing such broadsides and disseminating them among voters.

But an election this boisterous was sure to extend beyond the boundaries of print. Federalists liked to hold military parades, while Republicans planted liberty poles. Both parties threw picnics and barbecues where they plied voters with copious amounts of alcohol. At a Republican dinner in Lancaster, Pennsylvania, guests drank sixteen toasts—one for each state of the Union—before digging into a half ton of beef and pork.

Adams held out hope for a great victory, but at the time most politicians considered Jefferson the sure winner. The ubiquitous Alexander Hamilton, Adams's nemesis, tried to make that outcome certain. In October, Hamilton published a most astonishing document, *Letter from Alexander Hamilton Concerning the Public Conduct and Character of John Adams, Esq., President of the United States*, fifty-four pages of what one historian has called unremitting vilification. "If we must have an enemy at the head of the government, let it be one whom we can oppose . . . who will not involve our party in the disgrace of his foolish and bad measures," wrote Hamilton.

Though Hamilton had long been known for his machinations, the letter shocked everyone. To try to understand the impact, imagine if Hillary Clinton sent an e-mail to Democratic Party faithfuls under the subject "E-mail from Hillary Clinton Concerning the Public Content and Character of Barack Obama" and then went on to accuse the president—the leader of his party—of suffering from "distempered jealousy," "extreme egotism," and an "ungovernable temper."

Some historians feel that Hamilton had temporarily lost his mind; others think the publication was a calculated ploy to throw votes away from Adams and to Charles Pinckney, who would be more sympathetic to Hamilton's extreme Federalist agenda. It is even possible the letter was stolen and published without Hamilton's consent. Regardless, Hamilton was attacked by both parties and retired from politics after the election. Four years later, he was shot and killed in a duel with Vice President Aaron Burr.

## THE WINNER (EVENTUALLY): THOMAS JEFFERSON

On Election Day, December 3, electors met once again in their respective state capitals to cast their votes. As usual, the law stipulated that ballots could not be opened until early February, when both houses of Congress were in session. And again as usual, word leaked about the outcome: Jefferson had won. "The Jig Is Up!" cheered one Republican Party newspaper. Another writer declared: "Here ends the 18th century. The 19th begins with a fine, clear morning."

There was just one small problem. By the end of December it

was clear that Republican candidates Jefferson and Burr each had 73 votes (Adams received only 65). The problem with the two-vote system was knottier than ever. In past elections, Republican electors might have "wasted" a handful of votes on Adams or Pinckney or even a minor candidate so that Burr would not receive an equal number as Jefferson (ensuring his position as VP). But in such a close contest every vote mattered, so all the Republicans voted for Jefferson and Burr. The result was a tie.

To make matters worse, the Constitution dictated that the Republican runoff election should be resolved by the House of Representatives—which, ironically, was controlled by the Federalists! Burr initially declared he would be happy to serve under Jefferson, but only because he mistakenly thought he had lost by one vote. His spirit of cooperation vanished upon realizing he had a fair shot at the presidency. In fact, many Federalists offered their backing—anything to keep out Jefferson—making Burr's chances of winning rise exponentially.

On February 11, during a massive snowstorm, the House of Representatives met in Washington, D.C., to vote for a president. All members were present, even one so ill he had to be carried two miles on a stretcher and then laid on a bed in an adjoining chamber. Vice President Jefferson, who was also Senate president, counted the electoral ballots and certified the vote at 73 apiece for him and Burr. Next, the House deliberated. The slate was now blank.

Each of the sixteen states had a single vote, and the winner needed a majority of nine to take the prize. Over the next six days, thirty-six ballots were recorded. For the first thirty-five, the results were the same: eight states for Jefferson, six for Burr, two undecided. No winner. In the back rooms of taverns and the antechambers of the House, behind-the-scenes maneuverings were intense. Federalists wooed Burr, but he refused to agree to their agenda in exchange for a chance at becoming president. The deadlock continued.

Finally, on February 17, a Federalist congressman from Delaware who opposed Jefferson abstained from voting, as did Federalists from Maryland, Vermont, and South Carolina. With these states out of the balloting, Jefferson was quickly elected, winning ten out of sixteen votes. Burr would be his vice president.

No records survive to confirm these events because almost everything that occurred during those six historic days took place in the utmost secrecy. Yet many suspected that Jefferson cut a deal with the Federalist Party to become president. He would always deny it, but his policies while in office—which included continuing the Bank of the United States set up by Hamilton, financing a national debt, and keeping certain Federalists in office—seemed to confirm that a secret agreement had been brokered with the opposition.

★★★

**The Only Thing Missing Is Monica** . . . The Federalists couldn't get enough of attacking Jefferson personally; indeed, their assaults sound like the insults leveled at Bill Clinton, another Southerner, almost 200 years later. "Jefferson is a mean-spirited, low-lived fellow, the son of a half-breed Indian squaw, sired by a Virginia mulatto father," claimed one leaflet. And a Connecticut paper raised the specter of the French Revolution, supposedly beloved by Jefferson: "Are you prepared to see your dwellings in flames . . . female chastity violated, [your] children writhing on the pike? GREAT GOD OF COMPASSION AND JUSTICE, SHIELD MY COUNTRY FROM DESTRUCTION."

**King John** Republicans claimed that Adams planned to marry one of his sons to a daughter of King George III of England to start an American royal dynasty and reunite England and America. If that wasn't enough to make Anglophobes panic, Republicans also claimed that Adams sent his running mate, Charles Pinckney, to England to pick up four pretty mistresses—two for the president and two for Pinckney. When Adams heard the story, he exclaimed: "If this be true, General Pinckney has kept them all for himself and cheated me out of my two!"

**First "Blame It All on the Media" Attack** After the election, one Federalist poet decided that his party's defeat could be blamed entirely on the media, which in his opinion clearly favored the Republican Party: "And lo! In meretricious dress, / Forth comes a strumpet called 'THE PRESS.' / Whose haggard, unrequested charms / Rush into every blaggard's arms."

**Who's Your Daddy?** Alexander Hamilton was born illegitimate, a fact that John Adams—who had good reason to hate Hamilton's guts—never let him forget. On various occasions, Adams referred to Hamilton as "a Creole bastard," "the bastard brat of a Scotch peddlar," and "a man devoid of every Moral principle—a bastard."

**Never Again** In the election's aftermath, the Republicans and the Federalists all agreed on one thing: never again an election like that of 1800. Congress passed a resolution calling for a constitutional amendment stating that electors would henceforth vote separately for president and vice president, rather than allowing the top two vote-getters to take all. The resolution was quickly ratified and became the Twelfth Amendment.

# 1804

## THOMAS JEFFERSON vs. CHARLES PINCKNEY

Since Thomas Jefferson proved to be a highly skilled middle-of-the-road president, the election of 1804 was a bit of a snoozer. Despite Federalist howls, Jefferson did not turn the country into an atheistic society, instigate a Jacobean bloodbath, or abandon the New England merchant class. On the contrary, the new president made several popular decisions during his first term—most notably the Louisiana Purchase, in which Jefferson doubled the size of the United States for a mere $15 million (roughly three cents an acre).

On February 25, 1804, in what was the first official nominating caucus for a U.S. president, Republican congressmen met and renominated Thomas Jefferson for president, naming Governor George Clinton of New York as his running mate.

For their candidate the Federalists chose Charles Cotesworth Pinckney, Adams's running mate from 1800. A large, jowly man, Pinckney was respected by both parties but also half deaf and not terribly exciting. New York senator Rufus King got the nod for vice president.

**THE CAMPAIGN** Everyone could see that Jefferson and the Republicans had a lock on the election, but the Federalists—desperate to salvage votes in their base of New England—fought as hard as they could. The usual anti-Jefferson slurs were trotted out—he was an atheist, he had an affair with his slave, and on and on.

**THE WINNER: THOMAS JEFFERSON** It was no contest: 162 votes for Jefferson, 14 for Pinckney. The Federalists carried only two states: Connecticut and Delaware. Even Massachusetts voted Republican.

# 1808

## JAMES MADISON vs. CHARLES PINCKNEY

Thomas Jefferson's second term was a much different story from his first, primarily because of escalating hostilities between the French and the British.

The powerful British navy had returned to its antagonistic practice of stopping American ships on the pretext of looking for English deserters—the true purpose was to impress American seamen into duty. After an especially nasty incident off the coast of Virginia when a British warship attacked an American frigate, resulting in the death and wounding of twenty-one sailors, Jefferson prevailed upon Congress to pass the Embargo Act, thus preventing Americans from trading not just with Great Britain and France but with all of Europe. Unfortunately, the biggest victims of the embargo were American farmers who exported grain overseas. Also negatively affected were New England merchants whose lively trade in goods to Europe was suddenly cut off. Instead of being the shining hero, Jefferson became, as one newspaper put it, "an infernal villain."

Like George Washington before him, Jefferson knew when to shuffle off the public stage. Declaring that it was time to retire to "my family, my books, and farms," he recommended his close friend and secretary of state, James Madison, as the next Republican presidential candidate. Vice President George Clinton would remain as running mate.

Despite an impressive résumé, the fifty-seven-year-old Madison did not necessarily make a good first impression. At five feet four inches tall, he weighed less than a hundred pounds and suffered from a host of health complaints. "Little Jemmy," as his contemporaries called him, disliked eye contact and wore a dour expression most of the time; portraits seem to capture him having just bitten into a lemon.

Looks can be deceiving, however, for Little Jemmy was in fact a bright guy with an astute grasp of the problems facing the nation. If he lacked Jefferson's political charm and acumen, he possessed another valuable asset: his wife, Dolley. Seventeen years his junior, Dolley was beautiful and vivacious, the Jackie Kennedy of her day.

As for the Federalists, they brought back Charles Pinckney and Rufus King, the less-than-dynamic duo of 1804. This time around, the pair would not have to face off against the charismatic Thomas Jefferson. But in picking the same stolid candidates yet again, the Federalists showed they were a party in need of fresh talent.

**THE CAMPAIGN** By the summer of 1808, things were looking bad for the Republicans, mainly because of the embargo (dubbed the "Dambargo" by many opponents). Nevertheless, with the possibility of war against Great Britain looming on the horizon, the country rallied around the party in office.

**THE WINNER: JAMES MADISON** Madison received 122 electoral votes, Pinckney a mere 47. And on March 1, 1809, the departing president Thomas Jefferson gave Little Jemmy a gift—he signed a bill repealing the Embargo Act.

# 1812

## JAMES MADISON vs. DEWITT CLINTON

James Madison was not a colorful man; he was often eclipsed during his presidency by his wife, Dolley. Historically speaking, the same holds true. In America's litmus test of enduring presidential fame—otherwise known as Show Me the Money—Madison's likeness can be found on the $5,000 bill, a unit of currency that has been discontinued.

What Madison is renowned for is a law that sets high school students everywhere a-giggle. Taking the place of the repealed Embargo Act, the much more sensible Non-Intercourse Act allowed Americans to trade with everyone except for England and France. American merchants thus found other world markets, particularly in the Netherlands, and prospered.

War with Great Britain was in the air as the election season of 1812 heated up. What's more, a revolution had taken place in the congressional elections of 1810–11. Half the creaky and aging House members were voted out, replaced by such idealistic younger men as Henry Clay and John C. Calhoun. And these war hawks wanted England to pay for its insults over the years.

Madison understood that most of the country wanted to engage in hostilities with Great Britain and that it might behoove him to go along with the war hawks. He was nominated by the Republicans in May 1812. Vice President George Clinton had died in office just a few weeks earlier, so the Republicans nominated Elbridge Gerry, former governor of Massachusetts, as their new V.P. (Gerry's energetic redistricting of Federalist voting areas is how we got the term *gerrymandering*.)

What happened—or didn't—with the Federalist nominating

process provides the only element that passes for suspense in the election of 1812. The Federalists decided not to nominate their own candidate. Instead, they gave their support to a Republican.

That Republican was DeWitt Clinton, mayor of New York City, nephew of the late George Clinton, and implacable enemy of James Madison. Like another Clinton after him, DeWitt figured he could be all things to all people. He would appeal as an antiwar candidate to Federalists yet would also be attractive to New England Republicans sick of the "Virginia Dynasty" (as many described the chokehold the southern states seemed to have on the White House after the Washington, Jefferson, and Madison administrations). In August 1812, the Federalists met in great secrecy and decided to throw their support his way.

**THE CAMPAIGN** Clinton's supporters presented themselves as the peace ticket but assured voters that if Clinton were elected, he would still prosecute the war —only far more wisely than would Madison. (If you were paying attention in the election of 2004, this line of reasoning ought to sound familiar.) Clinton's supporters called the sitting president "a base wretch . . . who is for WAR," attempting to pound the drum of popular indignation. But the war against Great Britain had plenty of supporters, and ultimately the ploy proved unsuccessful.

**THE WINNER: JAMES MADISON** After the electoral votes from the eighteen states of the Union were counted, James Madison was declared the winner, with 128 votes to Clinton's 89. Not then—not ever—would Americans turn a "war president" out of office.

The 1812 election heralded the beginning of the end for the

Federalist Party, and over the next few years it faded from the political scene. Ironically, its demise was partially because so many of the Federalist ideas had already been, or would soon be, incorporated into the fabric of American life, including a national bank, a standing army, and a strong central government to ride herd on unruly states. Ultimately, the Federalist Party had allowed itself to become too narrowly defined as the party of the rich and the powerful, as a group who cared only about northern New England states. With Americans spreading out across the continent, they sought political representation that reflected a broader and more democratic view of the burgeoning new country.

# 1816

## JAMES MONROE vs. RUFUS KING

Even though the War of 1812 ended on a satisfactory note in 1814 with an American victory, Madison announced that he would follow the custom of leaving office after two terms. James Monroe stood ready behind the throne.

Monroe was the last of the revolutionary generation of Virginians—Washington, Jefferson, Madison—to become president. He had quite the résumé, too: Continental Congress, U.S. Senate, minister to France under Washington and Jefferson, secretary of state, and acting secretary of war under Madison.

Despite that laundry list, Monroe elicited a general dearth of enthusiasm. He may have been honest and hardworking, but he clearly lacked charisma. Still, in the absence of fierce party rivalries, there was no need to trumpet Monroe's virtues (or those of his vice president, Daniel Tompkins). Voters lacked much of an alternative.

The Federalists didn't even bother to make an official nomination, although three or four northern states banded together and decided it might be a good idea if Rufus King, the perennial vice-presidential candidate, ran for president against Monroe. It was a half-hearted gesture from a dying political party. "Federalists our age must be content with the past," King told a friend even before the election was over.

**THE CAMPAIGN** There was none. Rufus King sniped that Monroe had the "zealous support of nobody, and he was exempt from the hostility of everybody." The claim was accurate, but beside the point.

**THE WINNER: JAMES MONROE** A snap: 183 votes for Monroe, 34 for King. The "Era of Good Feelings" was about to begin.

# 1820

## JAMES MONROE VS. HIMSELF

In the inaugural address delivered by James Monroe in March 1817, he remarked how gratifying it was "to witness the increased harmony of opinion which pervades our Union. Discord does not belong to our system." Spoken like a true founding father—they never did like those pesky political parties.

There's nothing like a successful war, economic prosperity, and a lack of Federalists to make a Republican circa 1820 feel good. As in the wild when the natural enemy of a species is removed, the predator-free creatures thrive.

The most contentious issue facing the country was the northern states rapidly outstripping the south in terms of population and political clout. If the new states entering the Union from the Louisiana Purchase were admitted without slaves, the south would quickly become marginalized. The Missouri Compromise signed by Monroe divvied things up—states south of the 36°30' latitude could own slaves—but set the scene for further strife.

For now, however, all was well. Republicans nominated Monroe for president, with Vice President Daniel Tompkins continuing in his role. The Federalist Party, since it had ceased to exist, nominated no one. For the third, and last, time in history, a presidential candidate ran unopposed.

**THE WINNER: JAMES MONROE** James Monroe received all the electoral votes. Well, all but one. A curmudgeon in New Hampshire gave his one vote to John Quincy Adams, Monroe's secretary of state, so that George Washington would remain the only president ever elected unanimously.

SLEAZE-O-METER

## 1824

★

### JOHN QUINCY
# ADAMS

REPUBLICAN

## VS.

### ANDREW
# JACKSON

REPUBLICAN

★

"EVERY LIAR AND CALUMNIATOR WAS AT WORK
DAY AND NIGHT TO DESTROY MY REPUTATION."
—John Quincy Adams

L ike many presidents, James Monroe seemed to grow into the presidency just as it was time to leave office. His second term reached its apex in 1823 when he issued the historic Monroe Doctrine, declaring the Western Hemisphere closed to colonization by other powers. But despite this foreign relations coup, the real excitement during his second administration concerned the naming of his successor.

The election of 1824 has much in common with the elections of today, what with candidates running unofficially almost the minute Monroe was inaugurated in 1821. One newspaper, the *Niles Register*, counted seventeen who had thrown their hats in the ring; among them were some pretty influential personalities, including Secretary of War John C. Calhoun, Secretary of the Treasury William Crawford, former Speaker of the House Henry Clay, and Andrew Jackson, hero of New Orleans and supposed "friend of the common man." And then there was Secretary of State John Quincy Adams, the brilliant but aloof son of America's second president.

Crawford was considered the front-runner—Monroe favored him—and he was certain that when the time came, he would receive the nomination. But a funny thing happened on the way to the caucus.

Since 1804 small groups, or caucuses, of influential congressmen had picked the Republican Party presidential nominee, but public sentiment was changing. Many Americans perceived the caucuses as elitist. Residents of new western states such as Missouri, Kentucky, Tennessee, Ohio, and Illinois wanted a more direct say in electing the president and thus voted in congressmen who better represented their wishes. Certain states began to let citizens choose their electors by popular vote. Tennessee sent the half-literate coonskin-capped Davy

Crockett to Congress, declaring he was every bit as good as some bewigged aristocrat from Virginia.

Realizing the times were a-changing, all the candidates except Crawford simply boycotted the caucus procedure, lined up their own support, and started campaigning. The caucus did choose Crawford as the presidential nominee, but it didn't matter. These were wild and woolly times; the American electoral system was reinventing itself, and no one recognized Crawford as the sole candidate. The so-called King Caucus system was officially dead, and it would never again be used to choose a presidential candidate.

Instead, the election became a contest between John Quincy Adams and Andrew Jackson, with Henry Clay and William Crawford standing out as chief runner-ups––and Clay playing a controversial role as a spoiler.

## THE CANDIDATES (ALL REPUBLICANS)

**ANDREW JACKSON** Jackson was born in 1767 in South Carolina to poor Irish immigrant parents who worked a hardscrabble farm out in the boondocks, making him that most-coveted nineteenth-century commodity— a true "backwoods" presidential candidate (the first in American history). He was orphaned by the age of fourteen but became a successful lawyer, politician, and general; after destroying the British at New Orleans in 1815, Jackson became a bona fide national celebrity. He was tall, handsome, and, as many of his opponents on the battlefield and campaign trail discovered, extremely ruthless.

**WILLIAM CRAWFORD** Talk about a dream candidate. During Crawford's distinguished career, he had served as U.S. senator, minister to France, secretary of war (under Madison), and secretary of treasury (under Monroe). He was robust, good-looking, affable, and gregarious. Unfortunately, soon after being nominated, he suffered a stroke that left him paralyzed and nearly blind. Crawford eventually returned to his cabinet post, but he was no longer the front-runner for president.

**HENRY CLAY** A native Kentuckian, Clay had been the leader of the War Hawks in 1812 and was now a brilliant Speaker of the House. He was an ardent patriot who wanted a national bank and a standing army. He was also a debonair gambler known for holding card games that lasted until all hours.

**JOHN QUINCY ADAMS** Adams boasted distinguished bloodlines—his father was the second president of the United States—as well as a notable career. He helped negotiate the Treaty of Ghent, ending the War of 1812, and had labored tirelessly as James Monroe's secretary of state. Unlike his handsome opponents, however, Adams was short and bald, with a constantly running eye. Even he described himself as "a man of reserved, cold, austere, and forbidding manners."

## THE CAMPAIGN

In a word, nasty. Rumors were spread about Adams, in particular—that his father, the aging former president, had broken with him politically and that he was selling future patronage appointments in return for votes. Yet people smiled to his face. "My complaint," he wrote, "is not that attempts were made to tear my reputation to pieces," but that such slanders "were accompanied by professions of great respect and esteem."

After twenty years of sleepy presidential elections, the pamphleteers were relieved to again be slinging mud. They satirized Adams's sartorial inelegance (he was, admittedly, an eccentric dresser—when he couldn't find his cravat, he'd sometimes tie a black ribbon around his neck), called Clay a drunkard, and accused Jackson of murder for having executed mutineers in 1813 (charges that would follow Jackson into the next election). Crawford—still running, though paralyzed and sightless—was accused of malfeasance in his role as treasury secretary. If all these charges were true, one politician said, "our presidents, secretaries, and senators are all traitors and pirates."

# THE WINNER (EVENTUALLY):
# JOHN QUINCY ADAMS

The voting of the presidential electors was completed in early December, and it soon became clear that quite the horse race was still going on. Andrew Jackson pulled 99 electoral votes (he also led in the first popular vote ever, although six out of twenty-four states were still appointing electors in their state legislatures). In close pursuit were Adams with 84 electoral votes, William Crawford with 41, and Henry Clay at 37. Since no single candidate claimed a majority, the outcome of the race would be decided in the House of Representatives, with each state delegation casting one vote. (John C. Calhoun did win the majority of votes for vice president, so his position was a lock regardless of who became president.)

The voting was scheduled for February 9, 1825, and the candidates set to work lining up support in Congress. Because Jackson had received the most electoral votes, many were saying that he should be president, even if the Constitution disagreed.

The matter was finally resolved when Henry Clay pulled out of the race. He would throw the three states that had voted for him—Ohio, Missouri, and Kentucky—to John Quincy Adams. Clay had probably decided that between Jackson and Adams, the latter would be more likely to strengthen the west by providing money for road and canal construction, badly needed projects in the outlying states. Of course, many speculated that the two men had embarked on a "corrupt bargain"— votes for Adams in return for a cabinet position for Clay —but Adams always swore the accusation was untrue.

When the vote came down on February 9, Adams squeaked out a majority with thirteen states, as opposed to Jackson's seven and Crawford's four. He would be president, and the next four years would turn out to be an almost unmitigated disaster.

★★★

**To Be or Not to Be . . . President?** Like a medieval prince or modern analysand, John Quincy Adams was prone to deep ambivalence about success. At no time was that more evident than in the election of 1824. "Oh, the winding of the human heart," he wrote in his diary. "Whether I ought to wish for success is among the greatest uncertainties of the election." On the one hand, "the object nearest to my heart [is] to bring the whole people of the Union to harmonize together." On the other hand, winning and losing "are distressing in prospect, and the most formidable is that of success. The humiliation of failure will be so much more than compensated by the safety in which it will leave me that I ought to regard it as a consummation devoutly to be wished." Somehow one cannot picture his opponent Andrew Jackson (who preferred beating up other people to beating up on himself) muttering away in like fashion.

**Clay vs. Jackson** Henry Clay did not like Andrew Jackson—he thought he was a rash and boneheaded military thug—and made no secret of it: "I cannot believe that killing 2,500 Englishmen at New Orleans qualifies for the various, difficult, and complicated duties of the Chief Magistracy."

**Jackson vs. Clay** When Adams announced shortly after the election that Henry Clay would be his secretary of state, Jackson told a friend: "So you see, the Judas of the West [Clay] has closed the contract and will receive the thirty pieces of silver. His end will be the same. Was there ever witnessed such a bare-faced corruption in any country before?"

**The Duel** The election of 1824 was so contentious that a duel resulted from it. In April 1826, the hot-tempered Virginia senator John Randolph made a speech on the Senate floor accusing Henry Clay of throwing the election to John Quincy Adams. Specifically, he called him a blackleg, slang for a cheating gambler. It was too much for Clay, who challenged Randolph to a duel.

The two met early in the morning at a deserted spot along the Potomac River. They took their positions, backed up by seconds who included Senator Thomas Hart Benton, but a comedy of errors ensued. First, Randolph accidentally discharged his gun and had to be given another. Then both men shot and missed. They reloaded and then Clay fired. His bullet pierced Randolph's coat without hurting him. Randolph paused a moment, then turned and deliberately fired his pistol straight up into the air.

"I do not fire at you, Mr. Clay," he said. The two men shook hands and were thereafter friendly acquaintances. Senator Benton dryly remarked that it was "about the last high-toned duel" he ever saw.

SLEAZE-O-METER

**1828**

★

ANDREW
# JACKSON
DEMOCRAT–REPUBLICAN

## VS.

JOHN QUINCY
# ADAMS
NATIONAL–REPUBLICAN

★

"TO THE POLLS! TO THE POLLS! THE FAITHFUL
SENTINEL MUST NOT SLEEP—LET NO ONE STAY HOME—
LET EVERY MAN GO TO THE POLLS!"
—*United States Telegraph*

The election of 1828 begins with Andrew Jackson's anger. Jackson—the six-foot-tall ex-frontier hero of New Orleans, the man who as a boy of thirteen in the Revolutionary War received a saber slash across the head for refusing to shine the boots of a British officer, who then survived smallpox and the deaths of his mother and two brothers, and who grew up to defeat not only the British in 1814 but also the Creeks, Seminoles, and Spanish—well, this was not a guy you wanted to piss off.

But Jackson was convinced that John Quincy Adams had entered into a "corrupt bargain" with Henry Clay to win the presidency, and he was determined to make things right. Enthusiastically backed by his Tennessee delegation, which in its eagerness nominated him for president in 1825, Jackson resigned his Senate seat and went after the presidency with renewed fervor.

That spelled bad news for Adams, whose presidency was off to a rocky start. On his inauguration day, Adams had to compete for attention with a traveling circus that had come into town, no easy feat in the early 1800s. Then he and his wife, Louisa, discovered that the Monroes had left the White House in a shambles. The furniture was so battered, the place such a mess, that Louisa invited members of the public to take a look, lest she and her husband be blamed.

Adams began his administration with a few blunders. In his first State of the Union address, he focused not on foreign affairs or westward expansion but on establishing a national observatory, a series of astronomical outposts that would be "the lighthouses of the sky." To his credit, Adams was ahead of his time (he used the same speech to lobby for a regulated system of weights and measures), but this tack was akin to a contemporary president giving an hour-long address passionately advocating the adoption of the metric system.

Things quickly went from bad to worse. The whole administration, according to a sympathetic biographer, "was a hapless failure and best forgotten, save for the personal anguish it cost him." With cries of "Corruption and Bargain" ringing from Jackson allies in the west (including Adams's own vice president, John C. Calhoun), the president was on the defensive at every turn. No wonder he began to feel surrounded by "conspirators" and that he was being tried by a "secret inquisition." He was. A spiteful opposition in Congress thwarted him in matters both foreign and domestic.

With so much conflict and strife, it's no surprise that the Republican Party split in two. The National Republicans supported Adams and his vice-presidential pick, treasury secretary Richard Rush. They were the party of the old-line Republicans, the wealthy merchant classes, and the landed aristocracy. Opposing them were Andrew Jackson and his running mate, John C. Calhoun, backed largely by the western small farmers and the eastern laboring men. At first they called themselves the Friends of Andrew Jackson, then Democratic-Republicans, and finally Democrats. This group would form the core of the future Democratic Party.

Both groups would have to contend with a major change to the electoral process: the widespread use of the popular vote. The election of 1828 saw four times as many people casting a vote for president as in the election of 1824. All but two states (Delaware and South Carolina) would use this form of voting to select their candidates, which meant that presidential campaigns—crazy enough to begin with—were about to get a whole lot crazier.

## THE CANDIDATES

**DEMOCRAT-REPUBLICAN: ANDREW JACKSON** The general—now sixty-one years old—was probably at the peak of his power. Driven by a belief that the White House had been stolen from him in 1824, as well as his life-long desire to wrest power from the privileged and place it in the hands of the people, Jackson envisioned himself as a president for the common man, leading with his beloved wife, Rachel, by his side. Only one part of this dream would come true.

**NATIONAL-REPUBLICAN: JOHN QUINCY ADAMS** It was possible that John Quincy Adams—also sixty-one—was running for president just for the sheer stubborn pride of it, because the previous years had been no picnic. At one point he was stalked by the first would-be presidential assassin, a crazed doctor who (in a day when any citizen could and did just walk into the White House to see the president) talked openly about killing him. To his credit, Adams met with the lunatic and gave him a stern talking-to. Many historians now speculate that Adams was clinically depressed going into the campaign.

## THE CAMPAIGN

With one party claiming to defend the nation against "howling Democracy" and the other battling "a lordly, purse-proud aristocracy," is it any wonder that things soon became extremely malicious?

The campaign began in September 1827, after both candidates were nominated. Since each party still operated without national nominating conventions, Jackson and Adams were put forward in a series of special state nominating conventions and mass meetings.

Jackson had the immediate edge because he understood the need for party organizations in each state. ("You must avail yourself of the physical force of an organized body of men," he told supporters.) Soon "Friends of Jackson" in all parts of the country were pushing for Old Hickory, the Hero of New Orleans. These "Hurra Boys" wrote political songs, printed pamphlets, and attacked Adams with a vengeance. Adams's "habits and principles are not congenial with . . . the notions of a democratic people," one Jackson supporter wrote. They also spread rumors about his mysterious "foreign wife" (Louisa was English). When the president bought a billiard table and set of ivory chess pieces, Jackson supporters accused him of purchasing a "gaming table and gambling furniture" for the White House. They called Adams a monarchist and antireligious because he traveled on the Sabbath. And of course he was smeared for his association and friendship with Secretary of State Henry Clay, who supposedly owed his position to the "corrupt bargain." (Clay was not a statesman, snarled the *New Hampshire Patriot*, but "a shyster, pettifogging in a bastard suit before a country squire [Adams].")

Adams supporters organized themselves and returned fire. Jackson, they said, had aided Aaron Burr when the latter conspired against the Union in 1806, invading Florida and nearly starting an international incident. They claimed Jackson had the personality of a dictator and that he couldn't spell (he supposedly spelled Europe as "Urope").

The Republicans also published an extremely nasty but delightfully titled pamphlet called "Reminiscences; or, an Extract from the Catalogue of General Jackson's Youthful Indiscretions between the Age of Twenty-three and Sixty." It enumerated all of Jackson's purported fights, duels, brawls, and shoot-outs. It described him as an adulterer, a gambler, a cockfighter, a slave trader, a drunkard, a thief, a liar, and the husband of a really fat wife.

The campaign saw little serious examination of the issues, such as rural America's desperate need of public works projects or tariff protection for New England manufacturers. Jackson was known for being evasive, a fact that he tried to turn into a virtue: "My real friends want no information from me on the subject of internal improvement and manufactories. . . . Was I now to come forward and reiterate my public opinions on these subjects, I would be charged with electioneering for selfish purposes."

Adams's positions were well-known—he was in favor of tariffs and public works—but his voice was lost in the din of battle. No wonder the guy was depressed.

## THE WINNER: ANDREW JACKSON

Balloting took place on different days in different states, from September through November 1828. Results indicated a clear victory for Jackson, with 642,553 votes compared to 500,897 for Adams. The campaign had been so bitter that neither candidate made the customary postelection courtesy calls on the other, and John Quincy Adams became the second American president, after his father, not to attend his successor's inauguration.

Jackson took the oath of office in March. The streets of Washington were filled with massive crowds of common people who had come from hundreds of miles away to view this historic day. Supporters famously surged into the White House, wiped their feet on delicate rugs, broke antique chairs, and ate and drank everything in sight. Thousands of dollars' worth of glass and china were broken, fights ensued, and women feared for their virtue. In the end, an exhausted Jackson slipped out the back door and into a local inn to get some sleep.

★★★

**John Q. Adams, Pimp** When people really want to get dirty, they hit below the belt. Jackson supporters claimed with utter seriousness that the prudish Adams, when serving as minister to the Russian court of Czar Alexander I, had offered his wife's maid to the ruler as a concubine. That there was a kernel of innocent truth—Adams had introduced the young woman to the czar—made the lie easier to swallow.

**Andrew Jackson, Bigamist** The Republicans returned fire with a vengeance, targeting not only Jackson but also his wife, Rachel. She had been previously married to the abusive and pathologically jealous Lewis Robards, who had finally left her in 1790 to get a divorce. Jackson married Rachel in 1791, thinking that the divorce was final, except it wasn't because Robards had delayed getting the necessary decree. The clerical oversight went undiscovered for nearly two years; once it surfaced, she and Jackson were forced to remarry just to make everything legal.

Rachel—whom Jackson loved deeply—later fell victim to the ugliest slanders imaginable. Republicans called her a "whore" and a "dirty, black wench" given to "open and notorious lewdness." The *Cincinnati Gazette* asked, "Ought a convicted adulteress and her paramour husband be placed in the highest office of this free and Christian land?"

Adams supporters hoped that Jackson might lose his cool and challenge someone to a duel, or perhaps even kill one of his tormentors. But what happened was that Rachel, who was overweight and suffering from health problems, took the attacks quite literally to heart. In December 1828, after Jackson had won the election, she died of a heart attack. Jackson grieved profoundly and was as wrathful as an Old Testament prophet. At her funeral, he intoned: "In the presence of this dear saint I can and do forgive all my enemies. But those vile wretches who have slandered her must look to God for mercy."

**Most Vicious Broadside** Perhaps the nastiest political attack on Jackson was the infamous Coffin Handbill, a widely circulated broadside displaying six coffins under the headline: "Some account of some of the Bloody Deeds of General Jackson." It went on to tell the story of the six militiamen whose order of execution Jackson had approved during the War of 1812. The men were the leaders of a mutiny of 200 militiamen who thought their terms of service were up. The army disagreed. The men were court-martialed; nearly all were merely fined, but the six ringleaders were sentenced to death. Jackson signed the execution papers, and at the time, few objected.

During the campaign, however, the Coffin Handbill painted Jackson to be bloodthirsty and merciless: "Sure he will spare! Sure JACKSON yet / Will all reprieve but one— / O hark! Those shrieks! That cry of death! / The deadly deed is done!"

**Most Comprehensive "Why You Shouldn't Vote for Him" Statement** This, from an anti-Jackson pamphlet, pretty much covers it all: "You know that Jackson is no jurist, no statesman, no politician; that he is destitute of historical, political, or statistical knowledge, that he is unacquainted with the orthography, concord, and government of his language; you know that he is a man of no labor, no patience, no investigation; in short that his whole recommendation is animal fierceness and organic energy. He is wholly unqualified by education, habit, and temper for the station of the President."

SLEAZE-O-METER

1 2 3 4 5 6 7 8 9 10

# 1832

★

## ANDREW
# JACKSON

DEMOCRAT

## VS.

### HENRY
# CLAY

NATIONAL–REPUBLICAN

★

*"THE KING UPON THE THRONE: THE PEOPLE IN THE DUST!!!"*
**—Anti-Jackson headline**

One of the supreme ironies about Andrew Jackson is that although he was the first president to be born in a log cabin and he saw himself primarily as the champion of the common man, his enemies claimed he was a dictator.

After Jackson paid for the damage to the Executive Mansion caused by the *Animal House*-style antics of his inauguration, one of his first acts was to try to rid the civil service of incompetent bureaucrats with lifelong sinecures. Claiming that "the duties of all public officers . . . are so plain and simple that men of intelligence may readily qualify themselves for their performance" (translation: any idiot can do these jobs), he initiated what he called rotation in office. His opponents dubbed it the spoils system because, naturally, any fired officeholder was replaced by a Democrat. Only some 10 percent of federal officeholders lost their jobs, but the new president became feared throughout the bureaucracy.

The 1832 election would change the political landscape by introducing the first national party conventions—an attempt to regulate nominations currently being held by state legislatures, which tended to fracture into local sectional disputes.

The first convention was held by the Antimasons, a third political party that had sprung up in opposition to such powerful secret societies as the Masons. Their candidate was the well-known orator William Wirt; the party was also the first to introduce such lasting convention features as the party platform and rules committee.

The National-Republicans—soon to start calling themselves the

Whigs—held their convention in December 1831. They nominated Congressman Henry Clay for president, with former Attorney General John Sergeant as his running mate.

The Democrats met in a hotel saloon in Baltimore in May 1832, and naturally they renominated Jackson for president. Martin Van Buren was his handpicked V.P. The Democrats also came up with an innovation in political conventions, declaring that the majority of delegates from each state would henceforth designate the single nominee.

## THE CANDIDATES

**DEMOCRAT: ANDREW JACKSON** In many ways, Andrew Jackson was a hollow man without his beloved Rachel. Although he could be chivalrous and courteous in private, his public persona was increasingly cold, unbending, and given to fits of rage. In fact, much of the time Jackson's opponents gave in to him because they were afraid of his temper.

**NATIONAL-REPUBLICAN: HENRY CLAY** Clay was the silver-tongued senator from Kentucky who had been a bitter enemy of the Democrats ever since the election of 1824, when Jackson accused him of entering into a "corrupt bargain." He and Jackson had something in common, however. Both were dueling men—Clay had fought against Senator John Randolph, and Jackson had dueled anywhere from twice to (if you believed the smears proffered by his opponents) more than a hundred times.

## THE CAMPAIGN

The American public was decidedly uninterested in the election of 1832, for two reasons. First, a deadly cholera epidemic had struck the eastern United States that summer; most people were finding it hard to focus on politics with a plague spreading across the land. Second, the main election issue was Jackson's attack on the Bank of the United States, an important concern but not exactly one that drove voter turnout.

Alexander Hamilton, the first secretary of the treasury, had established the Bank of the United States to accept tax revenue deposits to fund the national debt and issue paper money. Jackson, by contrast, liked coins that clinked in his pocket; he hated the Bank of the United States and, in particular, its president, Nicholas Biddle, a Republican old-money man. Jackson (with some accuracy) felt the bank was an elitist institution with too much power, one that made "the rich richer and the potent more powerful."

He vetoed the bank's recharter, essentially trying to put it out of business. None of which made Republican Party hounds very happy, and so they began baying. "A more deranging, radical, law-upsetting document was never promulgated by the wildest Roman fanatic," wrote one New England editor about the veto. A mob of anti-Jacksonians went to the bank's headquarters in Philadelphia to announce that the president had "wantonly trampled upon the interests of his fellow citizens." Noah Webster proclaimed that in vetoing the recharter, Jackson had announced: "I AM THE STATE!"

But Jackson continued his attack. He hated banks that issued paper money, or, as he put it, "wretched rag money." His followers made toasts to "Gold and silver, the only currency recognized by the Constitution." Jackson branded Nicholas Biddle as Czar Nick. (No wonder Biddle used funds from the bank—monies deposited by the U.S. government—to support Jackson's enemies, including Henry Clay.)

Republicans responded by tagging Jackson as King Andrew I. They also spread stories about illnesses—his health, in the blunt phrase of former vice president John C. Calhoun, was "deranged"— and attacked him for traveling on Sunday (ironic, since the same slur had been used against John Quincy Adams by the Democrats).

Nevertheless, Jackson's party organization won the day. One visiting French official saw a torchlight parade for Jackson in New York City that was a mile long. Jackson even won over Clay's home state of

Kentucky, where one disheartened Clay supporter reported that large crowds held hickory bushes and sticks in honor of Old Hickory.

## THE WINNER: ANDREW JACKSON

In the end, Jackson ran away with the election—he won 701,780 votes to Clay's 484,205. He had defeated "the overwhelming influence" of the "corrupt Aristocracy" of the Bank of the United States and continued—in a way that would influence the way Americans thought about their future presidents—to amass executive power for himself.

★★★

**Lampooning Jackson** Commercial lithography had taken hold in America in the 1820s, making it easier to turn out newspaper cartoons; before then, all illustrations had to be engraved or cut into wood or copper, a time-consuming process. And something in Andrew Jackson's tall, spare demeanor, with his Woody Woodpecker thatch of gray hair, made Republican cartoonists salivate. During the campaign of 1832, Jackson was painted as a pig about to be dissected at a barbecue by a ravenous Clay and Webster; a decrepit old man playing poker with opposition candidates Clay and William Wirt (the cards in Jackson's hand read "Intrigue," "Corruption," and "Imbecility"). He was also depicted as a king with a crown and scepter, wearing royal robes and stomping on the Constitution and Bank Charter, under the heading "Born to Command."

**Zounds!** Much like Thurston Howell III on the television show *Gilligan's Island*, Andrew Jackson was given to wonderfully apocalyptic oaths. "By Almighty God!" "By the Eternal!" and the Shakespearian "S'blood!" The only other president to match him for such rich cursing was probably Lyndon Johnson—in some ways, Jackson's twentieth-century counterpart—who was known to rip off a few choice phrases from time to time (see page 228).

**The Gallant Jackson** During his first term, Jackson lost almost his entire cabinet to the so-called Peggy Eaton Affair. When Jackson's close friend and Secretary of War John Henry Eaton married Peg O'Neale, the beautiful but notoriously unvirtuous daughter of a Washington tavern keeper, the wives of Jackson's cabinet members and Vice President John C. Calhoun shunned her. Jackson—still hurting from the attacks made against his wife, Rachel—defended Peg as "chaste as a virgin," causing much hilarity among his enemies. Secretary of State Martin Van Buren saw it as a wonderful opportunity to forward his own ambitions for the presidency and so defended Peg Eaton at every turn.

The colorful Peg Eaton continued to be a legend in her own time. Her husband died, leaving her a fortune; later, as a much older woman, she married an Italian ballet master who turned around and ran off with her granddaughter.

SLEAZE-O-METER
1 2 3 4 5 6 7 8 9 10

## 1836

★

### MARTIN
# VAN BUREN

DEMOCRAT

## VS.

### WILLIAM HENRY
# HARRISON

WHIG

★

"HIS MIND BEATS ROUND LIKE A TAME BEAR
TIED TO A STAKE, IN A LITTLE CIRCLE."
—Davy Crockett, on Martin Van Buren

The year 1836 was a volatile one in American history. Davy Crockett fought at the Alamo in March, Samuel Colt received a patent for what would soon be America's favorite "peacemaker," and Andrew Jackson, gaunter and more pissed-off than ever, continued his campaign against Nicholas Biddle and the Bank of the United States. He refused to deposit tax revenues into the bank's coffers and instead placed the money into his own "pet" banks, institutions run by his cronies. Naturally, many of these banks made unwise loans, and government revenues were lost. When Jackson's first two treasury secretaries protested against this plan, he fired them and eventually found one who would cooperate.

Jackson followed the tradition of leaving office after two terms and made sure that Democrats nominated Martin Van Buren, his handpicked successor. He insisted that the Democrats hold a national convention in Baltimore in May 1835, a good year-plus before the election. Van Buren was nominated in good order, although problems arose when Jackson pushed through the nomination of the vice-presidential candidate, Richard M. Johnson. Johnson was a hero of the War of 1812 Battle of the Thames, where he supposedly killed the Indian leader Tecumseh. He had openly lived with a black woman named Julia Chinn and had two daughters with her. Because Johnson had the nerve to present his family in public, he was reviled by Southern Democrats, who "hissed most ungraciously" when his name was presented.

Meanwhile, Jackson's enemies, the Republicans, had coalesced into a new party. The Whigs were composed of Republicans, Antimasons, and disaffected Democrats who all shared one thing in common: their dislike of Andrew Jackson and his policies. The Whigs (named after the British Reform Party that battled for the supremacy of Parliament over the king) skipped a nominating convention and instead threw three candidates at Van Buren and Johnson, hoping to keep Van Buren from a majority victory and force the election into the House of Representatives. The Whig candidates were Senator Daniel Webster of Massachusetts, Senator Hugh White of Tennessee, and William Henry Harrison, the sixty-three-year-old former Indiana Territory governor and hero of the Battle of Tippecanoe. Of the three contenders, Harrison was by far the strongest.

## THE CANDIDATES

**DEMOCRAT: MARTIN VAN BUREN** At fifty-three years old, Van Buren had been New York's governor and senator. He was a bit of a dandy who took on aristocratic airs, even though (or because) he had come from a solidly middle-class family; his father had been a popular tavern-keeper near Albany. His chief qualities, according to both his friends and his enemies, were his loyalty to Andrew Jackson, whom he served well as vice president, and his political astuteness, which is how he earned the nickname "Little Magician."

**WHIG: WILLIAM HENRY HARRISON** A congressman and senator from Ohio, Harrison was the son of a signer of the Declaration of Independence. Despite a tendency to get into personal financial trouble, he was picked to run for president because of his status as a hero of the War of 1812; destroying the Shawnee Indians at the Battle of Tippecanoe had earned him the nickname "Old Tip." In addition, having three or more Anglo-Saxon names has never hurt a presidential candidate before or since. Consider John Fitzgerald Kennedy and Lyndon Baines Johnson and George Herbert Walker Bush and, well, you get the picture.

# THE CAMPAIGN

The campaign kicked into high gear early in 1835 as the Whig rag the *New York Courier* and the *Enquirer* got beastly on Van Buren, comparing him to the "fox prowling near the barn; the mole burrowing near the ground; the pilot fish who plunges deep in the ocean in one spot and comes up in another to breathe the air." One cartoon shows Van Buren and Harrison, both bare chested and boxing. Van Buren, getting the worst of it, cries: "Stand by me Old Hickory or I'm a gone Chicken!"

Feeling confident of victory, Democrats had a hard time rousing their ire against the Whig candidate triumvirate. They labeled them "Federalists, nullifiers, and bank men" but otherwise depended, as usual, on their superb state organizations to carry the day. However, as with many elections that follow the presidency of a popular and charismatic chief executive, the 1836 contest was not so much about Van Buren or Harrison as it was about Andrew Jackson. If you liked him, you voted for Van Buren. If not, you chose Harrison or one of the other Whig candidates.

## THE WINNER: MARTIN VAN BUREN

Victory was easy for Van Buren, who pulled 764,176 votes against 738,124 for the Whig candidates combined. The Whigs did manage to confuse the vice-presidential contest; because no clear majority was attained by any one candidate, the outcome was decided by the Senate, which voted for Richard Johnson. The Whigs were further encouraged by William Henry Harrison's 550,816 votes, and they knew that Van Buren's election win was a triumph of party politics plus the power of Andrew Jackson. Van Buren the man inspired no passion. It all boded well for the election of 1840.

★★★

**Davy Crockett, Attack Dog** Reading about Davy Crockett's career in politics, one sees a starkly different picture from that of the honorable homespun hero of 1950s-TV coonskin cap fame. Crockett was a Whig attack dog, the Ann Coulter of his time. In his insanely spurious *The Life of Martin Van Buren, Heir-Apparent to the 'Government,' and the Appointed Successor of General Andrew Jackson. Containing Every Authentic Particular by Which His Extraordinary Character Has Been Formed. With a Concise History of the Events That Have Occasioned His Unparalleled Elevation; Together with a Review of His Policy as a Statesman*, Crockett (or his ghostwriter) claims that Martin Van Buren "is fifty-three years old; and notwithstanding his baldness, which reaches all round and over half down his head, like a white pitch plaster, leaving a few white floating locks, he is only three years older than I am. His face is a good deal shrivelled, and he looks sorry, not for any thing he has gained, but what he may lose." He goes on to administer the coup de grace: "Martin Van Buren is laced up in corsets, such as women in a town wear, and if possible tighter than the best of them. It would be difficult to say from his personal appearance, whether he was a man or a woman, but for his large red and gray whiskers."

Unfortunately, dear Davy was skewered on a Mexican bayonet before he could observe if his skewering of Van Buren hit home.

**Old Executioners Never Die, They Just . . . Wish They Had Killed More** On the day after Van Buren's inauguration, Andrew Jackson sat reminiscing over his presidency. He remarked to his friend that he had only two regrets. One, he should have shot Henry Clay. Two, it would have been nice if he'd had a chance to hang John C. Calhoun.

SLEAZE-O-METER

1840

★

WILLIAM HENRY
# HARRISON

WHIG

## VS.

MARTIN
# VAN BUREN

DEMOCRAT

★

"PASSION AND PREJUDICE PROPERLY AROUSED
AND DIRECTED WOULD DO ABOUT AS WELL AS PRINCIPLE
AND REASON IN A PARTY CONTEST."
—Thomas Elder, Whig politician

Martin Van Buren didn't know it when he entered the presidency, but he was a "gone chicken" before he had barely begun—all thanks to the Panic of 1837, the worst economic recession the country had yet seen. And the reason the Whigs started joking about Martin Van Ruin.

That this crisis was partially the result of Andrew Jackson's monetary policies made things even worse for Van Buren. Under Jackson, the U.S. government made millions by selling land to speculators. The government then deposited the money in Jackson's "pet" banks— run by his cronies—instead of the Bank of the United States, which Jackson had gutted. Those local banks then gave large loans, often to speculators who bought even more land from the government. Add to this vicious circle high inflation, a crop failure in 1835, and a new "hard money" law forcing banks to repay money borrowed from the government in specie rather than currency, and by the summer of 1837 America's economic life had ground to a standstill. The ensuing recession would last several years, forcing factories to close and sending families to beg on the streets.

The Whigs held their first national nominating convention in December 1839 in Harrisburg, Pennsylvania. A strange thing happened. The boisterous convention, attended by farmers, disgruntled bankers, protariff and antitariff forces, slaveholders and abolitionists, resembled nothing more than a passionate Democratic rally. Henry Clay hoped to be the Whig candidate (a young Illinois lawyer in attendance, Abraham Lincoln, pronounced him the "beau ideal of a statesman"), but because Clay was a Mason, the Antimasons refused to vote for him. The nomination instead went to Old Tip, William Henry Harrison. His vice-presidential ticket-balancer was Senator

John Tyler of Virginia.

The Democrats knew they were in trouble when they met in Baltimore in May to pick their candidate, and thousands of Whigs were waiting for them in the streets, marching and chanting, "With Tip and Tyler / We'll bust Van's biler."

Well, maybe you had to be there, but the demonstration certainly got the Democrats' attention. The times they were a-changin' but Van Buren won the nomination anyway. Many Democrats balked once again at Richard Johnson (who "openly and shamefully lives in adultery with a buxom young negro," as one anonymous letter writer saw it), but in the end, Johnson was nominated as well.

## THE CANDIDATES

**DEMOCRAT: MARTIN VAN BUREN** Van Buren was basically a decent guy with a lot of government experience who didn't know how to handle an economic crisis. And after four years in the presidency, many people still perceived him as Andrew Jackson's lackey. The first cartoon portraying the Democratic Party as a donkey appeared during this election. Jackson rode the animal and Van Buren walked behind it, hat in hand, saying obsequiously, "I shall tread in the footsteps of my illustrious predecessor."

**WHIG: WILLIAM HENRY HARRISON** At age sixty-eight, Harrison was getting up there in years, but his reputation as a war hero still inspired much loyalty. And just as George H. W. Bush would one day transform himself from New England preppie to Texas "aw-shucks" oilman, this Virginia aristocrat portrayed himself as a "just-folks" guy with a log cabin constituency. Voters bought it.

## THE CAMPAIGN

The Whigs were handed a wonderful gift at the beginning of the 1840 campaign. Just after their convention, the *Baltimore Republican* published a remark about Harrison supposedly made by a Whig backer of Henry Clay: "Give him a barrel of hard cider and settle a pension of two thousand a year on him and, my word for it, he would sit the remainder of his days in a log cabin, by the side of a 'sea-coal' fire, and study moral philosophy." It was meant to be an insult, but the Whigs turned it into the campaign's greatest asset. In almost no time, Harrison became the "log cabin and hard cider" candidate, a guy who hung out with the coonskin-cap boys, plowed the back forty with his own hands, and was always ready to raise a glass of cider. Never mind his Virginia ancestry and ownership of at least 2,000 acres—Harrison was now a man of the people. The Whigs organized huge rallies attended by thousands and held parades four miles long. The log cabin symbol was everywhere, from log-cabin-shaped newspapers and pamphlets to songbooks and badges. You could buy Log Cabin Emollient or whiskey in log-cabin-shaped bottles from the E. C. Booz distillery (incidentally, this is how the word *booze* entered the English language).

The Democrats protested, mostly in vain, that Harrison wasn't born in a log cabin, didn't drink hard cider, and, when you came right down to it, wasn't much of a war hero (a mediocre strategist, Harrison sustained heavy casualties in the fight at Tippecanoe). It didn't do a bit of good. Crying "Tippecanoe and Tyler, too!" the Whigs charged onward. With Democrats whispering that Harrison did nothing without his political handlers—that he was "An Old Gentleman in Leading Strings"—the Whigs had their candidate make a few stump speeches, the first presidential candidate ever to do so. Democrats groaned that the man talked about nothing, but crowds everywhere gathered to hear him anyway.

## THE WINNER: WILLIAM HENRY HARRISON

The popular vote was closer than some expected: Harrison's 1,275,390 votes won out over Van Buren's 1,128,854. But Old Tip killed it in the Electoral College, with 234 votes to the president's 60. An incredible 78 percent of eligible voters turned out.

The contest had been so vitriolic that there was no kissing and making up afterward. "We have been sung down, lied down, and drunk down," wrote the *Wheeling Times*. "Right joyous are we that the campaign of 1840 is closed." The Whigs were not exactly gracious in victory. Harrison's election, they proclaimed, was proof that voters had "placed their seal of condemnation upon a band of the most desperate, aspiring and unprincipled demagogues that ever graced the annals of despotism."

★★★

**Running Off at the Mouth** A congressman named Charles Ogle made a three-day-long speech in the House of Representatives, arguing that the White House was "as splendid as that of the Caesars, and as richly adorned as the proudest Asiatic mansion." According to Ogle, Van Buren had mirrors nine feet tall, slept on fine French linens, ate from silver plates with forks of gold, and, most incredibly, constructed on the White House grounds a pair of "clever sized hills" that resembled "an Amazon's bosom, with a miniature knoll on its apex, to denote the nipple."

These were, as Democrats and even some horrified Whigs protested, some of the strangest and most twisted lies ever argued in the House of Representatives. Nevertheless, the speech was distributed nationwide and further established the dichotomy between the supposedly aristocratic Van Buren and his supposedly countrified opponent Harrison.

**Mum's the Word** The Democrats attacked Harrison for the way his handlers—among them Thurlow Weed, the brilliant Tammany operative who was managing the campaign—kept him from replying to even the most innocuous queries about political issues. Was "Granny Harrison" senile? Was he a "man in an iron cage"? The Whigs denied the charges, but in private, the prominent Whig Nicholas Biddle cautioned, "Let the use of pen and ink be wholly forbidden [to Harrison] as if he were a mad poet in Bedlam."

**Old Kinderhook, Okay?** The election of 1840 may have given America its enduring expression "okay." Van Buren hailed from Kinderhook, New York, and some of his supporters started a new organization called the O.K. Club to promote Van Buren's candidacy—O.K. standing for Old Kinderhook. Some etymologists believe the expression existed before Van Buren's campaign (many think it began as an abbreviation of "all correct"), but the boy from Old Kinderhook certainly helped popularize it.

SLEAZE-O-METER

**1844**

★

JAMES K.
# POLK

DEMOCRAT

## VS.

HENRY
# CLAY

WHIG

★

"A MORE RIDICULOUS, CONTEMPTIBLE, AND FORLORN
CANDIDATE WAS NEVER PUT FORTH BY ANY PARTY."
—*New York Herald*, on James Polk

U nfortunately for the Whigs, the good times stopped rolling very quickly. One month into his term, William Henry Harrison was dead of pneumonia. His illness was supposedly the result of his 100-minute inaugural address, presented without hat or coat on a blustery March day.

The Whigs were bereft, the Democrats joyous. So strong were the ill feelings lingering from 1840 that most Democrats failed to even pause for a hypocritical moment of silence in honor of the fallen president. Poet William Cullen Bryant said he regretted Harrison's death only because "he did not live long enough to prove his incapacity for the office of President." And former president Andrew Jackson turned his eyes heavenward, calling Harrison's death "the deed of a kind and overruling Providence."

The Whigs turned to John Tyler, the first vice president ever to replace a sitting president, a man whom John Quincy Adams tartly dubbed "His Accidency." What occurred next proved to future political generations that choosing a vice-presidential candidate is a lot like picking a spouse—after the honeymoon, things change.

Once in power, Tyler started acting far more like a Democrat than the "firm and decided" Whig he had declared himself to be. He vetoed a Whig bill for a new Bank of the United States (to replace the one Jackson had gutted) and went head-to-head with Whig leader Henry Clay, who resigned his Senate seat in protest. All but one member of Tyler's cabinet would soon quit. Essentially, the party disowned its own president, declaring in an extraordinary statement: "Those who bought the President into power can no longer, in any manner or degree, be justly held responsible or blamed for [his actions]."

Naturally, Tyler's chances of being Whig candidate for president in 1844 were less than zero. He made overtures to the Democrats, but they didn't trust him either, and he was left out in the cold. But he still had one surprise up his sleeve. In 1843, Tyler negotiated a treaty to annex the slaveholding Republic of Texas, an issue that had been sidestepped by both parties because of the volatile slavery issue. But Tyler put a patriotic spin on it—if we don't grab Texas, he proclaimed, Mexico will. Although his treaty was vetoed by the Senate in 1844, the debate over annexation was the pivot around which the election revolved.

The Whigs assembled in Baltimore on May 1, 1844, and nominated Henry Clay for president. For vice president they picked New Jersey politician Theodore Frelinghuysen, a so-called Christian gentleman who was supposed to balance Clay's reputation for high living, boozing, and playing cards.

The Democrats met a month later, also in Baltimore, and their convention was stormy to say the least. Martin Van Buren was considered the front-running candidate, but many didn't like that he opposed the annexation of Texas. Finally, after eight rounds of balloting, former Speaker of the House and Andrew Jackson protégé James K. Polk was picked as a compromise candidate. The vice-presidential nod went to Pennsylvania lawyer George M. Dallas.

## THE CANDIDATES

**DEMOCRAT: JAMES K. POLK** James K. Who? That's what most Americans were saying after the Democratic pick was announced. But Polk, former governor of Tennessee as well as House Speaker, was admired by many Democrats as a solid and loyal party member. Not surprisingly, the Whigs hated him. On Polk's last day as Speaker, Henry Clay had made a special trip from the Senate to shout from the visitor's gallery: "Go home, God damn you. Go home where you belong!"

**WHIG: HENRY CLAY** Clay had influenced American politics for twenty-five years as Speaker, senator, and party leader. This was his third try for the presidency, after 1824 and 1832, and he wanted it bad.

## THE CAMPAIGN

The Whigs immediately targeted James K. Polk's obscurity and made derisive comments to newspaper editors all over the country: "Who is James K. Polk?" they cried. "Good God, what a nomination!" They claimed that the very raccoons in the forests of Tennessee were now singing: "Ha, ha, ha, what a nominee / Is Jimmy Polk of Tennessee!"

You couldn't call Henry Clay obscure, but the Democrats fired back at something else—the candidate's supposed baggage train of gambling, dueling, womanizing, and "By the Eternal!" swearing. An alleged Protestant minister wrote a letter published in many Democratic papers claiming to have heard Clay curse extensively during a steamboat trip. A popular leaflet titled *Twenty-One Reasons Why Clay Should Not Be Elected* listed as reason two that "Clay spends his days at the gambling table and his nights in a brothel." Clay was also accused of being a white slaver, and the Democrats hammered again at the "corrupt bargain" that he and John Quincy Adams supposedly made to steal the presidency from Jackson in 1824. Not much was true, but Clay played enough cards and drank enough liquor for the mud to stick. It was much harder to slander Polk, a man so thoroughly colorless that his nickname was "Polk the Plodder."

The Whigs tried to brand Polk as a man who owned slaves to elicit votes from abolitionists, but that was a little tricky because both Polk and Clay were slave owners. The Whigs got around the technicality by claiming it was all a matter of degree—that Polk was really an *ultra* slaveholder, in slavery "up to his ears." One Whig newspaper stated that Polk had branded the initials *J.K.P* onto the shoulders of a group of forty of his slaves, a claim so patently untrue that the paper later printed a retraction.

## THE WINNER: JAMES K. POLK

Although the term *Manifest Destiny* was coined by New York journalist John L. O'Sullivan only in 1845, that's essentially what the 1844 election was all about. Polk was firmly in favor of annexation—not only of Texas but of Oregon Territory as well—hence his famous campaign slogan, "Fifty-four Forty or Fight!" which referred to the northernmost latitude to which America should extend. Clay waffled on annexation, which cost southern votes and annoyed northerners. And there was one other factor, an effective third-party outing by the Liberty Party of New York, a group of abolitionists and radicals, who garnered 62,000 votes nationwide.

In the end, Polk beat Clay by only about 39,000 popular votes, although he bested him in the Electoral College 170 to 105.

★★★

**The Nasty Personal Smear That Henry Clay Only Wished Were True** Democrats accused Clay, an admitted lover of gambling, of having invented poker. In fact, Clay was only a superb practitioner of the newfangled bluffing card game, which was based on the English game of brag.

**Hey, Go Easy on That Stuff!** In desperation to find a way to defame Polk, Sam Houston, hero of the Texas war against Mexico, proclaimed that the moderate drinker was "victim of the use of water as a beverage." This tactic—attacking a candidate for not drinking enough—was unsuccessful and rarely used in subsequent presidential smear campaigns.

**Voter Fraud, 1844-Style** Since Polk had Scotch-Irish heritage, a group of key New York City Democrats used their influence to naturalize thousands of Irish immigrants, eager to have them vote in the election. The Whigs quickly pounced on these newly registered voters, telling them that Clay's name was in fact "Patrick O'Clay." And in what is probably the first incident of floating voter fraud, a Democratic Party boss in New Orleans sent a boatload of Democrats up the Mississippi River. They stopped and voted in three different places.

# 1848

---

**AT A GLANCE**

## ZACHARY TAYLOR VS. LEWIS CASS

Historians may say that Jimmy Polk lacked personality (all right, they really say that he was "colorless and methodical," "a loner," "not well liked," a "stern task-master," "inflexible," and "Puritanical"), but they all agree he worked his butt off. Elected at the age of forty-nine, Polk was the youngest president to date; he regularly put in ten to twelve hours a day and held two cabinet meetings a week. Polk put it this way: "No President who performs his duty faithfully and conscientiously can have any leisure."

Just how faithfully Polk performed can be judged by history: of the four goals he set for himself—reducing the tariff, reestablishing an independent treasury (a way to get money out of the hands of private banks without a national bank), acquiring Oregon from the British, and acquiring California from Mexico—he accomplished the first three in a year.

The last required a "small war," as Polk called it, against Mexico. The conflict turned out bigger and bloodier than Polk expected, for although the Mexicans lost all the major battles, they simply would not surrender. The nation grew increasingly tired of dead bodies returning home. By 1848 the war was won and the United States was significantly larger, but for the president's popularity, the damage was done.

Big and bloody conflicts often make heroes of military men, who then run for president. Such was the case with General Zachary Taylor, "Old Rough and Ready," hero of the battle of Buena Vista. The Whigs nominated Taylor for president when they convened in Philadelphia in June 1847. His running mate was Millard Fillmore, former congressman and comptroller of New York State.

The Democrats were having a much harder time finding a candidate. Polk had made few friends in his own party and decided not to run for reelection. The best the Democrats could come up with was Lewis Cass, former Michigan governor and U.S. senator, who picked General William O. Butler, another Mexican war hero, as his vice president.

**THE CAMPAIGN** The sixty-four-year-old Taylor had the perfect voting record for a presidential candidate—he had never voted, for anyone. He was as middle-of-the-road as you could get. He was a southerner but not too much of slaveholder; he was a war hero but not a man who started a war; he was a Whig but, as Taylor himself put it, "not an ultra Whig." No one could tell what "Old Rough and Ready" was thinking, but a few suspected the answer was "not much."

Lewis Cass was a nice enough fellow and had a distinguished career, but his name rhymed with *ass* and *gas*. Predictably enough, he was depicted in cartoons as "General Gass," with cannons farting noxious fumes out of his belly, or as "The Gas Bag," with an enormous rear end, ready to lift off into the sky like a hot-air balloon. Whigs claimed that Cass had sold white men into slavery (not true). They also said he was guilty of graft in a previous job as superintendent of Indian Affairs (another lie). Finally, they just gave up and called him a "pot-bellied, mutton-headed cucumber," which seemed to sum it up nicely.

Taylor also received his fair share of abuse. One cartoon showed a phrenologist measuring his head with a pair of calipers. The good scientist's judgment? Taylor was "Obstinate and Mulish" as well as "Utterly wanting in all Sympathy."

**THE WINNER: ZACHARY TAYLOR** Everyone now voted on November 7 because of a newly enacted federal law, and the majority voted for Taylor. The victor won the election 1,361,393 votes to Cass's 1,223,460. It was close, mainly because Martin Van Buren had leapt into the race with an antislavery splinter party, the Free Soilers, and garnered more than 290,000 votes. The campaign issue of slavery was quickly coming of age. (Interesting footnote: When the Whigs won, a Democratic appointee named Nathaniel Hawthorne was fired from his civil service position at the Salem Custom House, at which point the poor man had no choice but to write *The Scarlet Letter*.)

SLEAZE-O-METER

1852

FRANKLIN
# PIERCE
DEMOCRAT

VS.

WINFIELD
# SCOTT
WHIG

"TIS SAID THAT WHEN IN MEXICO,
WHILE LEADING ON HIS FORCE,
PIERCE TOOK A SUDDEN FAINTING FIT,
AND TUMBLED OFF HIS HORSE."
—Whig campaign song

Wow, those Whigs—they sure know how to kill a good party! Just a few years after William Henry Harrison became the first president to die in office, Zachary Taylor became the second. "Old Rough and Ready" gave his inauguration address on a raw windy day in March 1849 and then settled in for about sixteen months' worth of presidenting. On July 9, 1850, Taylor died of gastroenteritis supposedly brought on by eating tainted fruit and chugging iced milk and water after a blazing Fourth of July ceremony. Rumors lingered for years that he had been poisoned with arsenic, but these were disproved in 1991 when Taylor's body—now much more rough than ready—was exhumed and samples of his hair and fingernail tissue tested negative for large amounts of the toxin.

During his brief tenure, Taylor faced issues regarding new American territories that would permeate presidential politics for the next decade. With the Gold Rush beginning in 1849, the population of California swelled and soon started clamoring for admission to the Union. Henry Clay introduced his famous Compromise of 1850, which suggested that California be admitted as a free state, that New Mexico (which included present-day Utah and Arizona) be admitted "with no mention of slavery," and that a more vigorous Fugitive Slave Law be enacted.

Clay's Compromise pleased neither northern radicals, who abhorred the Fugitive Slave Law, nor southern ones, who were already talking about secession. After Taylor died, his vice president, Millard Fillmore, took over and supported the compromise measures. Big mistake. In June 1852, the Whigs held their national convention in Baltimore. A splinter group of more than sixty delegates opposed to the Clay Compromise threw their votes to General Winfield Scott of

Virginia, a hero of the Mexican War. Chaos ensued. It took fifty-three ballots, but in the end, Scott triumphed over both Millard Fillmore and Nathaniel Webster. Secretary of the Navy William Graham would run as his V.P.

Typically, the Whigs did not run firmly on an antislavery platform. They waffled, saying they would support the compromise "until time and experience shall demonstrate the necessity of further legislation."

Things were equally chaotic on the Democratic side when the party met, also in Baltimore, to pick its nominee. This time, delegates bypassed party warhorses like Lewis Cass and James Buchanan and, after much boisterous debate, picked the little-known Franklin Pierce of New Hampshire. His running mate was Senator William King of Alabama. The Democrats came out firmly in favor of the compromise.

## THE CANDIDATES

DEMOCRAT: FRANKLIN PIERCE Pierce, the son of a New Hampshire governor, was a good-looking and well-liked congressman and senator. He had fought in the Mexican War and, at forty-eight years old, was a relatively youthful presidential candidate. Yet he was dogged by alcoholism and tragedy, which at this point included the deaths of two of his three children. Pierce pledged, along with his party, to execute all the provisions of the compromise, including the Fugitive Slave Law.

WHIG: WINFIELD SCOTT The good general was sixty-six years old, six feet five inches tall, and looked every bit the Mexican War hero he was. Scott was essentially against the compromise but waffled on his public pronouncements. Like Clay before him and many a presidential candidate after, he would pay the price for being afraid to come down clearly on one side of an important issue.

# THE CAMPAIGN

Everyone is quick to congratulate a war veteran for bravely serving his country, until that same war veteran decides to run for president. Once your name appears on a ballot, all your so-called heroism comes into question. Franklin Pierce was attacked with as much vehemence in 1852 as John Kerry was excoriated by Bush supporters in 2004.

The attacks centered on Pierce's apparent "fainting fit" during a battle in Mexico, which caused him to be carried off to safety. Ignoring the fact that Pierce suffered severely from a knee injury the day before, the Whigs had a field day with the rumor, calling him the Fainting General and asking voters if they wanted a coward for a president. In one satirical cartoon, General Scott rides a proud cock and Pierce sits atop a goose, with the former sneering at his rival, "What's the matter, Pierce? Feel 'Faint'?"

The Democrats, for their part, assailed Scott as "Old Fuss and Feathers," a nickname invented by his officers, who saw firsthand that the general was, to put it mildly, a bit of a pompous ass. Using his waffling on the compromise issue, they took him to task for supposedly being a puppet of New York senator William H. Seward, a radical antislavery Whig.

With the number of Irish immigrants growing, Catholicism had also become a campaign issue. Democrats laughed at Scott's attempts to curry favor with Irish Catholics by telling them that one of his daughters, since deceased, had been a nun. (The story was true, but such blatant pandering made it sound like a lie.) The Whigs retaliated by digging up a clause in the New Hampshire constitution prohibiting Catholics from holding public office and then accused Pierce of writing it.

Scott went a step further by addressing crowds of immigrants during a speaking tour, still uncommon practice for candidates. He spoke with all the unctuousness of the most politically correct twenty-first-century presidential candidate: "Fellow citizens. When I say fellow citizens I mean native and adopted as well as those who intend to become citizens." When Scott heard an Irish accent, he would exclaim: "I hear that rich brogue. It makes me remember the noble deeds of Irishmen, many of whom I have led to battle and victory."

## THE WINNER: FRANKLIN PIERCE

Scott's wearing of the green did little good. In the end, Americans preferred a candidate who at least said what he thought, and perhaps some wished that Henry Clay's compromise would end the battle over slavery. With thirty-one states voting, Franklin Pierce took all but four, receiving 1,607,510 votes to Scott's 1,386,942. At his inauguration, the new president said: "I fervently hope that the question [of slavery] is at rest, and that no sectional or ambitious or fanatical excitement may again threaten the durability of our institutions."

★★★

**The Well-Fought Bottle** Franklin Pierce was known to have a drinking problem, which he kept at bay as a congressman and senator by joining the Temperance League. But his alcoholism was fair game in the campaign, just as Senator Thomas Eagleton's alcoholism and "nervous exhaustion" became an issue in 1972. The Whigs called Pierce the "hero of many a well-fought bottle" and ferociously stoked the issue throughout the campaign. Ultimately, Pierce's well-fought bottle was a losing one. He died of cirrhosis in 1869.

**It Helps to Have a Great American Author on Your Side** Or does it? Franklin Pierce and Nathaniel Hawthorne were buddies from Bowdoin College who became lifelong friends. In 1852 Hawthorne—thrown out of work by the Whig victory in the last election—wrote a campaign biography for Pierce, who rewarded him with the job of consul to Liverpool. Unfortunately, having the dark and self-doubting Hawthorne write your bio is a bit like hiring Franz Kafka to pen press releases for your good cause. Below is an excerpt from the preface to *The Life of Franklin Pierce:*

"THE AUTHOR of this memoir—being so little of a politician that he scarcely feels entitled to call himself a member of any party—would not voluntarily have undertaken the work here offered to the public. Neither can he flatter himself that he has been remarkably successful in the performance of his task, viewing it in the light of a political biography . . . intended to operate upon the minds of multitudes, during a presidential canvass. This species of writing is too remote from his customary occupations—and, he may, add, from his tastes—to be very satisfactorily done, without more time and practice than he would be willing to expend for such a purpose."

SLEAZE-O-METER

## 1856

★

### JAMES
# BUCHANAN

DEMOCRAT

## VS.

### JOHN
# FRÉMONT

REPUBLICAN

★

**"I DID NOT INTEND TO KILL HIM, BUT
I DID INTEND TO WHIP HIM!"**
—South Carolina Congressman Preston Brooks,
after nearly beating to death Massachusetts Senator
Sumner in Senate Chambers

Franklin Pierce was sworn in on a blustery March day, amid swirling snow and biting winds. Only weeks before, he and his family had been in a train accident. The single casualty was his eleven-year-old son, Bennie, the last of his children, who died before his eyes. Distraught, his wife was unable to accompany her husband to Washington; Pierce, though deeply religious, became the only president in U.S history who refused to place his hand on the Bible during the swearing-in. Pierce's vice president–elect, William King, also was absent from the inauguration. He was in Cuba, ill with tuberculosis, and died a month later.

Pierce took to hard drinking again and soon revealed himself to be a weak president unable to hold his party together. Democratic senator Stephen A. Douglas of Illinois, interested in pushing through a transcontinental railroad that would please his powerful Chicago constituency, persuaded Pierce to go along with a bill that reorganized lands west of Missouri into the Kansas and Nebraska Territories, which would soon be divided into the bill's two eponymous states. In his desire to accomplish this goal, Douglas made the mistake of bowing to powerful southern interests. At their behest, he pushed through what became known as the Kansas-Nebraska Act, which abrogated the Missouri Compromise, wherein slavery was kept below latitude 36°30′. Instead, Kansas and Nebraska would decide by "popular sovereignty" whether to be free or slave-holding states.

All hell broke loose. The parties split along slavery and antislavery lines, with the Whigs simply disintegrating. Disgusted by election losses and the party's inability to take a firm stance against slavery, dissident Whigs and antislavery Democrats met in February 1854 in Ripon, Wisconsin, to form a new political organization known as the

Republicans, named in honor of Jefferson's old party.

The Republicans gained strength as the party was joined by additional former Whigs (mainly from the north and west). They held their national convention in Philadelphia in June 1856, nominating John C. Frémont, hero of Western exploration, for president and Senator William L. Dayton of New Jersey as his running mate. Their platform was based on admission of Kansas as a free state and opposition to any new slave states.

The Democrats met in Cincinnati in June. They ruled out the possibility of reelecting the current president (one popular campaign slogan was "Anyone but Pierce!") and instead settled on James Buchanan, secretary of state under James Polk and Pierce's minister to England. Buchanan had been out of the country during most of the Kansas-Nebraska Act fight, thus avoiding death by association in the eyes of the public.

## THE CANDIDATES

**DEMOCRAT: JAMES BUCHANAN** Buchanan was a sixty-five-year-old bachelor and frequent presidential contender. He had been a possible candidate for president in 1844, 1848, and 1852, but each time someone else got the nod. This time he was, as one prominent Democrat said, "the most available and most unobjectionable choice." His V.P. was Senator John C. Breckinridge of Kentucky.

**REPUBLICAN: JOHN C. FRÉMONT** Frémont was forty-three, handsome and dashing, and a former army officer whose pioneering exploration of the West earned him the nickname "The Pathfinder." The Republicans were determined to turn Frémont into a political matinee idol; they sold poster-size colored lithographic likenesses of him for a buck apiece. John Greenleaf Whittier even wrote an adoring poem called "The Pass of the Sierras." His vice president was William Dayton, a former senator from New Jersey.

# THE CAMPAIGN

The campaign of 1856 revolved around the serious matter of slavery—not until the Vietnam War would a single issue so polarize presidential politics. The subject aroused such intense passion in Americans that outbursts of violence were common. One bloody incident occurred when proslavery forces raided an antislavery newspaper office in the town of Lawrenceville, Kansas, killing five men. In response, John Brown and other men attacked a proslavery town, killing five more. An eye for an eye.

Republicans held mass meetings and marched through the streets, joined by such northern thinkers and writers as Ralph Waldo Emerson and Henry Wadsworth Longfellow. Abraham Lincoln, who had been a potential Republican candidate for vice president, beat the drums for the party.

The Democrats responded by hurling the usual assortment of insults at Frémont. They claimed he was a drunkard and a slave owner, guilty of brutal treatment of California Indians. They accused him of lying or exaggerating his discoveries in the West. They parodied his election slogan of "Free Soil, Free Men, Fremont, and Victory!" chanting: "Free Soilers, Fremonters, Free Niggers, and Freebooters!" One thing Frémont's accusers said made sense to a lot of people: his radically antislavery stance made him a polarizing candidate. His election would surely cause the south to secede from the Union.

# THE WINNER: JAMES BUCHANAN

Almost 80 percent of eligible voters participated in the election, the third highest turnout in American history (1876 holds the record with 81.8 percent, followed by 1860 with 81.2 percent). James Buchanan won with 1,836,072 votes, compared to Frémont's 1,342,345. For the new and underfunded Republican Party, however, Frémont's respectable tally suggested that 1860 might hold great promise.

★★★

**Gay Bashing, Nineteenth-Century-Style** James Buchanan never married. His longtime roommate in Washington (then, as now, many members of Congress shared apartments to cut down costs) was Senator William Rufus King of Alabama. As far back as the Jackson administration, rumors circulated about a possible homosexual liaison between Buchanan and King. Andrew Jackson called Buchanan "Miss Nancy," and the nickname stuck. (Buchanan was a Jackson supporter, but Jackson disliked him in the extreme. He made him minister to Russia only because, he told a friend, "it was as far as I could send him out of my sight.") Henry Clay liked to taunt his fellow senator to his face, saying to Buchanan, "I wish I had a more ladylike manner of expressing myself."

**The Crime of Catholicism** William T. Seward once said that John C. Frémont was "nearly convicted of being a Catholic." Frémont's wife, the daughter of Senator Thomas Hart Benton, was a Catholic, and though Frémont was a staunch Episcopalian, he had allowed a priest to marry them (for want of another available clergyman). In pamphlets such as "Frémont's Romanism Established," the candidate was attacked as a secret Catholic, one who would surface with allegiances to the Roman pope. At the time these were serious charges, and they hurt Frémont in some political circles. But Frémont felt that to respond to the slurs would be to give them credence, and he suffered in silence.

**Hang It All!** James Buchanan suffered a from congenital palsy that caused his head to tilt to the left. Frémont supporters claimed the slight slope was really a result of Buchanan's bungled attempt to hang himself. And a man who couldn't even do away with himself should never be president, should he?

SLEAZE-O-METER

1860

★

ABRAHAM
# LINCOLN
REPUBLICAN

VS.

STEPHEN
# DOUGLAS
DEMOCRAT

★

"THE CONDUCT OF THE REPUBLICAN PARTY IN THIS
NOMINATION IS A REMARKABLE INDICATION OF A SMALL
INTELLECT, GROWING SMALLER."
— *New York Herald*

I n 1860 the U.S. population was just over 31 million, and every man,
woman, and child was anticipating the terrible storm of war.

Throughout James Buchanan's term, his administration had
been held hostage by the boiling factional dispute over slavery.
Two days after his inauguration, the Supreme Court handed down
judgment in the *Dred Scott* case, declaring that a freed slave who had
moved back to Mississippi could be legally enslaved. The result was
that when it came to new states, all bets were off—no more Missouri
Compromise, no more "popular sovereignty." If a man in Kansas or
Nebraska wanted to own a slave, so be it. The southern states were
ecstatic, the north was enraged, and political debate soon became
tinged with violence.

The Democrats held their convention in Charleston, South
Carolina, in April. Senator Stephen A. Douglas from Illinois—pro-
ponent of popular sovereignty, famous for his 1858 Senate race debates with his old buddy and adversary Abraham Lincoln—was the
leading candidate of party moderates. He refused to put a proslavery
plank in the party platform. But radical southern delegates vowed
they would not apologize for slavery—in fact they would "declare
it right" and "advocate its extension." Refusing to support Douglas,
the delegates of Alabama, Mississippi, Florida, Texas, and most of
Louisiana, South Carolina, Arkansas, Delaware, and Georgia—45
delegates in all—withdrew from the convention. Without the two-
thirds majority required to elect a candidate, the Democrats were
forced to adjourn until June, when they met again in Baltimore. This

time, they nominated Douglas for president, with Herschel Johnson, former governor of Georgia, as his running mate. The candidates would run on a relatively moderate popular sovereignty platform.

The Republicans met in Chicago at the "Wigwam," a massive two-story wooden structure that could accommodate ten thousand; it was the first building ever constructed especially for a political convention. They knew they were in a strong position to win the election, thanks to all the Democratic disarray. As the convention began, the chief contender was William Seward, former governor of New York and a powerful antislavery speaker who had the backing of New York City boss Thurlow Weed and his Tammany machinery. So sure of victory were Seward's supporters that a cannon had been set up on Seward's lawn in Albany, ready to blast a celebratory shot at just the right time. But then conventioneers began to wonder whether a tall skinny former congressman named Abraham Lincoln might be a good compromise. Lincoln, who was remembered for his debates against Douglas in the 1858 senatorial race, was the more moderate candidate many delegates were seeking.

As the nomination battle heated up, dirty tricks abounded. Thurlow Weed promised $100,000 to the Indiana and Illinois delegations (which supported Lincoln) if they threw their votes to Seward. No deal. Lincoln backers waited until Seward's delegates were marching in demonstration around the convention hall and then distributed counterfeit tickets to other Lincoln backers waiting outside. When Seward's men returned, they found they could not get back into the building to vote.

The Wigwam was set for a rocking, rolling, reeling ride the likes of which would not be seen again in Chicago until 1968. When the voting began, ten thousand people were inside the hall, with another twenty thousand screaming and chanting on the streets. One observer described the noise inside: "Imagine all the hogs ever slaughtered in Cincinnati giving their death squeals together, plus a score of steam whistles going." After four rounds of balloting, the vote went to Abraham Lincoln.

Lincoln, waiting anxiously in Springfield, was informed by telegram of his victory but advised to stay away. Seward backers, many weeping profusely, were in such a state that it was unadvisable for the new nominee to meet with them in Chicago. The party's judicious choice for Lincoln's vice president was Hannibal Hamlin, senator from Maine and a friend of the defeated Seward.

The stage was set for the most important presidential campaign in U.S. history.

## THE CANDIDATES

**REPUBLICAN: ABRAHAM LINCOLN** Unlike William Henry Harrison, the six-foot-four-inch Lincoln really had been born in a log cabin, and he capitalized on his humble upbringing. He may have received minimal formal schooling while living the hardscrabble life in Kentucky, Indiana, and Illinois, but he had worked his way up to become a circuit lawyer, state legislator, and member of the U.S. Congress. His folksy exterior concealed a brilliant political mind, which would prove to be his most valuable campaign asset.

**DEMOCRAT: STEPHEN A. DOUGLAS** Officially five feet four inches tall (although some estimates erroneously capped him at five feet), Stephen Douglas was as short as Lincoln was tall. In fact, the Illinois senator was known as the "Little Giant." He earned the nickname as much for his bulky boxlike torso and head as for his declamatory abilities and outsized political stances. "Let the people rule!" was his famous cry, which meant allowing each state to decide whether slavery should be allowed within its territory. But for much of his political career, Douglas had to hide that he had married a North Carolina woman who owned a large slavery-driven cotton plantation.

## THE CAMPAIGN

The Republicans held massive rallies and organized marches several miles long, with hordes of Wide Awakes—the Republican faithful who would save the Union—holding torches and likenesses of "Honest Abe" while sporting oilcloth capes and strange black enamel caps to protect themselves from dripping torch oil. In surviving lithographs, they bear a weird resemblance to certain members of the Village People. Boston Republicans organized a rail-splitter's battalion; in homage to Lincoln, each member stood exactly six feet four inches tall. Throughout the campaign, partisan newspapers published countless jokes at Douglas's expense, including the low blow "Lincoln is like a rail; Douglas is the reverse—rail spelled backwards—liar."

Already at a disadvantage, the Democrats tried to riposte. Lincoln, they said, had participated in duels. As a congressman during the Mexican War (which Lincoln opposed), he failed to vote for troop provisions. One claim purported that he had slandered Thomas Jefferson by saying that Jefferson had sold his own children (by Sally Hemings) into slavery.

Lincoln denied these lies privately but was too smart to be lured into public debate. He remained in Springfield while Douglas stumped mightily, riding a railcar all over the country. Douglas told audiences that a Republican win would mean secession. If only Andrew Jackson were alive, he bellowed, "he might hang Northern and Southern traitors on the same gallows."

## THE WINNER: ABRAHAM LINCOLN

After November 7, when the votes were counted, Lincoln was the president-elect, with 1,865,908 votes to Douglas's 1,380,202. It was a strong victory, but it came with a powerful quotient of caution. Lincoln had not received a single vote from a southern state.

★★★

**They're Grrrreat!** Lincoln did not debate Douglas during the 1860 campaign; however, if their 1858 debates were any indication, Lincoln would have come out on top. Honest Abe could be quite droll. He had a habit of mocking Douglas's rolling stentorian tones, surely sounding like Tony the Tiger as he satirized the Little Giant's "gr-r-r-r-r-r-reat pur-r-rinciple" of popular sovereignty. What popular sovereignty really meant, Lincoln pointed out, was that "if one man chooses to make a slave of another man, neither that other man nor anybody else has a right to object."

**Lost Boy** Douglas took a lot of heat for his whistle-stop election tour. In the next century, of course, such journeys would become standard for presidential candidates, but back in 1860 they still had an unseemly reputation. Douglas didn't help matters by claiming that he wasn't so much electioneering as making a few stops on the way to visit his dear mother in New York. It took him about a month to finally see her, and Republicans wouldn't let him forget it. One pamphlet, purporting to be a "Lost Boy" handbill, announced: "Left Washington, D.C., some time in July, to go home to his mother . . . who is very anxious about him. Seen in Philadelphia, New York City, Hartford, Conn., [and] at a clambake in Rhode Island. Answers to the name of Little Giant. Talks a great deal, very loud, always about himself."

**Mutt and Jeff Square Off** Lincoln took some hard hits because of his appearance—he was gaunt and far taller than most people of his day. Photographs made him look dreadfully serious, almost spectral. It's little wonder that Democrat-leaning papers caricatured him with a vengeance. He is a "horrid-looking wretch," wrote the Charleston *Mercury*, "sooty and scoundrelly in aspect, a cross between the nutmeg dealer, the horse-swapper, and the nightman." The Houston *Telegraph* added: "Lincoln is leanest, lankest, most ungainly mass of legs and arms and hatchet face ever strung on a single frame." Not to be outdone, Republicans described Douglas as "about five feet nothing in height and about the same in diameter the other way. He has a red face, short legs, and a large belly."

**Race Card** While Douglas waffled on the slavery issue, making such strange pronouncements as, "I am for the negro against the crocodile, but for the white man against the negro," Lincoln was plainly antislavery, which left him open to attack from racist elements of the Democratic Party. In one Democratic poster, he was pictured being carried into the lunatic asylum by "supporters." One was a black man dressed in fancy clothes who was saying: "Da white man hab no rights at collud pussuns am bound to spect." To make the whole poster even more offensive, the artist included a feminist screeching: "I want women's rights enforced and man reduced in subjugation to her authority!"

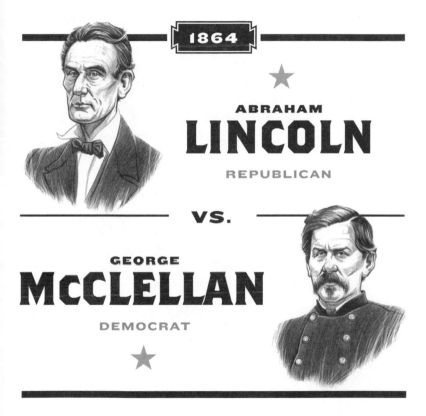

SLEAZE-O-METER

**1864**

★

## ABRAHAM
# LINCOLN

REPUBLICAN

## VS.

### GEORGE
# McCLELLAN

DEMOCRAT

★

"IT IS BEST NOT TO SWAP HORSES
WHILE CROSSING THE RIVER."
—Abraham Lincoln

**A** braham Lincoln took office under stresses endured by no other president before or since. A month after his inauguration, Confederate batteries opened up on Fort Sumter, and the Civil War began.

Until then, America could claim only one wartime president, James Madison, and the War of 1812 was nothing compared to the bloody struggle that threatened to destroy the young American republic. Lincoln was forced to learn on the job, and early results were mixed. As the Civil War heated up, partisan politics in the North reached a temporary cease-fire. Lincoln's opponent in the 1860 election, Stephen Douglas, supported him wholeheartedly. But as fighting continued and casualties increased, opposition to the president was inevitable.

Lincoln's chief critic among the Democrats was General George G. McClellan, commander-in-chief of the Army of the Potomac and youngest of the Union generals. Lincoln had appointed "Little Mac" early on to replace General Winfield Scott, the aging Mexican War hero, who had a little habit of napping during major battles. McClellan turned out to be a disaster. He continuously overestimated enemy strength and moved at such a glacial pace that Lincoln once sent him a note that read: "If you don't want to use the army, I should like to borrow it for a while." In 1862, after the bloody battle of Antietam, Lincoln fired McClellan, and the Democrats immediately starting talking up an embittered Little Mac, hoping to win him as their candidate.

Lincoln had problems within his own party as well. Many so-called Radical Republicans disagreed with his conduct of the war. They called him a dictator—and not a very good one at that. "How vain to have the power of a god and not use it godlike," Senator Charles Sumner wrote. Some pointed out that in the past thirty years, since Andrew Jackson, no president had served more than one term, so why should Lincoln be any different?

Even Union victories at Gettysburg and Vicksburg in 1863 didn't satisfy the Radical Republicans. They eventually splintered away to form the Radical Democracy Party. Meeting in Cleveland in May 1864, they chose as their nominee the 1856 Republican candidate, John C. Frémont. Their platform demanded one-term limits on the presidency and congressional participation in wartime and reconstruction decision-making.

The Republican Convention was held in Baltimore in June. Though Lincoln was renominated, no one was really sure he could again win the presidency. Despite Union victories in the summer of 1863, the war seemed to be turning in the Confederacy's favor. Countless party luminaries asked Lincoln to step aside, including Horace Greeley ("Mr. Lincoln is already beaten") and Boss Thurlow Weed ("I told Mr. Lincoln that his election was an impossibility"). Lincoln, understandably nervous, chose his running mate carefully. He picked Andrew Johnson, former Democrat and senator from Tennessee, as a ticket-balancer who might win votes in the border states.

The Democrats met in Chicago in August, at a convention controlled by antiwar Democrats known as the Copperheads. George McClellan was nominated as their presidential candidate, although he wisely refused to endorse the "peace at any cost" plank the Copperheads had inserted into the platform. His vice-presidential nominee was George Pendleton, congressman from Ohio.

## THE CANDIDATES

**REPUBLICAN: ABRAHAM LINCOLN** At fifty-five years old, Lincoln was looking much older than his age. He was worn down not only by the war but also by the death of his young son Willie, who died at age eleven in 1862. Yet Lincoln fervently pursued his goals, issuing the Emancipation Proclamation in 1862 while desperately searching for the right generals to lead the Union to victory.

**DEMOCRAT: GEORGE B. MCCLELLAN** When George McClellan was first appointed commander-in-chief of the Army of the Potomac, at the remarkably young age of thirty-four, the handsome and dashing general wrote to his wife: "I find myself in a new and strange position here—Presdt., Cabinet . . . & all deferring to me—by some strange operation of magic I seem to have become the power of the land. . . . I almost think that were I to win some small success now I could become Dictator." No wonder McClellan earned the nickname "Little Napoleon." But the reality of the man was at odds with his image. A plodding general, he was insubordinate to Lincoln (whom he openly despised) and became a divisive presence within the army he led.

## THE CAMPAIGN

McClellan started things off with a bang: "The President is nothing more than a well-meaning baboon," he roared. "He is the original gorilla. What a specimen to be at the head of our affairs now!" It was hard to match this level of rhetoric, but other Democrats tried their best. "Honest Abe has few honest men to defend his honesty," wrote the New York *World*, accusing Lincoln of corruption. They published a truly perfidious campaign biography, *The Only Authentic Life of Abraham Lincoln, Alias Old Abe*, accusing Lincoln of being interested only in the money: "Abraham thought [being president] was a good chance to make twenty-five thousand a year." The same circular went on to describe him personally: "Mr. Lincoln stands six-feet-twelve in his socks, which he changes once every ten days. His anatomy is composed mostly of bones, and when walking he resembles the offspring of a happy marriage between a derrick and a windmill."

A pamphlet war ensued between the two parties. In "The Lincoln Catechism, Wherein the Eccentricities & Beauties of Despotism Are

Fully Set Forth," Democrats asked a series of mock questions:

Q. What is the constitution?
A. A compact with hell, now obsolete.
Q. By whom hath the constitution been made obsolete?
A. By Abraham Africanus the First.

Republicans fired back with "The Copperhead Catechism":

Q. What is chief Aim of a Copperhead in life?
A. To abuse the President, vilify the administration, and glorify himself.

In July, Confederate forces under Jubal Early came within five miles of the White House. Lincoln stood on a parapet to watch their battle with Union forces and was told repeatedly to seek shelter as bullets flew and nearby men fell wounded. Despite the show of bravery, Early's raid was bad political news for the president, who began to despair of winning the election. Late in August, Lincoln made each cabinet member sign a note he had written stating they would cooperate with the new president-elect, whoever that person might be.

## THE WINNER: ABRAHAM LINCOLN

Fortunately for Lincoln—or not so fortunately, considering he would be assassinated in six months' time—the gods of war finally smiled on the Union. In early September, Admiral Farragut captured Mobile Bay ("Damn the torpedoes, full speed ahead!") and Sherman marched into Atlanta. When the tide turned, so did the election. In November, Lincoln easily bested McClellan 2,218,388 votes to 1,812,807. The soldiers of the Army of the Potomac, whom McClellan bragged would vote for him to a man, voted for Lincoln by a margin of almost four to one.

**Honest Abe's Dirty Tricks** Most history textbooks portray him as a martyred American icon, but Lincoln was not above a little double-dealing. In 1864 Lincoln feared that John C. Frémont's third-party candidacy would drain votes from the Republican ticket. With Senator Zachariah Chandler of Michigan acting as broker, a deal was struck: Frémont would withdraw his presidential bid if Lincoln would fire his controversial postmaster general, Montgomery Blair, who hated Frémont and the Radical Republicans. Though some doubt exists whether Lincoln knew about Chandler's actions beforehand, he certainly acquiesced once the deal was made known. On September 22 Frémont quit the election, and on September 23 Lincoln fired Blair, using the excuse that the latter had already offered to resign: "You have generously said to me more than once that whenever your resignation could be a relief to me, it was at my disposal."

Lincoln still needed to please powerful Tammany boss Thurlow Weed and his New York City conservative Republicans. To help his cause, the president ousted several appointees in New York's port and custom houses, replacing them with Weed's handpicked men. As the New York *Herald* dryly pointed out: "It is remarkable to note the change which has taken place in the political sentiments of some of these gentlemen in the last forty-eight hours—in fact, an anti-Lincoln man could not be found in any of the departments yesterday."

Lincoln also believed in getting out the vote in whatever way he could. On Election Day, he sent a federal steamer down the Mississippi to collect the ballots of gunboat sailors and furloughed federal employees in Washington, D.C.

**Mixed Marriage** Only Lincoln could have the charm to joke about interracial marriage during the Civil War and get away with it. Responding to continuous Democratic smear charges that Republicans favored intermarriage of blacks and whites, Lincoln joked: "It's a democratic mode of producing good Union men, and I don't propose to infringe on the patent."

**Little Mac to the Rear** Republicans noted how far Little Mac kept to the rear of his army during combat. Lincoln called the Army of the Potomac McClellan's bodyguard, and another Republican said that, during a retreat, "McClellan for the first time in his life was found in the front." That was mainly a canard—McClellan had performed bravely during the Mexican War—but it was true that, compared to some Civil War generals, he did spend a good deal of time back with the camp wagons.

**Is Nothing Sacred?** After Lincoln delivered his famous Gettysburg Address, the *Harrisburg Patriot and Union* wrote: "We pass over the silly remarks of the President; for the credit of the nation we are willing that the veil of oblivion shall be dropped over them."

SLEAZE-O-METER

**1868**

★

ULYSSES S.
# GRANT

REPUBLICAN

## VS.

HORATIO
# SEYMOUR

DEMOCRAT

★

"GRANT HAS BEEN DRUNK IN THE STREET
SINCE THE FIRST OF JANUARY."
—a Democrat attack on Ulysses S. Grant

ome vice presidents—like Harry Truman and Lyndon Johnson—
take a tragedy like the death of a sitting president and make the
most of it. Others—like Andrew Johnson—well, they get impeached.

Not that it was entirely Johnson's fault. Abraham Lincoln was
assassinated on April 14, 1865, among the most tumultuous and
confusing times in American history. Robert E. Lee had surren-
dered to Ulysses S. Grant at Appomattox Court House and the war
was over—good news, indeed. But now what to do? Many Radical
Republicans, who had feared Lincoln would be too kind to the
South, urged Johnson to slam the hammer on the defeated rebels.
But Johnson quickly announced he would follow the path laid down
by Lincoln. He set the steps for Reconstruction by calling a general
amnesty for all Confederate combatants, taking back into the Union
the "restored loyal governments" of Tennessee, Louisiana, Arkansas,
and Virginia. He then moved to restore the civil governments of the
other seven Southern states once they rewrote their constitutions to
revoke slavery.

Johnson also put into place the so-called Black Codes, a limited
form of freedom for ex-slaves that prohibited them from voting or
acquiring property. The Radicals wanted full civil rights for former
slaves, including the right to vote. And since they controlled Congress
after midterm elections, they set about voting down every one of
Johnson's Reconstruction bills. When the president vetoed Congress,
they overrode his veto. The fighting grew increasingly intense until, in
the spring of 1868, the Republicans finally assembled enough votes to

impeach the president. Though they failed to convict by just one vote, Johnson was finished.

The Republican Party's new standard-bearer was Ulysses S. Grant, the plain-spoken hard-drinking former Civil War general whose dogged tactics and brilliant strategizing had sealed victory for the Union. His iconic stature is comparable to that of Dwight D. Eisenhower after World War II. On May 20, four days after Johnson's impeachment trial, Grant was nominated for president at the Republican convention in Chicago. The vice-presidential nod went to Speaker of the House Schuyler Colfax. Facing a national election, the Radicals in the Republican Party started to waffle on the "Negro question": full suffrage for freed blacks was supported, but it was declared that each state should be in charge of voting in the measure—at best an iffy prospect.

The Democrats—a party many now equated with the Confederacy—met in New York on July 4 in blazing hot weather. After twenty-one ballots and no agreed-upon candidate, a dark-horse nominee was engineered by Samuel Tilden, the aggressive head of the New York delegation: Governor Horatio Seymour of New York. The reluctant Seymour became overwhelmed, first mounting the platform to decline the nomination in inadvertent rhyming couplet ("May God bless you for your kindness to me, but your candidate I cannot be."), then bursting into tears backstage ("Pity me . . . pity me!"), and finally accepting the job. His running mate was Francis Blair. The Democrats stood on a platform opposing the harsh Reconstruction plans formulated by the Radical Republican Congress, wherein Southern states were organized into five military districts and corrupt legislatures, and state governments were set up, which were soon swarming with carpetbaggers.

## THE CANDIDATES

**REPUBLICAN: ULYSSES S. GRANT** The forty-six-year-old Grant was a legend, his career the stuff of American dreams. After graduating from

West Point and serving in the Mexican War, he passed through a period of obscurity in his father's Galena, Illinois, leather store before rejoining the army in the early days of the Civil War and rising to commander-in-chief. Grant was the general whom Lincoln and the country had longed for. That he smoked, drank, and gambled to excess made it even better. In the eyes of many, he truly was "United States" Grant.

**DEMOCRAT: HORATIO SEYMOUR** "The fault, dear Brutus, is not in our stars, but in ourselves." This line from *Julius Caesar* might well be applied to Horatio Seymour, one of the most obscure presidential candidates ever to take the political stage. Seymour was in desperate need of a good PR machine and stumbled through a number of blunders. Aside from becoming weepy when drafted as his party's presidential nominee, he also addressed a mob of draft rioters in New York in 1863 as "my friends," an opening gambit that calmed the crowd but failed to bring good press.

## THE CAMPAIGN

Republicans seized on Seymour's tentative acceptance of his nomination by gleefully mocking "The Great Decliner" in what became a famous little ditty:

> *There's a queer sort of chap they call Seymour,*
> *A strange composition called Seymour,*
> *Who stoutly declines,*
> *Then happiness finds*
> *In accepting, does Horatio Seymour.*

Some Republicans hinted that hereditary insanity ran in his family. And, of course, he was a Democrat. "Scratch a Democrat," the line ran, "and you'll find a rebel under his skin."

Republicans also went after V.P. nominee Francis Blair, a war

hero from a distinguished political family. A private investigator discovered that Blair had spent two days in a Hartford hotel, where his
room came to only $10 but he spent $65 on whiskey and lemons.

The Democrats were not idle, of course, and Grant presented an inviting target, especially his habit of hard drinking. Though
many people, including reporters, had downplayed his bouts of blind
drunkenness during the Civil War, stories abounded. His enemies
called him a soak (slang for an alcoholic), and as one popular song
tittered:

> *I am Captain Grant of the Black Marines,*
> *The stupidest man that ever was seen.*
> *I smoke my weed and drink my gin,*
> *Paying with the people's tin.*

The slur concerned Grant's supposed support for Negro suffrage, although both he and Seymour tried to downplay the volatile issue.

## THE WINNER: ULYSSES S. GRANT

The race was closer than expected. Grant had refused to make
speeches or say much of anything. When cornered by a reporter at
a train station in New Jersey and asked what he thought about his
presidential prospects, he replied, "I don't think of it at all right this
time. My principal object just now is to catch the train." He had tak-
en a trip to Indian Territory to be seen with former Civil War heroes
Sherman and Sheridan, but even then he refused to make speeches.

Meanwhile, three weeks before the election, Seymour hit the circuit, in part because many Democrats feared a humiliating defeat and
wanted to replace him. His speechmaking efforts may have helped,
but not enough. Grant won 3,013,650 votes to Seymour's 2,708,744.
For the first time in U.S. history, half a million black men voted, and
it's safe to assume the overwhelming majority sided with Grant.

The Republicans finally saw self-serving benefit in the black vote.

They pushed through the Fifteenth Amendment, ratified in 1870, which stated that the right to vote should not be denied because of "race, color, or previous condition of servitude." Not until the Voting Rights Act of 1965, however, would many blacks vote freely in Southern states.

★★★

**General Order No. 11** Grant was branded an anti-Semite, an accusation that has some basis in truth. His infamous "General Order No. 11" of 1862 began: "The Jews, as a class violating every regulation of trade established by the Treasury Department . . . are hereby expelled." The order was quickly revoked by Lincoln, but it became campaign fodder anyway.

**The North's Dirty Little Secret** In 1868, even though an entire war had just been fought over slavery, black votes were counted in only sixteen of the thirty-seven states. Eight of these states were in the former Confederacy. (Black men were registered to vote in Mississippi, Texas, and Virginia, but the electoral votes did not count because these states had not yet been readmitted to the Union.) Connecticut did not allow blacks to vote, and New York made ownership of $250 worth of property a requirement before allowing a black man to cast his ballot.

# 1872

## ULYSSES S. GRANT vs. HORACE GREELEY

Most historians agree that Ulysses S. Grant was an honest guy. They also concur that he had a lot of dishonest acquaintances. Among them were Jay Gould and Jim Fisk, a pair of financiers determined to corner the gold market. Gould and Fisk managed to befriend Grant's brother-in-law Abel Corbin and assistant secretary of the treasury Daniel Butterfield, who gave them access to the president. The resulting "Gold Ring" scandal reached all corners of Grant's administration, as did affairs of the Whiskey Ring and Indian Ring. ("Ring," connoting a cabal of plotters, was the all-purpose scandal descriptive during the Grant years, much like "-gate" became the suffix of choice after Watergate in the Nixon years.)

Many Republicans had grown tired of the corruption and were fed up with Grant's failure to reform the civil service and present a serviceable Reconstruction policy. These so-called Liberal Republicans broke from the main herd and sought an uprising of "honest citizens" to sweep Grant from office. They were a little like the reforming Democrats of the 1960s, but instead of trying to empower the common man, they felt that the "intellectually well-endowed" should rule government. Holding their own table-thumping convention in Cincinnati in May, they nominated famous newspaper editor Horace Greeley for president and Missouri governor Benjamin Gratz Brown as vice president. The Democrats, meeting a month later, decided to throw in their lot with the Liberal Republicans, and Greeley became their candidate as well.

Greeley is one of the oddest presidential candidates in American history. A powerful newspaperman, editor of the *New York Tribune*, and crusading journalist, he had famously advised young men to "Go

West." He was also a balding, rotund vegetarian with tiny spectacles and big white sideburns (imagine a cross between a Dickens character, Truman Capote, and the musician David Crosby). On top of all that, he was also an atheist.

The regular Republicans, if you will, held their convention and renominated Ulysses Grant. Knowing that smart positioning for his campaign would be "Ordinary Guys against Stuck-Up Snobs," Grant chose as his running mate Henry Wilson of Massachusetts, a former shoemaker turned factory owner. Almost immediately posters billing the pair as "The Galena Tanner" (after the occupation of Grant's father) and "The Natick Shoemaker" started rolling off the presses.

**THE CAMPAIGN** With a legendary war hero running against an atheist vegetarian newspaperman, you can imagine how the campaigning went. New York Republican boss Thurlow Weed wrote to a friend, "Six weeks ago I did not suppose that any considerable number of men, outside of a Lunatic Asylum, would nominate Greeley for President." William Cullen Bryant echoed the sentiment, deciding that the only reason for Greeley's nomination was that "bodies of men as individuals sometimes lose their wits." For once, though, politicians were not accused of being sots. One reporter wrote that Greeley's nomination had to be the result of "too much brains and not enough whiskey" at the Cincinnati convention.

**THE WINNER: ULYSSES S. GRANT** Grant won 3,598,235 votes to Greeley's 2,834,761. All thirty-seven states voted, with thirty-one going for Grant. "I was the worst beaten man who ever ran for high office," Greeley declared. To make matters worse, his wife died just a week before Election Day. Soon after the election, Greeley began to suffer from hallucinations and was taken to a private sanitarium. "Utterly ruined beyond hope," as he wrote, he waited for "the night [to close] its jaws on me forever." He died on November 29. Grant attended his funeral.

"Never in American history," wrote historian Eugene Roseboom, "have two more unfit men been offered to the country for the highest office. . . . The man of no ideas was running against the man of too many."

SLEAZE-O-METER

### 1876

RUTHERFORD
# HAYES
REPUBLICAN

## VS.

SAMUEL
# TILDEN
DEMOCRAT

"IT SEEMED AS IF THE DEAD HAD BEEN RAISED."
—Zachariah Chandler, Republican National Chairman, 1876

**A**merica's centennial year, 1876, was a time of glorious celebration across the country. From May through November, people flocked to Philadelphia's Centennial Exposition, especially its vast Machinery Hall, which held thirteen acres of the era's engineering wonders, including electric lights and elevators, along with the typewriter, telegraph, and telephone. A visiting Dom Pedro, emperor of Brazil, held Alexander Graham Bell's device to his ear and immediately dropped it, exclaiming, "My God, it talks!"

The voice that shocked the good king signified American might and modernity, not to mention a century's worth of the grand triumph of American ideals and democracy. It is, therefore, ironic that one of the dirtiest and most brutal elections in nineteenth-century U.S. history was about to begin. It is a further irony that both candidates, Rutherford B. Hayes and Samuel J. Tilden, were so-called reform candidates whose goal was to wipe out government corruption.

In 1876 Ulysses S. Grant was hungering for a third term, but the stench of scandal and cronyism hung so heavily over his administration that Republicans said "no more." At their convention in Cincinnati in mid-June, they chose Rutherford B. Hayes, governor of Ohio, who would run on a platform of holding elected officials to rigid standards of probity and responsibility. His running mate was New York congressman William Wheeler.

The Democratic Party was desperate for a presidential victory—they hadn't won the White House in sixteen years—and members were certain they could take advantage of a Republican Party weakened by the series of corruption scandals that had rocked the Grant administration. They picked Samuel J. Tilden, governor of New York, as their nominee. Tilden was the Rudy Giuliani of his age—as a crusading Manhattan D.A., he had smashed Boss Tweed's powerful ring of corruption and sent its ringleader to prison. His V.P. was Thomas Hendricks of Indiana.

## THE CANDIDATES

**REPUBLICAN: RUTHERFORD B. HAYES** No one ever claimed that fifty-three-year-old Hayes was the world's most fascinating guy. But he was a former congressman and honest-to-goodness Civil War hero (four times wounded), a happily married father of seven, and just about as hardworking and sincere as a politician could be. Hayes would often write notes to himself, accusing himself of not being thrifty or "prudent" enough and of partaking in "too much light reading." He prayed with his family every morning and sang gospel hymns with them in the evening. No heavy partying for this guy.

**DEMOCRAT: SAMUEL J. TILDEN** Tilden had a brilliant mind, but you wouldn't want him kissing your baby. An icy, aloof bachelor, his penetrating intellect made even his friends uncomfortable. Plus he was prone to bouts of ill health. When he wasn't sick in reality, he imagined he was. An intense hypochondriac, he once visited his doctor every day for a month. One of Tilden's biggest political liabilities was that he had taken no part in the Civil War, instead setting out to amass millions from his railroad and iron mines.

## THE CAMPAIGN

Although the candidates still were not making public appearances, their political machines percolated. Tilden began a public relations campaign to overcome his cold-fish image. Hiring editors, writers, and artists, he set up a "Newspaper Popularity Bureau" whose sole purpose was to manufacture the image of a warm and lovable Samuel J. Tilden by issuing press releases to newspapers countrywide. As the election heated up, Tilden also created a so-called Literary Bureau in which teams of writers churned out anti-Hayes material, including a

750-page book that attacked his opponent for supposedly being party to Grantian scandals—"wicked schemes for peculation"—and for stealing $400 from a Union deserter about to be executed. (Strangely, Hayes really did take the money but he passed it on to the man's family, a fact Hayes was unable to prove until after the election.)

Tilden's dirty tricks couldn't hold a candle to the shenanigans of Zachariah Chandler, the bewhiskered, bejeweled, and often besotted Republican national chairman who also served as Hayes's campaign manager. Chandler kicked off the campaign with a menacing fund-raising letter sent to every Republican appointee holding office: "We look to you as one of the Federal beneficiaries to help bear the burden. Two percent of your salary is __. Please remit promptly. At the close of the campaign, we shall place a list of those who have not paid in the hands of the head of the department you are now in."

Unfortunately, none of this bad behavior comes anywhere near the dirty tricks perpetrated by both parties in the South. The Republicans—the party of the Great Emancipator, Abraham Lincoln—wanted freed blacks to vote and so prodded many of them to the ballot boxes at gunpoint. Democrats in South Carolina and elsewhere started violent race riots, in some cases shooting and killing blacks who attempted to exercise their franchise. On both sides, men voted ten or twenty times and local party bosses stood by ballot boxes, tearing up votes cast for the "wrong" candidate.

## THE WINNER: SAMUEL J. TILDEN?!?

By the time the polls closed on Election Day, Samuel J. Tilden was ahead by 250,000 in the popular vote (out of a total of 8,320,000 votes cast), garnering 184 electoral votes to Hayes's 165. One more electoral vote would put Tilden over the top, and since there were still twenty more to be had (divided among Florida, Louisiana, South Carolina, and Oregon), he seemed assured of victory. In New York City, Hayes went to bed certain he had lost; his party chairman, Zachariah Chandler, went out and got drunk.

But then came one of those curious moments upon which history pivots. Prominent Republican general Daniel E. Sickles, on his way home from the theater, stopped into the deserted Republican national headquarters to check the returns. Sickles was a notorious figure back then and remains so today—hero to some, villain to others. In 1859 he killed Philip Barton Key, son of Francis Scott Key, but was later acquitted of murder using the first-ever-in-American-history "not guilty by reason of temporary insanity" plea. Sickles then rose to the rank of general in the Civil War, lost a leg at Gettysburg, and was awarded the Congressional Medal of Honor, although many felt that his actions on the field nearly cost the Union the battle.

Whatever historians might think, Sickles was a man of action. He decided that Hayes could win if he somehow regained control of Florida, Louisiana, and South Carolina. Pretending to be Chandler, Sickles wired leading Republicans in those states, saying: "With your state sure for Hayes, he is elected. Hold your state."

By the time Chandler was roused from his whiskey-induced stupor, the race to win was on. The struggle over the remaining twenty electoral votes lasted from November 8, 1876, to March 2, 1877. Republican-controlled "returning boards" (groups in each state who tallied electoral votes) simply threw out enough Democratic votes to swing Florida, Louisiana, and South Carolina to Hayes. Democrats cried foul, officials of both parties flocked to the South, and President Grant sent federal troops, just in case. In the end, an Election Commission was established, consisting of five U.S. senators, five members of Congress, and five Supreme Court justices, all of whom split evenly along party lines. With the commission tied at 7–7, the Supreme Court justice who had the deciding vote resigned and a Republican justice took his place. Hayes was voted into office with 185 electoral votes to Tilden's 184.

★★★

**Who Really Won?** Had it been a truly fair election, would Tilden have won? Probably. Most historians believe that, at the very least, he carried Louisiana and Florida. In the end, fittingly enough, this dirtiest of all nineteenth-century elections finished with a secret dirty deal. Southern Democrats promised not to contest the Election Commission's results if Hayes, once in office, would pull federal troops out of the South and appoint at least one Southerner to his cabinet. Reconstruction collapsed—and the future of civil rights was set back for decades—but Hayes was awarded the presidency. March 5, 1877, was Inauguration Day, but the situation had become so heated—someone had already fired a shot through the window of Hayes's home—that the president had to be secretly sworn in.

**Take Aim at Mother** Desperate to discredit Hayes, the Democrats spread a rumor that he once shot and wounded his own mother "in a fit of insanity." Anonymous letters written to newspapers claimed that Hayes, in Ohio before the war, returned home from a night of drinking, pulled a gun, and shot Sophia Birchard Hayes in the arm. Hayes's mother had died in 1866, so she wasn't around to deny the reports, but no record exists of her suffering from a gunshot wound. Moreover, we know for certain that Hayes and his wife, Lucy, were not what you'd call heavy drinkers. Once ensconced in the White House, they banned all alcoholic beverages and served only water at state dinners. International visitors were horrified.

**An STD For SJT?** Because Samuel Tilden was a bachelor—and a New York City bachelor, at that—Republicans went to town claiming that he had enjoyed many affairs, including some with married women. The nastiest smear was contained in pamphlets published in early fall of 1876, which accused Tilden of having contracted syphilis years earlier from an Irish whore on the Bowery. According to the rumor, not only had the venereal disease affected his actions, but it also made him susceptible to blackmail. Tilden died of pneumonia in 1886, at age seventy-two, leaving behind no medical record of his ever having suffered from an STD.

**Most Viciously Hyperbolic Political Speech Ever!** While stumping for Hayes, writer Robert G. Ingersoll attacked the Democrats by claiming they were all Confederates at heart: "Every man that tried to destroy this nation was a Democrat. . . . The man that assassinated Abraham Lincoln was a Democrat. . . . Soldiers, every scar you have on your heroic bodies was given you by a Democrat."

SLEAZE-O-METER

**1880**

★

JAMES
# GARFIELD

REPUBLICAN

VS.

WINFIELD
# HANCOCK

DEMOCRAT

★

"[IN 1880] THE REPUBLICAN PARTY EXISTED [ONLY]
TO OPPOSE THE DEMOCRATIC PARTY."
—John D. Hicks, author of *The American Nation*

Under Rutherford Hayes, America sailed into the very heart of what Mark Twain dubbed the Gilded Age. A huge economic expansion was led by a few robber barons—er, industrialists—including Andrew Carnegie, John Rockefeller, John Jacob Astor, Jay Gould, and Cyrus W. Field. The rich got richer, the poor got poorer, and the disenfranchised were more disenfranchised.

Although contemporary historian Henry Adams called him "a third-rate nonentity," Hayes was not a bad president. He was relatively honest and had attempted (albeit with little success) to reform the highly corrupt, patronage-ridden civil service. But he was hamstrung by promises he'd made to Democrats to win in 1876. Hayes's fellow Republicans watched as their president withdraw troops from the South (troops that supported corrupt Republican carpetbag state governments), gave important positions to Southern Democrats, and approved money for Southern pork barrels, and they didn't like it. Not one bit.

Hayes wisely decided not to run for a second term, setting the stage for an internal Republican Party battle that has seldom been equaled in U.S. political history. The party split into two wings. One was called the Stalwarts, made up of those loyal to the old-line party of Ulysses S. Grant, who was fishing for a third term as president. The other was dubbed the Half-Breeds—moderates who wanted reform within the party and abhorred the thought of another four years of "Grantism," meaning the general's corrupt cronies dipping into the public trough at will.

As the Republican convention met in Chicago's brand-new glass and iron Exposition Building on June 2, 1880, Roscoe Conkling, the powerful and vain U.S. senator from New York, thought he had votes locked up for Grant. The famous general had been out of the country on a two-and-a-half-year world tour, long enough for people to forget the scandals of his administration and look upon him with nostalgic fondness. The Half-Breeds were led by Senator James G. Blaine of Maine, Conkling's sworn enemy (who had once called him "a majestic, supereminent, overpowering, turkey-gobbler strut").

At stake was the fate of the party as well as that of the nation, for most assumed the Republicans would win the White House, as they had since 1860 (one reason the editorial cartoonist Thomas Nast had recently caricaturized the Republican Party as a stolid dependable elephant, an image that stuck). Thousands crammed the convention halls as ballot after ballot was cast. Spontaneous demonstrations arose during the alphabetized roll calls, either for Grant or for Blaine for president. One female spectator even climbed a "Goddess of Liberty Statue" on the convention stage and began ripping off her clothes. After all was said and done, Conkling put Grant in nomination with a fiery speech culminating in a sappy poem:

> *Do you ask what State he hails from?*
> *Our sole reply shall be:*
> *He hails from Appomattox*
> *And its famous apple tree.*

But a new senator from Ohio, James A. Garfield, arose and nominated fellow Ohioan John Sherman, treasury secretary and brother of William Tecumseh Sherman. John Sherman was a favorite of the Half-Breeds, although not of the public at large, for reasons that are evident in his nickname: the Ohio Icicle. But as ballots were taken, an extraordinary thing happened: more and more delegates voted for Garfield, swayed by the idea of him as a moderating force between the two sharply divided factions. After thirty-six ballots—the most ever cast at a Republican convention before or since—the forty-eight-year-old Garfield became the dark horse Republican candidate for president. Chester Arthur, Stalwart machine politician from New York, was chosen as the vice-presidential candidate.

After that uproar, the Democratic convention seemed like an afterthought. On only the second ballot, they nominated General Winfield Scott Hancock, former Civil War hero and military governor. His running mate was William H. English, a banker from Indiana, a state both parties desperately needed for its large number of electoral votes.

## THE CANDIDATES

**REPUBLICAN: JAMES A. GARFIELD** The low-key and likeable Garfield was the last American presidential candidate to be born in a log cabin. During the summer of his seventeenth year, he drove mules on the towpaths of the Ohio Canal, hence his nicknames "Towpath Jim" and "Canal Boy." He rose to become president of Hiram College, then volunteered for the Civil War. He distinguished himself in battle and became a major general before being elected to Congress in the postbellum years.

**DEMOCRAT: WINFIELD SCOTT HANCOCK** Nothing came between Hancock and his feedbag. The general was described sarcastically by Republicans as "a good man weighing two hundred and forty pounds," and in truth he was a good man. He boasted such a strong military record during the Civil War that he had been known as "Hancock the Superb." However, he had never held public office or even dabbled in politics, and Republican machine politicians were ready to make mincemeat out of him.

## THE CAMPAIGN

As America surged toward the twentieth century, the country faced pressing issues: the need for child labor laws and an eight-hour workday, the plight of African Americans, the rights of women, and a graduated federal income tax, just to name a few. Democrat and Republican platforms addressed none of these concerns. Instead, both emphasized civil service reform, opposed aid to parochial schools, and called for curtailing Chinese immigration—"an evil of great magnitude," claimed the Republicans. (With nothing to lose, the Republicans also came out against polygamy, the "gay marriage" red herring of its day.)

Like punch-drunk fighters who don't know the bell has rung, the two major parties were still fighting the Civil War a decade and a half after it ended, running two heroic generals against each other. Trying to smear Garfield with Grantian scandals, the Democrats claimed he had taken $329 in bribes from a holding company for the Union Pacific Railroad during the Crédit Mobilier scandal. After Garfield provided an innocent explanation, Democrats switched tactics and assailed him for having an unpaid tailor's bill back in Troy, New York.

Ulysses S. Grant, stumping for Garfield, apparently forgot that he had called Hancock a "glorious soldier" during the Civil War and told a journalist the man was "crazy to be president. He is ambitious, vain, and weak." Nominating Hancock, a Republican newspaper wrote, "no more changes the character [of the Democrats] than a figurehead of the Virgin on Kidd's pirate ship."

## THE WINNER: JAMES GARFIELD

In a surprisingly close election, in which 78.4 percent of eligible voters went to the polls, James Garfield won 4,446,158 votes to Hancock's 4,444,260. But Garfield's Electoral College margin was 214 to 155. The modest and capable Half-Breed from Ohio was going to Washington—although within a few short months of his inaugural address, he would become the second U.S. president to be assassinated.

★★★

**Slick Business** "Soap" and "Soapy Sam" were 1880s slang for cash passed out to encourage voters to vote for a candidate. Soaping palms had been the custom in American elections for years, but money exchanged hands in an unprecedented fashion during the Garfield-Hancock contest.

One case of Soapy Sam coming to the rescue occurred in Indiana, one of the states that still had not coordinated local and congressional elections with the national Election Day. Rather than early November, it held elections on October 12; as a result, many people looked to Indiana as a bellwether of the countrywide election. Since Democratic vice-presidential candidate William English was a Hoosier, Republicans were terrified Indianans would go for Hancock and quickly sprang into action. After one Republican operative reported that, in his opinion, there were "30,000 merchantable votes in the State," James Garfield and Chester Arthur urgently requested cash from their Wall Street connections. A silver-tongued bagman named Stephen Dorsey was sent to Indiana carrying, by some accounts, as much as $400,000 in $2 bills.

To be fair, the Democrats also attempted to buy votes, but lacking similar access to Wall Street dough, they were mostly unsuccessful. Their biggest dirty trick consisted of sending in "repeaters" or "floaters" from outside Indiana to vote repeatedly in different precincts. In the end, Soapy Sam helped carry the state for Garfield.

**Truth And Consequences** On October 20, 1880, James Garfield fell victim to what is probably the first October Surprise in U.S. presidential election history. A newspaper improbably named the *New York Truth* printed a letter purportedly written by Garfield to an H. L. Morey of the Employers Union of Lynn, Massachusetts. In it Garfield wrote that the "Chinese problem" (the fears of whites in the West that Chinese immigrants would take their jobs) was not a problem at all and that employers had the right "to buy labor where they can get it the cheapest."

That pronouncement struck terror in those who had been trying to stop Chinese immigration, particularly into California. Garfield did not write the Morey letter and was able to refute it. Investigations further showed there was no Morey and no Employers Union, either. The letter was traced to the hand of one Kenward Philp, a *Truth* journalist who was later arrested and indicted for fraud.

Even though Garfield was able to prove his innocence, the Morey letter caused him to lose California, which nearly caused him to lose the entire election.

**The Three-Percent Solution** Chester "Chet" Arthur, a Stalwart from New York, may have been picked as vice president to placate party boss Roscoe Conkling, but he sure knew his job. New York was home to thousands of state and federal civil-service workers, all of whom held their jobs at the sufferance of the big bosses. The going rate to keep their livelihood? In 1876 the Republicans set the mandatory campaign contribution at 2 percent of annual salary, but Arthur upped it to 3 percent, delivering hundreds of thousands of dollars to the Republican treasure chest.

SLEAZE-O-METER

**1884**

★

GROVER
# CLEVELAND
DEMOCRAT

## VS.

JAMES G.
# BLAINE

REPUBLICAN

★

**"KIND REGARDS TO MRS. FISHER. BURN THIS LETTER."**
—James G. Blaine, Republican Candidate For President

Under the category of famous last words comes this utterance by James Garfield just before his inauguration: "Assassination can no more be guarded against than death by lightning, and it is not best to worry about either."

During his first four months in office, Towpath Jim had done quite well, making inroads in his battle to dismantle the patronage system strangling the country's civil service. But on July 2, 1881, Garfield was shot and seriously wounded by Charles Guiteau, a deranged man who is usually described by historians as a "disappointed office seeker." Guiteau had haunted Garfield for months, desperate to earn a position as consul to Paris even though he was supremely unqualified. "I am a Stalwart," he proclaimed after his arrest, "and Arthur shall be President!" When Garfield died on September 19 (helped along to eternity by his doctors' unwashed and constantly probing fingers), Guiteau's vision was realized: "Chet" Arthur was sworn in as the twenty-first president of the United States.

As president, the dapper and corpulent Arthur was well liked but barely energetic. His emerging Republican rival for the 1884 presidential nomination, James G. Blaine, called him a stalled ox. His party failed to nominate him for a second term, which left the field open for a deliciously scandal-ridden presidential race. In some ways it can be likened to Bill Clinton's 1992 outing against George H. W. Bush, when the whole Gennifer Flowers affair reared its pretty blonde head.

## THE CANDIDATES

**DEMOCRAT: GROVER CLEVELAND** Grover Cleveland was the picture of a Gilded Age politician—he had the well-fed look, the striped pants, the balding pate—with one critical exception. He was honest—so honest that he was known in the telling slang of the day as "ugly honest." A former reform mayor of Buffalo and governor of New York, Cleveland was chosen on the second round of balloting at the Democratic convention. For V.P., Cleveland chose Hoosier Thomas Hendricks, Samuel Tilden's 1876 running mate, who could assure the pivotal votes of the state of Indiana.

**REPUBLICAN: JAMES G. BLAINE** At last it was James G. Blaine's turn. This eloquent Maine-born former Speaker of the House, senator, and secretary of state under Garfield inspired deliriums of passion in his rabid supporters, who were known as Blainiacs. They had dubbed him the "Plumed Knight" for his courage and integrity, but many in the know thought that the good man was on the take. It was perhaps a bad sign that his pick for vice president, Illinois senator John Logan, was suspected of corruption and known far and wide as "Black Jack."

## THE CAMPAIGN

Talk about wishful thinking. The chaplain giving the opening invocation for the Republican convention in June 1884 prayed that the "coming political campaign be conducted with the decency, intelligence, patriotism and dignity of temper which becomes a free and intelligent people." Politicians nodded reverentially and then went at it tooth and nail.

Immediately after Blaine's nomination, a large portion of the Republican Party bolted to the Democrats, including such leading luminaries as Reverend Henry Ward Beecher, Charles Francis Adams, and Mark Twain. Called Mugwumps (an Algonquin Indian word meaning "big chief") by their enemies, these men reviled Blaine for corruption and being under the thumb of Republican party bosses. He had, as one editorialist put it, "wallowed in spoils like a rhinoceros in an African pool."

Blaine's dealings with the burgeoning railroads—whose owners pushed as much money into Washington as defense contractors do to-day—were particularly suspect. A damning moment occurred when Democrats uncovered a letter written by Blaine to Warren Fisher, a Boston railroad attorney. In it, Blaine appeared complicit in shady business dealings. To make matters worse, his hearty signoff read: "My regards to Mrs. Fisher. Burn this letter!" The Democrats impaled the Plumed Knight on his own lance, gleefully chanting "Burn this letter! Burn this letter!" and "Blaine, Blaine, James. G. Blaine, the Continental liar from the state of Maine!"

They thought they had a lock on the sleaze issue; their "ugly honest" candidate—a.k.a. Grover the Good—was known to have unimpeachable morals. But then on July 21, Cleveland's hometown paper, the *Buffalo Evening Telegraph*, published a sordid story with a grabber of a headline: "A Terrible Tale: A Dark Chapter in a Public Man's History—The Pitiful Story of Maria Halpin and Governor Cleveland's Son." Turns out that in 1874, when Cleveland was bachelor about town, he had embarked on an "illicit" affair with a thirty-six-year-old widow named Maria Halpin. She later gave birth to a boy, whom Cleveland gallantly supported despite privately acknowledged doubts about the child's true paternity.

The Republicans went wild over the story (much as their future compatriots would in 1992 when Bill Clinton's alleged dalliance with torch singer Gennifer Flowers made headlines). One Buffalo minister proclaimed: "The issue is evidently not between the two great parties, but between the brothel and the family, . . . between lust and law." Editorialists cried: "We do not believe that the American people will knowingly elect to the Presidency a coarse debaucher who will bring his harlots with him to Washington." Cleveland was called a "lecherous beast," a "moral leper," and, for good measure, an "obese nincompoop." (The man tipped the hay scales at about 250 pounds.) Republicans now had their own derisive chant: "Ma! Ma! Where's my pa?" Cartoons pictured Halpin plaintively searching for Cleveland while holding a baby—a trifle ridiculous since, by this time, the child was ten years old.

And so the 1884 presidential contest degenerated, as one foreign observer drolly noted, into a contest between "the copulative habits of one candidate and the prevaricative habits of the other." In other words, was it worse to be a fornicator or a liar and a thief? It was the first time this conundrum crystallized so clearly in an American presidential race, but by no means would it be the last.

When Democrats begged Cleveland to defend himself, he simply said: "Above all, tell the truth." And that is what they did. Cleveland simply acknowledged his support of the child (who had been adopted by others) and then refused to say anything more. Such a dignified response should have set an example for Bill Clinton a hundred years later. Of course, Cleveland had a few advantages over Clinton—he wasn't married, and Maria Halpin stayed in seclusion and refused to give statements—but above all it was his honesty that helped him weather the storm. The scandal also happened early in the campaign, leaving him time before Election Day to shift the focus to other issues.

Most Americans then, as now, were more forgiving of lechery than of hypocrisy.

## THE WINNER: GROVER CLEVELAND

The race was close. Grover Cleveland won 4,874,621 votes; Blaine came in with 4,848,936. It was the first time since the 1856 administration of James Buchanan that a Democrat sat in the White House. Gleeful Cleveland supporters could now chant: "Ma! Ma! Where's my pa? Gone to the White House! Ha! Ha! Ha!"

★★★

**Black Wednesday** October 29, 1884, is among the worst days a presidential candidate has ever had—worse than Nixon during that first 1960 debate, worse than Edmund Muskie weeping at a news conference in 1972, worse than the Howard Dean Scream in the 2004 primaries. If not for that day's events, James G. Blaine would have won the 1884 election.

Just as Cleveland weathered the Maria Halpin crisis, Blaine was busy overcoming charges that he was on the take. His stumping and passionate speechmaking seemed to be winning over voters. He arrived in New York with a slim lead in the state and, on that fateful Wednesday morning, sat down to a breakfast meeting at just another whistle stop on the campaign trail.

Unfortunately, during the seemingly unending meeting, a local Presbyterian minister by the name of S. D. Burchard got carried away in attacking the Democrats; Burchard called them the party of "rum, Romanism, and rebellion," essentially slurring them as Irish Catholic drunks. Even more unfortunately, Blaine apparently wasn't listening and failed to denounce Burchard's intemperance when he rose to speak. A Democrat at the meeting took down Burchard's words and raced to local party headquarters. Campaign operatives immediately set to work printing thousands of handbills describing Blaine as a "Catholic-hater." In a city full of Irish Catholic working-class immigrants, that did not sit well.

That evening, Blaine—who still had no idea what was happening—attended an entirely different sort of event: a dinner at the stylish Delmonico's restaurant, in the company of Republican tycoons the likes of Jay Gould, John Jacob Astor, and Cyrus W. Field. The next day, just as the "Rum, Romanism and Rebellion" handbills were hitting the streets, newspaper headlines described "The Royal Feast of Belshazzar Blaine and the Money Kings."

The brutal one–two publicity punch cost Blaine the election. He lost New York by a mere 1,149 votes. Had it not been (as he later put it) for "an ass in the shape of a preacher," he would have won the state and the White House as well.

**Mark Twain and Ladies of the Night** Mark Twain deserted the Republican Party over the nomination of James G. Blaine, whom he considered hopelessly corrupt. When news of the whole Cleveland–Halpin affair broke, he derided the hypocrisy of those criticizing the Democratic candidate: "To see grown men, apparently in their right mind, seriously arguing against a bachelor's fitness for President because he has had private intercourse with a consenting widow! These grown men know what the bachelor's other alternative was—& tacitly they seem to prefer that to the widow. Isn't human nature the most consummate sham & lie that was ever invented?"

# 1888

## BENJAMIN HARRISON vs. GROVER CLEVELAND

The election of 1888 was close and it was dirty. In one corner was Grover Cleveland, the Democratic president who had for four years labored stubbornly to continue civil service reform and put an end to high import tariffs. (Along with many Democrats, he thought the protective barriers lined the pockets of tycoons while making the cost of goods prohibitive for working people.)

In the other corner was Republican nominee Benjamin Harrison, a distinguished Civil War veteran and Indiana senator. The aloof fifty-four-year-old Harrison was a second choice for many Republicans (1884 nominee James G. Blaine still had plenty of supporters), but Harrison had good bloodlines. He was the grandson of President William "Old Tippecanoe" Harrison, who had died in 1840 after only a month in office. He also supported the high tariffs that made the Republican tycoons so rich.

**THE CAMPAIGN** No one talked much about the Maria Halpin affair anymore because President Cleveland had married during his first presidential term (the first such ceremony ever performed in the White House). Nevertheless, Republicans seized on the fact that Cleveland had wed his former ward, Frances Folsom, the daughter of his late law partner—she was twenty-one years old, and some twenty-eight years younger than the man she once referred to as Uncle Cleve. Many Republicans were titillated by the incestuous nature of their union; they referred to Cleveland as the "Beast of Buffalo" and even spread rumors that he beat Frances. In one of the most extraordinary official utterances made by a first lady in the nineteenth century, Frances issued a statement calling the charges "a foolish campaign ploy without a shadow of foundation."

Democrats nicknamed the difficult and aristocratic Harrison "Kid Glove," but in truth, they had a hard time laying a glove on this smart veteran campaigner. Harrison had learned from the mistake of Blaine's Black Wednesday that too much campaigning could leave one vulnerable to the Reverend Burchards of the world.

And so he began the nation's first front-porch campaign, allowing crowds to gather at his Indianapolis home for a brief address once a day, and then sending out a carefully worded version of his remarks to the Associated Press for nationwide dissemination. This early form of spin control kept his message in the public while letting him rest comfortably in his own bed at night. (Cleveland chose not to campaign, even from his front porch, and relied instead on his inept running mate, seventy-five-year-old Allen G. Thurman, who, during speeches, would forget what he was supposed to be talking about and start complaining about his rheumatism.)

Of course, Benjamin Harrison also had the benefit of Republican money. Lots of it. The Republican national campaign manager, Matthew S. Quay, remarked that he would "fry the fat" out of Republican businessmen who benefited from the protective tariffs—and he did, collecting more than $3 million, much of it from the American Iron and Steel Association. At the same time, millworkers received slips tucked into their pay envelopes threatening the loss of their jobs if tariffs were abolished and cheap foreign goods allowed to flood the country.

**THE WINNER: BENJAMIN HARRISON** It took a lot of dirty tricks—including more vote buying in Indiana, where Republican "floaters" were now paid as much as $15 a head and literally marched to the polls by party operatives before they got too drunk to vote—but Benjamin Harrison was elected president in 1888. Even though he lost the popular vote by 90,000, garnering 5,443,892 votes to Cleveland's 5,534,488, Harrison won in the Electoral College 233 to 168. One big victory was in New York State, where thirty-six electoral votes went to Harrison after the state's Democratic candidate for governor made a deal with Harrison's people: in return for enough Republican votes to win him the gubernatorial victory, he would deliver New York to Harrison.

The dirty tricks in this campaign were such that Republican bigwig Matthew Quay remarked pointedly that Harrison would never know how many Republicans "were compelled to approach the gates of the penitentiary to make him president."

# 1892

## GROVER CLEVELAND vs. BENJAMIN HARRISON

The 1892 election was transitional—not the most exciting presidential battle in history. But major changes were shaking the country.

The U.S. population had risen to more than 62 million; even more significantly, the population center had shifted westward. Six western states had been admitted to the Union in 1889 and 1890: North Dakota, South Dakota, Montana, Washington, Idaho, and Wyoming. A telephone line now stretched between New York City and Chicago. Thomas Edison had invented the kinetoscope, the first moving picture camera. And a new portable Kodak camera was put on the market in 1888; instead of using dry plate negatives, it employed a spool of flexible film with a hundred exposures that could be developed at a dealer or sent directly to Kodak headquarters in Rochester, New York. Suddenly, everybody was a shutterbug.

Unfortunately, there wasn't much to be photographed in the election of 1892. Benjamin Harrison spent most of his White House tenure controlled by the corrupt Republican bosses who had helped him win in 1888. The bosses couldn't stand the prickly born-again Christian president, claiming that Harrison was "as glacial as a Siberian stripped of his furs" and that talking to him even in warm weather made a person feel like putting on "winter flannels, galoshes, overcoat, mitts, and earlap."

Cleveland, on the other hand, was still popular with millions of Americans—after all, this was the man whose baby daughter, Ruth, had a candy bar named after her. He hungered for a third nomination and second term, and so the race against frosty Ben Harrison was on.

**THE CAMPAIGN** Cleveland still did not take to the stump, although he broke with tradition to become the first presidential nominee to make a public speech in acceptance of his nomination, rather than simply sending out a letter of acceptance.

And Harrison, preoccupied with his ill wife (who died two weeks before Election Day) did not repeat his front-porch PR coup of the previous election. With running mate Whitelaw Reid, he spent most of his time emphasizing his support of high tariffs and protectionism. Unfortunately, a violent strike in Homestead, Pennsylvania, in July 1892—during which Andrew Carnegie's general manager, Henry Clay Frick, cut the wages of steel mill workers 20 percent and then hired armed Pinkerton agents to battle them when they struck—was a PR disaster and may have cost Harrison the election.

Homestead helped Cleveland (running with veep nominee Adlai E. Stevenson, grandfather of the future Democratic presidential candidate) with labor, demonstrating in action that high tariff barriers did not translate to high wages for workers.

**THE WINNER: GROVER CLEVELAND** Cleveland won convincingly, 5,551,883 votes to Harrison's 5,179,244. He carried seven northern states as well as the usual Democratic southern voting bloc, and he entered the record books as the first and only president to serve two nonconsecutive terms.

But change was in the wind. The new Populist Party, a grassroots amalgam of farmers and factory workers whose platform called for fair wages, public ownership of railroads, telegraph, and telephones, and a restoration of government "to the hands of plain people" had garnered more than a million votes for its candidate, James B. Weaver. Weaver had stumped throughout the country with a truly charismatic

American orator, the little-known Mary Elizabeth Lease, a woman who decried a "government of Wall Street, for Wall Street, and by Wall Street" and who told farmers in rallies that resembled religious revivals "to raise less corn and more hell."

This western groundswell was heading east. And party bosses, both Republican and Democrat, were about to see the beginning of the end of their storied power.

SLEAZE-O-METER

## 1896

★

WILLIAM
# McKINLEY
REPUBLICAN

## VS.

WILLIAM JENNINGS
# BRYAN
DEMOCRAT

★

"[BRYAN] IS AN IRRESPONSIBLE, UNREGULATED,
IGNORANT, PREJUDICED, PATHETICALLY HONEST AND
ENTHUSIASTIC CRANK."
—*New York Times*

**P**oor Grover the Good. No sooner had he begun his second term when much of the world slid into a horrific economic depression that would last from 1893 to 1897. In America, within just a year of Cleveland's second inauguration, fifteen thousand businesses went under and four million workers lost their jobs. A half million laborers went on strike against substandard wages and working conditions; most of the strikes were broken by the police and the military. Bands of homeless people wandered the country in search of shelter and employment. An army of poor people marched on Washington. A more dismal picture would not be seen until the Great Depression of the 1930s.

America was changing, and the political parties were changing with it. What many historians call the great realignment of 1896 was about to occur. In it, the Republican Party would finally reach out to blue-collar workers, in much the same way as it did when Richard Nixon ran on his "Silent Majority" theme in the 1960s. In another foreshadowing of 1968, the Democrats embraced a young, passionate, and extraordinarily charismatic candidate.

The campaign was all about currency standards and precious metal—gold clashing with silver—and the sparks were about to fly.

## THE CANDIDATES

**REPUBLICAN: WILLIAM MCKINLEY** The fifty-three-year-old McKinley—of the starched shirt, double-breasted coat, red carnation, and mainstream American Methodism—had a long political record as a congressman and then governor of Ohio. He was smart, dependable, and upstanding. If you were a certain class of American, you felt reassured just by looking at the guy and hearing his stentorian tones. His campaign was run by Mark Hanna, a powerfully astute political operator who pioneered many of the techniques used in modern campaigning.

**DEMOCRAT: WILLIAM JENNINGS BRYAN** At the age of thirty-six, Bryan was (and still is) the youngest man ever to receive a major party's nomination for president. He was known as "The Great Commoner"—a Nebraska native, evangelical Christian, and passionate speaker who traveled 18,000 miles (all by train, of course) through twenty-seven states, making up to thirty-six speeches a day on behalf of a new currency standard and the down-trodden farmers. The lean and handsome Bryan ate six meals a day just to keep up his strength during the grueling campaign. He also enjoyed relaxing rubdowns with gin, leading many people he met to believe he was a drunk.

## THE CAMPAIGN

William McKinley and Mark Hanna remembered the lessons of Benjamin Harrison's presidential campaign in 1888: Harrison had promised so many favors to eastern party bosses that he could hardly accomplish anything once he arrived in the White House.

They realized the times were changing. The decisive moment came in the months before the Republican convention, when party bosses Matthew Quay of Pennsylvania and Senator Thomas Platt of New York demanded that McKinley make Platt secretary of the treasury. And they wanted McKinley to put that promise in writing. McKinley simply told Hanna: "There are some things in the world that come too high. If I cannot be president without promising to make Tom Platt Secretary of the Treasury, I will never be president."

It was the tipping point. In a time of deep depression, the ordinary people were sick of party fat cats. They supported McKinley as the candidate against what was even then being called the machine — the grinding apparatus of party corruption. As Charles Dawes, one of McKinley's young campaign aides put it, McKinley's men would "make the machine sick before we get through with them."

Once nominated, however, McKinley's real enemy was William Jennings Bryan. The charismatic Nebraskan had stolen his party's nomination with his famous "Cross of Gold" speech, in which he advocated an expanded supply of money and silver coinage to alleviate the woes of working people. Bryan argued that "tight money"—in which each dollar was backed by its equivalent in gold—was keeping farmers and those deeply in debt from being able to make a decent living, while those bankers who controlled the gold wallowed like Scrooges in chambers of wealth.

"You shall not press down upon the brow of labor this crown of thorns, you shall not crucify mankind upon a cross of gold," Bryan thundered, and he was joined by not only Democrats but also the Populist Party, who later nominated him for president and became known as Popocrats.

The Republicans who feared Bryan's western populism branded him as an anarchist who would bring economic ruin to the country. During the summer of 1896, attacks on Bryan in GOP newspapers mounted in hysteria. Bryan, the *New York Tribune* snarled, "was a wretched, rattle-pated boy, posing in vapid vanity and mouthing resounding rottenness." Theodore Roosevelt, stumping for McKinley, compared Bryan to "the leaders of the Terror in France in mental and moral attitude." (Some Republicans also likened him to Charles Guiteau, Garfield's assassin.) Bryan's followers were labeled by one Philadelphia paper as "hideous and repulsive vipers." Antis-Semitic caricatures abounded in editorial cartoons—silver-loving Shylocks who would be "Sure Winners if Bryan Is Elected."

Like most political campaigns, however, the Republican efforts worked on many levels. Cheap shots in newspapers were all to the good, but party organization and discipline were just as important.

Mark Hanna, the Karl Rove of his day, came up with a brilliant strategy. Instead of trying to beat the peripatetic Bryan by stumping all over the country (not McKinley's style, anyway), Hanna had his candidate stay home in Canton, Ohio, and arranged for people to visit him. These front-porch meetings surpassed those of Benjamin Harrison's and were as orchestrated as any "town hall" meeting in today's electronic village. Hanna's railroad connections provided free excursion passes to Canton for carefully chosen groups of students, workers, farmers, merchants, and ex-soldiers, among others. The night before each event, the audience could submit questions in writing, and McKinley would respond the next day in short, carefully scripted speeches.

Leaflets extolling McKinley were printed in the millions (in seven or eight languages) and distributed nationwide. McKinley buttons were manufactured by the thousands. Billboards with McKinley's picture were planted alongside miles of roads. Fourteen hundred speakers were enlisted, ready to be sent into action if an area seemed to be going Democrat. McKinley's men aimed right at the breadbasket in these hard times—they boasted that McKinley was the man with the "Full Dinner Pail." He was "The Advance Agent of Prosperity." He was solid and dependable.

Democrats tried to fight back. They attacked Mark Hanna as "the most vicious, carnal, and unrelenting oppressor of labor . . . in existence" and hinted that he was capable of murder to achieve his ends. Bryan stumped so hard that he lost his voice. But in the end, as is almost always the story in American politics, money talked. Bryan's campaign purse was, at most, a million dollars; McKinley had three times that amount, maybe more.

## THE WINNER: WILLIAM MCKINLEY

McKinley beat Bryan handily, 7,108,480 votes to 6,511,495, with an electoral margin of 271 to 176. McKinley had managed the stupendous feat of keeping the upper middle class in his corner and garnering the votes of urban blue-collar workers, who would now form the core of the revised Republican Party.

Bryan had polled well in the West and, in fact, later estimated that appearances were deceiving. Had 18,000 votes in key states gone his way, he would have been president. Bryan's brand of populist politics would change the Democratic Party forever (even though Bryan, intimidated by the Southern voting base, would never do much for African Americans). Regardless, the Great Commoner began calling 1896 the "first" battle. He knew he would be back.

★★★

**Madman in the White House** In September, just as the election was heating up to a fever pitch, the McKinley-supporting *New York Times* published an interesting little article entitled "Is Mr. Bryan Crazy?" The story examined several of the Democratic candidate's utterances and claimed that they were not the workings of a rational mind. The *Times* editors also included a letter from a distinguished alienist stating that if Bryan won the election, "there would be a madman in the White House."

The paper then interviewed several more alienists and published the results two days later. These eminent medical geniuses said that Bryan suffered from megalomania (delusions of grandeur), paranoia querulent (complaining too much), and querulent logorrhea (talking about complaining too much). One other "expert" said simply, "I don't think Bryan is ordinarily crazy. . . . But I should like to examine him as a degenerate."

**Like a Virgin** In describing the canny, ahead-of-his-time political operator Mark Hanna, Theodore Roosevelt once remarked, "He has advertised McKinley as if he were a patent medicine!" Hanna was an Ohio political broker who spotted the young McKinley as early as 1884, when he was an Ohio congressman, and proceeded to groom him to become president.

Many observers thought that Hanna called the shots and could "shuffle [McKinley] and deal him like a deck of cards." But friends who knew both men disagreed. One contemporary said that Hanna, the hardened politician, felt about the pure-as-the-driven-snow McKinley as "a bashful boy [feels] towards the girl he loves." And McKinley's biographer, Margaret Leech, wrote: "Hanna was drawn to McKinley's idealistic standards like a hardened man of the world who becomes infatuated with virgin innocence."

**Campaign Financing** Eastern tycoons didn't particularly like the independent-minded McKinley, but they disliked Bryan and his silver standard even more. They began spending big money to keep the Boy Orator out of the White House. Led by James G. Hill, the powerful New York railway mogul, Wall Street pushed Republican businesses into line. In those days, political contributions were not left to chance. Banks were assessed one quarter of one percent of their capital. Most big businesses, especially life insurance companies, contributed similarly. Standard Oil—becoming very big business indeed in an increasingly machine-dependent age—put $250,000 into the Republican war chest. All told, the party collected some $3 million, although some estimates range even higher.

# 1900

---

## WILLIAM MCKINLEY vs. WILLIAM JENNINGS BRYAN

The year 1900 announced a new American century in which things were looking far rosier than they did four years earlier. McKinley had gotten lucky. The Depression ended soon after he took office, with the advent of good harvests, rising prices, and new gold discoveries in Alaska, Australia, and South Africa doubling the world's supply and allowing the Treasury Department to issue more banknotes. Arguments for a new silver currency standard were suddenly a lot less persuasive. McKinley could also take credit for the blossoming of American imperialism. In 1898, the United States fought the Spanish-American War, ostensibly to liberate Cuba. The U.S. victory resulted in the acquisition of the Philippines and Puerto Rico.

**THE CAMPAIGN** It was a foregone conclusion that McKinley was the Republican candidate—the only suspense was identifying his running mate. The main contender appeared to be Theodore "Teddy" Roosevelt, the "Rough Rider" hero of Cuba and governor of New York, but party architect Mark Hanna hated Roosevelt's manic energy and impulsiveness. During the Republican convention in Philadelphia, Hanna screamed to delegates, "Don't any of you realize that there is only one life between that madman [Roosevelt] and the presidency?"

Roosevelt pretended that he wasn't interested in the veep nod but showed up at the convention wearing a hat that looked suspiciously like his old broad-brimmed Rough Rider chapeau (leading one observer to smile and say, "Gentleman, that's an acceptance hat"). The prediction turned out to be true: McKinley stood with Roosevelt on the podium when the convention was done.

The Democrats again nominated William Jennings Bryan, dooming their candidate to another hopeless fight. The silver issue was dead, yet Bryan would not give it up, leading Republican Speaker of the House Thomas B. Reed to quip that Bryan would "rather be wrong than be president." Bryan went after McKinley on imperialism and the stranglehold of trusts and monopolies on American business, but people just didn't care. "Let well enough alone" was the Republican slogan, and that about summed it up. McKinley didn't even bother to make his front-porch appearances; instead, the fiery Roosevelt traveled 21,000 miles and rivaled Bryan in passionate speech-making (although Roosevelt chagrined Mark Hanna and the Republican faithful by referring to Bryan as "my opponent," as if Roosevelt were running for president).

**THE WINNER: WILLIAM McKINLEY** McKinley smashed Bryan 7,218,039 votes to 6,358,345, this time winning many of the agricultural states in the West. Bryan's career in politics wasn't over—he still had one more presidential campaign left—but his popularity was clearly trending downward.

Interesting footnote: In the summer of 1899, William McKinley posed for a photo with his first-term vice president, rich New Jersey businessman Garret A. Hobart, who died in office later that year. The photograph was so admired that another was issued in the next summer, with McKinley sitting in an identical pose with VP candidate Theodore Roosevelt.

Strangely, no one can remember McKinley and Roosevelt posing together for the photograph. Even stranger, the photo shows McKinley wearing the same clothes and sitting in the same chair as the McKinley/Hobart photo of a year before. There is also a barely discernable line running down the middle of the photograph, which has led some historians to speculate that the image was a composite assembled by the McKinley campaign—no doubt for the innocent reason that McKinley and Roosevelt didn't have time to sit down together. If so, it is most likely the first-ever doctored photograph used in a presidential campaign.

There would be plenty more.

# 1904

## THEODORE ROOSEVELT vs. ALTON PARKER

On September 6, 1901, President William McKinley attended Buffalo's Pan-American Exposition, afterward shaking hands with the public at a reception on a very hot day in which men and women alike pulled out huge handkerchiefs to wipe their brows.

One of these handkerchiefs concealed a .32 caliber Iver-Johnson revolver belonging to Leon Czolgosz, a young man who had been stalking McKinley all day. Czolgosz, who believed himself an anarchist, went by the name Fred Nieman (or Fred Nobody). He is easily the most pathetic of all presidential assassins and so lame-brained that real anarchists refused to hang out with him, thinking he was either insane or a police spy. When Czolgosz reached McKinley in the reception line, he shot the president twice. In a week McKinley was dead—the third president killed by an assassin in thirty-five years.

Czolgosz would fry in the electric chair, only the fiftieth person to be so executed; the new American century had begun with a bang and a sizzle. When forty-two-year-old Theodore Roosevelt was sworn in as president, he remarked: "It's a dreadful thing to come into the presidency this way, but it would be a far worse thing to be morbid about it."

Morbid he certainly was not. With his high-pitched braying voice, his obsession with exercise, and an abundance of natural energy, he was, in the words of historian Henry Adams, "pure act." The writer Henry James, who didn't like Roosevelt at all, called him "a monstrous embodiment of unprecedented and resounding noise."

**THE CAMPAIGN** In his first term as McKinley's successor, Roosevelt showed a political subtlety that many thought he did not possess (after all, this is the man who called the president of Venezuela a "villainous little monkey"). Understanding the deepening voter dissatisfaction with big business, Roosevelt publicly went after the "malefactors of great wealth" in antitrust suits while maintaining generally cordial relations with the Wall Street capitalists who would fund his 1904 campaign. He was nominated to great acclaim on the first ballot at the Republican convention in Chicago.

Roosevelt's Democratic opponent was the colorless Alton B. Parker, chief justice of the New York Court of Appeals and probably one of the most obscure presidential candidates of all time. Parker— whom Roosevelt referred to as "the neutral-tinted individual"—was chosen to appeal to Democrats as well as crossover Republicans sick of Roosevelt's progressive labor policies. Unfortunately, Parker had little skill in campaigning or speaking, and he spent much of his time alone on his Hudson Valley farm. The best the Democrats could claim was that their man would "set his face sternly against Executive usurpation of legislative and judicial functions."

Not exactly stirring stuff. There was a brief flurry of activity in the fall when Roosevelt thought he might lose in New York; he made a personal appeal to his Wall Street connections, which resulted in hundreds of thousands of dollars being bestowed upon him practically overnight. These enormous sums amassed so quickly embarrassed Roosevelt, who worried that tycoons like J. P. Morgan and Henry Clay Frick thought they were buying him. (In fact, after the election, Frick claimed, "We bought the son of a bitch and then he did not stay bought.")

Roosevelt could, and did, win without owing anybody anything. The election was a Republican landslide, with the president garnering 7,626,593 votes to Parker's 5,082,898. The electoral vote margin was even more lopsided at 336 to 140.

SLEAZE-O-METER

1908

★

WILLIAM
# TAFT
REPUBLICAN

VS.

WILLIAM JENNINGS
# BRYAN
DEMOCRAT

★

"WHAT DOES TAFT STAND FOR, BY THE WAY?
WHY, T.A.F.T. MEANS 'TAKE ADVICE FROM THEODORE!'"
—Democratic joke

In his exuberance on winning the 1904 election by such a gratifying margin, Theodore Roosevelt did something he would always regret. Accepting his country's nod for another term on election night he stated, "Under no circumstances will I be a candidate for or accept another nomination" for a second elective term.

In other words, the forty-six-year-old president had declared himself a lame duck at the moment of his greatest victory. It was perhaps one of the most foolish statements in presidential-elect history. Roosevelt's second term certainly had major successes—he won a Nobel Peace Prize for helping end the Russo-Japanese War, watched work on the Panama Canal begin, helped pass a Pure Food and Drug Act, and further curbed big business excess—but he was less effective than he might have been if he hadn't ruled out the possibility of a second full term.

At least he had the satisfaction of handpicking his successor—his good friend and secretary of war, William Howard Taft. At first Taft was reluctant, but Roosevelt convinced him. Taft was touched: "I must go over and thank Theodore," he said, to which the convivial president replied, patting Taft on the back: "Yes, Will, it's the thing to do."

Republicans were sorry to see Roosevelt go. When the party faithful met at their convention in Chicago, the mere mention of Roosevelt's name by the convention chairman led to a forty-nine-minute chanting of "Four, four, four more years!" But as per Roosevelt's wishes, Taft was nominated on the first ballot. His opponent would be the Great Commoner, William Jennings Bryan, a little older and a great deal balder, running for the third time on a very tired Democratic ticket.

## THE CANDIDATES

**REPUBLICAN: WILLIAM HOWARD TAFT** Taft was a well-liked jovial politico who had risen high in the ranks of the party, in large part thanks to his friendship with Theodore Roosevelt. Roosevelt had used the affable Taft as a sort of ambassador-at-large to smooth out difficulties all over the world—from the Vatican's claim to properties in the newly acquired Philippines to troubles getting the Panama Canal under way. Taft weighed 330 pounds, and his vice-presidential running mate—a conservative New York congressman named James "Sunny Jim" Sherman—tipped the scales at more than 200. Pound for pound, they offered the most political tonnage of any presidential ticket in history.

**DEMOCRAT: WILLIAM JENNINGS BRYAN** There was something both glorious and sad about seeing the old warrior running again for a third try. Even though the odds weighed heavily against him, Bryan hit the stump swinging, along with his running mate, an Indiana state senator named John Kern.

## THE CAMPAIGN

In retrospect, it is difficult to see how Bryan could have beaten any candidate backed by Roosevelt, but the Republicans weren't taking any chances. They immediately launched a vicious personal attack, with Teddy himself describing Bryan as "a kindly man and well-meaning in a weak way . . . but he is the cheapest faker we have ever proposed for president." Even First Lady Edith Roosevelt opined that Bryan was "a trifle too fat and oily for the fastidious."

Bryan struck back. His main campaign theme was "Shall the people rule?" and he hammered an argument that many Americans were beginning to support: far too many politicians were still in the pockets of big business. Bryan was aided by publisher William Randolph Hearst, founder of the new Independent Party and Roosevelt's enemy. In September, Hearst published secret letters from Standard Oil Company files proving that prominent Republican senator Joseph Benson Foraker had received sums as high as $50,000 for what were vaguely labeled as legal fees. (Ironically, these same secret letters implicated the treasurer of the Democratic campaign, Charles Haskell, who was forced to resign.)

The Democrats repeatedly argued that Taft was merely a proxy for Roosevelt. The accusation held plenty of truth. The president sent a steady stream of instructional letters to Taft, including one in which he urged the good-natured candidate to get out on the stump and "hit [Bryan] hard . . . attack him!" (Taft, tactful as always, replied by writing, "I have your letter . . . and if any [strategy] can elect me, I believe this letter can.")

For the most part, voters liked and trusted Taft. Although never a good orator and prone to gaffes (speaking to some old Union Army veterans, Taft kept harping on the fact that their hero, Ulysses S. Grant, drank too much), he had a childlike good humor. In speeches, he would proudly announce that he was "an honorary locomotive fireman" and boast that he was good friends with everyone in the International Brotherhood of Steam Shovel and Dredge Men. Taft found he had plenty of good friends among voters, too.

## THE WINNER: WILLIAM HOWARD TAFT

Taft's 7,676,258 votes outnumbered Bryan's 6,406,801 by a margin of 1,269,000 votes—not as big as Roosevelt's win in 1904, but still pretty impressive. "We beat them to a frazzle!" exclaimed not Taft but a giddy Roosevelt; the new president-elect headed straight to Hot Springs to play golf. His first public statement? "I really did some great work at sleeping last night."

The election was William Bryan's last presidential hurrah, but he would go on to influence the country in other ways—first serving a stint as Woodrow Wilson's secretary of state and later crusading against Darwinism (and Clarence Darrow) in the Scopes Monkey Trial.

★★★

**Teddy Knows Best** Theodore Roosevelt closely stage-managed William Howard Taft's run for president, including giving him sage advice in many letters: "I hope that your people will do everything they can to prevent one word being sent out about either your fishing or playing golf," he said in one missive. "The American people regard the campaign as serious business." He went on: "Let the audience see you smile always, because I feel your nature shines out so transparently when you smile. . . . You big, generous, high-minded fellow." He also remonstrated with Taft's advisers not to let the outsized presidential candidate be allowed on horses: "Dangerous for him and cruelty to the horse."

**Jobs for Taft** As usual, businesses were in the Republican corner during the 1908 election, and they made no secret about their loyalty. The vice president of the New York Central Railroad instructed that 2,500 freight and passenger cars be repaired—whether they needed it or not—to give jobs to employees and make the economy appear healthier. The president of a Midwestern fire insurance company sent out 2,000 of his door-to-door salesmen with instructions to always slip in a word for Taft while making a sale. A Missouri steel company added 400 men to its payroll just before Election Day in order, the chairman said, to pick up votes for Taft.

**The Perils of Being Unitarian** As a Unitarian—considered barely a religion by many Americans—Taft was attacked by Democratic and Republican religious newspapers. "Think of the United States with a

President who does not believe that Jesus Christ was the Son of God, but looks upon our immaculate Savior as common bastard and low, cunning impostor," cried one Midwestern editor.

The issue became so important that Theodore Roosevelt made a point of publicly attending Unitarian church services with Taft—in the hope, Roosevelt explained, "that it would attract the attention of the sincere but rather ignorant Protestants who support me."

Taft, to his credit, made no apologies for his mode of worship: "If the American public is so narrow as not to elect a Unitarian, well and good. I can stand it."

SLEAZE-O-METER

**1912**

WOODROW
# WILSON
DEMOCRAT

VS.

THEODORE
# ROOSEVELT
PROGRESSIVE BULL-MOOSE

VS.

WILLIAM HOWARD
# TAFT
REPUBLICAN

**"TAFT IS A FATHEAD . . . WITH THE BRAINS OF A GUINEA PIG!"**
**—Theodore Roosevelt**

I t's interesting to note that, with the exception of Grover Cleveland's two nonconsecutive terms, Republican Party candidates had occupied the White House since 1860—an astonishing 44 years. But things were about to change in an especially acrimonious election that saw the Republican Party literally tear itself apart.

After Taft's 1908 victory, Roosevelt headed off to Africa for big-game hunting—the ex-president was personally responsible for killing 9 lions, 8 elephants, 20 zebras, 7 giraffes, and 6 buffalos.

Back at home, progressive Republicans had a different kind of big game in their sights: William Howard Taft. The new president was more conservative than his predecessor and soon found himself under the sway of big business. Progressives complained that Taft was selling out, and the president whined in a letter to Roosevelt, "It is now a year and three months since I assumed office and I have had a hard time."

His former mentor was not an ideal confidant. As soon as Roosevelt returned home in 1910, he was besieged by progressive Republicans trying to convince him to run for a second full term. It didn't take much persuasion. Roosevelt began to criticize Taft's policies, claiming that he was a pawn of "the bosses and . . . the great privileged interests." Taft was stunned to hear such vehement attacks from a man he considered a personal friend (not to mention still referring to him as "the President"). "If only I knew what the President wanted," he told an aide, "I would do it."

What Roosevelt wanted became clear in February 1912, when

he declared his candidacy for the party nomination. "My hat is in the ring!" he roared (unwittingly coining a phrase in the process). "The fight is on and I am stripped to the buff!"

Taft picked up on the boxing metaphor when he issued his own statement: "I do not want to fight Theodore Roosevelt, but sometimes a man in a corner comes out swinging. . . . I was a man of straw but I have been a man of straw long enough. Every man who has blood in his body . . . is forced to fight."

At this point in American history, some states had already begun holding primary elections to pick delegates, a fairly pro forma procedure wherein delegates voted for the choice of their party bosses. All that changed during the election of 1912. In what can probably be considered the first-ever contested presidential party primaries, Roosevelt used his clout and charisma to beat Taft, nine states to one. Roosevelt even won in Taft's home state of Ohio. Arriving at the Republican convention in June, Roosevelt was on a roll, featured in newspapers all over the country, far better public fodder than Taft, who remained quietly in the White House.

It may be hard for us today, in an age of carefully orchestrated national political conventions, to understand the mayhem that occurred. But when you consider that Roosevelt showed up on the first day wearing a sombrero, smoking a cigar, and referring to the sitting president as "a rat in a corner," it's clear that a lot has changed in the last hundred years.

Even more action was happening behind the scenes. The delegates Roosevelt won in the primary elections were in the minority—Taft's conservative political bosses controlled the Republican National Committee and made a point of lining up Taft delegates from the states in the majority, which did not hold primaries. In back-room wheeling and dealing, they also purchased the support of as many as 200 to 300 delegates from southern states—these states would vote Democratic in a national election, but they did have Republican delegates they were willing to trade for favors or cold cash.

Roosevelt and his men made challenge after challenge when Taft's men tried to seat these delegates; their challenges were denied, so much so that progressives began to cry they were being "steamrolled" (another expression coined in 1912). Tensions ran so high that police squads were brought in and barbed wire strung around the stage. Finally, when Taft ended up with a commanding lead in delegates, 561 to Roosevelt's 107, Roosevelt and his supporters stormed out. They formed their own independent party, made up of everyone from social workers, reformers, and feminists to unhappy mainstream Republicans. They called themselves the Progressive Party but were known popularly as the Bull Moose Party because Roosevelt had proclaimed: "I am fit as a bull moose!"

Thus, the most successful political party of the last half century had managed to split itself in two—hardly a recipe for victory, since simple arithmetic showed that Democrats had about 45 percent of the national vote locked up. As one onlooker said, referring to Taft and Roosevelt, "The only question is, which corpse gets the flowers?"

## THE CANDIDATES

**REPUBLICAN: WILLIAM HOWARD TAFT** Although he tried to rally, calling Roosevelt a "destructive radical" and even (in what was becoming fashionable alienist-speak) "neurotic," Taft reacted poorly to hostility. He wrote to his wife: "Sometimes I think I might as well give up as far as being a candidate is concerned. There are so many people in the country who don't like me." His running mate was his vice president, James Sherman, who died just days before the election. Nicholas Murray Butler, president of Columbia University, agreed to replace him—but only, he told Taft, on the condition that Taft not win.

**PROGRESSIVE-BULL MOOSE: THEODORE ROOSEVELT** Roosevelt had made the infamous 1904 blunder of declaring that he would never seek another term, so now he had to backpedal. He told voters that what he really meant was he wouldn't run for three *consecutive* terms. In spite of this lame explanation, Roosevelt remained enormously popular in America. Had he wrested the nomination from Taft, it's likely he would have gone on to take the national election. For his running mate, Roosevelt chose Hiram Johnson, governor of California.

**DEMOCRAT: WOODROW WILSON** The Democratic convention, held in Baltimore shortly after the Republican slugfest, featured a battle between Missouri Congressman "Champ" Clark, Speaker of the House, and a new type of Democrat entirely: Woodrow Wilson, former president of Princeton University and then-current governor of New Jersey. A diffident but extremely smart and ambitious man, he was a product of William Jennings Bryan—not a Populist, but the model of a liberal progressive Democrat.

Wilson eventually got the nod on the forty-sixth ballot, partly because Champ Clark had made himself a figure of ridicule by doing testimonials for a patent medicine company ("It seemed that all the organs in my body were out of order, but three bottles of Electric Bitters made me all right!").

Ever the scholar, Wilson refused to be too joyous about his nomination: "I can't effervesce in the face of responsibility," he said. His vice-presidential candidate was Thomas Marshall, governor of Indiana, who is now known for having said, "What this country needs is a really good five-cent cigar." A statement as true today as it was then.

## THE CAMPAIGN

With three evenly matched candidates squaring off for the presidency—a scenario unlike any other in American history—personalities began to dominate. Taft was honest but passive, Roosevelt explosive but full of energy, Wilson coherent but cold.

Taft, while admitting it was hard to "keep myself in the headlines," tried anyway. He attacked Roosevelt by saying he "is to be classed with the leaders of religious cults who promote things over their followers by . . . any sort of manipulation and deception."

This accusation was not as far-fetched as it might sound since Roosevelt's ringing cry was: "We stand at Armageddon and we battle for the Lord!" His progressive followers had an almost religious fervor. He developed a program that he called the New Nationalism, in which he claimed the government would play a strong role in regulating the economy and overseeing greedy and corrupt corporations.

While Wilson attacked Taft and Roosevelt as "Tweedledum and Tweedledee," two sides of the same Republican coin, he knew that the latter posed a real threat, for Roosevelt's progressivism was close to his own. Wilson developed his own program, the New Freedom, which placed more emphasis on oversight of monopolies but far less of a powerful role for federal government. The plan would also seek more cooperation with labor unions.

In public appearances, Wilson didn't come off as a traditional politician—he was a bit stiff, hated kissing babies, and whenever a speech called for him to sound forceful, the results were unconvincing. But Wilson was able to laugh at himself ("It is a fine system when some remote, severe, academic schoolmaster may become President of the United States"), and people warmed up to him. He seemed like a good alternative to Roosevelt's increasing bombast, which had begun to strike many as strident and unnecessarily violent. In the last week of the campaign, gamblers set 5-to-1 odds in Wilson's favor.

## THE WINNER: WOODROW WILSON

Divided, the Republicans fell. Wilson pulled 6,293,152 votes to Roosevelt's 4,119,207 and Taft's 3,483,922. Although Wilson had won only 41 percent of the popular vote, he performed strongly in the Electoral College, with 435 votes (compared to 88 for Roosevelt and only 8 for Taft). Roosevelt was the first and only third-party presidential candidate in American history to pull more votes than a major party candidate. But though he remained a major force in Republican politics (having rejoined the party after 1912), he would never again run for president.

★★★

**Movie Man** New forms of technology began to take hold in the election of 1912, not only among the electorate, but among the candidates as well. Woodrow Wilson spent hours closeted in a tiny rudimentary recording studio making speeches that were pressed onto 78 r.p.m. phonograph albums and made available for home listening. Wilson was such a stickler for accuracy that he also brought along a primitive recording device while making campaign speeches so that he could correct mistakes by reporters who hastily scribbed down his words.

Roosevelt hired a moving picture man, whom he nicknamed "Movie," to film some of his own whistle stops. If he didn't have a prepared speech, Roosevelt would sometimes just spout nonsense—"Barnes, Penrose, and Smoot! Recall of judicial decisions! *Alice in Wonderland* is a great book!"—while waving his arms to fake scenes for Movie to shoot. To silent-movie audiences of the day, the results were convincing enough.

**A Dangerous Profession** Being a presidential candidate always has its risks, but 1912 was a particularly tough year. Wilson's Pullman car was hit by a freight train, which shaved off the little back porch from which the candidate usually spoke. On another occasion, Wilson's Model T overturned, and doctors had to stitch the candidate's scalp back together.

Roosevelt had his own share of train shenanigans: To the horror of reporters and politicians accompanying him, he once took the controls of a locomotive and drove it pell-mell down the tracks. His worst moment came in Milwaukee on the night of October 14, when a man named John Shrank walked up to him before a speech and shot him in the chest. (Shrank claimed that the ghost of William McKinley had appeared to him and told him to shoot Roosevelt for running for a third term.)

Shrank was apprehended, and amazingly enough Roosevelt insisted on carrying on with his speech. In one of the great dramatic moments in American politics, he ascended to the platform and said: "Friends, I shall ask you to be as quiet as possible. I don't know whether you fully understand that I have just been shot; but it takes more than that to kill a bull moose."

He then pulled out his speech from his breast pocket. It was dripping with blood, and people gasped in horror. With a bullet inside him that fractured a rib and came perilously close to piercing his lung, Roosevelt still had the presence of mind to blame the shooting on his opponents. "It is a natural thing that weak and violent minds should be inflamed . . . by the kind of artful mendacity and abuse that have been heaped upon me for the last three months."

He made his speech and then went to the hospital, where doctors said he was saved by the folded papers, a glasses case, and his thick chest muscles. Roosevelt rested for two weeks; in sympathy, the other candidates stopped campaigning during that time as well.

**Just a Peck** The only hint of a romantic scandal in this campaign came when Woodrow Wilson's longtime friendship with a lovely divorcée named Mary Allen Peck was made public. Many Democrats suspected (but never proved) that Republican operatives stole Wilson's valise, hoping to find incriminating letters and concoct a scandal. No letters were ever produced, but Wilson (who was married) apparently thought they might be. He solemnly assured an aide that "we Southerners like to write mush" but explained that nothing had gone on between him and Peck.

This was probably true. As Theodore Roosevelt, who could be quite mean, said, "It wouldn't work. You can't cast a man as Romeo who looks and acts so much like an apothecary clerk."

# 1916

## WOODROW WILSON vs. CHARLES HUGHES

During Woodrow Wilson's first term in office, Congress passed the Sixteenth Amendment, providing for a federal income tax. Horrible as that was, the worst news in the world was that a massive bloody war was going on in Europe. Most people in the United States, including Woodrow Wilson, wanted to stay out of the conflict, but avoidance was becoming increasingly difficult, especially after a German submarine sank the British passenger liner *Lusitana* in 1915, killing 124 Americans. Wilson would manage to avoid the war for another two years, but he couldn't stop the escalation of anti-German hysteria.

On other fronts, Wilson was an active liberal president. During his first term, he backed several bills that helped ease the plight of workers in America, including the Child Labor Bill, which forbade children under the age of fourteen from working in factories. He was also responsible for federal laws allotting funds for new highways and schools. The economy boomed, although this was in part because of the high price American companies could demand for their goods in war-ravaged Europe. With Wilson swearing to keep Americans out of the war, he was nominated with deafening applause on the first ballot at the Democratic convention in St. Louis in June. His vice president continued to be Thomas Marshall.

The Republicans sought their own "intellectual" in the White House and nominated Supreme Court justice Charles Evans Hughes, with Theodore Roosevelt's former vice president Charles Fairbanks as his running mate. Roosevelt hemmed and hawed before offering Hughes his backing—he called the former justice a "whiskered Wilson" and suggested that the only difference between the two was "a shave." But in the end, he came around and supported Hughes.

**THE CAMPAIGN** Wilson chose the now somewhat old-fashioned route of refusing to campaign, and at first it seemed like he didn't need to. The Democratic slogan—one of the finest in all American presidential history—was "He kept us out of war." It played exceedingly well, particularly in western states where more and more women had won the right to vote. (The Nineteenth Amendment would give voting rights to all women in 1920.) Wilson supporters claimed "a vote for Hughes is a vote for war!" although, in fact, Hughes wanted to keep the country at peace. He was undermined at every turn by Theodore Roosevelt, who, while ostensibly stumping for his party's nominee, kept making bellicose anti-German statements.

Nevertheless, the GOP managed to hurt Wilson on several issues. Americans may have wanted peace, but they wanted their country to be prepared and respected by the world as well. Republicans, led by Roosevelt, successfully suggested that Wilson had not done enough to respond to the *Lusitania* attack or build up American armed forces. Wilson's reputation was also sullied in the eyes of many religious Americans because of his personal life. His wife, Ellen, had died in 1914, and Wilson shocked the country by marrying again in December 1915—this time to a forty-something widow named Edith Bolling Galt. Republicans quickly spread rumors that the president had engaged in an affair with Galt before Ellen's death. Some even argued that she had died of a broken heart.

**THE WINNER: WOODROW WILSON** The race was surprisingly close. Election Day was November 7, and with much of the east reporting, by late in the evening Hughes had won almost all the electoral votes he was going to need—just one more state, California, would put him over the top. Democratic-leaning newspapers conceded defeat, while

Republican ones carried huge headlines that read "THE PRESIDENT-ELECT—CHARLES EVANS HUGHES." Wilson confessed to a friend a feeling of relief that he no longer had to shoulder the weighty responsibility of being president, yet, cautious as ever, he decided not to concede until the next morning, when returns from the west (notoriously slow in reporting) were in.

It was a good thing. It turned out that Wilson had won California by 3,800 votes and swept the West. Nationwide, he beat Hughes 9,126,300 votes to 8,546,789, an amazing instance of snatching victory out of the jaws of defeat.

SLEAZE-O-METER

**1920**

★

WARREN G.
# HARDING
REPUBLICAN

## VS.

JAMES
# COX
DEMOCRAT

★

"[HARDING] IS A VERY RESPECTABLE
OHIO POLITICIAN OF THE SECOND CLASS."
—*New York Times*

**W**ilson may have promised to keep the country out of war, but by the time of his inauguration in 1917, new circumstances forced him to break his word. The Germans had opened unrestricted submarine warfare against merchant shipping, and several American vessels were sunk by U-boats. Even worse, Wilson discovered that Germany had proposed a secret alliance with Mexico. In return for joining the Axis powers, Mexico would be given most of the southwestern United States.

Wilson declared war on Germany in April of 1917, sending thousands of "doughboys" to France to join in the hostilities. America's role in the conflict lasted just eighteen months, but combat cost the lives of 53,000 American soldiers. When the armistice was signed in November 1918, Wilson tried to get Senate ratification of the Treaty of Versailles, which included his cherished League of Nations, but the Republicans thwarted him at every turn. Worn out, Wilson suffered a stroke and spent the rest of his administration partially disabled.

The end of the war brought higher costs for goods and widespread unemployment. Worse, the recent Russian Revolution had left many Americans on edge. It was just the opportunity the Republicans hungered for—a chance to reposition themselves as the party of the full dinner pail and the good old uncomplicated prewar days.

## THE CANDIDATES

**REPUBLICAN: WARREN G. HARDING** Warren G. Harding was the most libidinous candidate to run for president until Bill Clinton waltzed in from Arkansas seventy years later; the good-looking Harding was particularly popular among female voters, who were now casting their ballots in large numbers. When Republican operatives decided to nominate the fifty-five-year-old Ohio senator, they asked if he had anything hidden in his personal life that would "disqualify" him from winning the presidency. Harding asked for some time to reflect, and he may have pondered that he chewed tobacco, played poker, loved to drink (Prohibition had just been voted in), and was having affairs with not only the wife of one of his friends but also a young woman thirty years his junior, with whom he had an illegitimate daughter.

Then he said, nope, nothing to hide guys—it's all good.

Harding's vice-presidential running mate was almost his polar opposite; Calvin Coolidge was the hard-nosed and taciturn governor of Massachusetts. When Coolidge received word that he had received the vice-presidential nod, he told his wife, "I've been nominated for vice president." She said, "You aren't going to take it, are you?" To which Coolidge replied, "I suppose I'll have to."

**DEMOCRAT: JAMES. M. COX** The Democrats faced a serious disadvantage in 1920. They couldn't part company with the recently crippled Woodrow Wilson—it would seem like they were abandoning their man when he was down. So their nominee was James Cox, the liberal governor of Ohio and former newspaper editor, who promised to campaign for Wilson's pet project, the League of Nations. His running mate would be the young and charismatic assistant secretary of the navy, Franklin D. Roosevelt, distant cousin and nephew-in-law of Theodore.

## THE CAMPAIGN

With a candidate like Harding, the Republicans knew they had to act quickly. The first thing they did was get rid of the evidence. They sent his married lover, Carrie Fulton Phillips, on an extended all-expenses-paid tour of Asia, along with her entire family. And just to be completely safe, Republicans also sent Harding's brother-in-law to Europe, because the guy had just married a Catholic (and Catholics didn't play well in the conservative Midwest).

Now it was time for "a return to normalcy," as Harding explained in one of his campaign speeches. His speechwriter had written "a return to normality," but Harding pronounced it "normalty." Benevolent journalists translated it as "normalcy," and the phrase became a popular Republican campaign slogan.

Normalcy apparently meant small-town turn-of-the-century American values—Harding was never terribly clear about this—but the phrase played well in a country that was becoming increasingly conservative. James Cox worked incredibly hard, campaigning 22,000 miles in thirty-six states, giving 400 speeches before two million people, but he was handicapped by association with Woodrow Wilson and his anti-Prohibition stance. (Harding, of course, loved his booze, but he expressed public support for Prohibition, echoing popular sentiments throughout the country.)

Democrats furiously attacked Harding. They called him "weak, colorless, and mediocre," along with "a dummy, an animated automaton, a marionette." They said he was part of a "Senatorial cabal" of "pygmies" and "white-livered and incompetent politicians." But nothing worked. Despite Harding's excesses, he knew what he was doing. An admiring biographer wrote that he was a brilliant politician, shrewd when it came to "vacuity"—giving people satisfying emptiness.

## THE WINNER: WARREN G. HARDING

In the fall of 1920, in the first-ever poll taken during a presidential campaign, *Literary Digest* magazine sent out millions of postcards to its readers, asking whom they would vote for. Harding won by a huge margin, especially among women. The same held true on Election Day. Harding and Coolidge won by a landslide, defeating the Democratic ticket 16,153,115 votes to 9,133,092, with a huge margin in the Electoral College of 404 to 127.

The Roaring Twenties were about to begin, with just the man for the job at the helm—a president who knew how to have a good time.

**Advent of the Adman** When Albert Lasker signed on as a Harding campaign consultant, the playbook for presidential elections was rewritten forever. Lasker was the head of a Chicago advertising and public relations firm and a true innovator; he coordinated a PR blitz for Harding that included movies, radio, photography, newspapers, and magazines. Some sample Lasker ad headlines:

"America First!"

"Independence means Independence, now as in 1776."

"Let's be done with wiggle and wobble!"

"This country will remain American. Its next President will remain in our own country."

These utterances may strike us as inane, but in 1920 they spoke to an American public that was becoming more insular in an uncertain world.

Then, as now, people liked their movie stars, and Lasker helped Harding populate his front porch in Marion with Hollywood names. Long before Al Gore got chummy with Sean Penn and Susan Sarandon, newsreel cameras captured Harding at home, hamming it up with the likes of Al Jolson, Lillian Russell, Douglas Fairbanks, and Mary Pickford. The same cameras caught James Cox doggedly, grimly stumping away. People had no trouble deciding which candidate was more fun.

**Jumping the Fence** Harding had so many skeletons in his closet, it's hard to imagine why any of his opponents would feel compelled to invent new ones. But that's what happened when William Chancellor, a racist professor from Wooster, Ohio, claimed that he had thoroughly researched Harding's past and discovered that the candidate had African American ancestors.

In a paper entitled "Genealogy of Warren G. Harding of Marion, Ohio," Chancellor claimed that Harding's great-grandfather and great-grandmother were black and that his father was a mulatto who had married a white woman. As part of his "evidence," Chancellor cited Amos Kling, Harding's father-in-law—an unbalanced man who hated Harding—saying that Harding was "colored."

Woodrow Wilson and James Cox forbade the use of this material (although it was rumored that the latter whispered the story on more than one occasion). Most newspapers refused to touch it, although the slurs did appear in Democratic handbills. Harding was unruffled. When one newspaper reporter asked him directly, "Do you have any Negro blood?" Harding answered, to the horror of his party operatives, "How do I know, Jim? One of my ancestors may have jumped the fence."

**A String of Wet Sponges** What's in a word? Warren G. Harding's long meandering speeches, full of archaic nineteenth-century turns of phrase, satisfied his admirers but drove his opponents crazy. (A sample: "What is the greatest thing in life, my countrymen? Happiness. And there is more happiness in the American village today than in any other place on the face of the earth.") After listening to one such speech, the great American humorist H. L. Mencken wrote that it "reminds me of a string of wet sponges; it reminds me of tattered washing on a line; it reminds me of stale bean soup, of college yells, of dogs barking idiotically through endless nights. It is so bad that a sort of grandeur creeps into it. It drags itself out of a dark abysm. . . . "

# 1924

## CALVIN COOLIDGE vs. JOHN DAVIS

Warren Harding worked and played hard—late-night poker games and his supposed trysts in White House closets with his young mistress, Nan Britton, were balanced by an attempt to keep the country moving into prosperity as the effects of the crisis after World War I wore off. But Harding was hit by a virulent flu in early 1923, and the symptoms may have hidden a heart attack. Doctors became concerned about the president, whose systolic blood pressure readings routinely topped 175.

Pressures on Harding's administration continued as scandals began to unfold, including one in which Charles Forbes, head of the new Veterans Bureau, was found to have stolen $2 million from World War I veterans (a *New York Times* reporter came across Harding with his hands literally around Forbes's neck, shouting, "You double-crossing bastard!"). Returning from an Alaska vacation prescribed by his doctors, Harding collapsed and died in a San Francisco hotel room on August 2, 1923.

This left the country under the care of "Silent Cal" Coolidge. Coolidge inherited Harding's scandals, including the infamous Teapot Dome Affair, in which government oil fields were leased to private business in return for bribes. Not much of this rubbed off on Coolidge, who was the epitome of rectitude. He was easily nominated for president when Republicans convened in Cleveland in June 1924. His vice-presidential running mate was Charles Dawes, budget director and former bright young political operative for William McKinley.

The Democrats allowed their New York convention to be broadcast over the radio—the first time this had ever happened—and more than one million listeners were treated to endless days of squabbling from Ku Klux Klan members. The KKK had made major inroads into southern and western Democratic circles and wanted a platform amenable to their racist agenda. But after an astonishing 103 ballots (the most ever cast in a presidential party convention, before or since), anti-Klan forces prevailed and nominated John W. Davis, former solicitor general under Woodrow Wilson. His running mate was Charles Bryan, governor of Nebraska and brother of William Jennings Bryan.

**THE CAMPAIGN** Say what you will about Calvin Coolidge, the man was smart enough to keep his mouth shut. "I don't recall any candidate for president who ever injured himself very much by not talking," he told reporters hungry for a quote. When it came to America, he was "for the economy. After that, I am for more economy." The Republican campaign slogan "Keep Cool with Coolidge" seemed to sum it up.

John Davis hit the campaign trail, but he was a lackluster speaker who didn't think he would really win ("I went all around the country telling people I was going to be elected," he later wrote, "and I knew I hadn't any more chance than a snowball in hell.") Democrats did discover that twenty-seven Republican ambassadors were AWOL from their duties in foreign countries while campaigning for Coolidge. And it was found that Silent Cal had quietly pocketed a $250 speaking fee when he was vice president. (But then so had Woodrow Wilson's veep, Charles Marshall, who claimed he was so poorly paid as the nation's second in command that "I had to do it, steal, or resign.")

Radio continued to play a growing role in the American electoral

**ANYTHING FOR A VOTE**

process. After Harding's death, the newly formed National Broadcast Association approached Coolidge and told him that both Woodrow Wilson and Harding had basically worn themselves into sickness and death by traveling too much. Perhaps Cal might like to avail himself of the radio?

Silent Cal got the message. On election night, he stayed home and broadcast over a national radio hookup, ending with a very folksy goodnight to the country, "Including my father, up on the Vermont farm, listening in."

**THE WINNER: CALVIN COOLIDGE** Americans ate it up. Calvin Coolidge became the country's thirtieth president by beating John Davis 15,719,921 votes to 8,386,704, an almost two-to-one margin. Supreme Court chief justice Oliver Wendell Holmes summed up everyone's feelings quite nicely: "While I don't expect anything very astonishing from [Coolidge], I don't want anything very astonishing."

SLEAZE-O-METER

**1928**

HERBERT
# HOOVER
REPUBLICAN

VS.

AL
# SMITH
DEMOCRAT

*"ROME SUGGESTS THAT POPE MOVE HERE!"*
**—Headline in Republican newspaper**

On August 2, 1927, while vacationing in his "Summer White House" in the Black Hills of South Dakota, Calvin Coolidge walked outside to waiting reporters and handed them a slip of paper that read: "I do not choose to run for President in nineteen-twenty-eight." Taking no questions, Silent Cal walked back inside his house—and out of the presidency.

No one could quite figure out why Coolidge had made this decision. The economy was booming, and the president, despite or because of his rock-bottom New England reticence and many eccentricities, was popular. Perhaps he still harbored grief from the death by blood poisoning of his sixteen-year-old son Calvin Jr. in 1924. Or perhaps it was because, as Mrs. Coolidge allegedly said, "Papa says there's going to be a depression."

Whatever the reason, Coolidge's choice not to run set the scene for an election that was, in the words of one historian, "one of the most revolting spectacles in the nation's history."

## THE CANDIDATES

**REPUBLICAN: HERBERT HOOVER** Herbert Hoover would later gain a reputation as a man who twiddled his thumbs while America's greatest economic crisis set in—but in 1928, he was a formidable candidate. He was the secretary of commerce and a self-made millionaire who had become known for overseeing humanitarian aid to thousands of starving Europeans during and after World War I. Unfortunately, he was also was one of the stiffest, most stilted, most machinelike candidates ever to run—so much that Republicans were forced to plant articles with headlines like "That Man Hoover—He's Human."

**DEMOCRAT: AL SMITH** Al Smith was the polar opposite of Hoover, a politician born and bred within New York's Tammany Hall system. Smith loved meeting people and pressing the flesh. Going into 1928, he was the four-time governor of New York strengthened by a national following and the support of up-and-coming political stars like Franklin Delano Roosevelt and his wife, Eleanor. Al had two problems, however, and they were big ones. He supported the repeal of Prohibition, and he was America's first Catholic presidential candidate.

## THE CAMPAIGN

Neither party was hurting for money in the election of 1928, which may explain why things became so nasty. The Republicans would ultimately spend $9.4 million, the Democrats $7.1 million (the Democrats also ponied up $500,000 on radio time, at the rate of $10,000 an hour for a coast-to-coast hookup).

Republican ads underscored the prosperity Americans were feeling. "Hoover and Happiness or Smith and Soup Houses" or, even more effective, "A Chicken in Every Pot—Vote for Hoover." The message, as one Republican pamphlet put it, was "Your Vote Versus the Spectacle of Idleness and Ruin."

Hoover's handlers often filmed him romping with a large dog to loosen up his image, but he was a man who always wore a full suit and stiff collar, who read his speeches in a perfunctory monotone. ("I can only make so many speeches," he once said. "I only have so much to say.") During interviews he would restrict himself to answering questions without elaborating, and when he was finished, he looked at the questioner blankly, "like a machine that has run down," as one startled reporter put it.

Hoover wisely stayed away from debating the more colorful Smith (he refused even to mention his opponent's name) and presented himself as a smart businessman who would run the government like an efficient corporation.

But the election soon took a sickening turn. The Ku Klux Klan continued to be a powerful force in America, with a membership that historians now estimate as high as two to four million. When Smith's campaign train headed west, it was met by burning crosses on the hills and explosions from dynamite charges echoing across the prairies. Klansmen and other religious bigots swayed ignorant voters by telling them that the Catholic Smith, having supposedly sworn fealty to the pope, would turn the United States over to "Romanism and Ruin." Protestant ministers told their congregations that if Smith became president, all non-Catholic marriages would be annulled and all children of these marriages declared illegitimate. Preachers even warned their congregations that if they voted for Al Smith, they would go straight to hell.

Hoover officially proclaimed that his opponent's religion had no bearing on his ability to be president, but even Hoover's wife, Lou, whispered that people had a right to vote against Smith because of his faith. She and many other Republicans spread rumors of Smith's alcoholism, which were already rampant because he favored the repeal of Prohibition or, at least, the right of states to choose for themselves. Republicans sneeringly referred to him as "Alcoholic Smith," told of public drunkenness, and claimed that he had already secretly promised to appoint a bootlegger as secretary of the treasury.

In truth, Smith was a moderate drinker who enjoyed a cocktail in the evening from legal, pre-Prohibition stock. But as we've seen, truth rarely factors in to presidential campaigns.

## THE WINNER: HERBERT HOOVER

Herbert Hoover won in a landslide that included five states from the usually Democratic South, beating Smith 21,437,227 votes to 15,007,698. A joke went around New York that on the day after the election, Smith wired the pope a one-word telegram: "Unpack!"

**How Bad Were the Anti-Catholic Slurs?** Consider the following: at the time of the election, New York's Holland Tunnel was just being completed. Republicans circulated pictures of Al Smith at the mouth of the structure, declaring that it led 3,500 miles under the Atlantic Ocean to Rome—direct to the basement of the Vatican.

In Daytona Beach, Florida, the school board instructed that a note be placed in every child's lunch pail that read: "We must prevent the election of Alfred E. Smith to the presidency. If he is chosen president, you will not be allowed to read or have a bible."

And this lovely poem spread in leaflets in upstate New York during the summer of 1928:

> *When Catholics rule the United States*
> *And the Jew grows a Christian nose on his face*
> *When Pope Pius is head of the Ku Klux Klan*
> *In the land of Uncle Sam*
> *Then Al Smith will be our president*
> *And the country not worth a damn.*

**The Babe** Smith was lucky enough to have the endorsement of the country's biggest sports hero, Babe Ruth. After the Yankees' victory in the World Series of 1928, Babe Ruth stumped for Smith from the back of a train carrying the team home from St. Louis. Unfortunately, Ruth wasn't the most dependable spokesman. He would sometimes appear in his undershirt, holding a mug of beer in one hand and a sparerib in the other. Worse, if he met with any dissent while praising Smith, he would snarl, "If that's the way you feel, the hell with you!" and stagger back inside.

**Dirty Dancing** When people got tired of attacking Smith for his religion, there were other fruitful areas for invective. One Protestant minister railed against him for dancing and accused him of doing the "bunny hug, turkey trot, hesitation, tango, Texas Tommy, the hug-me-tight, foxtrot, shimmy-dance . . . and skunk-waltz." Another minister claimed that Smith indulged in "card-playing, cocktail drinking, poodle dogs, divorces, novels, stuffy rooms, evolution . . . nude art, prize-fighting, actors, greyhound racing, and modernism."

**Mr. and Mrs. Smith** Al Smith met his wife, Kate, when they were both growing up in Tammany's impoverished Fourth Ward on New York City's Lower East Side. Though the couple shared a deep love, Kate was anything but sophisticated. During the 1928 campaign, she was slammed with barely disguised anti-Irish bigotry by prominent Republican women. They claimed that with Kate as first lady, the White House would smell of "corned beef, cabbage, and home brew." Mrs. Florence T. Griswold, Republican national committee member, made a speech in which she said, "Can you imagine an aristocratic foreign ambassador saying to her, 'What a charming gown,' and the reply, 'Youse said a mouthful!'" Her audience roared with laughter.

**Radioheads** By 1928, radio networks like the National Broadcasting Company (NBC) and the Columbia Broadcasting System (CBS) extended nationwide—any major political address could expect to reach forty million listeners.

Although Herbert Hoover was a far worse stump speaker than Al Smith, he was much better at talking in a studio, where the speaker had to stand very still, exactly ten inches away from the large "pie" microphone, to reduce distortion and extraneous noise. (It was not something Hoover liked, however. When someone asked him if he got a thrill out of speaking over the radio, he snapped: "The same thrill I get when I rehearse an address to a doorknob!")

Smith, far better at campaigning in person, had a much worse time on the radio. He could not refrain from moving around, which caused his voice to fade in and out. And his thick New York accent ("rad-deeo" for radio, "foist" for first) alienated many listeners in rural America. Campaign strategists in both parties took note.

# 1932

## FRANKLIN D. ROOSEVELT vs. HERBERT HOOVER

What a difference four years can make. The stock market crash of 1929 sent America reeling into the hangover of the Great Depression, the worst economic crisis the country has ever faced. Twenty-three hundred banks collapsed in 1931 alone. By 1932, more than 300,000 children were forced out of bankrupt school systems. The Depression steadily worsened until millions of Americans were out of work. The name Hoover became synonymous with desperation and poverty—Hoovervilles were shantytowns, Hoover blankets were newspapers, and Hoover Pullmans were boxcars in which, by some counts, 200,000 starving Americans rode around the country seeking jobs.

You know things are bad when *Time* magazine calls you "President Reject," but the Republicans were stuck with Hoover, even though he had started making Marie Antoinette-ish statements, such as "Many people have left their jobs for the more profitable one of selling apples." Hoover ran partnered by his vice president, Charles Curtis, who was seventy-two years old and whose main claim to fame was having Native American blood. Before he gave a campaign speech, Curtis would always have an Indian "maiden" recite Longfellow's poem "Hiawatha."

The Democrats had far more exciting prospects with their nominee, fifty-year-old Franklin Delano Roosevelt, governor of New York. Although crippled by a bout of polio in 1921, he possessed indefatigable reserves of energy as well as the not inconsiderable political gift of being able to tell people exactly what they wanted to hear. Roosevelt's vice-presidential candidate was "Cactus Jack" Garner, hard-drinking Texan and Speaker of the House.

**THE CAMPAIGN** It's possible that almost any Democrat could have beaten Hoover in 1932, but Roosevelt's well-oiled political machine left nothing to chance. Through radio, pamphlets, speeches, and direct-mail campaigns, Roosevelt reminded people of empty Hoover promises, namely "prosperity is just around the corner" and "the worst has passed." Of course, most Americans hadn't forgotten these promises, and they were still holding a grudge. Hoover had become so unpopular that the Secret Service warned him not to leave the White House. At a campaign stop in Kansas, voters threw tomatoes at his train, and a few people were arrested for pulling up spikes from the tracks. Mounted riot police had to break up a demonstration against Hoover in Detroit (tone-deaf as always to the country's mood, Hoover was traveling in a limousine procession provided by Henry Ford). Marchers demanded that Hoover be lynched. At one point, he broke down and said to his aides, "I can't go on with it anymore." In his final campaign appearance in New York City, he was surrounded by crowds screaming, "We want bread!"

Roosevelt—who had broken with long tradition to become the first presidential candidate to accept his party's nomination in person at the convention—traveled the country, spoke of his "new deal for the American people," and was continuously upbeat.

**THE WINNER: FRANKLIN ROOSEVELT** In a triumph that was almost literally a reversal of 1928, Roosevelt beat Hoover 22,829,501 votes to 15,760,684 and destroyed him in the Electoral College, 472 to 59. Roosevelt took 42 out of 48 states. Hoover, even a sympathetic biographer has written, was not just beaten, "he was excommunicated." And a powerful new era in American history was about to begin.

# 1936

## FRANKLIN D. ROOSEVELT vs. ALFRED "ALF" LANDON

After declaring in his inaugural address that the only thing Americans had to fear was "fear itself," Roosevelt sent his "brain trust" of advisors to Congress, desperate to stem the disastrous inroads of the depression. In record time, he had established the Works Projects Administration (WPA) to give work to jobless Americans, the Social Security Act to provide unemployment and old-age insurance, the Tennessee Valley Authority (TVA) to harness the power of the Tennessee River and provide electricity to seven southern states, and the Civilian Conservation Corps (CCC) to send young urban men into rural areas to plant trees and fight forest fires.

These measures had an immediate effect on the nation's recovery, but naturally Roosevelt's political enemies didn't like them. Conservatives thought the president was flirting with communism, while progressives claimed the New Deal didn't go far enough. Nevertheless, Roosevelt easily won his party's nomination in 1936. He was the most popular Democratic president in memory, holding twice-weekly easygoing press conferences in his office and making national radio addresses in his satiny reassuring voice.

Faced with Roosevelt's star power, the Republicans did the best they could. They nominated Kansas Governor Alf Landon, who presented himself as the everyday American. He embarked on a "holy crusade" against the excesses of the New Deal, which, according to Landon, had centralized government too radically in Washington and gave too much power to labor.

**THE CAMPAIGN** One of Alf Landon's problems was that he never seemed terribly presidential. Even his first name had a rumpled doggy quality to it. Republicans hired a film director named Ted Bohn—a forerunner of modern candidate groomers—to teach Landon not to smile with his mouth hanging open, to walk slightly ahead when in a group to dominate pictures, and to shake hands with his chin up to give the impression of firmness. The training did little good.

Roosevelt—who privately referred to Landon as "the White Mouse who wants to live in the White House"—didn't have to do much campaigning. But when he did, he was met by vast throngs of Americans, as many as 100,000 during some speeches, who voiced their approval for his policies. Desperate, the Republicans tried to manipulate the media, asking the Associated Press to always identify Landon in its stories with the tag "budget-balancer." (The AP said it would, but only if it could tag Roosevelt as "humanity's savior.")

**THE WINNER: FRANKLIN ROOSEVELT** Despite the Republicans spending nearly $9 million on the campaign, Roosevelt kicked butt. He beat Landon 27,757,333 votes to 16,684,231, the biggest voter plurality until 1964, with a stupendous 523 to 8 margin in the Electoral College.

The 1936 election brought a harbinger of dirty tricks to come. Republicans had prepared a powerful radio ad called "Liberty at the Crossroads," which took the form of a short drama in which a marriage-license clerk reminds a prospective bridegroom that he would, in the future, have to deal with a large national debt created by Roosevelt's New Deal programs.

"Someone's giving us a dirty deal," the bridegroom whines. "It's a low-down mean trick." A dark voiceover (marked in the script as

"The Voice of Doom") intones: "And the debts, like the sins of the fathers, shall be visited upon the children, aye, even unto the third and fourth generations."

Neither NBC nor CBS, the two largest radio networks, would air the ad, claiming that it was unethical to "dramatize" real-life politics, but plenty of smaller stations with unsold air time quickly snapped it up. They knew a good political soap opera when they saw it, and so did the more than sixty million people who now had access to radios. "Liberty at the Crossroads" was ahead of its time in dramatizing (and manipulating) people's fears. You can trace a direct line from it to Lyndon Johnson's notorious "Daisy" ad in the presidential campaign of 1964.

SLEAZE-O-METER

1940

★

**FRANKLIN D.**
# ROOSEVELT
DEMOCRAT

VS.

**WENDELL**
# WILLKIE
REPUBLICAN

★

"WE CAN'T HAVE ANY OF OUR PRINCIPAL SPEAKERS REFER TO IT, BUT THE PEOPLE WAY DOWN THE LINE CAN GET IT OUT. I MEAN THE CONGRESS SPEAKERS, AND STATE SPEAKERS, AND SO FORTH. THEY CAN USE THE RAW MATERIAL. SHE'S AN EXTREMELY ATTRACTIVE LITTLE TART."—President Franklin Roosevelt musing aloud on how to smear Wendell Willkie by making public news of his mistress

**D**id Franklin Delano Roosevelt want a third term as president? Of course not. Who was he to break with powerful tradition and aspire to something even Washington and Jefferson never had? People would say he suffered from unreasonable ambition. It was time the country stood on its own two feet, with a new leader to guide the way. No, sir, Roosevelt told an aide, he was "violently and vividly" opposed to another term.

All this meant that—if you understood anything about Franklin Roosevelt—he was almost certainly going to run for an unprecedented third term in 1940.

When members of his cabinet, including Postmaster General Jim Farley and Roosevelt's vice president, John Garner, lined up for Roosevelt's job, Roosevelt smiled but quietly sabotaged their plans. Farley was a brilliant ward politician, but he knew too little about the international scene. Garner had turned virulently antilabor— perhaps the $200,000 dollars he "won at poker" from industrialists and coal mine owners had something to do with it—making him an embarrassment to Roosevelt's liberal administration.

America was emerging from the Depression but seemed to be heading directly into another war. By the spring of 1940, the Nazis had sliced through France and were poised to invade England. In private, FDR began to muse that perhaps his country still needed him. When the Democratic convention started on July 15, he demonstrated his political brilliance by telling the chairman, "I have not had today and have never had any wish or purpose to remain in the office of president . . . after next January." At the same time, Roosevelt dispatched his close aide, Harry Hopkins, to Chicago with a private message to Democratic bosses, such as Chicago Mayor Ed Kelly: he would accept the nomination, but only on the first ballot and only if he won by more than 150 votes.

The next night, the convention chairman read Roosevelt's message declining the nomination to the assembled delegates, who reacted with an uproarious, deafening demonstration in favor of Roosevelt (all secretly prepared in advance by Mayor Kelly). One evening later, Roosevelt was nominated for president in one ballot, beating both Farley and Garner. Roosevelt then immediately ousted Garner and made Agriculture secretary Henry Wallace his running mate.

## THE CANDIDATES

**DEMOCRAT: FRANKLIN DELANO ROOSEVELT** Franklin Roosevelt was the first American president to even consider running for a third term and probably the only one, short of George Washington, who could have pulled it off. He was at the height of his popularity—a dazzling yet wholly human figure whose "fireside chats" reached more than 60 million listeners and whose New Deal programs had begun to revive the sagging U.S. economy.

**REPUBLICAN: WENDELL WILLKIE** Wendell Willkie was a forty-eight-year-old utilities executive who, until 1939, had been a Democrat and even a delegate at the 1932 Democratic National Convention. Although he had never held elective office, he was a maverick politician with a strong following of avid supporters who loved his crusading, aggressive style. Willkie was tall, shambling, folksy, and charismatic. Taking his grassroots organization into the Republican National Convention in June 1940, he beat out experienced campaigners, including District Attorney Thomas E. Dewey of New York and Senator Robert Taft of Ohio, son of the twenty-seventh president.

## THE CAMPAIGN

Willkie literally rolled up his sleeves and launched a powerful whistle-stop campaign, traveling 19,000 miles in fifty-one days and making more than 500 speeches. His dramatic speaking manner—hair tousled, arms waving wildly—earned him plenty of favorable press, as did his populist stance against political bosses. "Bosses don't hurt me," he once said. "All I ask is a fair shake."

He attacked Roosevelt for being a "third-term candidate" in favor of "one-man rule." Although Willkie agreed with Roosevelt on the need to provide aid to Great Britain (currently being bombed by Germany), he preferred a more isolationist stance. "A vote for Roosevelt is a vote for war," he cried in impassioned speeches across America. An FDR victory meant "wooden crosses for sons and brothers and sweethearts." Like a reeling and weaving Rocky Balboa, he begged Roosevelt for a chance to debate. "Bring on the champ!" he cried.

Naturally, the Democratic machine was not prepared to allow Roosevelt to debate the underdog. In the early stages of the campaign, the president didn't even stump. Democrats sarcastically called Willkie "the simple, barefoot, Wall Street lawyer" whose utility company had used spies to bust up labor unions. It wasn't long before the smears got a whole lot worse. Democrats claimed that Willkie's hometown of Elwood, Indiana, had signs that read, "Nigger, don't let the sun go down on you." And numerous Democratic pamphlets featured a photograph of Willkie's father's grave to show that the man had been buried in a neglected potter's field.

But Willkie's fevered campaigning began to pay off. Early pollsters like the American Institute of Public Opinion showed Roosevelt leading by a surprisingly slim margin; some newspaper surveys even put Willkie on top. Roosevelt, who had not taken Willkie seriously at first, now began to exaggerate his opponent's isolationist stance and told reporters that "anyone who is pro-Hitler in this country is also pro-Willkie." The Republican candidate stepped up his campaigning, even though his throat was so hoarse he had to be accompanied everywhere by a doctor. FDR finally took to the stump, giving five fiery speeches in the last week of campaigning, telling aides that Willkie "didn't know that he was up against a buzzsaw."

# THE WINNER: FRANKLIN DELANO ROOSEVELT

Roosevelt, up against the strongest opponent he had ever faced, won the election 27,313,041 votes to Willkie's 22,348,480, a substantial margin but not quite as good as his previous victories. It was a sweet win for Roosevelt, but he was about to face one of the biggest challenges an American president has ever faced.

★★★

**The Great (Untold) Republican Smear** Henry Wallace was Roosevelt's secretary of agriculture and a pretty good one, too—but this liberal politician had a dreamy, spiritual side. To the horror of President Roosevelt's men, just after Wallace accepted the VP nod, Republicans discovered photostats of letters written by Wallace to a strange Russian mystic named Nicholas Roerich. In one note, Wallace wrote: "I must read Agny Yoga and sit by myself once in a while. We are dealing with the first crude beginnings of a new age. May the peace of the Great One descend upon you."

Another letter to Roerich talked about current events in a weird code: "The rumor is the Monkeys are seeking friendship with the Rulers so as to divide the Land of the Masters between them. The Wandering One thinks this is very suspicious of the Monkeys." Translation: The Japanese (the Monkeys) wanted to divide Manchuria (the Land of the Masters, which the Japanese had invaded) with the British (the Rulers). And Roosevelt (the Wandering One) didn't like it.

The Republican national chairman, Joseph W. Martin, told the Democrats that the original copies of the letters were being held by the treasurer of the Republican National Committee in a bank vault. He threatened to make them public. Did the Democrats want people to know that a lunatic like Wallace was only a heartbeat away from the presidency?

The news alarmed the Democrats greatly, but oddly enough, at Wendell Willkie's personal order, the letters were never used. Was it because Willkie held his own "secret"?

**The Great (Untold) Democratic Smear** Roosevelt knew that the married Willkie had a mistress in New York City, a writer and editor named Irita Van Doren. As it turned out, Irita used to be the mistress of Jimmy Walker, the flamboyant New York mayor. This liaison outraged Walker's wife so much that Jimmy was forced to pay her $10,000 each time she made a personal appearance with him.

Roosevelt wondered humorously to aides if Willkie's wife had to be hired in the same fashion to smile at the press during campaign stops. Perhaps, he suggested, the voters might be interested to learn about Willkie's girlfriend.

But voters never did, just as they never learned about Henry Wallace's letters. No evidence exists of direct communications between Roosevelt and Willkie, but it's only natural to suspect that some agreement was worked out. Russian mystics? Coded messages? New York mistresses? In a race this close, campaign managers would have been foolish to let such opportunities go to waste.

**Playing the Race Card** African Americans had been able to vote since the post–Civil War period, but often, especially in the South, they were discouraged from casting ballots by white segregationists using poll taxes and other means of intimidation. But the rise of black labor leaders and the unionization of many black workers in the 1930s helped turn out blacks to vote for Roosevelt in record numbers. Roosevelt was considered a friend of the working man, and it didn't hurt that his wife, Eleanor, was an outspoken advocate of civil rights. But as the country geared up for war, black leaders were concerned that blacks would be segregated into jobs as cooks and support troops, as they had been in World War I, and not given a chance to prove their mettle on an equal basis with whites.

At Eleanor's suggestion, Roosevelt met with black leaders William White of the NAACP and A. Phillip Randolph of the Brotherhood of Sleeping Car Porters. Roosevelt gave them the impression that he was going to help end military segregation—in return for black votes, of course. But then Roosevelt's press secretary, Steve Early, later announced that blacks and whites would not be integrated; worse, Early claimed that this policy had been approved by White, Randolph, and others who had met with the president.

White and Randolph were furious, and Roosevelt hastily tried to make amends. He met with Secretary of the Navy Frank Knox and made this suggestion: "Since we are training a certain amount of musicians on board ship—the ship's band—there's no reason why we shouldn't have a colored band on some of these ships, because they're darned good at it."

Race relations took another turn for the worse just a week before the election, when the president made a rousing speech at Madison Square Garden in New York City and then returned to Penn Station to board his train back to Washington. Press Secretary Steve Early attempted to get on the train, but a black New York City policeman named James Sloan didn't know who he was and prevented him from boarding. Whereupon Early, a Southerner, kicked Sloan in the groin, sending the cop—who had just returned to work after a hernia operation—straight back to the hospital.

The tussle made headlines, and Republicans distributed leaflets showing pictures of Sloan in his hospital bed, with a caption that read: "Negroes: If you want your President to be surrounded by Southern influences of this kind, vote for Roosevelt. If you want to be treated with respect, vote for Wendell Willkie."

Fortunately for Roosevelt, Early apologized, Sloan declared himself a tried-and-true Democrat, and the entire incident was defused.

**Special Delivery by Air** When making appearances in factory towns and other Democratic strongholds, Willkie found himself attacked consistently with flying vegetables and other projectiles. Commentators noted that never before had any candidate had so many objects hurled in his direction—they included, by one reporter's count, cantaloupes, potatoes, tomatoes, oranges, eggs, ashtrays, rocks, chairs, a phone book, and even a bedspread. Willkie usually took such attacks in stride, but outside Detroit he lunged at one protestor who had spattered his wife with an egg.

**Image Control** Stricken by polio in 1921, Franklin Roosevelt was partially paralyzed from the waist down and forced to use a wheelchair and heavy leg braces for the rest of his life. Yet the American public almost never saw him that way, thanks to a carefully orchestrated campaign to make the president seem as vital as anyone else. Roosevelt arrived at least an hour early for public speaking events, so people did not view him being lifted out of cars, and he used his Secret Service agents and his sons as supports when he stood to make speeches. When Roosevelt had to attend the funeral of a prominent congressman, the street outside the church was raised to the level of the church floor so that Roosevelt might appear to walk in under his own power. And one reason his wife, Eleanor, became so prominent in politics at a time when most first ladies kept to domestic White House matters was because she was his "eyes and ears," going out to give speeches and gather reaction from around the country.

Of course, none of this would have worked had the press not cooperated. They almost never took pictures of the president's wheelchairs and braces. When they did, their cameras were quickly destroyed by the Secret Service.

# 1944

## FRANKLIN D. ROOSEVELT vs. THOMAS DEWEY

By the summer of 1944, Franklin Roosevelt had led America through the deadliest war in history, bringing the nation to the brink of a victory he would not live to see. At the age of sixty-two, the president suffered from heart disease and high blood pressure, and he was prone to bouts of bronchitis that worsened his chronic insomnia. Nevertheless, he managed to keep his health problems under wraps, and his doctor, Vice Admiral Ross McIntire, issued reassuring public announcements that Roosevelt was in tip-top shape.

If the country had not been at war, Roosevelt almost certainly would not have sought a fourth term. But he told friends and advisors that he would not stand to see a Republican victory, which would mean a Republican president presiding over what promised to be a powerful postwar era. At the Democratic National Convention, Roosevelt was nominated on the first ballot. The only suspense came in the choice of a vice president, for it was likely that Roosevelt might not live out a full term. After some debate, Roosevelt ended up choosing Senator Harry Truman of Missouri, a well-liked politician who had received national attention for rooting out corruption in defense contracts.

Meanwhile, Republicans toyed with the possible candidacy of General Douglas MacArthur, hero of the Philippines, but his presidential boat was sunk when he was found to have criticized Roosevelt, his commander-in-chief, in letters to a Nebraska congressmen. (Also working against him were some recently discovered letters of a different sort, written by MacArthur to an ex-Singapore chorus girl who called him "Daddy.")

In search of safer waters, Republicans nominated forty-two-year-old Thomas E. Dewey, governor of New York, with Ohio governor John Bricker as his running mate. Dewey had a record as being an honest governor (and he had been an aggressive New York D.A. who prosecuted mobsters like Legs Diamond and Lucky Luciano). The first presidential candidate to be born in the twentieth century, he had an air of efficiency that struck some people as drably modern, especially compared to Roosevelt.

**THE CAMPAIGN** This was America's first war-time general election since 1864, and the Democrats made war the issue, praising Roosevelt's successful management of the conflict and his worldwide status as a leader to show the inadvisability of changing commanders at that time. And the economy, buoyed by defense contracts, was booming.

As in 1940, FDR did little campaigning until the last weeks of the election, but Dewey stumped hard. Roosevelt called him "the little man on the wedding cake" because of his pencil moustache, slim stature, and neatly combed black hair. The line has been attributed to everyone from actress Ethel Barrymore to Alice Roosevelt Longworth (Teddy Roosevelt's daughter), but FDR made full use of it.

Dewey returned fire, saying Roosevelt was a leftist who had become the darling of American communists. And though he rarely mentioned Roosevelt's health, he harped on the "tired old men" of Washington and how they needed to be replaced by young and energetic visionaries like himself.

Then Republicans made the mistake of repeating an apocryphal story about Roosevelt and his Scotch terrier Fala. According to the tale, Roosevelt was visiting the Aleutian Islands and accidentally left Fala behind; he later sent a destroyer to pick up the animal. The

Republicans tried to use the anecdote to illustrate the president's extravagance, but Roosevelt diffused the charges with gentle sarcasm in a national address: "I don't resent attacks and my family doesn't resent attacks, but Fala does resent them . . . he has not been the same dog since."

**THE WINNER: FRANKLIN ROOSEVELT** Roosevelt beat Thomas Dewey 25,612,610 votes to 22,117,617, winning in the Electoral College 432 to 99. On hearing the news, the president quipped: "The first twelve years are the hardest." And perhaps he was right. On April 12, 1945, he died suddenly of a cerebral hemorrhage at the presidential retreat in Warm Springs, Georgia.

SLEAZE-O-METER

1948

★

HARRY
# TRUMAN
DEMOCRAT

## VS.

THOMAS
# DEWEY
REPUBLICAN

★

"I KNOW EVERY ONE OF THESE [REPORTERS].
THERE ISN'T ONE OF THEM HAS ENOUGH SENSE TO
POUND SAND INTO A RAT HOLE."
—Harry Truman, on the journalists who predicted he would lose

The presidential election of 1948 is, to date, the most amazing political upset in American history. It contains one of the best campaigns ever run by anyone—President Harry Truman's give-'em-hell extravaganza—as well as one of the worst—that of New York governor Thomas Dewey. But throughout 1948 and right up to Election Day, November 2, there was not a reporter, pollster, or political expert in the country who thought Truman had any chance of winning.

Why was Truman held in such low esteem? After all, he had presided over victory in World War II and the hopeful beginnings of the United Nations, faithfully carrying on FDR's New Deal policies. But with the artificial wartime price controls rescinded, inflation had driven up prices by nearly 40 percent, war with the Soviets was close to breaking out over Stalin's blockade of Berlin, the southern wing of the Democratic Party was upset by Truman's support of civil rights, and a Republican-dominated Congress blocked Truman's every move.

The Gallup poll gave Truman a 36 percent approval rating—the kind of rating that takes you deep into Nixon/Watergate, Carter/Iran Hostages, and George W. Bush/Iraq War territory. Jokes spread across the country: "I wonder what Truman would do if he were alive." Democratic-leaning newspapers posed rhetorical headline questions like, "Must It Be Truman?" *Life* magazine published admiring profiles of Dewey with speculation on which worthies would make up the Dewey administration. And Truman's own party made overtures to Dwight D. Eisenhower, the immensely popular supreme commander of Allied forces during the war, since Eisenhower had not committed to being a member of any political party.

The Republicans were delighted to see Truman in such dire straits. At their national convention, Congresswoman Clare Boothe Luce called Truman "a gone goose" and suggested (in a nod to a popular Coca-Cola ad) that his time in office had not been "the pause that refreshes." The Republicans happily renominated their 1944 candidate, Thomas E. Dewey, along with the liberal Earl Warren, governor of California and future Supreme Court justice, to balance the ticket.

All these insults simmered inside Truman. By the time he was nominated by his dejected party in July 1948, with Kentucky senator Alben Barkley as his running mate, he was ready, in the most famous sound bite from 1948, to "Give 'em hell!"

## THE CANDIDATES

**DEMOCRAT: HARRY TRUMAN** Early in the campaign, the sixty-four-year-old Truman had occasional moments when his confidence vanished (meeting up with Dewey in New York, he whispered, "Tom, when you get to the White House, for God's sakes do something about the plumbing!"). But he was fired by an almost superhuman confidence. He was determined to win this election, even though his own mother-in-law told him he should quit.

**REPUBLICAN: THOMAS DEWEY** Dewey had a lot going for him. At the young age of forty-six, he had established a national reputation as both a crime-buster in New York and a respectable presidential candidate from 1944. This time around, Dewey assembled a team of young political experts to help put him over the top. Their chief (and fatal) advice to him: say nothing that will get you in trouble, and you will win the election in a walkover. The presidency is yours.

# THE CAMPAIGN

Truman had more to worry about—he had to fend off challenges from splinter groups within his own party. Henry Wallace, former Roosevelt vice president, was the candidate of the Progressive Party, which ran on a world peace platform and attracted quite a few liberal Democrats, students, unionists, and American Communists. On the other side of the spectrum, anti–civil rights Southerners, led by Governor Strom Thurmond of South Carolina, formed the so-called Dixiecrat Party.

With the Democrats so divided, Dewey didn't think he could lose. He ran a careful campaign on what he called a unity platform, speaking vaguely of America's greatness and portraying himself as a meticulous, upstanding, honest administrator. Elmo Roper, a pollster as famous in his day as George Gallup, had Dewey 44 to 31 percent and announced that he was going to stop polling: "My whole inclination is to predict the election of Thomas E. Dewey by a heavy margin and devote my time and energy to other things." *Newsweek* published its own poll of fifty respected political reporters. Who would win the election? Dewey, said the pundits, fifty to zero.

Truman refused to let his opponent get away with vagueness, and he started out on an incredible whistle-stop train tour of more than 31,000 miles and 350 speeches. He attacked Republicans as "gluttons of privilege," "bloodsuckers with Wall Street offices," and "economic tapeworms." His main target, interestingly, was not Dewey but the Republican-dominated eightieth Congress, which he called "the donothing Congress" and which he castigated for not helping to stop rising food and housing prices. Truman spoke to crowds of thousands in towns big and small all across America. He had one thing going for him that Dewey did not: he struck people as authentic. He used words like "damn" and "hell" while Dewey uttered "good gracious" and "oh, Lord."

Truman introduced his wife, Bess, as "the Boss" (at least until she told him not to do it anymore) and sometimes blurted out incredibly dumb things. Carried away by enthusiasm at one rally, Truman said of Stalin, "I like old Joe. He is a decent fellow." But when Republicans tried to use it against him to prove he was sympathetic to Communists, they were disappointed. Truman was not the Teflon president that Ronald Reagan would be, all smooth and shiny surfaces. Instead, as he campaigned to more and more enthusiastic crowds, he seemed like granite. Anything coming his way simply bounced off.

## THE WINNER: HARRY TRUMAN

The press had Truman measured for his loser's suit right up to and including Election Day, which, in 1948, was November 2, two days after Halloween. On November 1, Gallup gave the election to Dewey by five points. The *Wall Street Journal* published an article listing who Dewey's chief advisers would be. One writer wrote, "We're going to miss lil' ole Harry." Columnist Stewart Alsop wondered in the *New York Times* "how the government can get through the next ten weeks" with Truman as lame-duck president. Overseas in Great Britain, Alistair Cooke wrote an article about Truman entitled "A Study in Failure."

On November 2, Truman went to bed a loser, and on November 3 he woke up a winner. He beat Dewey 24,79,345 votes to 21,991,291 and was pictured in a photo that immortalized forever the foolish confidence of a press swayed by polls rather than the true desires of ordinary people—a grinning Truman holding the *Chicago Tribune* with a front-page headline reading, in big bold letters, "DEWEY DEFEATS TRUMAN."

Why did Truman win? Perhaps, as Dewey later claimed, it was because voter turnout was light for that era—only about 51 percent, which indicates that many Republicans were convinced by the polls and stayed home on Election Day, too confident of victory. Or maybe he won because Wallace's Progressives made Truman appear less liberal, while Thurmond's Dixiecrats made the president's civil rights record look even better than it was, especially to blacks.

Or maybe he won because, as the underdog in the fight of his life,

he simply went out, threw caution to the wind, and "gave 'em hell."
It was a lesson that future Democratic campaigners like Al Gore and
John Kerry failed to learn, to their peril.

★★★

**The Federal Bureau of Dewey** FBI Director J. Edgar Hoover was no
fan of Harry Truman, and—as he would do later with members of
the Kennedy family—he attempted to find incriminating confidential information to use against the president to influence the outcome
of the election. Hoover secretly put agents to work to find stuff that
would be detrimental to Truman because, being a longtime friend
of Thomas Dewey, he hoped that "President Dewey" would name
him as attorney general. One FBI agent remembered that they didn't
find much, but the agency had the nerve to prepare position papers
for Dewey on Truman's supposed "softness" on Communism, which
Dewey then released to the press as if they were written by his staff.

**Hands Off!** In the weeks leading up to Election Day, Dewey became
so sure of his victory that he began to act like the presidency was already his. He became enraged when Truman announced that he was
going to send a personal emissary to Stalin to try to mediate with the
Soviet leader. Dewey fumed to reporters: "If Harry Truman would
just keep his hands off things for another few weeks! Particularly, if he
will keep his hands off foreign policy, about which he knows considerably less than nothing."

**Truman to Dewey: Bite Me!** Well, maybe those weren't his exact
words—but Truman went after Dewey with a vengeance. During his
stump speeches, he loved to act out both sides of an imaginary dia-
logue between a doctor (Dewey) who diagnoses his patient (America)
as having a great deal of troublesome but not-quite-specified "issues."

"I feel really good, Doc," America would say. "I've never been stronger. What could be wrong with me?"

"I never discuss issues with a patient," Dr. Dewey said, "but what you need is a major operation."

Here Truman made a moustache-twirling motion.

"Is it serious, doc?" the patient asked.

"Not very," Dr. Dewey said, "it just means taking out your entire brains and replacing them with Republican ones."

**For the Birds** In 1946, only about 7,000 homes in America had televisions. By 1948, technology had made televisions both better and cheaper, and 148,000 people had shelled out for the big black box. Presidential candidates on both sides were quick to take advantage of technology. Both Truman and Dewey bought air time, but the honor for the first presidential candidate to do a paid political ad goes to Harry Truman, who gave a televised speech on October 5, 1948, from Jersey City, New Jersey.

Both 1948 political conventions were televised on the East Coast. To facilitate this, Republicans and Democrats agreed to hold their events in Convention Hall in Philadelphia—the Republicans in June, the Democrats a month later. For the first time in history, television cables ran over the convention floor, with batteries of hot lights arched over the stage (in the non-air-conditioned hall, the temperature at the podium was 93 degrees). Speakers wandered around wearing thick pancake makeup (women were told that brown lipstick showed up better on black-and-white television sets, so most female orators looked like they'd just bitten into a big piece of chocolate).

But people seemed to understand the medium—TV was theater, TV was spectacle. When India Edwards, executive director of the Women's Division of the Democratic National Committee, reached the podium, she waved a steak in the air to emphasize the high price of meat.

But the biggest spectacle did not come off the way it was intended. At two in the morning, when Harry Truman was about to go onstage to accept his party's nomination, a flock of pigeons was released from underneath a huge floral Liberty Bell. The birds, who had been trapped all night in the hot and humid bell, went berserk. In a scene straight out of Alfred Hitchcock's film *The Birds*, the pigeons began dive-bombing delegates, smashing into the rafters of the hall and flying straight into the television lights.

After a moment of stunned silence, Truman and everyone in the hall broke into uproarious laughter. The few people awake and still watching were privileged to see one of the most wonderful moments of live television ever recorded.

SLEAZE-O-METER

1952

★

DWIGHT
# EISENHOWER
REPUBLICAN

VS.

ADLAI
# STEVENSON
DEMOCRAT

★

"GENERAL EISENHOWER EXEMPLIFIES WHAT
THE FAIR SEX LOOKS FOR IN A MAN—A COMBINATION
OF HUSBAND, FATHER, AND SON!"
—Clare Boothe Luce

The 1950s are often remembered as a time of peace, security, and a big car with tail fins in every driveway, but the decade was also shaped by pervasive national fear and paranoia. During Truman's administration, America became embroiled in the Korean War, a so-called police action fought to keep the Chinese communists and Russians out of the Korean Peninsula. Instead, it proved to be a highly unpopular and costly war for the United States.

Then there was Joe McCarthy. The junior senator from Wisconsin began inspecting the activities of "subversive Americans" and ruined countless lives and careers in a Red Scare witch hunt. He was a vocal opponent of the Truman administration and constantly repeated his charge that the Democrats were responsible for "twenty years of treason."

At age sixty-eight, Truman had decided that seven years of being president was long enough, thank you, and passed on another term. Because of his stunning upset in 1948, Truman was certain that anyone he anointed to follow in his footsteps could beat the Republicans (who, after all, had been out of power for two decades, their longest period without a president since the party's inception in 1856). Truman decided that Adlai Stevenson, governor of Illinois, would be his man. A Truman supporter and a man of charm and intelligence, Stevenson was a strong liberal with a good record.

Have you ever offered someone something you think they will thank you profusely for, only to have them say, "Um, can I think about it?" That's how Stevenson responded to Truman's offer—partly because he knew that Dwight Eisenhower would be the formidable Republican candidate. He also knew that if he accepted too eagerly, he might be perceived as the president's lapdog—and, despite Truman's high opinion of himself, he wasn't all that popular anymore. Finally, in July Stevenson accepted the nomination during a powerful speech at the Democratic convention. The first presidential election dominated by television was about to begin.

## THE CANDIDATES

**REPUBLICAN: DWIGHT EISENHOWER** Dwight Eisenhower, known popularly as Ike, had been a brilliant commander-in-chief during World War II and later served as Columbia University's president and a NATO commander. He had spent most of his adult life surrounded by a staff that met virtually all his needs—in the morning, he was dressed from head to toe by a valet. Eisenhower didn't even know how to use a telephone. Yet, somehow, the average person on the street could relate to the general. Eisenhower radiated confidence and sincerity and a certain homely Americanism. His most famous campaign slogan—"I Like Ike"—said it all. His running mate was a young California senator named Richard M. Nixon.

**DEMOCRAT: ADLAI E. STEVENSON** Stevenson had a wonderful Democratic pedigree. His namesake grandfather had been vice president under Grover Cleveland in 1892 and William Jennings Bryan's running mate in 1900. Stevenson had been an assistant secretary of the navy during the war and was now the liberal Democratic governor of a populous and important state. But two significant characteristics were working against him. First, he spoke in elegant compound sentences. Second, he was divorced, and Americans had never voted a divorced man into the White House. (That would have to wait until Ronald Reagan in 1980). Stevenson's veep nominee was John Sparkman, a ticket-balancing senator from Alabama.

# THE CAMPAIGN

It's difficult to run against "the most admired of all living Americans" (as one Roper Poll found Eisenhower in 1952), and even given his underdog status, Stevenson conducted a poor campaign. Part of the problem was his vacillations over whether to accept the Democratic nomination; people saw him as weak and indecisive—like John Quincy Adams before him, a brooding Hamlet—not the person to fight communism and bring the country out of a nasty war.

Another problem for Stevenson was television. Simply put, Eisenhower's people understood the new medium, and Stevenson's didn't. In 1952, 40 percent of American homes, 18 million in all, owned a television. And Americans were buying the sets at the amazing rate of twenty thousand a day.

An eloquent campaign speaker, Stevenson would become the first American presidential candidate to be truly reduced—made less than he actually was—by television. To begin with, his people always bought thirty-minute segments, during which Stevenson gave set political speeches on various topics. A half hour is a long time to look at a single talking head, and Americans tuned him out. It didn't help that Stevenson hated cue cards and teleprompters and would often digress from his speech, almost always running over. The networks were draconian about time, never granting a second more than what was purchased. Those still watching Stevenson got used to seeing him cut off midsentence.

Eisenhower's television ad men, who included the legendary Ben Duffy, knew that simpler and shorter was better. They prepared a series of twenty-second spots titled "Eisenhower Answers the Nation." The camera would first go to a person or a married couple who had a concern: "Mr. Eisenhower, what about the high cost of living?" Then it would pan to Eisenhower: "My wife, Mamie, worries about the same thing!"

Eisenhower shot these segments in a studio. Shorn of his glasses, which tended to glare and hide his eyes, he read from cue cards written in giant letters. Eisenhower hated doing the spots—"To think that an old soldier has come to this," he said—but they were brilliantly effective. When George Ball, a disgusted Stevenson aide, griped that soon "presidential campaigns would have professional actors as candidates," he unknowingly predicted the future.

It wasn't that Ike didn't make mistakes. He was photographed shaking hands with Senator Joseph McCarthy, whom many people of both parties then considered a national disgrace. What's more, McCarthy probably didn't help by doing a televised endorsement speech for Ike in which he repeatedly referred to Adlai Stevenson as "Alger"—a smarmy reference to the supposed State Department spy Alger Hiss, whom veep candidate Richard Nixon had helped convict as a member of the House Committee on Un-American Activities.

With the world looking increasingly like a dangerous place— the United States had just tested the first hydrogen bomb and the Soviet Union had atomic weapons—the American people were forced to choose between a plain-spoken modern man of action or a long-winded "egghead" who couldn't end a speech on time.

## THE WINNER: DWIGHT EISENHOWER

At 10:30 on election night, CBS's powerful UNIVAC computer called victory for Eisenhower. The Democrats kept hope alive as Stevenson made gains in Pennsylvania and Ohio, but then the Republican "streamroller" headed west, completely flattening its opponents. Stevenson took only nine states. Eisenhower beat him in the popular vote 34,936,234 to 27,314,992.

Stevenson conceded graciously, quoting Abraham Lincoln, who said after a losing election that he was too old to cry but it hurt too much to laugh. He didn't abandon his dreams of the presidency—but for the next four years, the beaming face of Ike would come to symbolize a secure, happy, ordinary America.

★★★

**Adlai Stevenson, Homosexual** Eisenhower had a boring and unassailable personal life—few people at the time knew that his valet John Moaney pulled up Ike's underwear every morning—so the divorced Stevenson became the target of smears. Stevenson loved women and dated a number of them, but that didn't stop Republicans from spreading rumors that he was gay—especially since, as the campaign began, a friend and aide named Bill Blair had arrived to live in the Illinois governor's mansion. Truman was so alarmed by these rumors that he sent an aide to Illinois to investigate. The man returned to assure the president that Stevenson was straight.

The rumors continued as the campaign wore on. A strange man pretending to be an FBI agent called on a friend of a member of Stevenson's staff to "officially" investigate the latter's supposed homosexuality. No one ever found out who he was. But new rumors spread that Stevenson's former wife, Ellen, had left him because he was gay (Ellen didn't help matters when she threatened to write a tell-all memoir entitled *The Egghead and I*. Their divorce was caused mainly by Stevenson's devotion to his career and Ellen's impatience with his lack of attention.)

**Adlai Stevenson, Murderer** One of the worst rumors that circulated in 1952 appeared in leaflets distributed in the Midwest claiming that Stevenson had killed a young girl "in a jealous rage." That part wasn't true, but much of the rest of the story was surprisingly accurate. The incident occurred around Christmas of 1912, when an almost thirteen-year-old Stevenson and some friends were playing with a .22 rifle they thought was unloaded. The official story was that, as Stevenson went to put the gun away, it discharged and killed a girl named Ruth Merwin. But children who were there said that Stevenson, fooling around, in fact pointed the gun at Merwin and pulled the trigger; the bullet hit her dead center in the forehead.

In either version the death was accidental, but Stevenson carried around the guilt of the incident for the rest of his life, so much so that he never even told his wife or any of those closest to him about it. It is unknown how the Republicans discovered the secret, but fortunately their leaflets were not widely circulated, and America as a whole was unaware of the episode.

**You're Making Me Ill** Saved for posterity were the notes Adlai Stevenson jotted down to himself one night in 1952 as he tried to figure out whether he should accept his party's nomination. They provide a fascinating (and slightly disturbing) look into the mind of a politician:

> *I would not accept the nomination if offered to me.*

> *I [illegible] that the Presidency is a duty from which no American should shrink in fear . . . but even if I had the self-confidence to aspire to [crossed out] for that dread office, I could not accept the Democratic nomination.*

> *I have repeatedly said, my only amb. is to be Gover. of Ill. I have a lot of unfinished business here in Ill. . . . that is the limit of my ambitions and probably the full measure of my competence too.*

> *I do not wish to be nominated for the Presidency. I am a candidate for reelection as Gov. of Ill. That is my only ambition.*

> *Would I accept the nomination of the Dem. Party? Yes, I would. I don't suppose one can refuse except in the most extenuating of circumstances. And I suppose the friendly people of Ill. would release me from my commitments in that event.*

# 1956

## DWIGHT EISENHOWER vs. ADLAI STEVENSON

By 1956 tensions in America had simmered down. President Eisenhower's Big Four summit in Geneva, in which America, France, England, and Russia made some accords, lessened fears on the cold war front. On the home front, Joseph McCarthy had been completely discredited (and would die of cirrhosis in 1957).

But all the work took a toll on the president's health. In September of 1955, Eisenhower suffered a heart attack. Although he recovered, people began to wonder if he was up to the strains of the office. Less than a year later, Eisenhower went back to the hospital for more surgery, this time for an intestinal disorder. Nevertheless, the Republicans nominated Ike on the first ballot at their convention. Eisenhower had tried to get rid of Richard Nixon by offering him a cabinet post, but the vice president refused. To avoid an unseemly public battle, Eisenhower agreed to keep him on as running mate.

Adlai Stevenson, who had worked diligently for the Democratic Party in the previous four years, wanted another shot. Despite a primary challenge from Senator Estes Kefauver of Tennessee, Stevenson won—and then picked Kefauver as his running mate.

**THE CAMPAIGN** Stevenson, gallant as ever, had his work cut out for him. One sign of Eisenhower's enduring popularity was a 1955 Gallup Poll, in which six out of ten Democrats said that if by some far-fetched chance the Republicans did not nominate Ike in 1956, the Democrats should. Stevenson's task was made harder still when his men tried to find an advertising agency to handle the campaign. Twenty major agencies in New York said no thanks to the lucrative deal—they were afraid of being dumped by their main clients, a bunch of Republican-supporting businesses.

Eisenhower, running on his "four more years of prosperity" theme, was almost unassailable. The Democrats hammered away at what they called his part-time presidency (doctors had prescribed plenty of rest and exercise for Ike) but had to be careful not to be seen as attacking a sick man. Their best ad line was "Defeat part-time Eisenhower and full-time Nixon," which raised the specter of Nixon as the power behind the throne. In fact 1956 marks the true beginning of that favorite Democratic sport: Nixon bashing. A series of radio and TV ads asked, "Nervous about Nixon? *President* Nixon?" In one, shopkeepers from Nixon's hometown claimed they had to choose between displaying Nixon campaign posters or eviction.

The nervous-about-Nixon campaign never ran. Stevenson, ever the gentleman, would not allow the ads to air.

**THE WINNER: DWIGHT EISENHOWER** Eisenhower beat Stevenson 35,590,472 votes to 26,022,752, thus ending the eloquent Illinoisan's career as presidential wannabe, although he did go on to become an effective and distinguished ambassador to the United Nations. When Stevenson was a little late conceding on election night 56, Eisenhower's arrogance showed through: "What in the name of God is the monkey waiting for?" he snapped. "Polishing his prose?"

But the Democrats—with ambitious senators like Lyndon Johnson, John F. Kennedy, and Hubert Humphrey currently jockey-ing for national prominence—would soon have their revenge.

SLEAZE-O-METER

1960

★

JOHN F.
# KENNEDY

DEMOCRAT

## VS.

### RICHARD
# NIXON

REPUBLICAN

★

"NOBODY KNOWS TO THIS DAY WHO THE
AMERICAN PEOPLE REALLY ELECTED IN 1960."
—Tom Wicker

The year 1960 represented a powerful changing of the guard in American politics—oldsters like Eisenhower and Truman were out, youngsters like John F. Kennedy, with his "New Frontier," and Richard Nixon, running as the "New Nixon," were in.

It was about time. Eisenhower, with his cabinetful of Republican millionaires (eight of them) and his penchant for smoothing things over without really fixing them, had left the country with more than a little hard work to do. The Russians had beaten the Americans to space with *Sputnik I*, and their belligerent premier, Nikita Khrushchev, was making threatening noises. Eisenhower sent federal troops to enforce school integration in Little Rock, Arkansas, but that did nothing to address the roots of the civil rights issue. And American advisers were gradually becoming a presence in a distant country called Vietnam.

The most explosive decade in the twentieth century was about to begin with an election that many feel remains, to this day, too close to call.

## THE CANDIDATES

**DEMOCRAT: JOHN F. KENNEDY** Scion of the fabled Massachusetts family, forty-three-year-old John F. Kennedy was a war hero who was first a congressman, then a senator, and now running for president, all in the short span of fourteen years. His was a meteoric rise—helped in good measure by family money, movie-star good looks, and a lovely wife, Jackie. But Kennedy had a big strike against him: he was Catholic. The last Catholic to run for president, Al Smith, had been practically burned at the stake.

Lyndon B. Johnson, Senate majority leader, was Kennedy's

running mate. Kennedy and Johnson hated each other, but JFK needed the Texan as a Southern ticket-balancer. So why did Johnson take the job? As he told a woman friend at the Democratic convention, "One out of every four presidents has died in office. I'm a gamblin' man, darlin', and this is the only chance I got."

**REPUBLICAN: RICHARD M. NIXON** The forty-seven-year-old Nixon's rise had been just as meteoric as Kennedy's, in exactly the same span of time, with two terms as Eisenhower's vice president to boot. His star had risen in the eyes of the American public after his so-called Kitchen Debate with Khrushchev at a trade show in Moscow in 1959. Standing in the mocked-up kitchen of a "typical American home," Nixon deftly parried Khrushchev's bullying sallies and came across as a hero for American ideals and democracy.

All that did not necessarily help him with his boss, who had distrusted his vice president ever since the Checkers Speech. When asked if Nixon had participated in any major decisions in his administration, Eisenhower replied, "If you give me a week, I might think of one."

Nixon's running mate was Republican Henry Cabot Lodge, ambassador to the U.N.

## THE CAMPAIGN

The battle of 1960 was hard hitting and fast moving. Instead of traveling by rail, candidates crisscrossed the country in chartered planes, visiting cities and towns selected via modern statistical analysis.

To combat his reputation for being devious and underhanded, Nixon created his New Nixon persona: mellow, mild, and reasonable. Democrats weren't buying it, particularly former president Harry Truman, who once remarked, "If you vote for Nixon, you ought to go to hell!"

Of course, Kennedy had his own share of image problems. His promise of a New Frontier had little meaning for most people, and his speeches played much better in urban centers than in the heartland. Most of America's farmers were unimpressed with his richboy charm. (After talking to an unsympathetic audience at a South Dakota state fair, Kennedy muttered to aides: "Well, that's over. Fuck the farmers.")

And then, of course, there was the problem of his Catholicism. The level of anti-Catholic bias in the country had sunk since the days of Al Smith, and Kennedy was able to skillfully defuse the issue. He went to Houston to address a prominent group of Protestant ministers and convincingly denied that he had any allegiance to the pope. To his credit, Nixon refused to make religion an issue; the Democratic forces under campaign manager Bobby Kennedy kept bringing it up, however. At one point, Bobby teared up during a speech and said, "Did they ask my brother Joe whether he was a Catholic before he was shot down?" (Joe Kennedy, eldest of the brothers, had been killed by the Nazis during the war.) Democrat campaign workers continued to make cynical use of the issue, asking voters (in a technique that today would be called push-polling): "Do you think they're going to keep Kennedy from being president just because he is Catholic?"

"Tricky Dick" Nixon ran a far cleaner campaign than Kennedy, even when faced with such attack ads as the glowering picture of his face over the headline "Would You Buy a Used Car from This Man?" Nixon hammered away at his opponent's "inexperience" in foreign affairs and lack of a viable agenda for the country. The election was being rated by pollsters as too close to call by September, when Nixon foolishly agreed to a series of four debates with Kennedy. The first one was broadcast from Chicago on September 26.

Sixty million Americans watched the debate, and millions more listened to the radio broadcast. Most listeners (not viewers) thought that Nixon had won. But those who tuned in to their televisions saw a poised, cool, and confident Kennedy and a strained, tired-looking Nixon whose makeup seemed to be streaking with sweat over his five o'clock shadow. Afterward, Nixon's mother called to ask if he was ill;

in fact, he was fighting off the effects of a debilitating infection that arose after he banged his knee on a car door earlier in the campaign.

Although the candidates had three more debates to go—in which Nixon looked much more refreshed and confident—it is the first one in Chicago that voters, and American history, remembered.

## THE WINNER: JOHN F. KENNEDY

Going into election night, many commentators were predicting a Kennedy victory, but by no means a landslide. An engaged American public went to the polls; it was one of the last elections in which more than 60 percent of eligible voters cast ballots. The outcome was Kennedy 34,226,731 votes and Nixon 34,108,157, a difference of 119,450, or less than one-tenth of one percent (although Kennedy won in the Electoral College 303 to 219). It was the closest election since the Benjamin Harrison–Grover Cleveland contest in 1888. (By contrast, in 2000 Al Gore won the popular vote by more than a half million votes over George W. Bush but lost in the Electoral College.)

After a nearly sleepless night, Nixon conceded and Camelot was ready to have its brief, shining moment onstage. But behind the glittering myth will always remain the question: Who really won in 1960?

★★★

**No Contest** Many Republican bigwigs could not understand why Nixon refused to contest the election results of 1960. He certainly had good reason to be suspicious. Immediately after the election, Earl Mazo, an investigative reporter for the *New York Herald Tribune*, began a series of highly convincing articles detailing voter fraud in two key states, Texas (Lyndon Johnson's home state) and Illinois (home to the powerful Democratic machine run by Chicago mayor Richard Daley).

In Texas, there was widespread evidence of stolen ballot paper, dead men voting, and phony registering. "A minimum of ten thousand votes for the Kennedy–Johnson ticket were simply nonexistent," Mazo wrote, with certain polling stations reporting thousands more votes than they had registered voters.

In Chicago, Mayor Daley held back on releasing statewide election returns, probably to see just how many votes Kennedy needed. It would later become apparent that Nixon had taken 93 of the state's 102 counties, yet somehow he managed to lose in Daley-controlled Cook County by 450,000 votes. (Nixon would end up losing the state and its twenty-seven electoral votes by just over eight thousand votes, out of 4.7 million cast.) In the early morning hours, Daley called Kennedy and said: "Mr. President, with a bit of luck and a few close friends, you're going to carry Illinois." In Illinois, Mazo found evidence of cash payments for votes by precinct captains, dead voters, duplicate voting, and "pre-primed" ballot machines, which would automatically record three votes for every one cast.

Had the election gone the other way in both these states, fifty-one electoral votes would have found their way to Nixon's total, making him the president.

Mazo had published only four parts of his proposed twelve-part series and was about to examine possible Democratic fraud in other states, such as Alabama and California, when Richard Nixon asked him to visit him in the vice president's office. When Mazo showed up, Nixon implored him to stop writing the series in the interest of national unity. "No one steals the presidency of the United States," Nixon told him.

In an age when the press was far more cooperative with politicians than it is now, Mazo agreed to discontinue his articles. But did Nixon really believe that Kennedy had not stolen the presidency? Probably not, but faced with the difficulty of proving the charges, and the uproar of a recount, Nixon made the wise choice to walk away.

The Democrats had out-tricked Tricky Dick. And Nixon would not soon forget.

**How to Prepare for a Nationally Televised Historic Presidential Debate** As your school teachers undoubtedly told you, there is a right way and a wrong way to prepare for the big test.

The "wrong" way: Richard Nixon shows up in Chicago at midnight the day before the debate, exhausted from barnstorming through eleven states and plagued by a recurrent fever. The next morning, instead of resting, he gives a major speech and then spends six hours in his hotel room by himself, studying policy reports and refusing to see anyone. Then he heads for the television studio, once again banging his already infected knee on the way. His temperature is over 100 degrees. Instead of wearing regular makeup for television, he insists on smearing something called Lazy Shave, a kind of talcum powder, which casts his face in a ghostly pallor. And he agrees that the debate can take place with both candidates standing—something the Democrats, aware of his hurt knee, insist on.

The "right" way: Kennedy shows up in Chicago a day and a half before the debate and asks an aide, "Any girls lined up?" On the day of the debate, he gets a suntan on the roof the Palmer House Hotel, has lunch with some friends, and then "studies" in his hotel room by doing Q&A sessions with staff while lying on the bed in his underwear. Ninety minutes before the debate starts, Kennedy slips into a room where a call girl awaits and emerges fifteen minutes later, according to an aide, "with a big grin on his face." Then he dashes to the television studio, arriving only moments before the debate.

**Jumpers, Runners, Clutchers, and Screamers** It's hard to think of a presidential candidate with more sex appeal than John F. Kennedy— and his appearances on national television only underscored the phenomenon. Journalists accompanying Kennedy on his campaign would divide the women into categories—"jumpers," who would try to leap on his campaign car, "runners," who would chase after him, "clutchers" who, given the chance, would grab his arms and not let go, and "screamers," who would let out loud wails of, "Oh, Jack, I love you! I love you!"

Kennedy, of course, was never averse to taking advantage of adoring groupies. One day, after his voice gave out from too much campaigning, Kennedy wrote down a few notes on an envelope for a staffer, who preserved them for posterity. "I got into the blonde," one said. Another plaintively read: "I suppose if I win—my poon days are over?"

He would win—but those days were far from over.

SLEAZE-O-METER

**1964**

⭐

LYNDON
# JOHNSON
DEMOCRAT

## VS.

BARRY
# GOLDWATER
REPUBLICAN

⭐

"WE CAN'T LET GOLDWATER AND THE
RED CHINESE BOTH GET THE BOMB AT THE SAME TIME.
THEN THE SHIT WILL REALLY HIT THE FAN!"
—Lyndon Johnson

After the tragic events of November 22, 1963, when President Kennedy was shot down by assassin Lee Harvey Oswald, many thought that his mainly ignored vice president didn't have the strength or savvy to unite the country. Among the doubters were plenty of East Coast liberals who—in Lyndon Baines Johnson's own bitter words— thought he was "corn pone," an uncouth West Texan hillbilly who lifted his beagles by the ears. The disdain was mutual. Johnson loved to tell "liberal" jokes along the lines of: "What's the difference between a liberal and a cannibal? A cannibal doesn't eat his friends."

Johnson was uninterested in reform as an intellectual exercise. He was a tried-and-true New Deal Democrat, which meant, as a friend said, that he was an old-fashioned, roll-up-his-sleeves do-gooder. He continued policies begun by Kennedy, declared war on poverty with a slew of government-assistance programs, and helped pass a strong Civil Rights Act. The mood of the country was positive. America was more secure than it had been in a decade because of the Nuclear Test Ban Treaty. Johnson was gradually committing more troops to Vietnam, but most Americans, for the time being, were indifferent to this fact. The liberals may not have liked Johnson, but he still had plenty of support from the nation at large.

He also deeply wanted another term, and he was prepared to wage one of the twentieth century's dirtiest campaigns to get one.

## THE CANDIDATES

**DEMOCRAT: LYNDON BAINES JOHNSON** The man known as LBJ—the last of the midcentury Democratic three-initial presidents—was a garrulous Texan whose folksy back-slapping manner hid an extraordinary desire for power and an intimate knowledge of how to get it, honed during twenty years spent in the U.S. Congress. His vice-presidential running mate was Hubert Humphrey, a true liberal and civil rights activist whom Johnson treated as shabbily as possible. On choosing Humphrey for veep, he said: "If you didn't know you were going to be vice president a month ago, you're too damn dumb to have the office."

**REPUBLICAN: BARRY M. GOLDWATER** The fifty-five-year-old Goldwater was born in Arizona to a Jewish father and Presbyterian mother. He worked in the family's successful department-store business, served as an air force pilot, and became a U.S. senator in 1952. Goldwater was an ultraconservative who favored giving army field commanders the right to use tactical nuclear weapons. He liked to make provocative statements, such as, "Sometimes I think this country would be better off if we could just saw off the Eastern seaboard and let it float out to sea."

These were not the beliefs of Republicans like Eisenhower or even Nixon, but in 1964, the Republicans were controlled by ultra-conservatives—and Goldwater was the result. His running mate was a complete unknown, William E. Miller, a conservative ideologue and upstate New York congressman.

## THE CAMPAIGN

When Barry Goldwater was nominated at a Republican convention that saw moderates and conservatives fighting tooth and nail, the Democrats were gleeful. One Democratic politician laughed that the Republicans were on a "kamikaze mission."

Johnson knew he was going to beat Goldwater, but a simple victory wasn't enough—he wanted to destroy his opponent and thereby gain a huge mandate for his first elective term. At the campaign's outset, Johnson received a report from his media advisers that the way to really cremate Goldwater was to portray him as "ridiculous and a little scary: trigger-happy, a bomb-thrower . . . to keep fear of Goldwater as unstable, impulsive, [and] reckless in the public's mind."

The president didn't lose any time. At campaign stops, he would point to the sky and say that John F. Kennedy's spirit was "there in heaven watching us!" Who would the martyred JFK, and this audience, like to see in the White House—Johnson or Goldwater? "Which man's thumb do you want to be close to the button . . . which man do you want to reach over and pick up that hotline when they say, 'Moscow calling'?"

This might seem like alarmist rhetoric, but Goldwater only encouraged the remarks when he said things like, "Let's lob one into the Kremlin and put it right into the men's room." He also played to the racial tensions increasingly present in America, particularly in urban areas. "All men are created equal at the instant of birth," he said, "but from then on, that's the end of equality." Goldwater struck at white America's fears of black criminals: "I don't have to quote the statistics to you. You know. Every wife and mother—yes, every woman and girl knows what I mean."

Since Goldwater would often couple these announcements with statements like, "You know, I haven't got a really first-class brain," many Americans were terrified of him. *Newsweek* called him "the fastest gun," and *Life* said he was a man of "one-sentence solutions." A nationwide survey of American psychiatrists found that a sizable percentage thought Goldwater was unfit to serve as president because he suffered from clinical paranoia.

As the campaign heated up, Johnson instructed his staff to influence the press in whatever way they could ("reporters are puppets," he told them). When Goldwater attacked vice-presidential candidate Hubert Humphrey as a draft dodger (Humphrey had in fact registered for the draft in World War II but received a deferment), top Johnson staffer Walter Jenkins and press secretary Bill Moyers influenced editors at the *Washington Post* and *New York Times* to report on how degrading the Republican charges were. White House aide Walter

Heller wrote a secret memo to Johnson in which he suggested that "it might be healthy to get some respected columnist to give wider circulation to adverse Goldwater impact on the stock market." The person he picked was syndicated financial columnist Sylvia Porter, who wrote two columns about how a Goldwater victory would be bad for America's economy.

Goldwater fought back. His campaign produced a scurrilous book entitled *A Texan Looks at Lyndon: A Study in Illegitimate Power*, which brought together all the nasty stories about Johnson and, in its free-swinging slurs, harkened back to nineteenth-century campaign pamphlets. Johnson, according to author J. Evetts Haley, was guilty of all types of vote buying and sleazy politicking; even worse, he was responsible for the murder of several business associates and even the assassination of John F. Kennedy. In the first year of its publication, the book supposedly outsold the Bible in the state of Texas.

Two conflicting bumper sticker slogans of the time say it all:

Goldwater Supporter:
IN YOUR HEART YOU KNOW HE'S RIGHT.

Johnson Supporter:
IN YOUR GUT YOU KNOW HE'S NUTS.


## THE WINNER: LYNDON JOHNSON

In the end, the American people were suitably frightened. By 6:30 p.m. on November 3, NBC News called the race for Johnson in a landslide well before the polls closed. Sixty-two percent of voters showed up and Johnson received the biggest percentage of the popular vote in U.S. history (61.1). His 16 million-vote margin (43,129,566 to 27,178,188) was the largest to date (it was later eclipsed by Richard Nixon's 1972 and Ronald Reagan's 1984 totals). Republicans were horrified, Democrats were joyful. It looked like a long reign for the corn-pone president.

But in the 1960s, things had a way of changing quickly.

★★★

**"Daisy"** What may well be the most famous and effective campaign commercial of all time debuted in the 1964 election. On September 7, during NBC's top-rated "Monday Night at the Movies," viewers were treated to a lovely shot of a blonde girl walking through a field. She stops to pick a daisy and begins pulling off the petals and counting in her high innocent voice, "1 . . . 2 . . . 3 . . . 4." As she finishes, a military voice begins counting in reverse: "10 . . . 9 . . . 8 . . . 7 . . . 6 . . . " As the countdown reaches zero, the little girl looks up, startled. You stare into her frozen face and then a huge mushroom cloud explodes, filling the screen. Over the cloud, Lyndon Johnson's voice says, "These are the stakes. To make a world in which all of God's children can live, or to go into the dark. We must love each other, or we must die."

Johnson's team paid to air the ad only once—but to the delight of the Democrats, newscasts continuously replayed the spot in its entirety, driving home the message and offering free exposure. The more the Republicans screamed, the worse it was. Perhaps the ad was overkill. Yet no one who saw it could ever forget its stark simplicity.

**If It's 5:00, It Must Be Dirty Tricks Time** It is amazing that Lyndon Johnson wasn't impeached for some of the dirty tricks he pulled on Barry Goldwater. They were as bad as the unethical tactics that got Richard Nixon thrown out of office ten years later.

To smear his opponent, Johnson set up a top-secret sixteen-member committee, dubbed the "anti-campaign" or the "five o'clock club" because of its after-hours business practices. Johnson directly controlled the committee through two of his aides, who chaired each meeting. Among their activities were:

• Developing books to smear Goldwater, with such titles as *Barry Goldwater: Extremist of the Right*; *The Case against Barry Goldwater*; a Goldwater joke book entitled *You Can Die Laughing*; and even a children's coloring book in which the wee ones could color pictures of Goldwater dressed in the robes of the Ku Klux Klan.

• Writing letters to columnist Ann Landers under the guise of ordinary people terrified of Goldwater becoming president.

• Secretly feeding hostile questions to reporters on the Goldwater campaign.

• Sending CIA agent E. Howard Hunt (later infamous for his role in the Watergate break-in) to infiltrate Goldwater campaign headquarters. Hunt got access to advance texts of Goldwater speeches and fed the information to the White House staff, who undercut Goldwater initiatives on several occasions.

**The Republicans Fight Back** The Republicans didn't just sit on their hands, of course. They fought back with plenty of dirty tricks of their own:

• The Republican National Committe planted numerous newspaper articles asking how Johnson had amassed a personal fortune of up to $14 million during a lifetime in public service. One innocent answer was that his wife, Lady Bird, owned a radio station, but Johnson was also not above taking advantage of sweet real estate deals offered by admiring Texan friends.

• A Republican congressional aide spread the probably false story that Johnson had been given a large sum by the State Department for his personal use while visiting in Hong Kong as vice president in 1961.

- Republican ads in Western newspapers spread rumors that Johnson had kidney cancer and speculated on how long he had to live.

- A poll published in October showed Goldwater making gains in many states. The group taking the poll was called Opinion Research When suspicious Democrats questioned the results, other pollsters proved that Opinion Research worked for the Goldwater campaign and appeared to be falsifying results.

**Choices** A group calling itself Mothers for a Moral America made an extremely controversial pro-Goldwater film called *Choices*, which showed Americans that they had a "choice between good and evil."

On the positive side, the film portrayed conservative young people having good clean fun, the American flag flying high, the Statue of Liberty gleaming in the sun, and Barry Goldwater giving impassioned speeches.

The bad side included pornographic books with such names as *Jazz Me Baby* and *Men for Sale*, dances like the twist, women in topless bathing suits, black kids dancing and throwing rocks while rioting, and a speeding Lincoln Continental from the windows of which beer cans are hurled (this last bit was a knock at LBJ, who loved to drive at high speeds on his Texas ranch while tossing down a few cold ones).

Which side would you choose? Tough call. Mothers for a Moral America turned out, in the later words of a Goldwater aide, to be a "front group" for the Goldwater campaign. The film was scheduled to air on television late in the campaign, but Democrats found out about it and raised such a fuss about its racist content that Goldwater was forced to pull it.

**Johnson's Gaydar** In early October, the Goldwater campaign received an unexpected gift—the arrest of Walter Jenkins, Lyndon Johnson's top staffer, on a public morals charge for soliciting sex in the men's room of a Washington, D.C., YMCA.

The forty-six-year-old Jenkins had worked for Johnson for years. He was married with six children but mainly seemed to live for his work. On October 7, 1964, he went to a Washington party, drank about five martinis, and then went around the corner to the YMCA, where he encountered another man in a basement men's room. Just as things were getting hot and heavy, they found themselves surprised by three undercover cops.

Johnson was horrified. He later told a biographer, "I couldn't have been more shocked about Walter Jenkins if I'd heard that Lady Bird had killed the pope." The president was certain that the Republicans had framed Jenkins, although it was soon revealed that he had another arrest for soliciting sex in the same bathroom five years earlier.

Despite LBJ's best efforts to suppress the story, it hit the wire services. Jenkins resigned, and Goldwater, who had served in the air force reserve with Jenkins, publicly claimed that Republicans should make no use of this personal tragedy. Privately, he gleefully said to reporters: "What a way to win an election, communists and cocksuckers!" But before his operatives could use the Jenkins arrest to push home the message of immorality in the White House, larger events, including the explosion of China's first atomic bomb, took over the news.

There is one tragicomic footnote to the affair: some weeks after the incident, LBJ was talking to FBI Director J. Edgar Hoover about what had happened, a conversation that was captured on routine White House tape recordings and later released under the Freedom of Information Act. "I guess you're gonna have to teach me about this stuff," Johnson said, "I swear I can never recognize [gay people]".

And Hoover—long rumored to be gay himself, as LBJ must certainly have known—reassured his commander-in-chief: "There are some people who walk kind of funny that you might think may be queer. But there was no indication of that in Jenkins's case."

SLEAZE-O-METER

1968

RICHARD
# NIXON
REPUBLICAN

VS.

HUBERT
# HUMPHREY
DEMOCRAT

"I SAY CATEGORICALLY THAT I HAVE NO CONTEMPLATION
AT ALL OF BEING THE CANDIDATE FOR ANYTHING IN 1964, 1966,
1968, OR 1972.... ANYBODY WHO THINKS THAT I COULD BE A
CANDIDATE FOR ANYTHING IN ANY YEAR IS OFF HIS ROCKER."
—Richard Nixon, after losing the California gubernatorial race in 1962

By early 1968, Lyndon Johnson had become a prisoner of Vietnam. More than 500,000 American troops were caught up in the quagmire of a savage war that cost American taxpayers $80 million a day. The human price was far worse. Sixteen thousand Americans had died in combat in Vietnam as 1968 began. A thousand a month would die before the year was over.

Protestors disrupted almost every public appearance Johnson made, chanting: "Hey, hey, LBJ. How many kids did you kill today?" They demanded that he bring the troops home. It seemed that Johnson's "Great Society" was crumbling around him. In the last two years, black Americans had rioted in almost every major U.S. city, and Richard Nixon, the Republican Party's main hope after the Goldwater debacle, had called the "War on Poverty" a cruel hoax.

It was too much for Johnson. On March 31, 1968, he made the surprise announcement that he would not seek another term as president.

## THE CANDIDATES

**REPUBLICAN: RICHARD M. NIXON** Dick was back. After running for California governor in 1962 and being soundly beaten, he famously told reporters, "You won't have Nixon to kick around anymore because, gentlemen, this is my last press conference." ABC responded with a half-hour news show called "The Political Obituary of Richard Nixon." Nixon went off to practice law in New York.

Except he couldn't stay away. After Johnson pulverized

Goldwater, Nixon started to look attractive to moderate Republicans who wanted their party back. Nixon began fund-raising, put together a loyal staff including H. R. Haldeman, John Ehrlichman, and John Mitchell, and found media advisers who would remake his image. He entered several Republican primaries and won the nomination in August 1968 on the first ballot.

His only miscue was to pick as his running mate Maryland governor Spiro Agnew, a handsome but not very bright politician whose mouth was far too big.

**DEMOCRAT: HUBERT HUMPHREY** Johnson's refusal to run for another term left the Democrats scrambling. Humphrey, Johnson's vice president, was the anointed successor. Smart and committed to civil rights, Humphrey he projected a soft avuncular image. He was seen as such a lackey to LBJ that at one point in the campaign he was forced to declare: "The president has not made me his slave, and I am not his humble servant."

To make matters worse, Humphrey had two powerful antiwar opponents in Senator Eugene McCarthy of Minnesota and Senator Robert Kennedy of New York (the latter would almost certainly have captured the Democratic nomination had he not been shot down in Los Angeles in June 1968). During a tumultuous Chicago convention in August, while protestors rioted in the streets, the Democrats nominated Humphrey as their candidate, with Senator Edmund Muskie of Maine as his running mate.

## THE CAMPAIGN

As Joe McGinniss famously described in his book *The Selling of the President*, Richard Nixon surrounded himself with a team of media advisers who groomed him for success. No more relentless campaigning; Nixon would take frequent breaks for rest. No more debating, despite Humphrey's taunting him as "Richard the chicken-hearted." No more open press conferences in which Nixon might put his foot in his mouth. Now his handlers scripted television "panel shows" on which "ordinary citizens" (all Nixon supporters) lobbed him leading questions.

According to the polls, Nixon started the campaign with a good twenty-point lead over Humphrey, with especially strong support from blue-collar voters. He became the law-and-order candidate of the "Silent Majority"—the country's long-suffering working people who were fed up with hippies and rioting students and bra-burning feminists.

Humphrey was in a tough position. Blue-collar voters didn't like him, but the antiwar protestors didn't like him either. His campaign was chronically short on cash because Democratic fat cats didn't want to contribute to a losing cause. At one point, nearly in tears, Humphrey lamented, "Why me? What about Nixon?" But Nixon was much harder to reach, isolated in television studios and traveling the country in his private Boeing 727 named *Tricia*, after his eldest daughter. He had perfected the art of the modern candidacy, the sound bite, whereas Humphrey just couldn't stop talking. "I watched Humphrey give an eleven-minute answer to a question once," said a Nixon adviser. "Even the host was looking off-camera saying, 'What the hell did I ask this guy, I forgot.'"

By September, however, the race began to tighten. Nixon's vague pronouncements on ending the war—the vagueness of most of his stances, actually—began to wear badly on a public desperately seeking answers. At the same time, racist third-party candidate George Wallace, governor of Alabama, began making inroads with conservative Republicans.

Then President Johnson dropped a huge October surprise. On Halloween night 1968, he went on television to announce that Hanoi had agreed to begin peace negotiations in Paris in return for the cessation of bombing of North Vietnam. Suddenly, Humphrey shot ahead in the polls—with the Democrats actively involved in peace negotiations, who would want to break the line of succession?

Nixon bitterly (and cleverly) announced: "I am told that this spurt of activity is a last-minute attempt by President Johnson to salvage the candidacy of Mr. Humphrey. This I do not believe." In the last week of the election, some polls showed the Democratic candidate ahead for the first time—that is, until South Vietnam president Nguyen Van Thieu said that his country would not participate in the peace talks, and negotiations broke down.

## THE WINNER: RICHARD NIXON

In a close election, Richard Nixon beat Hubert Humphrey 31,785,480 to 31,275,166, a margin of about a half-million votes, although Nixon's electoral vote lead was 301 to 191. The fifty-five-year-old had made one of the most extraordinary political comebacks in American history. In his victory speech, Nixon said that the theme of his administration would be one he'd seen printed on a teenage supporter's sign during a campaign stop: "Bring Us Together."

It was typical of the era that this comforting story of unity was not quite what it seemed. The teenager was a girl named Vicki Cole, the daughter of a Methodist minister in a small Ohio town. She had first held a much more partisan sign that read, "LBJ Taught Us, Vote Republican," but after losing it, she found the "Bring Us Together Again" sign lying on the ground. It was a serendipitous occurrence that would win her a trip to the White House and a personal visit with President Nixon after the election. When reporters interviewed Cole, she revealed her true pick for president: slain Democrat Robert F. Kennedy.

★★★

**October Surprise?** It is generally believed that if Lyndon Johnson had successfully announced peace talks with North Vietnam in the last week of the 1968 election, Hubert Humphrey might well have won the election. But South Vietnam's president Nguyen Van Thieu refused, and negotiations broke down.

Many in Washington, LBJ among them, believed that Nixon had conspired with Thieu to break off the deal by convincing him that as president, Nixon would give better terms to South Vietnam. Despite some circumstantial evidence—Nixon's top adviser and, later, attorney general John Mitchell had made contact with a Thieu intermediary—the charges were never proved. Contemporary observers, including Hubert Humphrey, felt that Nixon would not have taken the risk of being seen as obstructing the peace talks; others emphasized that Thieu did not need any help in understanding that Johnson's announcement was indeed political, timed to meet the November elections and not necessarily in his country's best interest.

**Bow to the Enemy** After losing his California gubernatorial bid against Governor Pat Brown in 1962, Nixon pulled off some truly dirty tricks with the help of H. R. Haldeman, who would later become his chief of staff.

They set up a phony organization called the Committee for the Preservation of the Democratic Party, which mailed a half million postcards to registered Democrats, expressing concern over the "capture" of the party by a "left-wing minority" that included Brown. The Democrats discovered the ruse during the campaign, got a court order forcing Nixon to cease sending the postcards, and then sued the Republicans for damages, winning an out-of-court settlement.

Another ploy was stunning in its crudity. After finding a photograph of Brown kneeling to speak to a Laotian refugee girl, Nixon and Haldeman cropped out the refugee and put a picture of Russian Premier Nikita Khrushchev in her place, so that it looked as if Brown was kneeling in supplication to America's worst enemy.

**Cue Laugh Track** In Richard Nixon's carefully scripted campaign, VP candidate Spiro Agnew was the only one who ad-libbed—to disastrous effect. Agnew, the first Greek American candidate for vice president, had been picked for his staunch law-and-order stance as governor of Maryland, but Nixon soon realized that the man was a bit of a loose cannon. While on a flight to Hawaii, he saw a Japanese American reporter sleeping on the plane and shouted to a friend, "What's wrong with that fat Jap?"

Agnew, at least, was an equal-opportunity offender. He referred to Polish Americans as "Polacks" and commented, while visiting a ghetto, "when you've seen one city slum, you've seen 'em all."

Democratic ad men capitalized on his poor public image with a television commercial that simply showed the words "SPIRO AGNEW FOR VICE PRESIDENT," followed by thirty seconds of raucous laughter.

SLEAZE-O-METER

**1972**

★

RICHARD
# NIXON
REPUBLICAN

## VS.

GEORGE
# McGOVERN
DEMOCRAT

★

**"I COULD NOT MUSTER MUCH MORAL OUTRAGE
OVER A POLITICAL BUGGING."
—Richard Nixon**

In 1972 the Vietnam War was still raging despite Richard Nixon's campaign vows to bring it to a halt. In America, four student war protesters had died at Kent State University, in Ohio, shot by national guardsmen. Some 200,000 people marched on Washington in 1971, demanding an end to the hostilities. The 1972 election was pivotal. Americans, reeling from the unparalleled recent upheavals, sought a president with competence, integrity, and compassion. What they got was an election in which it seemed that all the smear tactics and nasty politics of the previous decade seemed to coalesce into a political campaign that would be forever synonymous with the words "dirty tricks."

## THE CANDIDATES

**REPUBLICAN: RICHARD NIXON** Nixon's triumphs had largely been on the foreign affairs front, with historical summit trips to China and Russia. At home, faced with growing opposition to his policies and an economy shored up by wage and price controls, he had walled himself inside his presidency, sticking close to the White House and relying on the same group of advisers and rich friends for comfort and advice.

**DEMOCRAT: GEORGE MCGOVERN** McGovern was a history and political-science teacher turned senator from South Dakota. He was affable and low-key, and he could be tough minded. Unlike Nixon, McGovern was a World War II hero who had won the Distinguished Flying Cross for piloting a bomber over North Africa and Italy.

But like Humphrey before him, McGovern was not terribly exciting. His nomination and acceptance speech at the Democratic convention in Miami took place at 2:48 a.m.—prime time, as one observer said, "in Guam." The nod for VP went to Senator Thomas Eagleton of Missouri.

# THE CAMPAIGN

The Republicans received a surprise early in the campaign when they learned that Thomas Eagleton had been hospitalized for clinical depression three times between 1960 and 1966—he had even been given electroshock therapy. Others rumors claimed that he'd been treated for alcoholism. At first, McGovern said he was behind Eagleton "one thousand percent," but eventually he succumbed to party pressures and replaced him with R. Sargent Shriver, a Kennedy intimate and former ambassador to France. It was easy for Republicans to paint McGovern as indecisive, a man who did not stand by his friends.

Nixon had decided to run as President Nixon, not as candidate Nixon; he made appearances only in the Rose Garden and at carefully controlled campaign events. Behind the scenes, his campaign swarmed with dirty tricks. When the *New York Times* opposed his mining of Haiphong Harbor in North Vietnam, a full-page ad appeared in the paper the next day, from fourteen concerned "citizens" supporting Nixon. The only problem was that the ad had been secretly placed by the Committee to Re-Elect the President (its true acronym is CRP, but it's so much more fun to call it CREEP). The names signed to the ad were those of relatives of CREEP team members. CREEP also sent thousands of pro-Nixon postcards to a Washington, D.C. based television station that was taking a public opinion poll on the mining of Haiphong, resulting in an outcome of three to one in support of the president's actions.

And these were only the more public actions. Nixon had also ordered a special team of the Internal Revenue Service (the ominously named Special Services Staff, or SSS) to conduct field audits on his enemies, who included Larry O'Brien, head of the Democratic National Committee. How did Nixon know who his enemies were? Because, of course, he had an "Enemies List," compiled by staffers John Dean and Chuck Colson. The list swelled to some 200 names— including Paul Newman (involved in "Radic-Lib causes"), black Congressman John Conyers ("known weakness for white females"), and Maxwell Dane, one of the partners in the advertising agency that had produced Johnson's famous "Daisy" spot.

And we haven't even mentioned the most famous group of dirty tricksters in American history, men whose actions far outsleazed LBJ's Five O'Clock Club: the Special Investigations Unit, a group known more informally as the "Plumbers." Nixon had told top adviser John Ehrlichman to "set up a little group right here in the White House" to fix leaks, and so Ehrlichman assembled a task force that included ex-CIA agents E. Howard Hunt and G. Gordon Liddy, among others.

On the night of June 17, 1972, a watchman would discover five Plumbers in the offices of the Democratic National Committee in the Watergate apartment and office complex in Washington, D.C. They wore surgical gloves and carried bugging equipment (tiny microphones hidden in phony ChapSticks), cameras, forty rolls of unexposed film, and $3,500 in brand-new consecutively numbered hundred-dollar bills.

When the press queried White House press secretary Ron Ziegler about this little episode, he dismissed it as "a third-rate burglary." If so, it was the only third-rate burglary to cause the resignation of a U.S. president. At the time, however, Americans paid surprisingly little attention to the news. The campaign went on, with Nixon taking a page from LBJ's 1964 playbook, marginalizing his opponent by making him seem to be a dangerous radical. Effectively caricaturized as the candidate of the "three A's: Acid, Amnesty [for draft dodgers], and Abortion," McGovern was getting the pants beaten off him. One McGovern staffer whispered to a reporter late in the campaign, "I just hope we can avoid a debacle."

## THE WINNER: RICHARD NIXON

And what a debacle it was. Richard Nixon won by the largest plurality of the popular vote, beating McGovern 47,169,911 to 29,170,383 and taking the Electoral College 520 to 17. But the party would soon be over, as revelations about Watergate over the next year drove

Nixon out of office by August 1974.

Nixon later dismissed Watergate as merely another "political bugging," and for a cold warrior who had been the victim of a lot of dirty tricks, that was no doubt true. He would admit in his memoirs that "I told my staff that we should come up with the kind of imaginative dirty tricks that our Democratic opponents used against us and others so effectively in previous campaigns." (The campaigns of Kennedy and Johnson were cases in point.)

But, at the time of Watergate, the revelation of the existence of tapes made in the Oval Office let Americans listen in, for the first time, to the sound of their president doing business. And what they heard was extremely unpleasant.

★★★

**The Destruction of Edmund Muskie** Early in 1972 President Nixon, whose approval ratings hovered at only about 48 percent, felt that he was vulnerable to a challenge from a strong Democratic candidate. So it became the goal of dirty tricks managers like Special Assistant to the President Dwight Chapin to "foster a split between Democratic hopefuls" in the primaries. Teddy Kennedy posed no problem. The last surviving Kennedy brother had pretty much blown his presidential chances by driving a car off a bridge in 1969, drowning the young woman with him.

Going into the New Hampshire primary in February, many predicted the big winner would be Senator Edmund Muskie of Maine (Hubert Humphrey's 1968 running mate)—in fact, most journalists had already anointed him the Democratic presidential nominee. Richard Nixon viewed Muskie as a formidable candidate.

But then strange things began happening. Suddenly, New Hampshire voters began receiving phone calls from rude black people—calls that came late at night or early in the morning—saying that they had been bused in from Harlem to work for Muskie. And then the conservative editor of the *Manchester Union Leader*, William Loeb, published a letter, purportedly written by an ordinary citizen, that accused Muskie of using the word *Canuck* to refer to French Canadians. In defending himself against this and other slurs, Muskie, standing outdoors before microphones and cameras, began to cry. Or, since it was snowing, perhaps a snowflake had landed in his eye—it's impossible to tell from tapes of the incident.

Muskie did lose his cool, however, and many voters wondered if he was unable to handle pressure. He won New Hampshire, but by a much smaller margin than predicted. Only later was it discovered that the "Canuck" letter was written by White House aide Kenneth Clawson.

Things only got worse when Muskie headed for the Florida primary. Many voters in that state received a letter, written on Muskie campaign stationery, stating (falsely) that Hubert Humphrey had been arrested for drunk driving in 1967. Other letters on Muskie stationery claimed that prominent Democratic senator and presidential hopeful Henry "Scoop" Jackson had fathered a child with a seventeen-year-old girl.

No detail was too small. Posters appeared on Florida highways that read: "Help Muskie in Busing More Children Now." Ads were placed in free shoppers' newsletters saying: "Muskie: Would you accept a black running mate?" At a Muskie press conference in Miami, someone released a handful of white mice wearing tags that read: "Muskie is a rat fink."

The person behind all the Florida mayhem was Donald Segretti, the dark prince of dirty tricks. Segretti, whose name means "secret" in Italian, was a California lawyer who had been law school pals with several Nixon staffers—in particular, Dwight Chapin, the man who hired him and paid him $16,000, plus expenses, to wreak havoc in the primaries.

Muskie placed fourth in Florida and was finished as a candidate. Segretti's role in the investigations was discovered after the Watergate break-in, and he served four and a half months in prison for misdemeanors associated with illegal campaign activities.

**Got a Leak? Get a Plumber!** The Plumbers came into existence at least partially because of the publication of the "Pentagon Papers" by the *New York Times* and *Washington Post*. These top-secret Defense Department papers traced the development of the U.S. involvement in the Vietnam War and showed how covert decisions had been made behind the backs of the American people. Although much blame could be laid at the feet of Democratic administrations, Nixon was concerned that such leaks could establish a precedent that might imperil his own secret decisions.

The leak was former Defense Department official Daniel Ellsberg, and the Plumbers were organized specifically to discredit Ellsberg—to "link him to a conspiracy which suggests treasonable conduct," as Nixon aide Chuck Colson put it. Their first operation was to break into Ellsberg's psychiatrist's office, which provided no information on Ellsberg and left behind a trail of destruction.

The clumsiness of the operation was rivaled only by that of the Watergate burgle of the Democratic National Committee offices on June 17, 1972. The group had already broken in on Memorial Day—undetected—to install listening devices. But the bugs weren't working properly, so the Plumbers went back. But this time, they carelessly taped the spring locks on the doors horizontally rather than vertically; the tape was seen by the night watchman, who called D.C. police. Two of the suspects had address books containing White House telephone numbers and, of course, they carried $3,500 worth of brand-new consecutively numbered hundred-dollar bills—not exactly walking-around money.

The five burglars had been recruited by E. Howard Hunt and G. Gordon Liddy, who were not present that night. But the trail now led directly to them, to CREEP, and to the White House. From there, the question for the nation in the televised congressional hearings the following year became: Did Richard Nixon approve or know about the burglary? His answer was that he did not, but it was apparent from the Oval Office tapes that he at least knew such dirty tricks were occurring.

# 1976

## JIMMY CARTER vs. GERALD FORD

Twenty members of the Nixon administration were convicted after the Watergate dust had settled; that's not including Vice President Spiro Agnew, who resigned after pleading no contest to non-Watergate-related tax-evasion charges. Nixon might have been indicted had it not been for his appointed successor, Gerald Ford, granting him a "full, free, and absolute" pardon for any crimes he might have committed.

That move was not popular with the American public, and it came back to haunt Ford in the bicentennial election year of 1976. Under Ford's watch, the country had suffered through significant inflation, rising unemployment, and the shocking end of the Vietnam War, in which American personnel fled the country in ignominy. They also had to deal with Ford's pratfalls—when he stumbled down the steps of Air Force One during official business, no one in the country let him forget it. Nevertheless, he became the Republican Party's nominee after narrowly beating out former California governor and neocon Ronald Reagan in the primaries. Ford's running mate was Senator Robert Dole of Kansas.

Reform laws passed in the wake of Watergate cleared the way for an untraditional presidential candidate: the former governor of Georgia, Jimmy Carter. With the passage of the Federal Elections Campaign Act (which went by the unlovely acronym FECA), individual campaign contributions were severely capped, but any candidate who could raise $100,000 in fifteen states could qualify for federal matching funds. In 1976 the Supreme Court declared one part of FECA unconstitutional, claiming that contributions were really a form of free speech and thus protected by the First Amendment.

Candidates were free to spend as much as they wanted on their own campaigns, as long as they refused federal matching funds. But the court did continue limits on individual contributions of federal candidates and upheld the part of FECA that called for public disclosure of campaign financing.

Because more money-strapped candidates could now qualify for federal matching funds, the primary season got longer and longer. Also, more primaries abandoned the traditional winner-take-all system in which the candidate who carried the state's primary received all the party's delegates. That meant a presidential candidate running second or third in a state primary could still take home a proportionate share of delegates.

The result was that a lot of politicians began throwing their hats into the ring, a process that continues to this day. And with so many relatively obscure candidates, Americans relied on television to make sense of them all. The first star of the new age of elections was James Earl Carter, a former peanut farmer and one-term governor of Georgia who liked to be called "Jimmy." A highly unusual dark-horse candidate, Jimmy Carter hailed from the Deep South (no American president had been elected from the South since before the Civil War), was a born-again Christian, and made speeches so boring that Senator Eugene McCarthy once called him "an oratorical mortician."

Yet along with his brilliant chief of staff, Hamilton Jordan, Carter understood that early victories in the extended primary process received a disproportionate share of press attention. Therefore, Carter went all-out to win the obscure Iowa caucus—and the next day, the *New York Times* anointed him Democratic front-runner, a position he would keep. His running mate was Minnesota senator Walter Mondale.

**THE CAMPAIGN** Carter ran on the theme that he was an outsider coming to clean up Washington. Most of his speeches began, "Hi, my name is Jimmy Carter, and I'm running for president." Yet the poor country boy did encounter a few problems. For one thing, he had done a *Playboy* magazine interview, which appeared during the campaign, in which he said: "I've looked on a lot of women with lust; I've committed adultery in my heart many times." The admission did not go over well with his born-again following. Carter didn't help himself with fellow Democrats either when, in the same interview, he stated that Lyndon Johnson was as guilty as Richard Nixon of "lying, cheating, and distorting the truth." The fact that both these statements were honest doesn't take away from their political foolishness.

Fortunately, Carter was running against Gerald Ford. The candidates held a series of debates—the first presidential debates since 1960 and the first time an incumbent president debated an opponent. Ford's men were careful to keep his klutziness in check, even demanding an especially deep well on the podium to hold his glass of water, lest he knock it over. But they couldn't control his tongue. America was amazed to hear him say that Eastern European states were not under Soviet domination.

Ford meant to say that his administration refused to accept such a situation as the status quo, but good intentions do not show up under the harsh glare of television lights.

**THE WINNER: JIMMY CARTER** Not only did Jimmy Carter become president, winning 40,830,763 votes to 39,147,793, a margin of just over 2 percent, but Democrats swept back into power in both the House and the Senate. On January 20, 1977, Carter got rid of his limousine and walked to his inauguration, making a statement that the country had to tighten its belt. Once again, he was delivering an honest message —but it wasn't one voters really wanted to hear.

**1980**

★

RONALD
# REAGAN
REPUBLICAN

## VS.

JIMMY
# CARTER
DEMOCRAT

★

---

**"STOP ME BEFORE I KILL AGAIN."**
—Sign on California redwood tree after Ronald Reagan
claimed that trees caused more pollution than cars

**A**h, the Carter years. Remember the "killer rabbit" Jimmy had to beat off with a paddle while fishing? Remember the Mr. Rogers cardigan sweaters he wore? Remember the double-digit inflation? Remember that weekend in July 1979 when 75 percent of New York gas stations had to close?

Heading into the election year of 1980, Carter was not having a good time. True, he had brokered the Panama Canal Treaty and the Camp David Accords between Israel and Egypt. But then students in Iran took Americans hostage, the Soviets invaded Afghanistan, and Mount St. Helens erupted.

In addition, Carter was about to run against the "Gipper," Ronald Reagan, former Hollywood actor, former governor of California, and future nonstick Teflon Man. With fifty-one primaries and caucuses, it was a long and extremely nasty campaign, with the mother of all October Surprises at its conclusion.

## THE CANDIDATES

**REPUBLICAN: RONALD REAGAN** Remember the disgruntled Adlai Stevenson campaign adviser who warned in 1952 that soon "presidential campaigns would have professional actors as candidates"? Well, the future had arrived. Ronald "Ronnie" Reagan—handsome smiling star of such movie classics as *Girls on Probation, Knute Rockne—All American*, and, of course, the beloved *Bedtime for Bonzo*—was sixty-nine years old as the 1980 campaign began. He had nearly beaten Gerald Ford during the 1976 primaries and now ran a well-oiled campaign with a large dollop of secrecy. William Casey, future CIA director, was his campaign manager, and George H. W. Bush, former CIA head, was his vice-presidential candidate.

**DEMOCRAT: JIMMY CARTER** At age fifty-five, Carter had been worn down by the burdens of a tough presidency and his own miscues. He seemed incapable of grasping that Americans didn't want to hear about a "crisis in confidence," nor did they want anything to do with the severe austerity measures he felt were necessary to revive the economy. One image of the Carter White House that resonated with a lot of voters came from the time that Carter, wearing a headband, tried to run a 10K road race near Camp David to encourage physical fitness and nearly collapsed. To put it bluntly, Jimmy was sort of a drag.

## THE CAMPAIGN

As the campaign began, America's "Misery Index" (a measurement created by a Chicago economist combining inflation plus unemployment) was at an all-time high, 22 percent (in late 2006, it was under 9, just to compare). Misery is tough on an incumbent, but it leaves a challenger plenty of opportunities. The theme of Ronald Reagan's campaign was "Are you better off today than you were four years ago?" Since the Misery Index was 13 percent in 1976, the answer was a miserable no.

Carter's strategy was to be presidential, yet strike hard at Reagan. A memo written by his media adviser told him how this was to be done:

| CARTER | REAGAN |
|---|---|
| Safe/sound. | Untested |
| Young. | Old |
| Vigorous. | Old |
| Smart. | Dumb |

Well, Reagan did come across as old and a little foolish. He claimed that the "finest oil geologists" had told him that the United States had more oil than Saudi Arabia. He stated that the eruption of Mount St. Helens released more sulfur dioxide into the air "than has been released in the last ten years of automobile driving." He also loved ethnic jokes. After the New Hampshire primary, reporters overheard him telling one that began: "How do you tell who the Polish fellow is at a cockfight? He's the one with the duck." When reports of this gaffe were published, Reagan claimed he had merely been providing an example of the kinds of jokes candidates shouldn't tell. And the Teflon Man actually got away with it.

Carter just couldn't win. When he attacked Reagan for supposedly having used code phrases like "states' rights" to imply a racist agenda and for being divisive (under President Reagan, Carter claimed, "Americans might be separated, black from white, Jew from Christian, North from South"), people thought he sounded mean. Reagan, it seemed, simply inspired friendly feelings in a lot of people. They didn't want to see him assailed.

The main issue of the election, however, was that Iranian students had captured fifty-three American hostages on November 4, 1979. The country was horrified. A bunch of foreign kids were thumbing their noses at the United States, and Carter seemed powerless to stop them. His approval ratings during the campaign sank lower than those of Richard Nixon's during Watergate—one Harris Poll put him at 22 percent.

It didn't help that a third-party candidate, long-time Illinois representative John Anderson, was pulling surprisingly well with his moderate National Unity Party. Anderson seemed to many a viable alternative, but he ultimately did more damage to Carter than to Reagan. Even the new fundamentalists, who were a growing power in the conservative wing of the Republican Party, attacked the born-again president . . . for being too liberal.

Carter had his debate with Reagan on October 28 to look

forward to, right? Wrong. It was bad enough a Republican spy stole Carter's secret debate briefing book and gave it to Reagan before the event. Reagan proceeded to dominate the debate in his usual affable, grinning manner, saying, "There you go again, Mr. President," whenever Carter said something Reagan found foolish. Carter didn't help his case by citing his thirteen-year-old daughter Amy as a source on matters of crucial global importance: "I had a discussion with my daughter Amy the other day, before I came here, to ask her what the most important issue was. She said she thought nuclear weaponry."

In the end, the sole hope for a Carter victory was the release of the hostages, and his administration fought valiantly to achieve it. The Reagan camp, in the meantime, kept warning that Carter might try to pull off a grandstanding October Surprise, but the event never materialized (for reasons that will soon be made clear).

## THE WINNER: RONALD REAGAN

Reagan cleaned Carter's clock, 43,904,53 to 35,483,838, and won the electoral votes of all but five states and the District of Columbia. John Anderson took about 5,700,000 votes, a respectable 7 percent showing for a candidate without major funding or the backing of a huge political organization. The victory was so bad that Carter conceded on national television at 9:50 p.m., Eastern Standard Time—or only 6:50 p.m. Pacific Standard Time, where the polls were still open, infuriating West Coast Democrats running for local office. Carter became the first incumbent Democratic president since Grover Cleveland to fail to retain his office (and even Grover got his back after a second try). Reagan was now president, and the era of "supply side" economics, Irangate, and the "Evil Empire" of the Soviet Union was about to begin.

Oh, yes, and the Iran hostages were released—moments after Reagan's swearing in.

★★★

**Held Hostage** In his controversial book *October Surprise: American Hostages in Iran and the Election of Ronald Reagan*, former Carter National Security Council staffer Gary Sick documents in copious detail how William Casey, Reagan campaign manager and later the CIA director, stalled the release of the Iranian hostages so that Carter would lose the election.

The Republicans had heard that the Iranians were seeking to negotiate with the Carter administration, which had thrown an economic cordon around Iran, freezing Iranian assets in U.S. banks and asking the international community to respect an arms embargo. Casey knew that the release of the hostages to Jimmy Carter would spell disaster for the Reagan campaign, and he moved swiftly to avert it. According to Sick, Casey used his and George H. W. Bush's old intelligence-community ties to establish a "back channel" of communications to Iran. Casey met with Iranian cleric Mehdi Karroubi in Madrid in August 1980 and offered military assistance—something Iran desperately needed since Iraq was threatening to invade—if the hostages were not released until after Ronald Reagan was elected. The Ayatollah Khomeini approved the deal.

Republicans were careful to monitor the situation, for they were afraid the Iranians would double-cross them and deal with Carter. Subsequent meetings between Iranian representatives, Casey, and other members of Reagan's campaign team took place in October, and the pot was sweetened: more guns and the unfreezing of Iranian cash in the United States, but only if the hostage release was delayed until after Reagan's swearing in on January 20, 1981, so that Carter would get absolutely no credit. In the meantime, a network of retired military officers who were friends of Casey monitored U.S. air force bases for any sign of unusual activity, which might indicate a Carter deal with some other faction in Iran.

On January 20, the hostages were loaded aboard a plane but forced to wait on the tarmac of Tehran Airport until the very moment of Reagan's swearing in. Then the plane took off for Wiesbaden,

Germany. Days later, the Reagan administration began sending military supplies to Iran.

Interestingly enough, Ronald Reagan, when asked in 1991 whether he had any knowledge of these types of secret dealings, said, "I did some things actually the other way, to try to be of help in getting those hostages . . . out of there." The questioner then asked him, "Does that mean contact with the Iranian government?" To which Reagan replied, "Not by me. No. [But] I can't go into details. Some of those things are still classified."

**Debategate** Discussing Carter's 1980 loss, former Carter speechwriter Hendrik Hertzberg pointed out that the debate had been a chief deciding factor, for Reagan came across as a pretty nice guy, not a conservative ideologue: "When people realized they could get rid of Carter and still not destroy the world, they went ahead and did it."

It's an indisputable fact that Carter's top-secret predebate briefing book was stolen and given to Reagan's people before the October 28 debate so that the Gipper would have all the right ripostes to Carter's sallies. But the question remains: whodunnit?

As recently as 2005, in an interview on National Public Radio, Carter blamed conservative writer George Will. In a scathing reply in his *Washington Post* column, Will, who did help Reagan prepare for the debate, said that a copy of the briefing book was in the room while he and others were working with Reagan, but Will claims he did not steal it or use it in his coaching.

Whether or not Will was responsible, there was certainly at least one spy in Carter's midst. A Congressional investigation in 1983 confirmed that Reagan campaign manager William Casey was receiving "classified reports on closely held Carter administration intelligence on the Carter campaign and the Democratic president's efforts to liberate the hostages." And Reagan never denied that the briefing book was stolen. He later said, "It probably wasn't too much different than the press rushing into print with the Pentagon Papers."

In hindsight, a lot of people wondered how a supposedly impartial journalist like Will could coach Reagan for his debate and then go on *Nightline* the same evening without mentioning his behind-the-scenes participation, praising Reagan's "thoroughbred performance." Although he defended himself at the time, Will now admits his role as Reagan coach was "inappropriate."

**Just Say Grrrrr!** Prior to 1980, presidential candidates used their wives to enhance their image as stable and well-rounded family men. But in 1980, for the first time in campaign history, a presidential candidate's wife appeared in an attack ad. This televised message from Nancy Reagan aired twice in the last few weeks of the campaign: "[I am upset that President Carter] is trying to portray my husband as a warmonger or a man who would throw the elderly out on the street and cut off their Social Security, when in fact, he never said anything of the kind, at any time, and the elderly people have enough to worry about now. They are scared to death of how they are going to live without this thrown on top of them. That's a cruel thing to do; it is cruel to the people; it is cruel to my husband. I deeply resent it, as a wife and a mother and a woman."

# 1984

## RONALD REAGAN vs. WALTER MONDALE

Welcome to "Morning in America," as the glowing 1984 Reagan campaign spot described the state of the nation. "In a town not too far from where you live, a young family has just moved into a new home. The factory down the river is working again. . . . Life is better. America is back."

Well, yes and no. In 1984 there were more jobs and interest rates were down, but the deficit was skyrocketing, tax cuts benefited only the very rich, and religious fundamentalists, intolerant of anyone who didn't share their beliefs, were in the ascendancy. Jerry Falwell of the Moral Majority gave the benediction at the Republican National Convention, calling Ronald Reagan and his vice president, George H. W. Bush, "God's instruments for rebuilding America."

Challenging God's instruments were Jimmy Carter's vice president Walter Mondale and the first female candidate for vice president, Geraldine Ferraro, U.S. representative from New York.

**THE CAMPAIGN** The 1984 campaign is one of the most boring on record and reminds many historians of 1956, when another Republican president, Dwight Eisenhower, ran in a time of prosperity. Even Mondale called the pace of the campaign "glacial." Reagan, who had been nearly assassinated in 1981, was loved by most of America, even though some speculated that his age (at seventy-three, he was the oldest U.S. president in history) might make him unfit for another full term.

In truth, he often seemed a bit forgetful. At a 1981 meeting of city mayors at the White House, Reagan greeted his Secretary of Housing and Urban Development, Samuel Pierce, as "Mr. Mayor."

He forgot the name of his national security adviser, Bud McFarlane. And he was prone to such misstatements as: "Now we're trying to get unemployment to go up. I think we are going to succeed."

No matter. Mondale lacked Reagan's charisma, and Ferraro's novelty as a woman candidate for high office wore off quickly when she stumbled on the issue of releasing her real-estate-developer husband's tax returns to the press.

**THE WINNER: RONALD REAGAN** In a landslide that hearkened back to FDR's annihilation of Alf Landon in 1936, Reagan took every state except Mondale's home bastion of Minnesota. The popular vote margin was 54,455,075 to 37,577,185, second only to Richard Nixon's victory in 1972. In the Electoral College, Reagan triumphed 525 to 13. Ouch.

SLEAZE-O-METER

1988

★

GEORGE H. W.
# BUSH
REPUBLICAN

## VS.

MICHAEL
# DUKAKIS
DEMOCRAT

★

**"I WILL STRIP THE BARK OFF THE LITTLE BASTARD!"**
—Lee Atwater, George Bush's campaign manager, speaking
"off-the-record" to reporters about Michael Dukakis

**O**n the face of it, 1988 should have been a campaign about issues. After eight years of Reaganomics, the budget deficit skyrocketed, the trade deficit was on the rise, and homelessness had become a serious problem in America. On the other hand, inflation had peaked and the cold war was coming to an astonishing end—almost as if the Gipper himself had scripted the movie.

Plenty of substantial issues for each candidate to sink his teeth into, right? Wrong, punk—and by the way, you sound like you're soft on crime! As it turns out, the election devolved into one of the bitterest, dirtiest, and meanest ever held in the United States—one that set the tone for much of the vicious mudslinging that characterizes Republican–Democrat contests right up to this day.

## THE CANDIDATES

**REPUBLICAN: GEORGE H. W. BUSH** George H. W. Bush had a long resume—rich New England kid, hero of World War II, ambassador to the U.N., head of the CIA, vice president—but Americans felt like they didn't know him. This was partly because many couldn't understand what the man was saying. Not only did he mumble but he also was prone to such elegant malapropisms as "I stand for anti-bigotry, anti-Semitism and anti-racism" and "I'm going to make sure that everyone who has a job, wants a job." But he was tall.

**DEMOCRAT: MICHAEL DUKAKIS** By contrast, Michael Dukakis was short—measuring about five feet eight inches—thus proving the truth of the ancient proverb: "It is easier for a camel to pass through the eye of a needle than for a short dude to enter the White House." He did have a pretty good record: as governor of Massachusetts he'd turned around that state's faltering economy by bringing in high-tech companies while resurrecting social programs to help the common-wealth's neediest citizens. (In this he was aided by his far more charis-matic lieutenant governor, John Kerry.)

In addition to being short, Dukakis was boring—stiff, straight laced, sincere to a fault—and sported the worst five o'clock shad-ow since Richard Nixon, the kind that looks like you've just smeared charcoal on your face before going out to trick or treat.

## THE CAMPAIGN

While Bush called for "a kindler, gentler nation" and "a thousand points of light," his campaign manager Lee Atwater pursued a strat-egy of "raising the negatives" by churning out a series of attack ads. The commercials portrayed Dukakis as being too liberal on drugs and soft crime and too much of a girly-man on defense.

Dukakis tried to fight back, but what did he have to propose? Massive cuts in defense spending? Programs for society's needy and disadvantaged? In a decade that made heroes of Rocky and Rambo, the Dukakis platform just wasn't sexy. While the Democrats struggled to formulate a counterattack, Atwater unleashed a sleazy ad cam-paign to end them all.

It focused on a thirty-nine-year-old black convict named William "Willie" Horton. During Dukakis's tenure as governor, Horton had taken part in a weekend furlough program in Massachusetts. Instead of returning to prison, however, Horton fled to Maryland, where he raped a white woman and stabbed her fiancé. The colors matter here because the Republicans proceeded to make the most racist series of attacks in modern American electioneering history.

To begin, Republicans renamed Horton. His real name was William. He was known to his mother, family, friends, enemies, cops, and parole officers as William. Newspaper accounts of his crimes referred to him as William. And yet the Republican attack ads called him "Willie."

What kind of attack ads? Here are a few samples:

**"Get Out of Jail Free Card"**: Modeled after the Monopoly card and distributed to 400,000 Texas voters, this tiny mailbox stuffer read: "Michael Dukakis is the killer's best friend and the decent honest citizen's worst enemy"

**"Pro-Family Letter"**: This was the Maryland Republican party fund-raising letter that featured photographs of Horton and Dukakis over the headline: "Is This Your Pro-Family Team for 1988?"

**"Weekend Passes"**: A sixty-second television spot with side-by-side pictures of Horton and Dukakis looking remarkably alike—and no wonder, since the ad makers used a dark photograph of a weary and unshaven Dukakis with his hair disheveled.

**"Revolving Door"**: Perhaps most famous of all, this stark black and white TV spot showed convicts marching through a turnstile into jail and immediately out again. No matter that the "convicts" were out-of-work Republicans instructed not to shave for the day. The point had been made.

## THE WINNER: GEORGE H. W. BUSH

With the lowest voter turnout since 1924, Bush took the popular vote 48,886,097 to 41,809,074 and won by a landslide in the Electoral College, 426 votes to 112.

Oops, make that 111. One Democratic elector from West Virginia was so disgusted with Dukakis that he cast his vote for vice-presidential candidate Lloyd Bentsen.

**Was It Good for You, Too?** Many Democrats tried to suggest that Bush had indulged in extramarital affairs and pursued shady oil connections, but these charges had no real impact on the campaign. In the end, the most scandalous charge uttered against Bush came from Bush himself, speaking in Detroit just weeks before the election: "I have worked alongside [President Reagan] and I am proud to be his partner. We have had triumphs, we have made mistakes, we have had sex . . . I mean, setbacks!"

**President Quayle** Building on fears that vice-presidential candidate Dan Quayle was not qualified to be president, Democrats created a television ad that began with grainy footage of vice presidents Harry Truman and Lyndon Johnson being sworn in as president. The voiceover intoned: "One out of five American vice presidents has to rise to the duties of commander-in-chief. After five months of reflection, Bush's choice: J. Danforth Quayle. Hopefully, we'll never know how great a lapse of judgment that really was." The soundtrack was an ominously thumping heartbeat.

**Totally Tanking** Sometimes even the best attempts at publicity can backfire—like the time Michael Dukakis, in an attempt to prove that he was no softie on defense, visited a General Dynamics plant in Michigan for a photo op with a tank. (Memo to future candidates: when poking your head out of the hatch of an M1 tank, do not grin and wave, do not wear a tie as well as a silly helmet, and do not, whatever you do, bear a striking resemblance to Alfred E. Neuman.) The photo op was such a disaster, Republicans recycled the footage for an attack ad. "Tank" showed Dukakis riding around and around in circles as a narrator intoned, with more than a touch of incredulity: "Now he wants to be our commander-in-chief? America can't afford the risk."

**Most Concerned Letter from a Serial Killer** After the Bush campaign claimed in an ad that Chicago mass murderer John Wayne Gacy would be released on furlough if Dukakis were elected, Gacy dispatched an angry missive from prison: "It is an insult to the voting public that [Republicans are] exploiting the name of John Wayne Gacy to scare people into voting for George Bush."

SLEAZE-O-METER

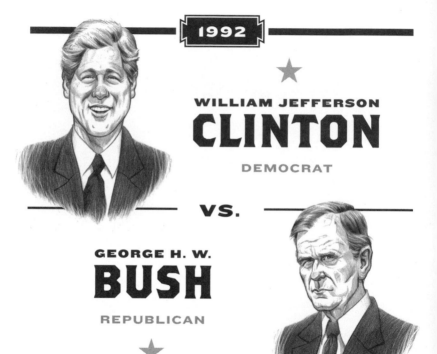

**1992**

WILLIAM JEFFERSON
# CLINTON
DEMOCRAT

VS.

GEORGE H. W.
# BUSH
REPUBLICAN

"ALL I'VE BEEN ASKED ABOUT BY THE PRESS ARE A WOMAN
I DIDN'T SLEEP WITH AND A DRAFT I DIDN'T DODGE."
—Bill Clinton

**J**ust after the successful completion of his hundred-hour Gulf War in the fall of 1990, George H. W. Bush's approval ratings reached an astonishing 90 percent; he seemed unbeatable. After twelve years of prosperous Republican rule, coupled with extremely weak Democratic presidential candidates, some pundits began to wonder whether the Democratic Party was heading toward political extinction, just like the Whigs or the Federalists.

But as the Bush administration progressed, the approval rating slowly started falling. War may have made Bush a hero, but he never earned the fanatically loyal following of a Ronald Reagan. He broke his famous 1988 pledge of "Read my lips: no new taxes," which left him open to Democratic attack. Reagan's legacy of a staggering $4 trillion national debt (up $3 trillion since 1980) didn't help much, either. There may have been an explosion of wealth in the top 1 percent of the U.S. population, but one in ten Americans was living on food stamps, and one in eight lived below the poverty level.

The relatively obscure field of Democratic candidates included Iowa senator Tom Harkin, Nebraska senator Bob Kerrey, Arkansas governor Bill Clinton, and Massachusetts senator Paul Tsongas. But Bush had more than Democrats to worry about. Conservative Christian columnist and former Nixon speech writer Pat Buchanan ran well in the primaries, showing that the religious right would not be denied its share of the action. And the fourteenth wealthiest person in the United States, billionaire Texan H. Ross Perot, decided to hell with federal matching funds, he'd pay for his own campaign—and then mounted the most successful third-party challenge since Teddy Roosevelt and his Bull Moose Party in 1912.

## THE CANDIDATES

**DEMOCRAT: WILLIAM "BILL" CLINTON** If there could be such a thing as a "log cabin" presidential candidate in the late twentieth century, that candidate was William Jefferson Clinton. He was born poor in Hope, Arkansas, in 1946. His father had died in a car accident when he was only three months old, and his stepfather was an abusive alcoholic. Clinton triumphed over all these circumstances to become a Rhodes scholar, attend Yale Law School, and in 1978 become the governor of Arkansas at thirty-two years old.

Married to Hillary Rodham Clinton, Bill Clinton was extraordinarily charismatic—six foot two, handsome, empathetic ("I feel your pain"), and a brilliant "policy wonk" with an impressive memory for details. According to Republicans, however, there was the little problem of his being "a pot-smoking, philandering, draft dodger."

Clinton's running mate was another southerner, Tennessee senator Al Gore.

**REPUBLICAN: GEORGE H. W. BUSH** By the time the election heated up in the summer of 1992, Bush's approval ratings had dropped to roughly 40 percent. Twenty-one years older than his Democratic opponent, he tried to run on his success in foreign affairs while glossing over his tax increase and the country's huge deficit, but he lacked both charisma and empathy. While Clinton "felt" the country's pain, Bush said, in his weird verbal shorthand, "Message: I care." Focus groups commissioned by the Republican National Committee found that his wife, Barbara, had higher approval ratings than the president—and his dog, Millie, wasn't far behind.

Even though Bush was told that dumping his hapless vice president, J. Danforth Quayle, would generate a net gain of as much as six points in the approval ratings, Bush refused to give the guy up.

## THE CAMPAIGN

Gossip had swirled around Clinton's womanizing for years, and it provided plenty of fodder for the campaign. Republican sleaze-meisters whispered that Clinton had fathered a child with a black woman, and rumors only worsened from there. He was a rapist. He was a sexual predator. He felt up a woman in the bathroom at his own wedding. And on and on.

The only sexual misconduct charge that stuck with Clinton in 1992 was an affair he supposedly had with a nightclub chanteuse and former Arkansas state employee named Gennifer Flowers (of whom he reportedly said, "She could suck a tennis ball through a garden hose"). Flowers revealed all in the *Star* tabloid in the winter of 1992. She claimed that their sexual relationship dated back twelve years; when Clinton denied it, Flowers held a press conference and played phone conversations she had taped with Clinton, in which they refer to each other quite cozily as "honey." In New Hampshire, the Arkansas governor was now met at every campaign stop by what his staff called "the clusterfuck"—a semicircle of reporters with microphones shouting leading questions.

Clinton worked quickly to control the damage. He appeared on the television news show *60 Minutes* with Hillary, admitted only that he caused "pain in my marriage," and managed to escape unscathed—as he would on the issues of smoking marijuana (he "didn't inhale") and draft-dodging back in the sixties ("dodge" was perhaps too strong a word, but he had avoided military service until he lucked into a high draft lottery number). No wonder Republicans dubbed him "Slick Willie." They hated him passionately and almost hysterically, the same way Democrats loathed Richard Nixon. One wealthy Republican businessman spent $40,000 at the beginning of the campaign digging for dirt that would torpedo Clinton. It did little good.

Bush had another problem, and that was the irrepressible Ross Perot. The historian Richard Hofstadter has written that American third parties are "like bees—once they have stung, they die." In 1992,

Perot put a pretty good sting on Bush.

Perot was quite a character. Born in 1930, the son of a Texarkana, Texas, cotton picker, he founded a data retrieval firm called EDS in 1962 and turned it into a billion-dollar company. Ignoring all traditional avenues of running for president, Perot announced his candidacy on the "Larry King Live" show. He called his campaign organization United We Stand America and crusaded mainly against national debt. With his squeaky drawl, jug-handle ears, and love of pie charts, he was a little like everyone's old high school math teacher. In some polls he began to lead both Clinton and Bush.

But Perot's campaign began to falter after he addressed the NAACP, during which he referred to them as "you people" and then falsely denied he knew about the case of an Orthodox Jew who had been fired from EDS for having a beard. In July, he abruptly withdrew from the race but returned in September alleging that Republican dirty tricksters had wiretapped his office and threatened to publish nude pictures of his daughter before her wedding. "There has been a ninety-day effort to redefine my personality by a group called opposition research," Perot said. "They're generally known as the dirty tricks crowd."

After Labor Day, Clinton jumped out to a thirteen-point lead in the polls. Desperate Republican strategists even sought advice from two aides to Prime Minister John Major of Great Britain, who had won despite a weak economy and poor personal ratings. (Their only suggestion: plaster pictures of Gennifer Flowers on billboards countrywide, with the words, "AND NOW HE WANTS TO SCREW THE COUNTRY, TOO.")

Bush tried in his own way to attack Clinton and the Democrats. They were "cultural elitists" and "tree huggers" and atheists (they "don't have the three letters G-O-D in their party platform"). He absurdly claimed that if Harry Truman were alive, he would vote Republican, something Truman's daughter Margaret vehemently denied. (Republicans since Ronald Reagan had adopted Truman as a plain-spoken paragon of the presidency, conveniently forgetting how viciously they had attacked him in 1948.)

Bush also proclaimed that "my dog Millie knows more about foreign affairs than those two bozos," referring to Clinton and Gore. But it was "THE ECONOMY, STUPID"—as the famous sign plastered in the Clinton–Gore "War Room" read—that Americans were really interested in.

## THE WINNER: WILLIAM JEFFERSON CLINTON

Election Day saw the largest voter turnout since 1960, with Clinton winning 44,908,254 votes to Bush's 39,102,343. Perot, running as an independent, pulled in 19 million votes, or almost 19 percent of the total. He didn't pull in any electoral votes but still managed the neat trick of hurting Bush and helping Clinton, though the latter was elected with the lowest percentage of popular vote (43 percent) since Woodrow Wilson beat Taft and Roosevelt (with 41 percent) in 1912. Who knows what would have happened had Perot not dropped out of the race in midsummer?

The forty-six-year-old Clinton, the youngest president since John F. Kennedy (his boyhood hero), was ecstatic. He could not have foreseen that his name would soon become synonymous with Kennedy for another reason: screwing in the White House.

★★★

**Oppo** Short for opposition research, "oppo" had become a separately funded part of the Republican Party by the election of 1992. The program was started by Lee Atwater, briefly chairman of the Republican National Committee, before his death in March 1991. The opposition resources center, located at the RNC headquarters in Washington, boasted a large room with state-of-the-art data-retrieval computers, a staff of some sixty people, and its own separate budget of $6 million. Operatives had developed huge files on the likes of

Mario Cuomo when it was assumed he would be Democratic candidate. They also investigated Pat Buchanan, fire-breathing conservative Republican, although it was considered not quite kosher to snoop around in the private lives of fellow Republicans. Then, of course, there was Bill Clinton.

Oppo men went all over Little Rock, Arkansas, searching for dirt on Slick Willie. They brought twenty years' worth of microfiche on Clinton from Arkansas newspapers and filled thirty file drawers with speculation on his sex life. The problem was that, after the primaries, George Bush wouldn't let them use the gossip they had gathered. Some felt he was taking the high road; others wondered if the president felt vulnerable about his own alleged adultery.

**You Spell Potato . . .** Vice President Dan Quayle was the butt of a lot of jokes. There was something so callow and ridiculous about the guy, even down to his name, J. Danforth Quayle, and the fact that, as one critic has said, "his pales eyes [look] like windows into an unfurnished room."

In 1992 Quayle picked the lack of "family values" in entertainment as his own particular issue. The music of rapper Tupac Shakur—a relatively easy target—had "no place in our society," according to Quayle. Then the VP made the mistake of going after the phenomenally popular television show *Murphy Brown*. Brown (played by actress Candace Bergen) was an anchorwoman who had decided to have a child out of wedlock. Quayle thundered that bearing a child alone "mocks the importance of fathers" and was an example of the "poverty of values" that afflicted television.

Not a smart move. Even Republicans loved to watch the show, and Quayle was weirdly acting as though this sitcom character was a real person. White House staffers decided that Quayle should change his tune and praise Murphy Brown for her courage in having the baby, rather than, say, having an abortion. Bush spared Quayle from this humiliation, and the situation died when, in early June, the vice president visited a New Jersey elementary school and corrected student William Figueroa's spelling of *potato*, claiming it was "potatoe." This new source of ridicule sent the *Murphy Brown* controversy spiraling into the old-news file.

# 1996

## WILLIAM JEFFERSON CLINTON vs. BOB DOLE

So many mini scandals plagued Bill Clinton's first term, you needed a scorecard to keep them straight. There was "Travelgate," in which several long-time workers in the White House travel office were fired for alleged improprieties and replaced with people having ties to Clinton. Then there was "Filegate," in which the White House head of security improperly requested and received FBI security clearance files on government employees; and, of course, Whitewater, a highly convoluted scandal about a Bill/Hillary Arkansas real estate deal, where no wrongdoing by the president was ever established by Kenneth Starr, the independent prosecutor assigned to investigate.

In July 1993 Clinton's close friend and deputy White House counsel Vince Foster committed suicide. Some six months later, in February 1994, Paula Corbin Jones, a low-level Arkansas state employee, sued Clinton for sexual harassment, claiming that as governor he had cornered her in a room, pulled down his pants, and asked for a blow job. ("I will never forget it as long as I live," she said. "His face was blood red, and his penis was bright red and curved.")

But according to Hillary Clinton, it was all part of a "vast right-wing conspiracy," and plenty of evidence backs up her claim, including indications that at least one conservative tycoon spent years funding efforts to discredit Clinton, to the tune of as much as $2 million.

Was there any time left to govern the country? Turns out there was. Clinton turned back the challenge of right-wing Republican congressmen by expertly moving to the center on most issues, from balancing the budget (a feat Clinton actually managed) to revamping welfare. When the time came for Clinton to run against Senator

Robert Dole in 1996, he was an incumbent at the helm of a robust economy. Translation: unbeatable, even with his satanic penis.

**THE CAMPAIGN** Kansas senator Robert Dole was a wounded World War II veteran with a dry sense of humor who, at age seventy-two, had spent thirty-five years in Congress and had been Gerald Ford's 1976 running mate. He was too moderate for the mood of the Republican Party and never quite convincingly endorsed the party's positions on abortion, crime, or state's rights. He later said of Clinton that "he was my opponent, not my enemy," a stance that did not endear him to Clinton loathers. On election night, the president took thirty-one states to Dole's nineteen, with a popular vote margin of 45,590,703 to 37,816,307. Ross Perot, running again, garnered about 8 million votes.

On January 23, 1996, a triumphant President Clinton gave an eloquent State of the Union address in which he thanked "the person who has taught me more than anyone else over twenty-five years about the importance of families and children—a wonderful wife, magnificent mother, and a great first lady. Thank you, Hillary." Clinton later inscribed an official copy of the speech to a friend: "To Monica Lewinsky, with best wishes, Bill Clinton."

SLEAZE-O-METER

2000

GEORGE W.
**BUSH**
REPUBLICAN

VS.

AL
**GORE**
DEMOCRAT

"ONLY AL GORE CAN BEAT AL GORE.
AND HE'S BEEN DOING A PRETTY GOOD JOB OF THAT."
—Green Party candidate Ralph Nader

**D** espite being impeached, but not convicted, of the crime of lying to Congress about his liaison with Monica Lewinsky, Bill Clinton left office in 2000 with a 68 percent approval rating—a score even higher than Ronald Reagan's final tally. It's not that voters approved of the president's extramarital affair or his claim that fellatio didn't constitute sex. The simple matter is that while Clinton was getting his hummer, the economy was humming, too—which left America sighing with relief.

But the Democrats faced a challenge ahead. Their new candidate was likely to be Vice President Al Gore, who, while undoubtedly smart and honest, lacked Clinton's charisma and political legerdemain. Just as Lee Atwater decided to make Willie Horton Michael Dukakis's 1988 running mate, Republican strategists tried to saddle Al Gore with the hulking shadow of his libidinous president.

First, though, the GOP had to pick a candidate. Big Republican money fell in behind George W. Bush, son of George H. W. Bush and the governor of Texas. With the help of his longtime top manager Karl Rove, Bush set out to win the primaries but ran into a roadblock in the form of Arizona senator John McCain, a former Vietnam POW who took New Hampshire by a 60-to-40 margin over Bush. The moderate McCain captured the votes of Independents and even some Democrats wearied by Clinton's behavior. Conservative Republicans were worried.

But Bush's men were waiting for McCain in the South Carolina primary, where they dragged out the sleazy old practice of push-polling. Voters in the state were asked: "Would you be more or less likely to vote for John McCain if you knew he had fathered an illegitimate black child?" (McCain and his wife had adopted a Bangladeshi girl.) This technique, which had the fingerprints of Karl Rove all over it, helped derail McCain; he lost in South Carolina, and Bush went on to capture the nomination.

On the Democratic side, Gore had little problem beating his strongest opponent, former New Jersey senator Bill Bradley, to take the nomination. But two third-party challenges would have serious consequences for Gore down the line: activist Ralph Nader, running as a Green Party candidate, and conservative Pat Buchanan, the Reform Party nominee.

## THE CANDIDATES

**REPUBLICAN: GEORGE W. BUSH** In 2000 George W. Bush—or "Dubya," as he is affectionately known—was fifty-four years old. Born into a wealthy Republican family (Bush's grandfather Prescott was a U.S senator, and of course his father, George H. W., had served as president of the United States), Bush attended Exeter and Yale and received his MBA from Harvard. A real New England Yank. But Bush is forever associated with Texas; it was there that he unsuccessfully ran an oil company, unsuccessfully ran for Congress, and partied very successfully. But in 1986, under the influence of the evangelist Billy Graham, Bush gave up drinking and became a born-again Christian, although he never relinquished his warm, fraternal, back-slapping manner, something that endeared him even to those who disagreed with his policies. In 1994 Bush beat Ann Richards to become governor of Texas, and in 2000 he was perfectly situated to seek the presidency. His vice-presidential candidate was Dick Cheney, his father's very conservative secretary of defense.

**DEMOCRAT: AL GORE** Al Gore also hailed from privileged political bloodlines. His father was senator from Tennessee; Gore attended elite private schools and, later, Harvard. A political junkie, he was fascinated by the electoral process and the history of government but could sometimes come across as stiff, intellectual, and a trifle arrogant, even to friends. The causes he espoused would qualify him for the tag "tree-hugger" in any Republican playbook, including the fight against global warming and a push to pass the Kyoto Protocol, which called for a reduction in greenhouse gas emissions.

Gore's running mate was Senator Joe Lieberman of Connecticut, a religious conservative Democrat and the first person of Jewish faith to run on a presidential ticket (if you don't count Barry Goldwater, whose father was Jewish).

## THE CAMPAIGN

Almost from the beginning, the race was neck and neck—but at first glance, it's a little hard to understand why. Gore could lay claim to being a part of an administration that had brought violent crime to a thirty-year low, balanced the budget, created a surplus, and in general kept the country in peace and prosperity. The big problem was Bill Clinton. Gore had been aghast at the president's White House "sex-capades" and probably felt it was necessary to distance himself—but in doing so, he distanced himself from the genuine accomplishments of the Clinton administration. Even Karl Rove later said that if Gore had paid more attention to the great shape the country was in, "we [the Republicans] should have gotten our brains beaten out."

Bush's strategists positioned their guy as a man who was out to bring back a sense of decency to America ("there's no question the president embarrassed the nation," Bush told journalists). Bush also became a "compassionate conservative" out to "reform" Medicare and Social Security and fix the environment, just like Al Gore—all of which made more than a few Democrats remember John McCain's remark about Bush during the primaries: "If he's a reformer, I'm an astronaut."

When they realized that Clinton-era scandals were not rubbing off on Gore as well as might be hoped, Bush strategists turned to portraying the vice president as a two-faced liar. They managed to do so quite successfully, creating controversy over most of Gore's political positions, including putting forth the widely accepted (but false) claim that Gore said he had invented the Internet. (What he actually said in a 1999 interview was, "During my service in the United States Congress, I took the initiative in creating the Internet." Okay, a bit of an exaggeration. But, according to some people involved in developing the technology, Senator Gore was instrumental in approving research funds for the "Information Superhighway," which helped transform it from a military communication system into a worldwide networking and information channel.)

The vice president didn't help his own cause by smirking and rolling his eyes during his first debate with Bush, which made it seem as if he were ridiculing his opponent (Ronald Reagan could get away with "There you go again!" but not the far-less-magnetic Gore).

Democratic strategists were hard at work, too. They resurrected Bush's 1976 bust for driving under the influence in Maine (Bush had gotten off with a $150 fine). And if Gore was a liar, well, Bush was an idiot, a sort of chuckling fool. Bush had once told reporters that his favorite book was the kid's classic *The Very Hungry Caterpillar*. He claimed that Democrats wanted "the federal government controlling Social Security like it's some kind of federal program!" He also said things like "Families is where our nation finds hope, where wings take dreams."

## THE WINNER (EVENTUALLY): GEORGE W. BUSH

Only some 50 percent of eligible voters turned out on Election Day 2000—November 7, a day that shall live in confusion. By late in the evening, it was clear that Al Gore would win the popular vote (the official tally would be Gore 50,996,582, Bush 50,456,062). The election was close, the difference being a half million votes, roughly the same margin by which Nixon beat Humphrey in 1968 and not even as close as Kennedy's edge over Nixon in 1960.

The problem, from Gore's point of view, was that pesky Electoral College. To win the 2000 election, a candidate needed at least 270 electoral votes. Not counting the state of Florida's 25 electoral votes, Gore was assured 267 votes, Bush 246. Whichever way Florida went, so went the presidential election.

About 7:50 p.m. EST on election night, major networks, relying on exit polls, announced that the state of Florida (whose governor was George Bush's younger brother, Jeb) had voted for Gore. (Some Republicans later said that calling the election ten minutes before polls closed in Florida kept Bush supporters at home, but there is little evidence of that.) By ten o'clock, Gore, in Nashville, thought he had won the presidency when New Mexico, Minnesota, and Michigan fell into line.

But gradually, as more returns from Florida came in, the situation changed. At 2 a.m., with 97 percent of the votes in, it appeared that Bush had won in Florida. Gore then made a serious tactical mistake. Anxious to seem statesmanlike and gracious, he called Bush, who was in Texas, and conceded the election. Then he made his way to Nashville's War Memorial Plaza, where he planned to make his concession speech and thank Democratic workers.

Just as he was about to give the speech, news came from frantic campaign staffers that Florida was too close to call—Bush's margin had narrowed considerably. Gore immediately telephoned Bush and, as the latter put it ruefully, "unconceded."

The following conversation is priceless because it proves that even big candidates sometimes act like squabbling teenagers. Insiders on both sides explain that it went something like this:

Gore: *"Circumstances have changed dramatically. The state of Florida is too close to call."*
Bush: *"Let me make sure I understand. You're calling me back to retract that concession?"*

Gore: *"You don't have to be snippy about it."*
*(Bush then explains that his brother, Florida governor Jeb Bush, has assured him of victory.)*
Gore: *"Let me explain something. Your little brother is not the ultimate authority on this."*
Bush: *"You do what you have to do."*

And the election after the election was on. For thirty-six days, no one knew who the next president would be.

★★★

**Republicans vs. Democrats** In Florida, automatic machine recounts are mandated by law when elections are as close as the Bush–Gore contest. Going into the recount, Bush led by 1,784 votes out of 5.9 million cast. Two days later, after the machine recount, his lead had shrunk to fewer than 300 votes. Democrats then cherry-picked three predominantly Democratic counties—Miami-Dade, Palm Beach, and Broward—and asked for a hand recounting of votes, which was allowed under Florida law.

Republicans argued that of course Gore was going to pick up Democratic votes in these three counties—in all elections, in all states, a few errors are made here and there. No doubt some errors were made in Republican favor in the extremely close contest in New Mexico (which had gone to Gore). Why not pick through votes there?

Bush followers, led by the extremely savvy James Baker, former secretary of state under George H. W. Bush and five-time Republican presidential campaign manager, claimed that the election was over. Bush was the winner, and Gore was the pretender to the throne. The election needed to be certified and done with.

**Overvotes, Undervotes, and Chads** Democrats, led by former Secretary of State Warren Christopher, pointed out that this was no ordinary case of a few ballots gone missing. The Votomatic system—in which voters punch out a hole on a paper ballot with a stylus to record their choice and then insert the ballot into a machine—was rife with problems.

In Palm Beach County, the two-page butterfly ballot (which looked like an opened book) was so poorly designed that more than 3,000 of the predominantly elderly, Jewish population had mistakenly punched the hole for ultraconservative Reform Party candidate Pat Buchanan, giving him 2,700 votes more than he won in any other Florida county. (Even Buchanan said that most of these votes were probably cast not for him, but for Gore.) Some voters saw their mistake and punched more than one hole to try to vote for Gore. These were known as overvotes.

There was not necessarily a lot anyone could do about the butterfly ballot errors—the ballot had been designed by a Democrat and approved by both parties ahead of time. But, in other counties, some ballots were only partially punched, leaving a hanging piece of paper (called a chad), which caused the vote not to be counted. This was known as an undervote. There were also ad nauseam "dimpled" or "pregnant" chads, which were still completely attached to the ballot on all four sides and corners, but bulged slightly in the middle, rendering those votes invalid.

In all, Democrats estimated, there were as many as 61,000 disputed undervotes. These had simply not been counted as votes cast, and they needed to be. For it was a matter of law in Florida that a voter's intent to vote be taken into consideration when recounting ballots, even if said voter made a procedural or mechanical mistake (that is, not punching the ballot fully) in casting a vote.

Hence, Democrats said, the hand recount was needed. But Florida Secretary of State Katherine Harris, a co-chair of the Bush campaign in the state, refused to allow the recounts—intent on certifying the election and moving forward. On November 21, the Florida Supreme Court voted to force Harris to let the recount proceed, approving manual recounts in the three Florida counties chosen by the Democrats. The hand count went on, but Republicans sent activists to demonstrate (many of them congressional aides flown to Florida). In Dade County, these "preppy protestors" were so militant that they managed to delay the counting, frightening the exhausted and overwhelmed poll workers.

When the deadline set by the Florida Supreme Court came and went without all votes being counted, Harris immediately declared Bush the Florida winner by 537 votes. But Democrats got another Florida Supreme Court decision not only to reopen the Dade County hand counting but also to hand count ballots for which no choice was recorded for president in all sixty-seven counties in Florida.

**And the Winner Is . . .** Republican lawyers appealed to the U.S. Supreme Court to hear their case, which the court agreed to do on December 1. In oral arguments, Bush's lawyers claimed that hand counting must be stopped because it failed to provide Bush equal protection under the law—the votes had already been counted, had been recounted automatically as per law, and the Democrats did not have a right to a hand count. Democrats replied that it was quite odd that the Republicans, fierce state's rights champions, should ask the court to intervene in what should essentially be an issue for the state of Florida to decide.

On December 9, the U.S. Supreme Court ordered a stay of the recount. The decision was made by a sharply divided court, with five conservative justices triumphing over four moderate ones. On Monday December 11, the Court heard arguments in *Bush v. Gore*. On December 12 they refused to allow the manual recounting to go forward, thus effectively handing the presidential election to Bush.

**How Dirty Was It?** Bush had lost the popular vote but won in the Electoral College 271 to 266, thus becoming president. Historians turned to 1888 to find the last time that a presidential candidate—Benjamin Harrison—lost the popular vote but won in the Electoral College.

If anything, the 2000 election most closely resembles the Rutherford Hayes vs. Samuel Tilden contest of 1876, which Tilden almost certainly won but had the election stolen from him by Republican "returning boards" in Louisiana, South Carolina, and, yes, Florida. The election was so dirty that Hayes never really recovered and became a one-term president.

In some ways, Republican efforts in Florida were not as sleazy as they have been made out to be. Roadblocks were not put up to keep blacks from voting, as has been reported. But no Republican official in Florida, entrusted with the votes of an entire state, acted in anything other than a partisan manner.

Had the tables been turned, had Democrats controlled the state, would they have acted in a less partisan fashion? No one knows. But other factors that helped Gore lose the election could not be blamed on the Republicans:

Had Gore been able to win his home state of Tennessee, which he did not, the whole Florida issue would have been moot.

Had Ralph Nader or even Pat Buchanan not run third-party challenges, Gore would have won.

Had Bill Clinton not acted as he did while in the White House (or had Gore decided to allow the still-popular president to campaign for him), Gore would probably have won.

And if Gore and his forces had decided to fight as dirty as Bush's forces did in Florida, they might have won. But from the moment of his too-early concession, Al Gore acted like a gracious loser rather than a tough-minded winner. A self-fulfilling prophesy, as it turned out.

**You Low-Down Dirty Rat!** One day during the summer of 2000, a Gore volunteer was watching a Republican ad attacking Gore's prescription drug plan when he saw the word "RATS" flash across the screen. He reported it to Gore campaign officials, who played the ad slowly and also noticed the word, written in big white capital letters, followed by the phrase "BUREAUCRATS DECIDE."

Was this an example of the so-called subliminal advertising that had first been tried in the 1950s, the art of hiding secret messages in television commercials? The FCC, while not specifically forbidding this type of advertising, does consider it deceptive.

Democratic Party operatives managed to make the story a cause célèbre. The Republican ad man who created the spot claimed, somewhat lamely, that he had merely flashed RATS because it was the last part of BUREAUCRATS, and wanted to make "a visual drumbeat. . . You want to get [viewers] interested and involved."

Bush, appearing on *Good Morning, America*, claimed that "rats" was meant to be seen—although most watchers did not notice it unless they were warned ahead of time—and further made the whole thing laughable by repeatedly mispronouncing the word "subliminal" as "subliminable."

The Republican National Committee yanked the ad, but it had already run more than four thousand times in different markets across the country.

SLEAZE-O-METER

**2004**

GEORGE W.
# BUSH
REPUBLICAN

VS.

JOHN
# KERRY
DEMOCRAT

"OUR ENEMIES ARE INNOVATIVE AND RESOURCEFUL, AND SO
ARE WE. THEY NEVER STOP THINKING ABOUT NEW WAYS TO
HARM OUR COUNTRY AND OUR PEOPLE, AND NEITHER DO WE!"
—President George W. Bush, in a 2004 campaign speech

Four years after the election of 2000, the mood of America had changed dramatically. The sexual scandals of the Clinton years now seemed like the hijinks of a bygone generation, as dated as raccoon coats or hippie headbands. In their place was the somber fact of September 11, 2001, when al-Qaeda terrorists flew planes into the World Trade Center and the Pentagon and crashed another plane, intended for the White House, into the ground in Pennsylvania. Three thousand Americans lost their lives.

Bush, who had been limping along, now enjoyed approval ratings into the ninetieth percentile, as high as those of his father after the first Gulf War. With broad bipartisan support, the president invaded Afghanistan and retook it from the Taliban, although American forces failed to capture Osama bin Laden, the mastermind of the 9/11 attacks. The president's approval ratings remained high even after he invaded Iraq in 2003—his rationale being that dictator Saddam Hussein supported al-Qaeda and possessed weapons of mass destruction that threatened the world.

The only problem was that neither of these allegations was true. As the insurgency took hold in Iraq and more and more U.S. soldiers died, Americans at home began to question Bush's judgment. And it didn't help any—it never does—that the stock market and economy were in a post-dot-com nosedive.

As 2004 approached, however, the Republican Party was firmly behind George Bush, to the tune of an $86 million campaign purse even before the primaries—where Bush ran practically unopposed—began.

The Democratic primaries were a different matter, a rough-and-tumble affair. Al Gore had announced in 2002 that he would not be seeking office, which left the field open to the likes of retired general Wesley Clark, Massachusetts Senator John Kerry, former North Carolina senator and trial lawyer John Edwards, and Vermont governor Howard Dean. Dean ran a grassroots campaign based on his early opposition to the Iraq war and support of new health-care initiatives in America. But Dean self-destructed in the Iowa caucus in January 2004, coming in third and essentially ending his campaign with a guttural primal yell that became known as the "Dean Scream." Senator John Kerry rolled to the nomination of his party.

## THE CANDIDATES

**REPUBLICAN: GEORGE W. BUSH** As progress in Iraq headed south, so did the presidency of George W. Bush. His manic performance shortly after the initial phase of the war ended—landing on a U.S. aircraft carrier wearing a full flight suit and making a triumphant speech in front of a banner that read, "MISSION ACCOMPLISHED"—was beginning to look more and more ludicrous as the fighting intensified. When it turned out that weapons of mass destruction were missing from Iraq, and the U.S. economy continued its dismal slide, the Bush presidency seemed to be in deep trouble.

**DEMOCRAT: JOHN KERRY** The Democratic candidate began his nomination speech at the national convention with the words: "I'm John Kerry, and I'm reporting for duty." This was no casual phrasing, for Democrats had recruited their first war hero candidate since George McGovern, another vocal opponent of an unpopular war. Raised in an upper-middle-class family in Massachusetts, Kerry attended Yale in the 1960s and then—an unusual choice at the time for someone of his age and background—enlisted in the navy and served two tours as a Swift boat skipper in Vietnam, where he earned a Silver Star, a Bronze Star, and three Purple Hearts.

Kerry was a bit wooden and at times even seemed a little detached. His handlers did their best to present him as a plain-spoken regular guy who loved ice hockey and hunting. But a great deal of Kerry's media attention was devoted to his wife, Teresa Heinz Kerry, the heir to the Heinz ketchup fortune. According to *Forbes* magazine, she was worth about $750 million.

## THE CAMPAIGN

As the fall of 2004 began, political signs began disappearing all over America. One night, you'd plant a candidate's sign in your front yard and by the next morning, poof! It had vanished. In one Pennsylvania town, nearly five hundred Bush/Cheney yard signs were ripped off. Hundreds of Kerry/Edwards signs were taken in Pensacola, Florida, where Kerry supporters responded by hanging Bush signs from tree limbs. There were also thefts in South Dakota, Wisconsin, Washington, Kentucky, Ohio, Colorado, Michigan, and Oregon.

One presidential historian wrote that whenever signs start to disappear, it's an indication of a divided and polarized country engaged in a tough, no-holds-barred election. That certainly describes the 2004 presidential battle. It raged 24/7 via Internet, cable news shows, talk radio, and newspapers. The Democrats were out to win back the presidency from a man they felt had stolen his seat and brought the country into a dangerous and unnecessary war. The Republicans were just as certain that Democrats would make a peace without honor in Iraq, leaving America open to more attacks like 9/11.

Senator John Kerry was supposed to blunt the quadrennial Republican smear that Democrats were not tough enough to face foreign enemies. Even before the campaign began, Kerry had the military bona fides to be able to criticize the president, saying he wasn't aggressive enough in using armed forces to capture Osama bin Laden. Senator Kerry had voted for the use of force in Iraq but later voted against $87 billion of additional military aid to the war effort; Bush's team seized on these facts and tried to brand Kerry as a "flip-flopper." (They were helped immensely when Kerry, trying to defend his position, said, "I actually did vote for the $87 billion before

I voted against it.")

Bush, in the meantime, ran as a tough guy, the man who told the terrorists, "Bring it on!" He refused to admit to any mistakes. As he said: "You may not always agree with me, but you'll always know where I stand."

Dirty tricks on a fairly minor level began as Kerry was alleged to have had an affair with a young woman (who denied the story). A picture widely circulated on the Internet showed a young Kerry and the actress Jane Fonda speaking together at a Vietnam War–era rally, except the photograph was a fake. For their part, Democrats sent out scare e-mails claiming that, if reelected, Bush would institute a military draft.

Kerry and Bush were running almost in a dead heat as Bush's approval rating sank to under 50 percent, the result of new setbacks in Iran. But on August 4, a self-styled "independent" group called Swift Boat Veterans for Truth, composed of some of the men who had served on the rivers of Vietnam with Kerry, announced that Kerry "was lying about his [military] record" and that he was "no war hero."

It's hard to understate the importance of the Swifties in the 2004 campaign. They thoroughly muddled the public perception of Kerry's military service and shifted focus away from the important campaign issues. The *Washington Post* published an article showing that one of Kerry's main Swift boat accusers had in fact supported Kerry's account of his wartime service, and Kerry was able to turn back the attacks with some force. But he'd spent two weeks of prime campaign time defending himself, and many undecided voters were now unsure what to believe.

Still, Kerry was able to best Bush in two debates. As the race headed for election night, there were predictions that the challenger might pull things off after all.

# THE WINNER: GEORGE W. BUSH

Exit polls agreed that Kerry had a fighting chance. Americans watching the networks during the evening of November 2 saw and heard commentators unanimously quoting exit polls that Kerry would be elected president.

Yet by midnight, Bush was shown as winning decisively, and Kerry conceded the next morning. The official tally was Bush 60,693,281, Kerry 57,355,978, with the incumbent winning in the Electoral College 286 to 251. It was not a huge margin of victory—a little more than 2 percent—but certainly the election was not anywhere near as close as 2000.

★★★

**Battleground Ohio** Ultimately the 2004 presidential election came down to the state of Ohio, which George Bush won by a margin of 118,601, giving him the state's twenty electoral votes and victory.

But reports of election irregularities began streaming out of the state even before the polls had closed. Representative John Conyers Jr., the ranking Democrat on the House Judiciary Committee (an original member of Nixon's Enemies List), performed the investigation. In his report to Congress in January 2005, he outlined "numerous, serious election irregularities in the Ohio presidential election, which resulted in a significant disenfranchisement of voters." To wit:

Early in September, two months before the election, Ohio Secretary of State J. Kenneth Blackwell, who—like Katherine Harris in Florida in 2000, was cochair of his state's Bush–Cheney reelection effort—used an outdated regulation to restrict voter registration. He claimed that the paper registrations needed to be printed on 80-pound unwaxed white paper (postcard paper). This might make sense for registrations through the mail, but Blackwell insisted that the regulation covered those delivered in person as well, and also that all registrations on different paper were retroactively invalid. According to the nonpartisan Greater Cleveland Voting Coalition, at least 15,000 voters lost their ability to vote as a result.

Among other things, according to Conyers, Republicans engaged in a deceptive direct-mail practice called "caging" to trim Democratic voters off the rolls. In the summer of 2004 the GOP, using ZIP codes, sent registered letters to 200,000 newly registered voters in urban areas more likely to vote for Kerry. Thirty-five thousand people who had refused to sign the letters or whose mail came back marked "undeliverable" were knocked off the voter rolls just two weeks before the election.

Some voters were forced to wait in line for more than twelve hours. Yet there were no long lines in Republican areas. In one county alone, the misallocation of machines reduced the number of votes by an estimated 15,000. Statewide, according to Conyers, African Americans waited an average of fifty-two minutes to vote, compared to eighteen for white Americans.

**Muzzling Teresa** Teresa Heinz Kerry, John Kerry's fabulously wealthy wife, was not what anyone would call the ideal campaign spouse. Unlike Laura Bush, whom the president's handlers trotted out at almost every turn, Teresa was not Mrs. All-American.

Born in Mozambique, Heinz moved to New York to work as a translator at the United Nations. In 1966 she met and married Senator John Heinz III, heir to the ketchup fortune. After Heinz died in an airplane crash in 1991, his widow inherited his vast fortune. She married Kerry in 1995 as a registered Republican, and she remained Republican until her husband ran for president.

While on the campaign trail, Heinz Kerry was often erratic and sullen. She once told a reporter to "shove it" and remarked that Laura Bush had never had "a real job." The biggest controversy took place behind the scenes at the Democratic convention. After Kerry gave his speech, tradition dictated that he be joined by his vice-presidential running mate. Instead, Heinz Kerry insisted that she go first. "I am the spouse," she said. "I go first." There was no dissuading her verbally, so as Kerry finished his speech, a young campaign aide blocked her with both arms and yelled at John Edwards: "Run!"

**Bulgegate** During Bush's first debate with Kerry, many viewers noticed a "bulge" underneath his suit jacket at about the center of his back. It set off much speculation. Some thought it might be a radio receiver. After all, Bush would often give long pauses before answering questions and once said, "Let me finish!" when no one had said anything to him. After the debates, a NASA scientist enhanced images of the area in question and expressed the opinion that what the president was wearing was indeed a receiver.

Others speculated that the bulge was either a bulletproof vest or, possibly, a cardiac defibrillator that Bush was forced to wear after he choked on a pretzel while watching a football game in January 2002. For the record, the White House claimed the bulge was "a wrinkle in the fabric."

SLEAZE-O-METER

**2008**

★

BARACK
# OBAMA
DEMOCRAT

**VS.**

JOHN
# MCCAIN
REPUBLICAN

★

"AS PUTIN REARS HIS HEAD AND COMES INTO THE AIR SPACE
OF THE UNITED STATES OF AMERICA, WHERE—WHERE DO
THEY GO? IT'S ALASKA. IT'S JUST RIGHT OVER THE BORDER."
—Republican vice-presidential candidate Sarah Palin,
explaining to CBS's Katie Couric why Alaska's proximity to Russia
gave her foreign policy experience

**P**olitical experts knew the election of 2008 would be unprecedented. To begin with, it was the first time in more than half a century (since the second Truman administration) that neither a sitting president nor his vice president was seeking reelection. That was because George W. Bush was a two-term lame duck and vice president Dick Cheney's health problems (not to mention his popular reputation akin to that of, say, Darth Vader) rendered him unable to serve. Furthermore, the Democrats' chief hope lay in a woman—two-term New York senator Hillary Clinton—who had put together a fat campaign purse and a formidable political machine (not the least of her assets was her husband, popular ex-president Bill Clinton). She was the first First Lady to run for president and the first woman to be considered the favored front-runner heading into a presidential campaign. But as the long election season kicked off in early 2007, there were other serious Democratic candidates vying for attention. The wealthy lawyer John Edwards, running mate of John Kerry in 2004, had announced his candidacy even before the end of 2006. And then there was the junior senator from Illinois, Barack Obama, who had delivered the sensational keynote address at the Democratic National Convention in 2004. Joe Biden, a malaprop-prone senator from Delaware also running for president, called him "the first mainstream African American who is articulate and bright and clean" and then immediately "deeply regretted" his remarks.

Meanwhile, the Republicans produced candidates like Rudy Giuliani, former mayor of New York; Mitt Romney, former governor of Massachusetts; and Arizona senator (and war hero) John McCain. But early front-runner Giuliani sank under rumors and gossip surrounding his three marriages (one of them to his first cousin). And

Mitt Romney never overcame the fact that, as one writer put it, he "came off as a phony even when he was perfectly sincere." This left McCain, rehabilitated after his lynching by Bush forces in the 2000 primary. McCain secured the nomination easily, despite (or because of) such gaffes as singing "Bomb, bomb, bomb, bomb, bomb Iran" to the tune of the Beach Boys' classic "Barbara Ann" during a campaign stop in South Carolina.

The Democrats would experience the most protracted and hard-fought primary battle of their party's history. In the Iowa caucus, Hillary Clinton placed third behind Barack Obama and John Edwards (the latter not yet been derailed by charges that he had sired a love child with a videographer hired by his campaign). Hillary fought back to win the New Hampshire primary by two points. After February 5—a.k.a. Super Tuesday, when 23 states held their primaries—Hillary and Obama ended up in a virtual tie and things started to get nasty. The Clinton campaign released a commercial that showed children sleeping peacefully while an ominous voice-over narrator asked, "There's a phone in the White House and it's ringing. Who do you want answering the phone?" It was a scare tactic that harkened back to 1964's Lyndon Johnson–Barry Goldwater smearfest. For his part, Obama was pilloried for telling an increasingly dour Hillary during one debate that she was "likeable enough." The primary fight was a divisive one, with old-line Democrats rallying behind Hillary Clinton (except for a few major Democratic powers like Senator Teddy Kennedy and New Mexico governor Bill Richardson, the latter of whom was called a "Judas" by Democratic activist James Carville) while, younger Democrats and African Americans lined up behind Obama as a candidate of change. By June of 2008, the exhausting primary battle—which Obama likened to "a great movie that's gone on about half an hour too long"—was settled. Barack Obama had become the first African American to receive a major party's nomination for president of the United States. He would face John McCain in what promised to be a long and bruising campaign.

# THE CANDIDATES

**DEMOCRAT: BARACK OBAMA** Barack Hussein Obama was one of the most unlikely presidential candidates in United States history—and not just because his name echoed two of American's sworn enemies, Saddam Hussein and Osama bin Laden. With a father from Kenya and a mother from Kansas, Obama was born in Hawaii and raised partly in Indonesia. He had brushes with drugs (marijuana and cocaine) before heading off to Occidental College in California, followed by Columbia University and eventually Harvard Law School, where he became the first African American president of the *Harvard Law Review*. A career as a community organizer in Chicago was followed by one as a civil rights attorney, Illinois state senator, and, finally, in 2004, United States senator. Obama was smooth, hip, and capable of seeming both cerebral and passionate—but he was a cipher to many Americans, some of whom found his mixed parentage and exotic childhood threatening. For his running mate he chose Joe Biden, even though many Democrats wanted Hillary Clinton in the vice-presidential slot. As Biden himself said, in his inimitable way: "Hillary Clinton is as qualified or more qualified than I am to be vice president of the United States of America. Quite frankly, [she] might have been a better pick."

**REPUBLICAN: JOHN MCCAIN** Born in the Panama Canal Zone in 1936 (making this the first presidential campaign in which both major party candidates were born outside of the continental United States), Senator John McCain was seventy-two years old in 2008, twenty-five years older than his opponent. His journey to the nomination was as traditional as Obama's was untraditional. McCain was the son and grandson of four-star Navy admirals, a wild young man who graduated near the bottom of his class at the Naval Academy before being assigned as a Skyhawk pilot flying missions over North Vietnam. He was shot down over Hanoi in 1967 and spent five and a half years in the infamous Hanoi Hilton prison, where his captors savagely torturcd him. After being released in 1973 with permanent physical damage—he was unable to lift his arms above his head—he eventually embarked on a career in politics as a Republican congressman from Arizona. He won the former Senate seat of Barry Goldwater in 1986 and soon became a national figure—a quick-tongued, mercurial, self-styled "maverick" who was perhaps a little further to the left than his party's right-wing base would have liked, but who polled well with moderates and independents. He survived some of the nastiest politicking in the modern history of campaigning—George W. Bush and Karl Rove's sleazy attacks on his character and morals in the South Carolina primary of 2000—but as the 2008 campaign reached its zenith, the question became: Would he survive his choice of a running mate, Alaska governor Sarah Palin, the most controversial vice-presidential pick in American history?

## THE CAMPAIGN

As with many other presidential campaigns—Clinton vs. Bush, Kennedy vs. Nixon—the 2008 campaign became a contest of experience (McCain) versus change (Obama). McCain's biggest disadvantage was his affiliation, as a Republican, with the highly unpopular sitting president, George W. Bush, a man whose 90 percent approval rating after the terrorist attacks of 9/11 had been squandered on such disasters as the protracted war in Iraq, his administration's lackluster post-Hurricane Katrina response, and a seriously tanking economy. Although Bush endorsed John McCain, he did not make a single campaign appearance for the Republican candidate, and only appeared at the September Republican Convention via video broadcast. McCain walked a tightrope between supporting the man who was, after all, his commander in chief—when a questioner at a town hall meeting asked him if he supported Bush's stated goal of keeping troops in Iraq for fifty years, he blustered: "Make it a hundred ... that would be fine with me"—and criticizing the president's policies. It didn't help any that the Democrats released pictures of a 2004 campaign appearance in which Bush embraced and kissed McCain, who leaned his head bashfully on the president's shoulder. What kind of "maverick" cozied up with a man whose operatives had once portrayed his wife, Cindy, as a drug addict?

In the meantime, Barack Obama faced his own problems. His longtime pastor was the fiery Reverend Jeremiah Wright, whose videotaped sermons reaped a bounty for Republican opposition researchers. Shortly after 9/11, Wright was captured on tape lecturing parishioners at his Trinity United Church in Chicago: "We bombed Hiroshima. We bombed Nagasaki. And we nuked far more than the thousands in New York and the Pentagon. . . . America's chickens are coming home to roost!" This played into the fears of some Americans that Barack Obama was a dangerous radical, fears that were heightened when Republicans linked Obama to Bill Ayers, a former member of the radical Weather Underground of the 1960s who, like Obama, had become a Chicago political activist. Although Obama refuted any close relationship between the two men—Ayers, he said, was merely "a guy . . . who engaged in detestable acts forty years ago, when I was eight years old"—many felt that Obama was a bit too left of center. He furthered this impression by telling a crowd in San Francisco that small-town Americans "cling to guns or religion or antipathy to people who aren't like them or anti-immigrant sentiment or antitrade sentiment as a way to explain their frustrations."

Heading into September 2008, both candidates had a chance at victory, but then McCain suffered twin disasters. The first was his choice of a running mate. Seeking to inject a shot of youth serum into his tired campaign—and to counter Obama's glam factor—he chose Alaska governor Sarah Palin as his vice-presidential partner. At first glance, the forty-four-year-old Palin seemed an inspired choice. Plainspoken, independent, and photogenic, she became the first Republican woman candidate for vice president. Her one-liners were soon the talk of America—she told a cheering crowd at the Republican National Convention that the difference between a hockey mom and a pit bull was "lipstick"—but it quickly became apparent that she was not yet ready for prime time. During the campaign, she was forced to reveal that her sixteen-year-old daughter, Bristol, was pregnant and that $150,000 in campaign contributions had been spent on Palin's wardrobe—both facts at odds with Palin's image as a straight-shooting, unfussy, family-values-oriented Alaskan. A disastrous interview with Katie Couric, in which Palin could not remember the name of even one periodical she read regularly, prompted many Americans to wonder if she should be a heartbeat away from the presidency.

Even worse for McCain, however, was the massive financial crisis that began in September, when the U.S. housing market bubble burst, financial institutions (including Lehman Brothers) collapsed, and the stock market began an accelerated decline. McCain's announcement that he was going to "set politics aside" to deal with the crisis (which reached its apex only two days before McCain's first nationally televised debate with Barack Obama) was widely considered a political publicity stunt. McCain made matters worse when he told an interviewer "the fundamentals of our economy are strong," even as President Bush was telling congressmen that "this sucker could go down."

It was all over but the whining. Barack Obama shot to a commanding lead in the polls, one that he would not relinquish.

## THE WINNER: BARACK OBAMA

Such is the nature of voting in the twenty-first century that by November 4, 2008, Election Day, 31 percent of the electorate had taken part in "early voting," an increase of almost 10 percent over 2004. In all, it was a good day for American democracy, as 131.3 million ballots were cast for president. Of those eligible to vote, 61.7 percent actually turned out, the highest percentage since the Goldwater-Johnson slugfest of 1964. The election was closely monitored for the polling irregularities that had plagued Ohio during the 2004 contest, but nothing significant turned up.

The winner, hands down, was Barack Obama. He beat John McCain by nearly 10 million votes, 69,456,897 to 59,934,814, earning 53 percent of popular vote—the most of any Democratic president since Lyndon Johnson—and winning in the Electoral College 375 to 163. Shortly after midnight on November 5, Barack Obama delivered his acceptance speech in Grant Park, in Chicago, before an audience estimated at 240,000 people, with millions more watching across the world. He was to be America's first African American president and he told the crowd, "It's been a long time coming ... but change has come to America."

★★★

**The Real Barack Obama?** By mid-October, Obama had taken a commanding lead in the polls over John McCain and many Republican voters were growing desperate. When John McCain and Sarah Palin went out stumping, they were met with Obama-hating crowds carrying signs that read "Treason!" Some people shouted "No Communists!" One man stood up at a McCain rally in Wisconsin and yelled: "It's not the economy. It's the socialists taking over the country.... When you have an Obama, [Speaker of the House Nancy] Pelosi and the rest of the hooligans up there [who are] gonna run this country, we've got to have our heads examined." After one woman in Minnesota referred to Obama as an Arab, McCain finally demurred: "No, ma'am, he's a decent family man." But his campaign was, at least in part, responsible for fomenting this type of anger. Earlier, Sarah Palin, in a script written for her by the McCain campaign, said of the Democratic candidate, "This is not a man who sees America as you and I do—as the greatest force for good in the world. This is someone who sees America as imperfect enough to pal around with terrorists [referencing former Weather Underground member Bill Ayers] who targeted their own country."

In the meantime, playing on fears that Obama was not what he appeared to be, McCain asked at campaign stops, "Who is the real Barack Obama?" Rumors swept through the Republican base that Obama had really been born in Kenya, not Hawaii, and so could not be president. People claimed that he had attended Muslim terrorist schools in Indonesia and that, now, as a secret Muslim, he intended to burrow into the infrastructure of American democracy and wreak havoc. (In fact, Obama had attended a public school in Indonesia and had not received Muslim religious training.) There were also those who said that Obama, if elected, would insist on being sworn in on a Koran instead of a Bible. And so on. In the end, these rumors did not keep Barack Obama from being elected, but they would follow him into his presidency.

**World's Biggest Celeb** Members of the McCain campaign felt that Obama's "elitist" image was a major political liability, so on July 30 they released a television spot to exploit this weakness. Called "Celeb," the attack ad featured pictures of Paris Hilton and Britney Spears intercut with shots of Obama waving to cheering crowds. "He's the biggest celebrity in the world," a female narrator whispered, "but is he ready to lead?" Accompanying the release of the ad was an e-mail to reporters from Rick Davis, McCain's campaign manager: "Only celebrities like Barack Obama go to the gym three times a day, demand 'MET-Rx chocolate roasted-peanut protein bars and bottles of a hard-to-find organic brew—Black Forest Berry Honest Tea' and worry about the price of arugula."

The ad was effective but the Obama team quickly struck back. On the day "Celeb" was released, Obama told a crowd in Missouri, "Nobody really thinks that Bush or McCain have a real answer to the challenges we face, so what they're going to try to do is make you scared of me. 'You know, he's not patriotic enough. He's got a funny name. You know, he doesn't look like all those other presidents on those dollar bills. He's too risky.'"

The McCain campaign then claimed that Obama was playing

"the race card" (by referring to "all those other presidents on those dollar bills") and responded aggressively by asserting (rather hilariously, given the nature of their ad) that Obama's Missouri comments were "divisive, negative, shameful and wrong." Still, "Celeb" helped McCain a good deal—by August, he had pulled even with Obama in most polls.

**"Um, All of Them"** There have been many disastrous media fiascoes by America's vice-presidential candidates—Spiro Agnew's referring to a Japanese American reporter as a "fat Jap" and Dan Quayle's misspelling of the word *potato* at an elementary school leap to mind. But none had more impact than Sarah Palin's three-part interview with CBS's Katie Couric in September 2008. Going into the interview, Palin was still riding fairly high from her appearance at the Republican National Convention earlier that month, until Americans witnessed exchanges like this one:

> **Couric:** *You've cited Alaska's proximity to Russia as part of your foreign policy experience. What did you mean by that?*
> **Palin:** *That Alaska has a very narrow maritime border between a foreign country, Russia, and, on our other side, the land boundary that we have with Canada. It's funny that a comment like that was kinda made to … I don't know, you know … reporters.*
> **Couric:** *Mocked?*
> **Palin:** *Yeah, mocked, I guess that's the word, yeah.*
> **Couric:** *Well, explain to me why that enhances your foreign-policy credentials.*
> **Palin:** *Well, it certainly does, because our, our next-door neighbors are foreign countries, there in the state that I am the executive of.*

And this one:

> **Couric:** *And when it comes to establishing your world view, I was curious, what newspapers and magazines did you regularly read before you were*

*tapped for this—to stay informed and to understand the world?*

**Palin:** *I've read most of them again with a great appreciation for the press, for the media—*

**Couric:** *But which ones specifically? I'm curious.*

**Palin:** *Um, all of them, any of them that have been in front of me over all these years.*

**Couric:** *Can you name any of them?*

**Palin:** *I have a vast variety of sources where we get our news. Alaska isn't a foreign country, where, it's kind of suggested and it seems like, "Wow, how could you keep in touch with what the rest of Washington, D.C., may be thinking and doing when you live up there in Alaska?" Believe me, Alaska is like a microcosm of America.*

In memoirs written later, Palin claimed that the McCain campaign left her unprepared for a national interview with an unsympathetic questioner; the McCain camp said that Palin didn't prepare adequately. Regardless of whom you believe, the interview was an instant disaster, making Palin a national laughingstock and calling John McCain's judgment into question at a time when he could least afford it.

SLEAZE-O-METER

2012

★

BARACK
# OBAMA
DEMOCRAT

VS.

MITT
# ROMNEY
REPUBLICAN

★

"I'M NOT FAMILIAR WITH PRECISELY WHAT I SAID,
BUT I STAND BY WHAT I SAID, WHATEVER IT WAS."
—Mitt Romney at a press conference, May 17, 2012

When president-elect Barack Obama delivered his acceptance speech in Chicago's Grant Park on November 5, 2008—having handily beaten John McCain—he famously proclaimed to the cheering crowd that "change has come to America."

Well, yes. But not the type of change he had presumably hoped for. As he entered office, Barack Obama was like a confident poker player on the winning streak of his life who suddenly confronts the worst hand he's ever been dealt. On Inauguration Day, Chief Justice John G. Roberts stumbled administering the oath of office—he and Obama needed a redo the next day—and it was downhill from there. The economic meltdown that had begun with the crash of financial institutions and the bottoming out of the home mortgage market turned into the Great Recession. The economy wasn't dead, quite, just consistently feeling flu-ish. Wages were stagnant, jobs hard to come by, and things just never seemed to get any better. (Unemployment in 2009 was 7.8 percent, a figure that would fluctuate to as high as ten percent before returning to 7.8 percent in December of 2012.) Not surprisingly, the 2010 midterms were an unprecedented Democratic bloodbath, with the Republicans gaining 63 seats in the House and six in the Senate.

There were some bright moments for the new president. He helped rescue Detroit's auto industry in 2009, the year he also won the Nobel Peace Prize; pushed through his Affordable Care Act (forever tagged Obamacare) in 2010; and managed to nail Osama bin Laden in 2011.

All of which bumped up his generally anemic approval ratings, but did nothing for his biggest problem of all: the intransigence displayed by the right-wing of the Republican party towards anything that even smacked of cooperation with Barack Obama. It was shocking for many Americans to hear Congressman Joe Wilson (R-SC) shout "You lie!" at the president when he addressed a joint session of Congress on his health care bill in September of 2009. Wilson was forced to apologize, but the anger was there for all to see. Many Republicans bruited about Obama's supposed foreign birth as if it were an accepted fact. Newt Gingrich seriously posed the question: "What if [Obama] is so outside our comprehension, that only if you understand Kenyan, anti-colonial behavior, can you begin to piece together [his actions]?"

It goes without saying that when the election year of 2012 rolled around Democrats and Republicans were ready for a major smackdown. The Supreme Court's 2010 Citizen's United decision, which ruled that government could not restrict private spending on elections, helped both parties. Almost immediately so-called super PACs arose, funded by almost unlimited amounts of money from corporate, union or individual donors. Although they are forbidden to donate money directly to any candidate—and have to identify their donors on a quarterly basis—independent super PACs, liberal and conservative, would spend more than $700 million dollars in 2012 trying to get candidates elected.

And what did the American people get for $700 million dollars?

Well, at the very least, a dirty and highly entertaining election cycle….

## THE CANDIDATES

**DEMOCRAT: BARACK OBAMA** Obama had turned fifty in the White House—still quite young as far as U.S. presidents are concerned—but his hair was rapidly graying and his face tauter in a way that bespoke enormous stress. His cool intelligence was now seen by many of his supporters as aloofness; worse, the president sometimes seemed indecisive and disengaged. Democrats sympathized with the shellacking (an Obama word) that he was taking from Republicans, but, hey, Bill Clinton had gotten it nearly as bad and was still able to outmaneuver his foes. Not so Barack, who could be too eager to be conciliatory to House Republicans, who, embarrassingly, treated his overtures with contempt. Obama's approval ratings generally hovered in the low 40s as 2012 began, and Republicans felt that his domestic malaise, combined with the lingering war in Afghanistan and an explosive series of crises in the Mideast, made him an easy target despite his incumbency.

But Obama had a crack re-election team and still sat squarely at the center of a sizeable demographic model built on women and Hispanic voters, two population segments Republicans had estranged with their policies on birth control, abortion and immigration.

Joe Biden, despite his classic vice-presidential tendency to place his foot in his mouth—*Washington Post* columnist Alexandra Petri commented that Biden "inspires the sort of discomfort one feels upon introducing one's fiancé to Grandpa after he has had a Scotch too many"—would once again be Obama's running mate.

**REPUBLICAN: MITT ROMNEY** Former Massachusetts Governor Mitt Romney was back, having recovered nicely from his failed run for the nomination in 2008. With vast wealth, his chiseled jaw, his perfect hair tinged with grey along the temples and his photogenic family—including five sons and wife Ann—Romney looked the very epitome of a presidential candidate. That is, if this were 1956. But in 2012, Romney had some liabilities. Perhaps his biggest success as Massachusetts governor had been a universal health care law that closely resembled Obamacare, forcing Romney into the awkward position of denying the basic tenets of his most effective program. His work for the private equity firm Bain Capital had made him millions but also turned him into an easy target for attack ads by his opponents claiming that he had gutted industries and put humble Americans out of work. But Romney's chief problem was that he simply wasn't far enough to the right for the right-wingers who controlled the Republican base. He attempted to move in that direction—claiming, to Democrat hilarity, that he was "severely conservative"—but never convincingly, and his old "flip-flopper" rep would come back to haunt him.

Romney's running mate was the photogenic, up-and-coming young congressman Paul Ryan of Wisconsin who, in the grand vice-presidential nominee tradition, started things off with a gaffe: he claimed that he had run a marathon in 2 hours and 50 minutes, thus shaving, oh, an hour off his actual time. He called the error "an honest mistake."

## THE CAMPAIGN

Barack Obama was a very beatable incumbent in 2012. The economy continued in the doldrums, Congress was in bitter deadlock, and the Affordable Care Act was under court challenge. Figures on the right—Donald Trump in particular—harped so continuously on the president's supposed Kenyan birth that Obama was forced into the unprecedented release of his "long-form" Hawaiian birth certificate. There was no question that Obama would be his party's nominee—with only token opposition, he had gathered the delegates he needed by early April—but as far as Mitt Romney was concerned the president was just waiting for someone, namely, Mitt, to come along and put him out of his misery.

Well, it didn't quite turn out that way. Because of Mitt's reputation as a moderate, the Republican primary season became a series of challenges by candidates positioning themselves far to the right of the former Massachusetts governor, thus forcing him to tack in that direction. Romney's chief opponents were former Pennsylvania senator Rick Santorum, who won a narrow victory over Romney in Iowa, and Newt Gingrich, who beat him soundly in South Carolina.

This left Mitt with only a New Hampshire victory out of the first big three primaries. Things got even worse when Santorum won three more states and began edging ahead of Romney and into the hearts of America's conservatives with his support for teaching creationism in schools and his infamous comparison of gay sex to "man on child, man on dog, or whatever the case may be."

Ultimately, Santorum couldn't sustain his campaign, nor could Gingrich, whose debate bite could be sharp—during one exchange he told Mitt to "drop a little bit of the pious baloney"—but whose verbosity and inability to stay on message, not to mention his sordid history of extramarital affairs, left him vulnerable. On Super Tuesday, Mitt pulled ahead to a lead that he never relinquished. But the primaries had, to some extent, left him damaged goods; the mood of the country at large called for a moderate candidate, but the primaries had pushed Mitt too far in the direction of the Tea Party. The flip-flopper Romney of 2008 came to the fore: Romney changed his positions on abortion, health care, and whether or not he'd advocated a bailout of the auto industry. And then there were the mistakes—his candid appraisal of the 47% of Americans he felt would never vote for him was caught on tape, and when he jumped in to criticize the president after the death of the American ambassador during a terrorist attack in Libya, he was seen as a callow political opportunist.

Even so, the race remained tight, especially after Romney aced a passive and apathetic-seeming Obama at the first presidential debate in Denver, on October 3. Obama redeemed himself in the next two debates, but then came the biggest October surprise of all: Hurricane Sandy, which hit New Jersey and New York on October 29. Suspending his campaign for four days, Obama got to play the role of commander-in-chief to the hilt, touring the stricken Jersey shore area in the friendly company of Republican Governor Chris Christie (the two even indulged in a famous bro-hug). By the time campaigning resumed, it was all over but the counting.

# THE WINNER: BARACK OBAMA

When November 6, 2012, rolled around, Barack Obama was re-elected president by a 51-47 percent margin, winning 332 electoral votes, and garnering more than 65,000,000 popular votes (compared to Romney's nearly 61,000,000). Despite everything, Romney and his team had expected to win; the size of their loss surprised them. Seemingly congenitally unable to look inward—to reflect on his own mistakes—Romney told disappointed donors during a November 14 conference call that "what the president's campaign did was focus on certain members of his base coalition, give them extraordinary financial gifts from the government, and then work very aggressively to turn them out to vote."

Mitt thought it was a private call, but, of course, someone leaked his comments. They sounded like very sour grapes indeed.

★★★

**Let the Suffering Begin** Whatever else can be said about it, 2012 was a bumper year for nasty or just plain weird campaign attack ads. Herman Cain's people produced a very strange commercial with a noir edge, which featured Cain's campaign manager Mark Block nervously puffing on a cigarette as he extolled Cain's virtues. (Cain appeared at the very end, staring into the camera with a creepy smile.)

The Democratic National Committee did a neat number on Mitt's greatest flip-flops (pro-choice, wait, pro-life! Global warming, er, no such thing!). A super PAC for Mitt retaliated nicely, using Obama's claim that there were bound to be "bumps in the road" along the way to economic recovery to imply that the president meant that ordinary Americans were, well, roadkill.

Mitt Romney's candidacy brought out what amounted to attack ad poetry in Newt Gingrich. One of his commercials lumped Romney with other "Massachusetts Moderates" like Michael Dukakis (a clip from the infamous 1988 Bush attack ad against Dukakis showed him riding in the tank with his tie on) and John Kerry. But coup de grace, as it were, was delivered at the end of the ad, when the narrator gravely intones: "Just like Kerry, [Romney] speaks French, too!"

But the 28-minute long "When Mitt Romney Came to Town" by the pro-Gingrich super PAC Winning Our Future ranks as the magnum opus of all 2012 campaign commercials. As dark thunderclouds hover over abandoned factories and portentous music plays, the video purports to trace the genesis of Romney's Bain Capital, which took "seed money from foreign countries" and then used it to gut companies and put ordinary Americans—several of whom appear in their front porches and living rooms—out of work. "Nothing was spared, nothing mattered but greed," intones the narrator. "For millions of Americans, the suffering began…when Mitt Romney came to town."

The video was so riddled with inaccuracies that The *Washington Post's* Fact Checker column gave it its worst possible rating: Four Pinocchios. Even Newt made noises about disowning it. But, like all effective attack ads, it left an indelible impression.

**The Infamous 47%** It was supposed to be a private fundraising dinner at the Boca Raton home of wealthy equity manager Marc Leder, but it didn't turn out that way. Despite the fact that Mitt Romney's team cautioned all guests not to use their cell phones as recording devices, someone—supposedly a bartender—get his phone video going while Mitt spoke. And he said a mouthful.

In response to question about how he was going to convince people to vote for him, Romney said: "All right, there are 47 percent who are with [Obama], who are dependent upon government, who believe that they are victims, who believe the government has a responsibility to care for them, who believe that they are entitled to health care, to food, to housing, to you-name-it. . . . And the government should give it to them. And they will vote for this president no matter what. . . . These are people who pay no income tax."

This was on May 17, and no one at the fundraiser or in Romney's campaign staff thought anything of it—just another day at work for a busy candidate. But fast forward exactly four months later, on September 17, when *Mother Jones* released the video of the 47% remarks just as Romney's campaign, postconvention, was heating up. Instant controversy, with Romney forced to call a press conference to attempt to ameliorate the impression that he was an elite rich white guy (speaking to a room full of other elite rich white guys) who was contemptuous of ordinary Americans. In the category of "remarks-that-merely-confirm-what-everyone-thinks-of-you-anyway," Romney's comments ranked right up there with Barry Goldwater's aside about dropping a nuke on the Kremlin men's room and Bill Clinton promising that he "didn't inhale" when he toked up in college.

**Another Hillary?** Yes, but this time with one "l". Early in April, Hilary Rosen, a Democratic CNN pundit, appeared on *Anderson Cooper 360* to talk about the problems Mitt Romney had appealing to women (a recent poll had found that only 38% of American women approved of him). She told Cooper: "[Romney] is running around the country saying, 'Well, you know, my wife tells me that what women really care about are economic issues, and when I listen to my wife, that's what I'm hearing.'" Okay so far, but then Rosen continued: "Guess what? His wife never actually worked a day in her life."

Reminiscent of remarks made in 2004 by Teresa Heinz Kerry, candidate John Kerry's wife, that First Lady Laura Bush had never had a "real job," Rosen's words were instantly controversial—Ann Romney was, after all, the mother of five boys and suffered from multiple sclerosis (she was also a breast cancer survivor). Hilary was forced to apologize the next day and the Obama's campaign stumbled over themselves trying to show how stay-at-home-mom friendly they were—"there's no tougher job then being a mom," Obama unctuously told a TV interviewer.

As for Ann Romney, she was more delighted than upset. Someone's tape recorder was running at a Florida fund-raiser when she described Rosen's gaffe as "an early birthday present."

**Bring in the Clowns** For months during the Republican primary season, it seemed that Mitt Romney—always the frontrunner if he could just pull it together—was playing a game of whack-a-mole with his opponents. As soon as he knocked down one challenger, another would arise.

Yet, truth be told, Romney really didn't need to do much whacking, since his opponents were more than happy to self-destruct.

• Herman Cain, CEO of Godfather's Pizza, whose beaming countenance, conservative values, and plan for a simplified tax code made him popular in early straw polls. But allegations that he had a lengthy affair with a female employee and had sexually assaulted a job applicant—"You want a job, don't you?" she claims he said as he directed her head toward his crotch—forced him to abandon his campaign in late 2011.

• Studly Texas governor Rick Perry (Bill Clinton called him a "good-lookin' rascal") was seen as a real threat to Romney, until it turned out he had a hard time counting. During a candidate's debate in Auburn Hills, Michigan, Perry huffed: "I will tell you, it's three agencies of government, when I get there, they're gone: Commerce, Education, and, uh, ummn . . . "

Befuddled, Perry stopped. Down the stage, Mitt Romney offered: "EPA?" "EPA! There you go," Perry exclaimed. But that wasn't it, either, and finally Perry gave up: "Oops," he said. Turns out he meant the Department of Energy, but it was too late. Perry was down for the count.

• Michele Bachmann, U.S. representative from Minnesota, won the Ames Straw Poll (an influential Republican poll in Iowa) in August of 2011, pushing Minnesota governor Tim Pawlenty (who once called her "insane") out of the race. But Iowa's love affair with Bachmann didn't last long, especially after she visited the town of Waterloo (where she was born) and told a reporter: "John Wayne was from Waterloo. That's the kind of spirit I have, too." Actually, it was the serial killer clown John Wayne Gacy, not the movie star, but never mind. Bachmann had already survived a trip to New Hampshire, which she apparently thought was Massachusetts. "You're the state where the shot was heard around the world at Lexington and Concord," she told a puzzled crowd. "She makes Sarah Palin look like Count Metternich," a GOP consultant sniped. After receiving only 5 percent of the vote in the Iowa caucuses in January 2012, Bachmann suspended her campaign.

**Religion, Again?** Obama's religion was vague in most people's minds (he is a Congregationalist, although in 2012 17 percent of registered voters counted him a secret Muslim), but Mick Romney was a Mormon, which made him the target of several attacks. (During the 2008 primaries, former Arkansas governor and preacher Mike Huckabee was forced to apologize for asking the sweetly rhetorical question: "Don't Mormons believe that Jesus and the devil are brothers?") In 2012, a Midwestern Democratic-leaning Catholic group did informal push-polling phone calls in which they asked: "How can you support a Mormon who does not believe in Jesus Christ?" Evangelicals on the Republican right were also not fond of the candidate's religion. Robert Jeffress, the Texas Baptist megachurch pastor and Rick Perry backer, said that Romney was not a Christian and that "every true born again follower of Christ ought to embrace a Christian over a non-Christian."

# APPENDIX

---

# BIBLIOGRAPHY

---

# INDEX

---

# ACKNOWLEDGMENTS

# APPENDIX

---

# TOP TEN CLASSIC ATTACKS IN PRESIDENTIAL ELECTIONS

**S**ome things never change—like the ways in which presidential candidates go after each other. Below are ten classic slights, slurs, and smears used almost continuously during two hundred years of presidential electioneering.

**10. "You're Not Tough Enough!"** This perennial attack suggests that—in a time of war—a candidate will probably turn tail like a yellow-belly chicken. The list of cowardly candidates in U.S. history is enormous: Thomas Jefferson was too soft on France; Franklin Pierce fainted in the heat of battle; Jimmy Carter couldn't stand up to Iran; and many of today's candidates aren't "man enough" to battle the terrorists.

**9. "You'll Drive Us Into War!"** The flip side of number 10. These candidates—say, Andrew Jackson, Teddy Roosevelt, Barry Goldwater, George W. Bush—are loose cannons who will drag us into bloody foreign wars and destroy our future, just to prove how tough they are.

**8. "You're Too Old!"** William Henry Harrison, Winfield Scott, Dwight Eisenhower, Ronald Reagan, Bob Dole—geez, you guys should be out playing shuffleboard! What if you fall asleep with your finger on that big red button? Let the young fifty-five-year-olds take over!

**7. "You're An Egghead!"** Thomas Jefferson, John Quincy Adams, Adlai Stevenson, Eugene McCarthy, Jimmy Carter, Al Gore, Barack Obama—all were way too smart for their own good, according to their opponents. Even worse, they were book smart—Jefferson loved architecture, Stevenson read poetry, and McCarthy wrote poetry, for Christ's sake.

**6. "You're An Idiot!"** On the other hand, candidates like Lewis Cass, William Howard Taft, Herbert Hoover, Alf Landon, and George W. Bush must have fallen down and bumped their heads when they were young. In the case of Gerald Ford, many Democrats speculated that he'd played too much football without a helmet.

**5. "You're A Slut!"** Apparently Thomas Jefferson, Grover Cleveland, Warren Harding (a rare Republican target for this attack), Woodrow Wilson, John F. Kennedy, Gary Hart, Bill Clinton, and John Kerry just couldn't keep their minds on business when the ladies were around.

**4. "You're Clearly Not Having Sex With Anyone!"** On the other hand, Americans do want their presidents to have a little red blood. It's bad form for the commander-in-chief to appear dry, shriveled, and sexless, like James Madison, Benjamin Harrison, Calvin Coolidge, Richard Nixon, and even Jimmy Carter, despite the lust in his heart.

**3. "You're At Least A Little Bit Gay!"** Not that there's anything wrong with it. But many felt that James Buchanan and Adlai Stevenson "played for the other team," and party operatives did their best to spread rumors.

**2. "You're Drunk All The Time!"** This favorite attack was used most notably against Ulysses S. Grant, but it was also leveled at the likes of Henry Clay, Franklin Pierce, Teddy Roosevelt, Warren Harding, and George W. Bush. Of course, Bush was clean and sober by the 2000 election, but who cares. Once a souse, always a souse.

**1. "You're Insane!"** Shrinks publicly stated that both William Jennings Bryan and Barry Goldwater were neurotic and paranoid; Horace Greeley died in an asylum right after Election Day 1872; Thomas Eagleton received shock treatments; and Nixon—well, all you had to do was look at the guy's 1952 Checkers speech. Diagnosis: Bonkers.

Ackerman, Kenneth D. *Dark Horse: The Surprising Election and Political Murder of President James A. Garfield*. New York: Carroll & Graff, 2003.

Aitken, Jonathan. *Nixon: A Life*. Washington D.C.: Regnery Publishing, Inc., 1993.

Ambrose, Steven E. *Eisenhower: The President*. New York, Simon & Schuster, 1984.

Auchincloss, Louis. *Theodore Roosevelt*. New York: Henry Holt & Company, 2001.

Balz, Dan, and Haynes Johnson. *Collision 2012: Obama vs Romney and the Future of Elections in America*. New York: Viking, 2013.

Balz, Dan, and Haynes Johnson. *The Battle for America, 2008*. New York: Viking, 2009.

Boller, Paul E. *Presidential Campaigns: From George Washington to George W. Bush*. New York: Oxford University Press, 2004.

Brands, H. W. *Andrew Jackson: His Life and Times*. New York: Doubleday, 2005.

Brodie, Fawn M. *Thomas Jefferson: An Intimate History*. New York: W.W. Norton, 1974.

Bourne, Peter G. *Jimmy Carter: A Comprehensive Biography from Plains to Postpresidency*. New York: Scribner, 1997.

Calhoun, Charles W. *Benjamin Harrison*. New York: Henry Holt & Company, 2005.

Cannon, Lou. *President Reagan: The Role of a Lifetime*. New York: Simon & Schuster, 1991.

Dallak, Robert. *Flawed Giant: Lyndon Johnson and His Times, 1961–1973*. New York: Oxford University Press, 1998.

Dean, John W. *Warren G. Harding*. New York: Henry Holt & Co., 2005.

Dershowitz, Alan M. *Supreme Injustice: How the High Court Hijacked Election 2000*. New York: Oxford University Press, 2001.

Donald, David Herbert. *Lincoln*. New York: Simon & Schuster, 1995.

Donovan, Robert J. *Conflict and Crisis: The Presidency of Harry Truman, 1945–1948*. New York: W.W. Norton & Co, 1977.

Ellis, Joseph J. *American Sphinx: The Character of Thomas Jefferson*. New York: Alfred A. Knopf, 1997.

———. *His Excellency: George Washington*. New York: Alfred A. Knopf, 2004.

Ferling, John. *Adams vs. Jefferson: The Tumultuous Election of 1800*. New York: Oxford University Press, 2004.

Goldberg, Robert Allen. *Barry Goldwater*. New Haven: Yale University Press, 1995.

Goldman, Peter, et al. *Quest for the Presidency 1992*. College Station: Texas A&M University Press, 1994.

Goodwin, Doris Kearns. *Team of Rivals: The Political Genius of Abraham Lincoln*. New York: Simon & Schuster, 2005.

Greenfield, Jeff. *The Real Campaign. How the Media Missed the Story of the 1980 Campaign*. New York: Summit Books, 1982.

Heilemann, John, and Mark Halperin. *Double Down: Game Change 2012*. New York: Penguin, 2013.

Heilemann, John, and Mark Halperin. *Game Change: Obama and the Clintons, McCain and Palin, and the Race of A Lifetime*. New York: HarperCollins, 2010.

Howe, George Frederick. *Chester A. Arthur: A Quarter-Century of Machine Politics*. New York: Frederick Unger Publishing Co., 1957.

Jamieson, Kathleen Hall. *Dirty Politics: Deception, Distraction and Democracy*. New York: Oxford University Press, 1992.

———. *Packaging the Presidency: A History and Criticism of Presidential Campaign Advertising*. Third Edition. New York: Oxford University Press, 1995.

Johnson, David E., & Johnny R. *A Funny Thing Happened on the Way to the White House: Foolhardiness, Folly and Fraud in Presidential Elections, from Andrew Jackson to George W. Bush*. New York, Dallas: Taylor Trade Publishing, Lanham, 2004.

Ketchum, Ralph. *James Madison: A Biography*. Charlottesville: University of Virginia Press, 1971.

Klein, Joe. *Politics Lost: How American Democracy Was Trivialized by People Who Think You Are Stupid*. New York: Doubleday, 2006.

Kutler, Stanley I. *The Wars of Watergate: The Last Crisis of Richard Nixon*. New York: W.W. Norton & Co, 1990.

Lorant, Stefan. *The Glorious Burden: The History of the Presidency and Presidential Elections from George Washington to James Earl Carter, Jr*. Lenox, MA: Author's Edition Inc, 1977.

Leech, Margaret. *In the Days of McKinley*. New York: Harper & Brothers, 1959.

McCoy, Donald R. *Calvin Coolidge: The Quiet President*. New York: Macmillan & Co., 1967.

McCullough, David. *John Adams*. New York: Simon & Schuster, 2001.

———. *Truman*. New York: Simon & Schuster, 1992.

McFeely, William S. *Grant: A Biography*. New York, London: W.W. Norton & Co., 1981.

Martin, John Bartlow. *Adlai Stevenson of Illinois: The Life of Adlai E. Stevenson*. Garden City & New York: Doubleday & Co., 1976.

Miller, Douglas T., and Marion Nowak. *The Fifties: The Way We Really Were*. Garden City, New York: Doubleday & Co, 1977.

Morgan, Ted. *FDR: A Biography*. New York: Simon & Schuster, 1985.

Morris, Edmund. *Theodore Rex*. New York: Random House, 2001.

Nagel, Paul C. *John Quincy Adams. A Public Life, A Private Life*. Cambridge, MA: Harvard University Press. 1997.

Patterson, James T. *Restless Giant: The United States from Watergate to Bush vs. Gore*. New York: Oxford University Press, 2005.

Phillips, Kevin. *William McKinley*. New York: Henry Holt & Co., 2003.

Pringle, Henry F. *The Life and Times of Howard Taft: A Biography*. New York, Toronto: Farrar & Rinehart, 1939.

Reeves, Thomas C. *A Question of Character: A Life of John F. Kennedy*. New York: The Free Press, 1991.

Robinson, Lloyd. *The Stolen Election: Hayes versus Tilden—1876*. Garden City, NY: Doubleday & Co. 1968.

Roseboom, Paul H., and Alfred E. Eckes Jr. *History of Presidential Elections: From George Washington to Jimmy Carter*. Fourth Edition.

New York: Macmillan Publishing Co, Inc., 1979.

Seigenthaler, John. *James K. Polk*. New York: Henry Holt & Company, 2003.

Shephard, Edward M. *Martin Van Buren*. New York and Boston: Houghton, Mifflin & Company, 1899.

Sick, Gary. *October Surprise: American Hostages in Iran and the Election of Ronald Reagan*. New York: Times Books, 1991.

Slayton, Robert A. *Empire Statesman: The Rise and Redemption of Al Smith*. New York: The Free Press, 2001.

Smith, Richard Norton. *An Uncommon Man: The Triumph of Herbert Hoover*. New York, Simon & Schuster, 1985.

Stephanopoulis, George. *All Too Human: A Political Education*. New York: Little, Brown & Co., 1999.

Toobin, Jeffrey. *A Vast Conspiracy: The Real Story of the Sex Scandal That Nearly Brought Down a President*. New York: Random House, 1999.

———. *Too Close to Call: The Thirty-Six Day Battle to Decide the 2000 Election*. New York: Random House, 2002.

Walworth, Arthur. *Woodrow Wilson*. New York: W.W. Norton & Co., 1978.

White, Theodore H. *Breach of Faith: The Fall of Richard Nixon*. New York: Atheneum, 1975.

Wicker, Tom. *One of Us: Richard Nixon and the American Dream*. New York: Random House, 1991.

# INDEX

## A

accidents, 166, 215–16
Adams, Charles Francis, 131
Adams, John, 10, 11, 14–18, 20–32
Adams, John Quincy, 24, 40, 41–55, 74, 76, 213, 322
Adams, Louisa, 49, 52
advertising. See political advertising
Affordable Care Act, 311, 314
Afghanistan, 292, 313
age, 13, 322
Agnew, Spiro, 238, 241–42
airplanes, 221
The Alamo, 63
Alien Act, 27
Alsop, Stewart, 206
Anderson, John, 257, 258
annexation, 75, 76–77, 78
Antimasons, 57, 68
anti-Semites, 111, 145
antitrust, 153
aristocrats, 17
Arthur, Chester, 125, 127, 128
assassins and assassinations, 240
    attempts, 51, 262
    presidential, 103, 107, 121, 126, 130, 152, 228
Astor, John Jacob, 123, 134
astronomical observatories, 49
atomic weapons, 214, 227, 232, 235
attack ads. See political advertising
Atwater, Lee, 264, 266, 275, 281
Ayers, Bill, 304, 306

## B

Bache, Benjamin Franklin, 23
bachelors, 89, 91, 117, 120
Bachmann, Michelle, 319–20
"backwoods" candidates, 43, 125.
    See also Lincoln, Abraham
Baker, James, 286
Ball, George, 214
ballots, 24, 29, 286–87
banks and banking, 17, 58–59, 63, 68, 74, 186
barbecues, 28
Barkley, Alben, 204
Barrymore, Ethel, 200
Beecher, Henry Ward, 131
Bell, Alexander Graham, 116
Benton, Thomas Hart, 47, 91
Bentsen, Lloyd, 267
Bergen, Candace, 276
Biddle, Nicholas, 59, 63, 71–72

Biden, Joe, 300, 302, 313
bigamy, 53–54
big game hunters, 161
bin Laden, Osama, 292, 294, 302, 311
biographies, 85–86
birds, 209
Black Codes, 107
blackmail, 195–96
Blackwell, J. Kenneth, 296
Blaine, James G., 124, 129–35, 136
Blair, Bill, 215
Blair, Francis, 108, 109–10
Blair, Montgomery, 104
Block, Mark, 316
Bohn, Ted, 189
books, 234
Booz, E.C., 70
boycotts, 43
Bradley, Bill, 282
break-ins, 246–47, 249, 250
Breckinridge, John C., 89
bribery, 94. See also vote tampering
Bricker, Jim, 200
Britton, Nan, 177
Brooks, Preston, 87
Brown, Benjamin Gratz, 112
Brown, John, 90
Brown, Pat, 241
Bryan, Charles, 178
Bryan, William Jennings, 142–51, 154–59, 178, 212, 323
Bryant, William Cullen, 74, 113
Buchanan, James, 83, 87–91, 93, 323
Buchanan, Pat, 271, 276, 282, 287, 289
bugs (listening devices), 9, 246–47, 249
Bull Moose Party. See Progressive Party
Burchard, S.D., 134
Burr, Aaron, 23, 27, 29–30, 52
Bush, Barbara, 272
Bush, George H. W., 69, 256, 259, 262, 264–77, 286
Bush, George W., 9, 10, 11, 280–98, 303, 322, 323
Bush, Jeb, 285
Bush, Laura, 297, 318
Bush, Prescott, 282
Butler, Nicholas Murray, 163
Butler, William O., 79
Butterfield, Daniel, 112

## C

Cain, Herman, 316, 319
Calhoun, John C., 36, 42, 45, 50, 59, 61, 66

## ACKNOWLEDGMENTS

I would like to thank Jason Rekulak, my astute and generous editor. Not only was this book his brainchild, but he has made many helpful suggestions along the way that have immeasurably improved it. Every writer should be so lucky.

I read innumerable books and articles while researching this book, but I relied heavily on Stefan Lorant's *The Glorious Burden*, Paul Boller's *Presidential Campaigns*, Kathleen Hall Jamieson's *Packaging the Presidency* and *Dirty Politics*, and Paul H. Roseboom and Alfred E. Eckes Jr.'s *History of Presidential Elections: From George Washington to Jimmy Carter*. All are treasure troves of information on every aspect of presidential politics.

# THE DARKER SIDE
# OF GENIUS

## Richard Wagner's Anti-Semitism

# THE DARKER SIDE OF GENIUS

## Richard Wagner's Anti-Semitism

# JACOB KATZ

Published for Brandeis University Press by
University Press of New England
Hanover and London, 1986

UNIVERSITY PRESS OF NEW ENGLAND

BRANDEIS UNIVERSITY       DARTMOUTH COLLEGE
BROWN UNIVERSITY       UNIVERSITY OF NEW HAMPSHIRE
CLARK UNIVERSITY       UNIVERSITY OF RHODE ISLAND
UNIVERSITY OF       TUFTS UNIVERSITY
CONNECTICUT       UNIVERSITY OF VERMONT

Ⓒ 1986 by Jacob Katz

PRINTED IN THE UNITED STATES OF AMERICA

LIBRARY OF CONGRESS CATALOGING-IN-PUBLICATION DATA

Katz, Jacob, 1904–
   The darker side of genius.

   (Tauber Institute for the study of European Jewry series; 5)
   Translation of: Richard Wagner: Vorbote des Antisemitismus.
   Bibliography: p.
   Includes index.
   1. Wagner, Richard, 1813–1883—Relations with Jews.
2. Composers—Biography. 3. Antisemitism. I. Title.
II. Series: Tauber Institute series; no. 5.
ML410.W19K3313    1986     782.1'092'4     85–40935
ISBN 0–87451–368–5

The Tauber Institute for the Study of European Jewry, established by a gift to Brandeis University by Dr. Laszlo N. Tauber, is dedicated to the memory of the victims of Nazi persecutions between 1933 and 1945. The Institute seeks to study the history and culture of European Jewry in the modern period. The Institute has a special interest in studying the causes, nature, and consequences of the European Jewish catastrophe and seeks to explore them within the context of modern European diplomatic, intellectual, political, and social history. The Tauber Institute for the Study of European Jewry is organized on a multidisciplinary basis, with the participation of scholars in history, Judaic studies, political science, sociology, comparative literature, and other disciplines.

## THE TAUBER INSTITUTE FOR THE STUDY OF EUROPEAN JEWRY SERIES

### Jehuda Reinharz, General Editor

1

GERHARD L. WEINBERG, 1981

### World in the Balance
Behind the Scenes of World War II

2

RICHARD COBB, 1983

### French and Germans, Germans and French
A Personal Interpretation of France
under Two Occupations, 1914–1918/1940–1944

3

EBERHARD JÄCKEL, 1984

### Hitler in History

4

Edited by FRANCES MALINO
and BERNARD WASSERSTEIN, 1985

### The Jews in Modern France

5

JACOB KATZ, 1986

### The Darker Side of Genius
Richard Wagner's Anti-Semitism

# Contents

# Preface

The impetus for writing this book came from the encouragement of my colleagues at the Leo Baeck Institute in Jerusalem. When I was invited by the Institute in 1979 to deliver the annual memorial lecture in honor of Siegfried Moses, I chose as my subject Richard Wagner's role in the emergence of modern anti-Semitism. Although I had dealt with this topic in a chapter of my book on the history of anti-Semitism (*From Prejudice to Destruction: Anti-Semitism, 1700–1933*, Cambridge, Mass., 1980), I felt that it deserved a special, expanded treatment, a feeling confirmed in subsequent conversations with friends.

My original intention had been to ascertain the role of Wagner in the history of modern anti-Semitism. My research, however, led me to inquire into another aspect of the problem—the role that anti-Semitism played in the life of Wagner. In the final run, both historical and biographical material elicited equal consideration, and their treatment in the book, I think, is kept well in balance.

A third dimension to the subject has preoccupied students of Wagner in the last generation—the question of whether or to what extent Wagner's anti-Jewish phobia left traces in his artistic creation. Instead of accepting as axiomatic that indeed it had left traces and then searching for indications to confirm this assumption, I inquired into the history of the assumption itself. It turned out to have been of quite recent origin and could be dated to the post-Hitlerite period. It was clearly a residue of the appropriation of Wagner by the Nazis, who for reasons of historical legitimation interpreted the entire oeuvre of the artist as a prophetic anticipation of their own Weltanschauung. Paradoxically, the critics of the post-Nazi period followed suit, seeing at times in Wagner's anti-Semitism the key to interpreting his art and in turn establishing his anti-Semitism on the basis of this interpretation. In fact, without forced speculation, very little in the artistic work of Wagner can be related to his attitude toward Jews and Judaism. His theoretical and journalistic writings, however, together with other contemporary sources, especially the recently published diaries of his wife, Cosima, permit us to draw as graphic a profile of his anti-Semitism as one could wish. This profile is what I have attempted in this book. I wrote the original text in German; for the English rendering I have to thank Allan Arkush, and for its publication the Tauber Institute for the Study of European Jewry of Brandeis University and its director, Professor Jehuda Reinharz.

*Jerusalem, Israel*                                                    J . K .
*October 16, 1985*

# Chronology

1813  Richard Wagner born 22 May in Leipzig

Wagner's father dies 22 November

1814  Wagner's mother marries Ludwig Geyer
28 August

1822  Wagner enters school in Dresden

1827  Returns to school in Leipzig

1830  Enters Leipzig University

1833  Becomes conductor in Würzburg

1836  Marries Minna Planer

1837  Becomes musical director and conductor,
Königsberg and Riga

1839  Has first encounter with Meyerbeer, Paris

1842  Returns to Dresden

1843  Becomes court conductor in Dresden

1849  Participates in the Dresden revolution, flees to
Zurich

1850  Second attempt to prevail in Paris fails

Has affair with Jessie Laussot in Bordeaux

Back in Zurich publishes *Das Judentum in der
Musik* (*Judaism in Music*) under a pen name

1852  Meets Mathilde Wesendonck

1855  Visits London

1857  Crisis with family Wesendonck, Cosima Liszt
marries Hans von Bülow

1859/60     Third sojourn in Paris, fiasco of *Tannhäuser*

1862/63     Visits Vienna, Prague, Saint Petersburg,
            Budapest

1863        Begins intimate relationship with Cosima von
            Bülow

1864        Ludwig, king of Bavaria, announces his
            protection of Wagner

            Wagner resides in Munich

1865        Forced to leave Munich, Wagner seeks asylum
            in Triebschen, near Luzern, with Cosima

1869        Republishes *Das Judentum in der Musik* under
            his own name

1870        Marries Cosima

1871        Visits Bayreuth, plans for establishing the
            Festspielhaus

1873        Wagners move to Bayreuth

1873        Stockmarket crisis

1875        Beginning of anti-Jewish press campaign

1876        Has encounter with Count Gobineau

1878        *Bayreuther Blätter*, edited by Hans von
            Wollzogen, established

1881        *Parsifal* conducted by Hermann Levi

1883        Wagner dies in Venice 13 February

# THE DARKER SIDE OF GENIUS

Richard Wagner's Anti-Semitism

# 1     The Problem

In contrast with most studies dealing with the subject of Richard Wagner and anti-Semitism,[1] this work does not owe its origin to biographical concerns. Wagner's biographers, like his contemporaries, were struck—justifiably—by the anti-Jewish sentiments revealed in *Das Judentum in der Musik* (*Judaism in Music*), for prior to its publication in 1850 his public statements, his many letters, and his apparent behavior showed no traces of such an attitude. In later decades as well, Wagner's approach to the Jews and Judaism, or, if one wishes, the Jewish question, was by no means clear-cut or consistent. In spite of his passionate outburst against Judaism and his attacks on musicians and writers of Jewish origin, he maintained friendly relations with other Jews. On this point, therefore, the biographer confronts a psychobiographical problem. It is difficult to say whether the many attempts to resolve it have brought this riddle closer to a solution.

But beyond the biographical queries, whose significance should not be underestimated, Wagner's anti-Jewish sentiments are of historical interest. Thus one may ask whether or to what extent Wagner's anti-Jewish utterances played a role in the history of anti-Semitism. If Wagner's anti-Semitic invective had remained a curiosity (and it was regarded as such by most of his contemporaries when *Judaism in Music* appeared under a pseudonym in 1850, and even when it was republished under his full name in 1869), the biographical problem would not have received the importance it has been given in the interpretation and assessment of Wagner's personality. His invective would have been dismissed as a craze, perhaps as a slip, occasioned by his ambivalent relations with Giacomo Meyerbeer, the real target of his first anti-Jewish salvos. The onset of the anti-Semitic movement at the end of the 1870s, however, makes such an innocent explanation appear implausible. What could have been seen during the years of the progressive integration of the Jewish minority into the life of the bourgeois-liberal society as altogether idiosyncratic, even self-contradictory behavior had already become, during Wagner's lifetime, a prototype of social conduct. Did Wagner's behavior serve as an example, did his anti-Jewish statements influence the ideology of the anti-Semitic movement or, at the very least, did his conduct on the individual plane anticipate later social developments? Many of the spokesmen of anti-Semitism, such as Houston Stewart Chamberlain, Alfred Rosenberg, and especially Adolf Hitler, believed themselves to have found in Richard Wagner a prototype of their anti-Semitic sentiments. Historians of anti-Semitism, and laymen in particular, who have traced the historical roots of the movement led by these men, with its horrible consequences, have often accepted them as chief witnesses when judging Wagner. Similarly, among the victims of the national socialist persecution of the Jews, it is often precisely Wagner's image that has been fixed as the symbol of mortal enmity toward the Jews—a development reflected, for example, in the resistance of broad sectors of the Israeli public to the performance of Wagner's music in their country.

A parallel phenomenon, situated more on the literary plane and having, to a certain extent, an antithetical tendency, is also to be noted outside of Israel, namely, in West Germany. There too the question of Wagner's role in paving the way to national socialism is discussed in connection with the problems of the present, namely, the so-called overcoming of the past. In order to remove obstacles and to facilitate access to Wagner's art, there has been a more or less conscious attempt to reconstruct a sanitized image of Wagner. In tune with the times, his anti-Jewish passion, if not exactly concealed, is more or less glossed over. This tendency is particularly visible in the popular biography of Wagner by Martin Gregor-Dellin, which occasioned in its turn a sharp protest from the other camp, energetically represented by the Germanist Hartmut Zelinsky. This school of thought holds that an overcoming of the past, if at all possible, can be achieved only through the merciless exposure of the guilt of individuals as well as whole groups in the anti-Semitic poisoning of the German people, which undermined the moral resistance to the barbarism of national socialism. Here too, in accordance with what the Nazis themselves said, a considerable degree of responsibility is ascribed to Wagner and his followers.

The historian who sees it as his duty to understand, present, and assess the past in the light of what was then known faces the difficult task of remaining independent of the tendencies of the present. He should be aware of the dangers confronting him. In the case of Wagner's anti-Semitism, its origin and development, the historian should observe, describe, and judge its role in Wagner's life and its effect on public affairs in the context of that time, and disregard the consequences that still lay in the future. In order to do so the historian must formulate and define as precisely as possible the questions that present themselves. At what point in Wagner's life do the first signs of his anti-Jewish sentiments turn up? What changes do they undergo in the course of time, and to what level do they rise, possibly influencing the artist's work?

Anti-Semitism, however, is not a matter of opinions and character traits of individual persons, and research into it can in no case be confined to them. It relates to a historical process in which individuals play a more or less active part. Wagner's anti-Semitism is of course not a pure idiosyncrasy. Wagner did not create his anti-Jewish arguments *ex nihilo*, nor is it possible to conceive his emotional reactions to Jews and everything Jewish without the negative associations that weigh upon Jewish phenomena. To be sure, in 1850, the year of the pseudonymous publication of Wagner's *Judaism in Music*, his first expression of hostility toward the Jews, there was no sign of an active, not to speak of an organized, anti-Jewish movement like the one in vogue in the last decades of the nineteenth century. But this movement did not drop from the sky; it was, as we know, the product of an animosity directed against the Jewish Diaspora from time immemorial. This animosity followed in a latent and dialectical manner as later generations of Jews began to extricate themselves from their ghetto existence and to make their way into the modern society of their respective countries, thanks to the modernizing and revolutionary turn in European history.

The first step in our investigation must therefore be to describe the historical scene at the time that Wagner began to take part in the revival of enmity toward the Jews, first with the anonymous publication of his article and then with his public avowal of it in 1869. For an understanding of his intellectual and emotional attitude, the events of preceding times are a legitimate key—more legitimate, in any case, than those that followed, in particular, the rise of the anti-

**4**       **The Darker Side of Genius**

Semitic movement and national socialism. However one evaluates the influence of Wagner's hostility toward the Jews on these movements, the relation is one of cause and effect. Any attempt to understand the former on the basis of the latter conceals within it the danger of a historically and critically inadmissible backdating. Attention to the chronological order in the presentation and interpretation of events is the first professional duty of the historian. This duty must be strictly observed especially in this case, which requires the overcoming of understandable resistance.

We must view the relation between chronologically distant events in a different light when we seek to determine the moral responsibility of a person acting at an earlier date for results that take place later. It is certainly impossible to predict all the consequences of one's actions, and full responsibility for them cannot be placed upon a person's shoulders. But even where one cannot have exact knowledge of the future, the mere supposition of what may follow from present actions entails a measure of moral liability. If, in addition, the first action itself is of dubious character, the question arises whether the initial, less serious but fully conscious behavior does not also include responsibility for the unsuspected consequences. Applied to the case of Wagner, the question is whether his hatred of the Jews, dubious both in itself and for his time, does not give him a share in the responsibility for the unforeseeable intensification of related tendencies. This question, which can only be mentioned here, will confront us in its full significance when our historical investigation of Wagner's hostility toward the Jews is completed. In anticipation of these conclusions, it can be said that the known facts dating from Wagner's lifetime prove to be incriminating enough, without burdening him in addition with the horrible deeds of Hitler.

# 2    Historical Background

From the middle of the 1870s on, an anti-Jewish mood had been on the rise in Germany. Nourished by a press campaign blaming the Jews for the severe economic crisis as well as all the other evils of the day, it had given birth by the end of the decade to a political movement under the leadership of the court preacher Adolf Stöcker. The emergence of this movement distressed many people, Jews as well as non-Jews. It signaled a departure from the relatively tolerant attitude of most Germans toward the Jewish minority living in their midst. This tolerance was based in a few cases on a belief in what later was termed religious and cultural pluralism. For the most part, however, it was rooted in the more or less emphatic hope that the Jewish minority, in its economic, social, cultural, and perhaps even religious particularity, would in the course of time disappear.

There had, of course, been those who had had their doubts about toleration since the entry of the Jews into the German social sphere in the last decades of the eighteenth century. It was then that the idea of the integration of the Jews into state and society, later designated as "emancipation," was conceived and, partially and experimentally, realized. The opponents of the idea were in their day dismissed by the ideological advocates of emancipation as reactionaries, adherents of a state of historical develoment that had already been overcome. However, in the light of the outbreak and expansion of anti-Semitism in the last third of the nineteenth century, the opponents of emancipation appear rather as the forerunners and pathbreakers of the coming epoch, with all its hostility toward the Jews.

In view of this continued enmity toward the Jews, one is entitled to conclude that modern anti-Semitism is by no means a mere defense against the rampant growth of Jewish influence in the wake of emancipation, as many anti-Semites portrayed it. The rapid socioeconomic rise of the emancipated minority may have been the occa-

sion for the outbreak of anti-Semitism, but the passion with which
the anti-Jewish campaign was conducted and its broad social reso-
nance point to the irrational roots of the phenomenon. We are apparently dealing with the revival of a prejudice with deep psychological roots and a wide sociological base—a prejudice whose roots
are to be sought in the age-old Jewish-Christian conflict.[1]

On the theoretical and theological level, both Judaism and Christianity may have carried on their struggle with equally sharp weapons of denial and condemnation.[2] But to the extent that the battle
was also a political and social one, Christianity had, overwhelm-
ingly, the upper hand. Even the physical existence of the branches of
the Jewish Diaspora depended on the willingness of their respective
surroundings to tolerate them. In Christian lands the Jews were
granted this tolerance in the hope that they would convert and step
forward as witnesses of the Christian truth, by the latest at the End
of Days. This provisional tolerance was of course attached to the
conditions of political powerlessness and social isolation and degra-
dation.[3] It is a sign of the often-admired resilience of Jewry that it
was still a living community, supporting its own culture, at the end
of the Middle Ages and the era of the ghetto, an epoch bearing the
stamp of religion. This survival was, to be sure, purchased at the
price of deep mutual alienation, which in the course of time continued to increase.

With the onset of modernity, the presuppositions for the separate
existence of the Jews seemed to have disappeared. The establishment of the secular state and a secular society—occurring contem-
poraneously with the undermining of the traditional theological
foundations of both Christianity and Judaism—seemed to have created the framework for the fusion of the Jewish minority with the
non-Jewish majority. The idea of Jewish emancipation was conceived on the basis of this analysis of historical developments and
their anticipated continuation. The essence of the idea was that the
alteration of the political status of the Jews, their transformation
from tolerated foreigners into legitimate members of the state, would
also lead to their social, economic, cultural, and perhaps religious
assimilation into the general population.[4] It was this hope for the
future that separated the advocates of emancipation from its opponents. Likewise, the Jews' assimilation into their environment became the standard for evaluating emancipation, once it had begun.

Although the idea of Jewish emancipation followed logically from the ruling tendencies of the time, there were also irrational, historically conditioned obstacles to accepting abstract logic. Precisely because the planned naturalization involved simultaneous economic cooperation, social contact, and cultural commonality with the hitherto despised and shunned aliens, many non-Jews recoiled from the demands of reason. But this reaction required a quasi-rational foundation. If the traditional theological justification for the ostracism of the Jews no longer appeared acceptable, it was necessary to adduce other religious—though undogmatic—or explicitly secular motives for their rejection. Thus arose the modern variants of the critique of the Jews, which are designated in the literature as religious, social, political, or racist anti-Semitism, depending on their ideological orientations.[5]

Such a classification of types of anti-Semitism may be of use in the analysis of the worldviews of individual anti-Semites or of entire currents of anti-Semitic thought. For a chronological presentation of their development, such as we require in order to be able to locate Wagner's enlistment among the anti-Semites in the context of his times, it certainly does not suffice. In reality, the anti-Semitic ideologies only rarely appear as monoliths, pure and unadulterated. For the most part, these ideologies employ arguments of different sorts, often in a blend full of contradictions. Their contentions do not, indeed, intend to reflect Jewish realities but rather aim at combating Jewish aspirations or gains already achieved. No argument that can convince oneself or others is scorned here.

If, therefore, one wishes to trace the development of hostility toward the Jews—even if not in a strictly chronological fashion but only in its shifting tendencies—one ought to disregard its ideological foundations and to concentrate on its goal. That goal, with some deviations and changes, was determined by the pace of the Jews' entry into the positions opened up to them. Protests and complaints coincided with the Jews' progress. In the first phase of this development, people avoided social contact with the former ghetto-dwellers and pariahs. Following the French occupation of Frankfurt, for instance, Goethe's mother reported disapprovingly that the Jews of that city were strolling proudly through the parks to which they had previously been denied entry. This aversion to sharing the social space with Jews was also shown by the proprietor of a Hamburg inn who forbade them to visit his establishment, as well as by the Freemason lodges that refused to grant membership or visiting privileges to Jews who were otherwise qualified.[6]

In the first phase of this development, in the late eighteenth century, the ambitions of the secularized segments of Jewish society were focused precisely on social contacts of this kind. Here and there the resistance to these contacts was broken—as eloquently demonstrated by the friendship of Moses Mendelssohn with Gotthold Ephraim Lessing and other prominent figures, and, even more significantly, the frequenting of Jewish salons by the most outstanding personalities of Berlin and Vienna. The surprise, not to say the amazement, that such contacts elicited from contemporary observers testifies, however, to their extraordinary character. To be sure, they by no means served as examples to the general public. Despite the progress in the area of political and legal emancipation—a grant of fully equal rights in the territories occupied by the French, and naturalization of the Prussian and Bavarian Jews by the edicts of 1812/13—social contact between Jews and non-Jews remained problematic.[7]

Nevertheless, once the taboo against social contacts was broken, the old condition of full social separation could no longer be restored, and in the course of the first decades of emancipation a kind of *modus vivendi* came into being. The enthusiastic expectation of a universal reconciliation of Jews and non-Jews was replaced by a slackening of mutual exclusiveness. Jews who wished to widen the radius of their social contacts were able to do so, provided they had adopted the generally accepted modes of speech and social behavior. They were no longer prevented from participating in public events, from attending theaters, concerts, and the like. They could have their children educated in gymnasiums and not infrequently they found entry into more or less closed social circles and associations.[8] Nevertheless, even after the establishment of formal legal equality, which still required struggle, the social acceptance of the Jews was by no means a matter of course.

This struggle began with practical measures and plans for reform, such as Joseph II's Edict of Tolerance in Austria and the proposals of the Prussian official Christian Wilhelm Dohm at the beginning of the 1780s. The Austrian measures and the Prussian suggestions proceeded from an awareness of the untenability of the existing situation, namely, the organization of the Jews as a sort of foreign colony living under special legislation on the margin of civil society. To adherents of the Enlightenment conception of the state as an entity based on rational and universal principles, this situation seemed to be an undesirable anomaly. That is why their preliminary measures and proposals must have appeared as the beginnings of a reform leading to the full incorporation of the Jews into the state and society,[9] even though at the time they aimed only at relatively minor alterations of the existing legislation concerning the Jews. That, at any rate, is how they were understood—correctly—by their opponents, who unleashed a corresponding reaction.

The process of naturalizing the Jews was accompanied at all times by a vocal, often hateful protest. The Jews' opponents advanced arguments of all sorts, both old and new. In fact, one can regard the battle against the political and social acceptance of the Jews as a stimulus to the recasting of the anti-Jewish ideology, which led to the transformation of the medieval, religious hostility toward the Jews into something new and secular, which was later called anti-Semitism.

The protest against the acceptance of the Jews took on particularly sharp forms during and after the Congress of Vienna, in the course of the great debate over the reorganization of the legislation concerning the Jews. At that time the question was whether the Jews should retain the legal equality that the German states had granted them, or had been compelled to grant them, in the revolutionary years. The citizenry of Frankfurt, Bremen, and other cities, irritated by the growth of Jewish economic activity during the period when the French had guaranteed the Jews equal rights, sought to drive the Jews back into their prerevolutionary position. The anti-Jewish agitation of this period ended, as is well known, in the summer of 1819 with the so-called Hep Hep Riots, which represented the culmination of the anti-emancipatory currents.[10]

With the liberal upsurge of the 1830s, the battle as well as the anti-Jewish argumentation accompanying it entered a new phase. In tune with the times, the advocates of Jewish emancipation believed themselves certain of ultimate victory. Their opponents' attempts to check their progress through propaganda and parliamentary maneuvers in cabinets and legislative assemblies struck them as the rearguard actions of a defeated army. Nevertheless, this period was especially rich in stormy debates concerning the Jews, in which the whole range of problems raised by their presence, now called the Jewish question, was fought with the sharpest instruments of rhetoric.[11] We have a particular reason to review these confrontations. Born in 1813, Richard Wagner was seventeen years old when the new debate about the Jews began. He must have received his impressions, ideas, and conceptions of Jews and Judaism during his formative years in this atmosphere of lively public discussion.

Two factors gave their special stamp to the situation of the Jews during this period. The first was the strategy developed by the opponents of emancipation during this phase of the battle; the second was the degree of adaptation, the degree of assimilation, that accompanied the process of emancipation. In a fundamental respect the struggle for the integration of the Jews had come to a head. Previous developments had assured the Jews of their right of domicile. People no longer thought of expelling the Jews, or reconstructing their ghettos, or ejecting them from the economic positions that they had conquered in the decades of their half-citizenship. The question that occupied the public, the legislative bodies, the press, and the pertinent literature was whether these halfway measures should remain in effect over the long run. The Jews and their partisans demanded that they be granted full and equal rights, including the right to participate in the political life of the state. In these debates the question of whether the Jews shared a common identity with the other sections of the population was once again raised and discussed on various intellectual levels.

In spite of the increasing secularization of public life, some circles continued to maintain that the state as such is bound up with the Christian idea. Hence, even if one granted Jews or perhaps deists the right of domicile and living space, the administration of the state had to remain in the hands of Christians. This idea received its philosophical underpinnings at the end of the 1840s in the work of the convert Julius Stahl. Long before that, however, it served conservative elements as a guidepost in the formation of their attitudes. For those who held this opinion, the full emancipation of the Jews was therefore out of the question.[12]

Nevertheless, the dominant trend of the times was toward the secularization of the state, which seemed to imply the granting of equal political rights to the Jews. That, at least, was how things stood when viewed in the light of the idea of the state. But if the criterion for the Jews' acceptance became their capacity to take part in the political life of the non-Jewish community, everything depended on how one evaluated the Jews' ability and readiness to adapt themselves. Arthur Schopenhauer, for example, declared that in view of the Jews' tribal consanguinity and solidarity, he could not believe in their integration into the ranks of another nation (*Staatsvolk*).[13] It is not necessary to determine whether such statements were based primarily on observation of Jewish behavior patterns or whether they were simply ideological facades for one or another of the variants of the anti-Jewish phobia. The outcome was in any case the rejection of the idea of equal political rights for the Jews.

Others expressed their doubts concerning the Jews' aptitude for fully identifying themselves with their surroundings. They made their approval of political equality for the Jews contingent on visible indications of changes in the Jews' way of thinking, or on a fundamental change in the existing social order, which would automatically tear down the barriers separating Jews from non-Jews. The radical rationalist theologian of Heidelberg, Heinrich Eberhard Gottlob Paulus, demanded that the Jews abandon all the irrational articles of faith and rites reminding them of their national past. Only when Judaism reached the level of a rational religion would the time come for political union.[14]

Bruno Bauer went a significant step further in the radical-critical phase of his development at the beginning of the 1840s. The society of the future, he believed, should be based on the overcoming of every religion. If this precondition were fulfilled, the Jews would not have to fight any battle for equal rights; following the abolition of religious cleavages, they would automatically come into possession of such rights. If the Jews recognized their true interests, they would make common cause with the critical pioneers of the society of the future and fight against all religion. Since they accepted the existing conditions, did nothing to oppose the Christian religion, and sought only to obtain for the adherents of Judaism rights equal to those of the Christians, their demands were, in view of the particularistic traits of the Jewish religion, hopeless and unjustified.[15]

These arguments as well as many others did not, of course, spring from a fundamental attitude toward emancipation. They were accompanied by socioeconomic observations and religious, cultural, and moral judgments concerning Jewish behavior and the Jewish mentality. Now, in contrast to earlier epochs, the object of these observations was not the poor and contemptible Jewish secondhand dealer but the rich banker. This was, after all, the epoch of the half-emancipated but economically rising financiers, represented by the Rothschild brothers. To be sure, much of the taint that formerly clung to the secondhand dealers was transferred to the now-envied financial potentates, as if all economic transactions performed by Jews were of equally dubious character. This attitude was often indicated by the notion of "huckstering" (Schacher), which was reserved for Jewish secondhand dealing.

The moral judgments of those who held out the prospect of a full emancipation were also, for the most part, negative, perhaps even more so than the judgments of those who rejected it. The future improvement of the status of the Jews was always made dependent on their fundamental transformation, so that the present situation could be safely criticized.

The peak of this dialectical appraisal of the Jews was reached with Karl Marx, although in his view the anticipated transformation concerned not the Jews as individuals but the economic system supported by them. Marx's On the Jewish Question (1844) continued the polemic of Bruno Bauer's pamphlet bearing the same name. While Bauer held out the prospect of the emancipation of the Jews as a consequence of their voluntary self-liberation from the burden of their religion, religion did not seem to Karl Marx to be an independent factor. For him, religion was only the spiritual reflection of material and economic realities. The Jewish religion, in particular, was the expression of the capitalistic monetary economy, in which the Jews occupied a central position. The Jews would be freed (i.e., emancipated) only when the monetary economic system, together with its religious mirror image in Judaism, was superseded by a new phase of economic development. Until then they would be enslaved to the "huckstering," which was, in addition, morally corrupting. One would have to castigate them, together with the system they supported, in order to expose publicly their obdurate self-deception.[16]

Thus the fundamental acceptance of Jewish emancipation in no way ruled out a simultaneous antipathy to the Jews and Judaism. Such a combination was, on the contrary, highly characteristic of the years during which Wagner was maturing. It should therefore not astonish us if Wagner, looking back on his early years, presented himself as having been a partisan of Jewish aspirations and, at the same time, spoke of having kept his distance from Jews.[17] Just how great this distance was can be established only on the basis of contemporary sources.

Before turning to such an investigation, however, we must consider the second factor characterizing Wagner's early years: the level of Jewish cultural adaptation.

Without doubt, remnants of the traditional Jewish society still existed in the second quarter of the nineteenth century in all the cities and villages inhabited by Jews. In their outward appearance as well as in their inner spiritual and mental outlook, those Jews still adhering to the traditional ways were clearly recognizable as such. The Christian world still perceived their opposition to their surroundings in the usual, religiously defined terms. But alongside these remnants already appeared Jews who had adapted themselves to the culture of their environment. Through private or public schooling or through university attendance they had modeled their conduct, thought, and cultural interests after the parallel stratum of non-Jewish society. In most cases these Jews had neglected or entirely abandoned the Jewish religious prescriptions restricting social contact, a process of alienation that not infrequently culminated in conversion to Christianity. This process of adaptation corresponded to the expectations of the liberal proponents of emancipation. If it had encompassed all sections of Jewry, it would have finally solved the so-called Jewish question. The desire for a gradual assimilation now took the place of the Christian hope for a general conversion of the Jews.[18]

Confidence in the fulfillment of this process proved, however, to be at least as problematic as the eschatological belief in the conversion of the Jews. That belief was based on a theological assumption that could not be shaken, despite repeated disappointments. The process of assimilation, however, was one whose success could be measured and judged on the basis of obvious facts. Thus the process of Jewish assimilation was exposed to constant supervision and accompanied by more or less suspicious questions: Is Jewish assimilation fast enough? Isn't it limited to only one stratum on the margin of Jewish society? Does the apparent transformation affect the inner being of the Jews or only their outward appearance? Even when assimilation led to a conversion to Christianity, that action by no means silenced all doubts. In earlier epochs the Christians believed in the transformative power of baptism. The Jewish convert was regarded as having been reborn, detached socially from his community of origin and transplanted into Christian society. If, however, the motive for baptism was solely the desire to assimilate into the environment, one could not assume that a spiritual transformation had taken place, nor would the convert enjoy unqualified acceptance into his non-Jewish surroundings. He would remain, for the most part, bound to his Jewish origins, even in his own eyes, and the Gentile world would still regard him with skepticism.

The more or less latent skepticism concerning Jewish assimilation was based on the inherited judgment that Judaism and everything Jewish were corrupt and corrupting. Consequently, the acceptance of the Jews into the political and social system appeared to be bound up with the disappearance of any traces of the Jewish mentality. If de-Judaization, so to speak, was a precondition for passive participation in the life of the emancipating society, this demand had to emerge still more forcefully when the Jews presented themselves as potential collaborators in the further development of the national culture. That this active participation would sooner or later take place was unavoidable. As soon as acculturation had made sufficient progress and a generation of Jews at home in the language and cultural tradition of its surroundings had arisen, its gifted members would surely make their contributions to the arts and sciences. These contributions were greeted with a certain skepticism, especially by artists, long before that skepticism rose to the level of paroxysm in the statements of Richard Wagner.[19]

The emergence of Jewish composers and poets provoked some astonishment even among those who were favorably disposed toward the Jews. In a letter to Goethe, Carl Friedrich Zelter mentioned his gifted pupil, Felix Mendelssohn-Bartholdy, but could not refrain from remarking: "He is, to be sure, a Jewboy [*Judensohn*] but no Jew. It would really be something rare [*eppes Rores*] if a Jewboy were to become an artist."[20] The use of the two German-Jewish words here reflects a stereotype of the Jews as not belonging completely to the realm of German culture, a view that was maintained in spite of the baptism of the "Jewboy." Baptism is a precondition for tearing down the barriers, though it does not guarantee the convert an artistic career, even when he possesses great gifts.

The artistic success of Mendelssohn, attested by the judgment of his contemporaries, appeared to contradict the prognosis of his teacher. And yet that prognosis did not remain without ironic fulfillment. For Felix Mendelssohn was, as we shall see, one of the figures whom Wagner used to demonstrate his thesis of the Jew's incapacity to take part creatively in the culture of his environment. Thus, in spite of his baptism and success, Mendelssohn was not spared the accusation of Jewish inadequacy. Did this accusation spring, as if by accident, from Wagner's very idiosyncratic persecution mania, or was it the result of a certain observable factuality? More generally, where is the boundary between the factual judgment of the conduct of an individual Jew and the attribution of his characteristics to a collective Jewish stereotype?

Anti-Jewish prejudice, more or less deeply rooted in the consciousness of the critic, can certainly influence the answer to this question. Nevertheless, a definite rule must be applied in this matter. As long as the critic does not find himself involved in a conflict with the object of his investigation, he can make an evaluation based on fact. But if such a conflict develops, he easily succumbs to stereotyping. Wagner, too, arrived at a derogatory generalization concerning Jewish artistic accomplishment as a result of his upsetting conflict with a Jew, Giacomo Meyerbeer. The validity of the rule is already proved, however, by the biographies of two contemporaries, Ludwig Börne and Heinrich Heine, whom we will encounter again in Wagner's reckoning with the Jews.

Börne and Heine are leading figures of Jewish origin who played a significant role in the early nineteenth century in German society and beyond. Both of them held conversion to Christianity to be an indispensable condition for reaching their goals. It is scarcely possible to determine whether they were correct or whether they could have maintained their positions—Börne as a journalist and editor and Heine as a writer and a poet—as Jews. It is certain, however, that their conversion to Christianity did not make them into Christians in the eyes of the world. They themselves continually remarked, complainingly or ironically, that they were invariably discussed and treated as Jews. That situation did not, however, bar their paths to literary activity, indeed to success and fame.[21]

Despite Germany's authoritarian regime and its powers of censorship, a relatively free press came into being. Benefiting, in all probability, from the division of the country into a number of states, this press was supported by the bourgeoisie. Those who wrote for it were not, of course, chosen on account of their origins. The decisive factors in their selection were talents and abilities corresponding to the expectations of the reading public. Heine and Börne were gifted, and their spirit and cast of mind suited the needs and the taste of wide strata of the bourgeoisie. Thus their journalistic and poetic talents rendered them immune to the consequences of their Jewishness. This immunity held as long as their opinions were accepted. Readers or critics who took offense at their views, however, quickly remembered their Jewish origins.

This process was revealed with the greatest possible clarity by the attack of the gymnasium instructor Dr. Eduard Meyer on Börne on the occasion of the publication of Börne's Parisian letters in 1831. The title of Meyer's pamphlet, "Against L. Börne, the Letter Writer Oblivious of Truth, Right and Honor," did not betray its author's intention to single Börne out as a Jew.[22] Meyer objected to Börne's lack of respect for the prince of German poets, Goethe, whose political conservatism Börne had attacked. The first indication that Meyer was planning to attribute Börne's conduct to his Jewishness was his association of the writer with Heinrich Heine and Moritz Gottlieb Saphir, who were guilty of similar things.[23] Excited by the recitation of the catalogue of Börne's sins, Meyer ended his litany with the characteristic utterance: "This is, then, once again carrying impudence very far, and a righteous indignation may excuse the following words, which otherwise perhaps would better have been suppressed: *Börne* is a *Jew*, like *Heine*, like *Saphir* [emphasis in the original]. Baptized or not, it is the same thing."[24]

Good manners, apparently, would have required overlooking an opponent's Jewish origin in a complaint about his conduct. Meyer first had to pull himself together in order to overcome his inhibitions. But then the suppressed animosity against individual persons and against all of Jewry broke out all the more fiercely: "It is not the faith of the Jews that we hate, as they themselves would like to make us believe in order to exculpate themselves, but the many hateful characteristics of these Asiatics, which cannot be laid aside so easily through baptism—the impudence and arrogance so frequent among

them, the immorality and wantonness, their forward nature and their often mean basic disposition."[25] Here we have in its pristine form the shifting of the ideological foundation from religion to character. In view of phenomena like the three baptized Jews who could not be regarded as Christians in any ecclesiastical or even in any secular sense, either by themselves or by others, the distinction between Jews and Christians must not be made to rest on a purely religious basis.

Venomously, but in fact not incorrectly, Meyer characterized Börne and Heine as "interlopers" who belonged to "no people, no state, no community" and who, unencumbered by the necessary piety, became radical critics of existing conditions.[26] In this time of rapid political and social changes, Jewish intellectuals were of course not the only ones who settled, so to speak, outside the existing order. Typically, however, the conservative Meyer connected the radical tendency of the social critics with a Jewish origin and mentality. In this way the social criticism itself was dismissed and neutralized as a Jewish product, and its opponents were thereby spared a confrontation with it. That we are dealing here not merely with a personal tactic but with a method rooted in the situation is proved by the role played by the Jewish factor in the debate over the "Young German" movement.

The Young Germans, a group of writers in the 1830s who were connected neither organizationally nor in any other way, were radical critics not only of existing conditions but also of the dominant concepts of religion and morality. If it is at all possible to speak of a leadership of this group, it must be said to have been non-Jewish. Its most prominent figure was Karl Gutzkow, who was judicially prosecuted because of his novel *Wally* (1835), which was declared immoral. A not insignificant role was played by Heinrich Laube, who contributed to the creation of the name "Young German" with his novel *Young Europe* (1833), and who was likewise sentenced to a term of imprisonment because of his radical statements.[27]

Börne and especially Heine can be numbered among this group insofar as the Young Germans took up many of their ideas—for instance, the notion of the liberation of the flesh from the spirit, expounded by Heine during one stage of his development. That the Young Germans' opponents decried their orientation as Jewish, although most of them were undoubtedly of Christian origin, can be

explained only by the tendency to employ Jewish names to discredit one's adversaries.

The literary assault began with a remark by Wolfgang Menzel. In his polemic against the Young Germans, he referred to a saying, supposedly in circulation, that the Young German movement should rather be named the "Young Palestinian" movement.[28] Menzel accepted this imputation without seeking proof for it.

Menzel's omission was the concern of two anonymous pamphlets, *A Vote on Young Germany* and *The Jeune Allemagne in Germany*, both appearing in 1836. The author of the first pamphlet dedicated the greater part of his writing to Gutzkow's notorious novel, although he attributed its amoral tendency to a "sympathy and elective affinity to that people," the "children of Israel." He then uncovered Jewish character traits in Gutzkow's mentality, "the disorganized talent, the caustic corrosive intelligence."[29] The title of the second pamphlet reflects its author's belief that France must be the source of the Young German mentality. The German spirit, thanks to its religious foundations, could not have produced such a growth. Who, then, transplanted it to Germany? It was the Jews, who, like the French, are pliant and frivolous.[30] Here, therefore, the Jewish spirit was represented as a carrier. As a result of cultural contact with Jews, the Jewish essence is also found among non-Jews—a thesis that we will find Richard Wagner repeating many times.

This is not to say that Wagner was influenced by the opponents of the Young Germans; in his developmental years he felt himself rather drawn to the radical movement, and he was in close personal contact with some of the Young Germans, above all Heinrich Laube. Paradoxically, while the Young Germans were in fact attacked for their supposed affinity to Judaism, they themselves by no means had any sympathy for it. Though Karl Gutzkow had many personal relationships with Jewish intellectuals and followed attentively the religious ferment that gripped the Jewish community in the 1830s and 1840s, he was very far from sympathizing with the Jewish efforts at reform, which sought to give Judaism a modern stamp and thereby to grant it greater vitality. Convinced of the absolutely anachronistic character of Judaism, perhaps also of its original corruption, he demanded of the Jews the full sacrifice of their inheritance.[31]

Heinrich Laube had a similar attitude. In his opinion "there are only two ways to solve the Jewish question: One must either fully annihilate the Jews or completely emancipate them." During the Wagner controversy in 1869 one of Wagner's partisans cited this sentence as a parallel to the Wagnerian idea.[32] Complete emancipation refers here to the disappearance of all traces of a Jewish mentality and a Jewish nature. But apart from this general negation of things Jewish, a statement of Laube's identifies him as a direct predecessor of Wagner's in his conflict with Meyerbeer and his defamation of the Jews. This passage, unnoticed by the Wagner researchers, is found in Laube's introduction to his drama *Struensee*, which appeared in 1847.[33] Michael Beer, the gifted, short-lived brother of Meyerbeer, wrote a play by the same name. The two pieces thus fell into a sort of competition with each other. Laube's efforts to have his drama produced were, he believed, foiled by Meyerbeer's intrigues in favor of his brother's play. He maintained that Meyerbeer's conduct was an offense against "German style." "It is fundamentally repugnant to all of us to haggle openly over objects of art and science in such a way that a so-called competitor—the word is intolerable to us in literature—can be disadvantaged."[34] Laube then explained that the source of Meyerbeer's inappropriate and un-German conduct was to be sought in his Jewishness: "In recent time a foreign element has penetrated everywhere in our midst, and into literature as well. This is the Jewish element. I call it foreign with emphasis; for the Jews are an Oriental nation as totally different from us today as they were two thousand years ago." Laube then presented his theory of how the Jews ought to be treated: "Either we have to become barbarians and expel the Jews to the last man or we have to incorporate them." He chose, of course, the second possibility, and at the same time indicated what means were required for its realization. It is "our sacred duty to reveal repeatedly and mercilessly what it is in their innermost maxims of life that does not suit us."[35] The diagnosis as well as the supposed cure is repeated almost literally in Wagner's argumentation. We thus have a philological proof that Wagner's anti-Jewish invective drew upon the sources available to him, although it ultimately stemmed from private motives.

# 3    Wagner's "Philo-Semitism"

Wagner's life, in its outward course as well as its internal development, can be divided into two parts: the period up to his flight from Dresden to Switzerland because of his participation in the revolution in 1849, and the following thirty-three years. In Switzerland he developed the radical critique of contemporary artistic life that found expression in his essay "The Work of Art of the Future" and in his book *Opera and Drama*. At the same time he distanced himself from the work of Mendelssohn and completely rejected that of Meyerbeer. From the point of view of musical history, that is the real content of his essay *Judaism in Music*.[1] To be sure, his critical attitude toward both composers is not simply based on a judgment of their achievements but is rather associated with their Jewish origin. The obvious weaknesses of Mendelssohn's music and the complete inadequacy of Meyerbeer's operas were no accident, according to Wagner. As members of the Jewish tribe and as bearers of the degenerate synagogal cult and Jewish culture, both composers, like all other Jewish artists, were excluded from the path to supreme achievements. Even greatly gifted individuals like Mendelssohn in music and Heine in poetry were excluded. To substantiate this assertion Wagner described the obvious deficiencies supposedly found in all things Jewish, in speech as well as in song, in music as well as in poetry. Almost unconsciously he transferred the odium of inferiority to the entire ethnic community. Wagner thus penned an anti-Jewish tract that is rightly numbered among the classics of anti-Semitism.

At the time of its initial pseudonymous publication in 1850, as well as in 1869, when it was reprinted under Wagner's own name, *Judaism in Music* was almost entirely without parallels. The twenty years between the revolution of 1848/49 and the Prussian constitutional granting of equal rights to citizens of all religions in 1869 can be seen as the calmest phase of German-Jewish integration.

During this period the resistance to the equalization of political and legal rights visibly subsided, and the rapid process of social and cultural assimilation was only rarely disturbed by discordant voices.[2] Wagner's attack was considered completely out of step with the times.

From a biographical point of view, too, Wagner's anti-Jewish remarks are striking. Nothing in his letters and other statements during the previous decades presages anti-Jewish sentiments. In contrast to the period following it, the years from 1830 to 1848, which corresponded to Wagner's formative years, were eventful and exciting for the Jews and their concerns. At that time, as we saw in the previous chapter, there was still much dispute concerning the Jews' fitness for citizenship and social equality. The next chapter will show that much of what was said then against the Jews entered Wagner's consciousness and then broke through to the surface in his anti-Jewish phase.

Since Wagner made no anti-Jewish utterances in the period before *Judaism in Music*, the scholars who have looked into Wagner's anti-Semitism have completely—and wrongly—neglected this period. If we wish to grasp the motivation and the extent of Wagner's hostility to the Jews, we must understand how it grew out of his relations with Jews and Judaism. To do so, we must examine and judge Wagner's subsequent statements concerning his earlier stance vis-à-vis Jews and Judaism in the light of contemporary testimony. Every biographical study must be cautious in the face of retrospective self-appraisals. In the case of a nature as passionately subjective as Wagner's, one must treat such statements with particular mistrust.

In *Judaism in Music* Wagner declared that he was among "the fighters" for the cause of the Jews during the struggle for Jewish emancipation (i.e., in the 1830s and 1840s).[3] We do not, however, have any evidence that he participated actively in the public discussions or even that he engaged in any political action in favor of the Jews. In making this statement Wagner probably had in mind the general sympathy for the civic equality of the Jews which he, as a liberally minded person, had shared with its protagonists. But Wagner's simultaneous statement that "in real active contact with Jews" one always felt "repelled" by them[4] is contradicted by the facts, at least in relation to the educated Jews with whom he had dealings.

Wagner had frequent contact with Jews, unbaptized as well as baptized (in his eyes, as in the eyes of most of his contemporaries, the act of baptism in no way altered a person's Jewishness). With some his contact was formal, with others familiar or even friendly. In none of these cases can we detect even a trace of a feeling of distance, not to speak of distaste, on Wagner's part. As early as his Riga period (1837/38) Wagner hoped that August Lewald would sponsor his literary and musical publications. Not without a touch of flattery he referred, in a letter to Lewald, to "the brilliant position that you occupy in German journalism." He alluded to Lewald's well-known readiness to help budding artists and hoped that in his case, too, Lewald would show "what a German can do for a German." In fact, the well-remunerated publications in Lewald's *Europa* were a welcome source of income during Wagner's difficult days in Paris.[5]

Lewald's Jewish origin—he was baptized in his youth[6]—was certainly not unknown to Wagner, but he never so much as hinted at it. One can, to be sure, attribute Wagner's silence to the fact that no conflicts or tension ever arose between him and Lewald. But before Wagner's anti-Semitic period, he left the Jewish origin of his partner unmentioned even when his relations with him were encumbered by accusations and suspicions. In 1838, during the first phase of his difficult struggle for existence in Magdeburg, Berlin, and Königsberg, Wagner felt himself to have been unjustly importuned by one of his creditors, Mr. Gottschalk, without doubt a Jew. Wagner threatened that if Mr. Gottschalk insisted on his terms of payment, he would turn the matter over to a commisioner of justice to clear up the nature of the debt, "which certainly will make him more flexible."[7] The debt was assigned, obviously, under unlawful conditions, and Gottschalk appeared as the epitome of the wicked usurer. In Wagner's later anti-Semitic period he would have attributed a much lesser offense on the part of a Jew to his ethnic peculiarities. In 1838, however, he assigned all the guilt to the usurer himself as an individual.

Wagner's lack of anti-Jewish feeling prior to the 1850s is especially clear in his relations with the musical publisher Maurice (Moritz) Schlesinger in Paris. Wagner had been recommended to Schlesinger by Meyerbeer, who had probably intended to provide Wagner with a source of income at a time when the composer was fighting for his bare existence.[8] In fact, after all his failures to succeed as a composer, the connection with Schlesinger was a godsend. Even at a later date, Wagner gratefully acknowledged his debt to Schlesinger. "Keep your sympathy for me, which has so often brought me help in distress," he wrote in his first letter to Schlesinger after his departure from Paris in 1842.[9]

Schlesinger's crucial assistance consisted in having Wagner commissioned to correct musical proofs. That work enabled him to survive, but at the same time it made him feel déclassé. Such wage labor was surely degrading for a young man driven by artistic ambition, a man who was firmly convinced of his future fame and who made no bones about this conviction in his dealings with his employer. In one of his frequent requests for an advance Wagner wrote: "A hundred francs, dearest Mr. Schlesinger, you must necessarily lend to me anew, otherwise I simply don't know how you'll be able to stand before the seat of judgment of posterity at a time when it might well be said: Moritz Schlesinger, the beneficent and circumspect Moritz Schlesinger, refused Richard Wagner, who was in any case destined to be so very famous, an advance of one hundred francs."[10] In spite of the intimate tone of this letter, Wagner's economic dependency obviously placed a strain on the relationship between the two men. Wagner could not rid himself of the feeling that Schlesinger was taking advantage of his exigency, as he put it—not maliciously, but clearly enough—in his correspondence with friends. "He is a scoundrel," he wrote in a letter to a mutual acquaintance in Paris, when Schlesinger acted high-handedly, in Wagner's opinion, in the settlement of an account.[11] In his anti-Semitic period he would certainly have mentioned the Jewish origin of the "scoundrel."

*Völkisch* biographers of Wagner have sought to identify his disgraceful dependence on Schlesinger as one of the causes of his conversion to anti-Semitism.[12] Such an interpretation can at best find support in a later remark in Wagner's autobiography in which he characterized Schlesinger as an unpleasant Jewish type, without, however, blaming Schlesinger for his sufferings.[13] There Wagner is obviously backdating his antipathy to everything Jewish, which took hold of him later and which elsewhere, too, as we shall see, led him to distort his memories.

Through Schlesinger Wagner became acquainted with the French Jewish composer Fromental Halevy. His note copying was mostly connected with Halevy's works, of which a few enjoyed great public success. Wagner, of course, had his own opinion of them. In a letter from Paris to Robert Schumann, which, though anonymous, was intended for the public—around this time Schumann edited the *Neue Zeitschrift für Musik*—Wagner judged Halevy's work favorably and praised him as a man. Relying on Halevy's own statements, Wagner asserted that the composer occupied himself with the popular genre of opera only out of economic necessity. If he were wealthy, Wagner wrote, Halevy would devote himself to the higher kinds of music, symphonies and oratorios. In any case, Halevy was no humbug: "He is open and honest and not a deliberately cunning deceiver like Meyerbeer." [14] Wagner's judgment in his *Autobiographical Sketches*, composed after his return home from Paris, runs much the same, although it is less forgiving of Halevy's choice of musical genres. [15] It is possible that Halevy profited from the contrast with Meyerbeer, in whom Wagner, as we shall soon see, began to lose faith around this time. Both Halevy and Meyerbeer were Jews, and Wagner was fully conscious of that fact. His judgment of them, positive or negative, remained untouched by it.

Wagner's later assertion that he had always felt an instinctive antipathy to the Jewish character of his acquaintances is decisively refuted by his relations with one of his Parisian fellow sufferers, Samuel Lehrs. Before the baptism of his family in the 1820s, this philologist from Königsberg bore the name Kaufmann. In Paris he belonged to Wagner's closest circle of friends, a circle united by particularly warm ties as a result of its members' shared distress and their isolation as emigrants. A year after Wagner's departure from Paris, Lehrs succumbed to consumption, probably caused, in part, by a life of deprivation. In his memoirs Wagner called his acquaintance with Lehrs one "of the most beautiful friendships of my life." This statement is unequivocally confirmed by his correspondence with Lehrs, and especially by his anxious expressions of concern for his sick friend in his letters to other Parisian companions. [16] It is true that he never mentions Lehrs's Jewish origin, neither in the contemporary testimonies nor in his subsequent memoirs. It is not that the fact itself was unknown or that Lehrs himself made a secret of it. After his baptism Lehrs received the name Siegmund, but he still preferred to be called Samuel. [17] Wagner's silence concerning Lehrs's Jewish origin can be attributed to the fact that during the philologist's lifetime Wagner was still scarcely concerned with the Jewish problem, and the later change in Wagner's sentiments was unable to tarnish the memory of his lamented friend. It was an entirely different matter with the friends and acquaintances who lived to see Wagner's change of mind.

After his return from Paris in 1842 Wagner settled in Dresden. During the following year he became the court conductor there. At that time he became friendly with the baptized and wealthy Ferdinand Hiller, whom he apparently considered to be not entirely without significance as a musician, and whom he praised unreservedly as a conductor.[18] Because he "felt no pain or shyness whatever" in turning to him, he applied to Hiller for a large loan—two thousand thalers for the printing of his musical works. Considering Wagner's well-known lack of restraint in monetary matters,[19] that request may not say very much. In any case, Hiller's refusal did not disrupt their friendship. Wagner may have had his own selfish reasons for recommending Hiller as composer for the libretto of a poet whose name we do not know and as conductor for the Dresden choral society.[20] He probably wished at least to give good advice to the poet, who was recommended to him, and the choice of Hiller as musical director of the choral society released Wagner himself from a burdensome and unsalaried sideline. Be that as it may, the tone of the letters to Hiller and the statements about him betray not the slightest trace of reserve because of Hiller's Jewish origin. Such judgments of Hiller, which we will encounter further on, must therefore be understood as projections of later sentiments.

Even more opposed to one another are Wagner's judgments of Berthold Auerbach before and after his anti-Semitic period. The first encounter of the two men was marked by mutual enthusiasm. On 9 October 1846 Wagner wrote to a friend: "For some days I have been quite friendly with Auerbach: he read us his new story and I obliged him with 'Tannhäuser.' He is an excellent poet, and he has such joy in himself and his poetry."[21] That this sympathy was reciprocated is attested in a letter of Auerbach's to an acquaintance one week later: "I have just come back from a stroll with M.[eissner] and with the court conductor Richard Wagner. I have forgotten to name this friend to you, but he is a very significant phenomenon, full of an almost feverish vitality and spirituality."[22] Auerbach then reported on the subjects of common interest to them, and from Wagner's autobiography we learn that questions concerning Judaism

were among them.[23] Wagner stressed that Auerbach was the only
one of his Jewish acquaintances who willingly and without embarrassment discussed Jewish matters. When Wagner wrote these words
he was already under the sway of his anti-Jewish ideas. Consequently, his report has a deprecatory undertone even when it is dealing with a proud Jew like Auerbach. At the time of their meeting in
Dresden, however, Wagner's enthusiasm about him was unreserved,
despite Auerbach's open profession of Judaism, or perhaps precisely
on account of it.

Wagner's change of heart is most striking in his assessment of
Heinrich Heine. In *Judaism in Music* Wagner assigned Heine a
position in poetry analogous to that of Meyerbeer in music, and he
continued to direct poisonous barbs at Heine in later statements as
well, as we shall see in the next chapter. Yet in the Parisian period
Wagner's relations with Heine were entirely positive. Wagner was
first introduced to Heine by Heinrich Laube. Evidence of the impression Heine's writings made on him can be found in his imitation of
his style, which scholars have frequently detected in his literary
work dating from this period. These imitations follow Heine's
model, in part even in their subject matter, that is, conditions in
Paris. Wagner set Heine's poem *The Two Grenadiers* to music, and
it is well known that he borrowed Heine's motifs for his *Fliegende
Holländer* and *Tannhäuser*.[24] For Wagner's judgment of Heine,
however, we need not resort to indirect evidence. One of the many
newspaper articles Wagner wrote to eke out a living in Paris was
devoted to a vindication of the frequently attacked poet. The immediate occasion for the article published in the *Dresdener Abend-
Zeitung* in August 1841 was the much-publicized duel between
Heine and Salomon Strauss, the husband of Ludwig Börne's friend.
Wagner saw the opportunity to castigate the Germans for the ban-
ishment of a talent "the likes of which Germany has few to boast
of," and "which with more fortunate care would have attained the
level of the greatest names of our literature."[25] This praise stands in
stark contrast to his later defamation of Heine's poetry and character. As far as we know, his estrangement from Heine was in no way
the result of any personal disappointment. It was rather a by-product
of the anti-Semitic transformation that was directly connected to
Wagner's relations with his musical predecessors, Mendelssohn and

Meyerbeer. The history of these relations has therefore a claim to our special attention.

As a fledgling composer Wagner undoubtedly saw Mendelssohn as a shining example. In 1835, at the age of twenty-two, he wrote to a friend of his youth: "Perhaps I'll do something like Mendelssohn." [26] Seven years later, after his return from Paris, he lauded Mendelssohn's achievement, this time in the carefully considered formulation of his *Autobiographical Sketches*, as marking a new beginning after Beethoven, who had set "the keystone of a great artistic epoch," to which nothing was to be added. Mendelssohn was guided by a correct self-understanding "when he came forward with the new musical genre of the small orchestral composition." [27] Wagner regarded this self-understanding as obligatory for himself as well.

As is well known, Wagner's relations with Mendelssohn later went beyond Platonic veneration. During his days in Magdeburg he had already approached Mendelssohn, who was at that time named to be conductor at the Leipzig Gewandthaus. In order to interest Mendelssohn in his later works and, generally speaking, in order to draw nearer to him, Wagner sent an early work—a symphony he had written at the age of eighteen—to the composer, who was scarcely older than himself but who had already "arrived." [28] The symphony got lost. Wagner later blamed Mendelssohn for that loss and even, on occasion, suspected him of having deliberately destroyed his copy. [29] One of Wagner's modern biographers believes that this episode marks the true origin of Wagner's resentment of Mendelssohn, [30] but the course of relations between the two musicians refutes his supposition. Even after his return from Paris Wagner relied on the assistance of Mendelssohn—"who receives me in every respect in a very friendly manner" [31]—in his attempts to establish himself in Berlin or Dresden.

Only when the Leipzig *Allgemeine Musikalische Zeitung*, "that organ of Mendelssohn's," silently passed over the two operas *Rienzi* and *Der fliegende Holländer*—which elsewhere, too, met with little understanding—did Wagner grow resentful of Mendelssohn. Typically, he at once deduced the "true character" of "the widely adored tone-setter" and attributed his conduct to jealousy. [32] Shortly thereafter he found himself engaged in a kind of competition with Mendelssohn. At the unveiling of a monument in honor of Friedrich

August, king of Saxony, there were performances of vocal music by both artists. Wagner emerged from this competition with the feeling that he had carried off the victory. "Only *one* opinion can be heard," he wrote to his wife, his brother, and his sister, namely, "that my composition, which was simple and edifying, trounced the Mendelssohnian, which was complicated and artificial." [33] By the next time they met, at the extremely successful performance of *Der fliegende Holländer* in Berlin, the tension had eased. "Mendelssohn . . . came onto the stage after the presentation, embraced me, and congratulated me very warmly," he reported in a letter to his wife. In a three-line letter to Mendelssohn, Wagner noted, "I have come a little closer to you . . . the best thing about my entire Berlin expedition." [34] This effusiveness obviously bears witness to the insecurity of a musician fighting for recognition alongside his artistically celebrated and socially as well as financially better placed rival.

A lasting intimacy did not develop between the two men. Only a businesslike occasion—the formation of a committee for the erection of a Weber monument—led to the renewal of the correspondence, in which Wagner felt he had to excuse himself on account of his "hyperactivity" for not having sustained the relationship. [35] Wagner experienced one of his many disappointments in the realm of musical collaboration when the Leipzig performance of the *Tannhäuser* overture under the direction of Mendelssohn was a complete fiasco. [36] That event can only have strengthened the negative component in his ambivalent relationship to Mendelssohn, and Wagner was not a man to keep completely to himself any reservations he felt regarding a rival. What he said about Mendelssohn and his musical achievement during his colleague's lifetime we do not know. Upon the early and unexpected death of his rival, Wagner wrote to a friend, "What did you have to say about Mendelssohn's death?—May we both remain alive for some time," without adding a word of sympathy. Shortly afterward he told his friend of an anonymous "letter from Leipzig in which I am reproached most crudely for the way in which I am supposed to have commented on Mendelssohn's death." He ascribes this calumny to enemies, "of which [I] have a large number in Dresden." [37] This reproach appears to have a basis in fact.

The sources therefore prove that Wagner's relations with Mendelssohn were already under great stress during Mendelssohn's lifetime. From the point of view of our investigation it is important to note that Mendelssohn's Jewishness plays no role in Wagner's early reservations about him—in contrast to his later disparaging judgment. We will see the same thing when we examine the changes in Wagner's relations with Meyerbeer.[38]

Meyerbeer was almost a generation older than Mendelssohn. During the years when Wagner was in need of support Meyerbeer stood at the peak of his fame, a fame based primarily on success in the Parisian Grande Opéra. Wagner was fascinated by the course of Meyerbeer's life and believed that he had to follow in his footsteps, that is, to seek his fortune in Paris. Unknown as he was, he sought to advance his career by drawing Meyerbeer's attention to his compositions and by receiving his recommendations for appropriate positions. Though Meyerbeer made diverse efforts on Wagner's behalf, they failed to have any positive results. Wagner did not initially attribute this failure to an insufficient zeal of his mentor. After all, Meyerbeer had given Wagner direct financial assistance and had introduced him to men like Maurice Schlesinger, who had at least enabled him to survive. Nor did Wagner feel inhibited about seeking Meyerbeer's help in his varied and mostly unsuccessful attempts to have his works performed in Berlin, Dresden, and other places. His appeals to Meyerbeer were accompanied by expressions of adulation and self-abasement that went well beyond the inflated style of that time. One can read them only with a sense of embarrassment even when Wagner's personal situation is taken into account. He wrote to his "adored protector," "My head and my heart, however, no longer belong to me . . . [they are yours,] my master. . . . I must be your slave in body and soul . . . for I openly confess that I have a slavish nature." This and more like it appear in a single letter.[39]

This self-abasement did not lead to the success for which Wagner hoped. That it would ultimately turn into resentment for the man who had inspired it was only natural. In fact, the turnabout had already taken place in Wagner's Parisian days, and it was stimulated and sharpened by the radical shift in Wagner's judgment of his mentor's artistic merits. His earlier admiration turned into a denial of any originality on the part of the other composer. Wagner attributed Meyerbeer's unheard-of success with the public to a deliberate fishing for effects as well as the weight of his purse with the venal makers of public opinion. This negative assessment of Meyerbeer was also shared by other contemporary critics, including Heinrich Heine.[40] Whether or not these evaluations were just may remain undecided in the course of our investigation and may be left to the experts in musical history. In any case, Wagner based his judgment on certain artistic considerations and his own sense of artistic superiority, which lent a particular edge to his criticism of Meyerbeer. This negative opinion had to coexist in one breast with the grateful adoration of Meyerbeer as a selfless protector.

Wagner tried to keep the contradictory tendencies apart. In a letter to Robert Schumann he called Meyerbeer an "intentionally cunning deceiver" but warned "that you do not, however, abuse him! He is my protector—and joking apart—a lovable man."[41] One year later, when Schumann "very calmly" said that much of *Der fliegende Holländer* "smacks of Meyerbeer," Wagner reacted with a passion that reveals how much of a sore point this charge was for him. His "*external* living conditions" alone had brought him into "contact with the *man* Meyerbeer" (emphasis in the original). In any case, there could be no question of Meyerbeer influencing Wagner's "creative power," since "except perhaps for a *refined* striving after superficial popularity," nothing could be regarded as specifically "Meyerbeerian." Everything in Meyerbeer's productions was borrowed from his predecessors—Rossini, Bellini, and others. From his knowledge of Wagner's dependence on Meyerbeer's support, Wagner wrote, Schumann had drawn conclusions concerning the quality of his artistic work.[42] This misunderstanding only strengthened Wagner's sense of the heavy burden resulting from his relations with Meyerbeer.

This correspondence with Schumann took place after Wagner's return to Germany and his appointment as conductor in Dresden. Despite the economic security that the post brought him, Wagner was extremely unsatisfied with the progress of his reputation as an artist outside of Dresden, especially in Berlin. For the advancement of his cause, Meyerbeer's support still seemed indispensable, and despite Wagner's growing contempt for his patron, he did not shrink from dispensing praise—though this time more reserved—in his letters of entreaty. The discrepancy between his inner convictions and his outward conduct became more and more oppressive. When he traveled to Berlin in the fall of 1847, it required visible self-control for him to seek out Meyerbeer, and when he finally reported to his wife that he had been invited to dinner at Meyerbeer's, he added, "He departs immediately—so much the better."[43]

The estrangement of the two men had already progressed this far in Wagner's Dresden years. When Wagner subsequently fled to Switzerland after taking part in the revolution in 1849, and from Zurich proceeded once again to try his luck in Paris, he counted on the help of Franz Liszt. Meyerbeer he now saw as an insidious antagonist, one who thwarted his success through intrigues. An accidental encounter at Schlesinger's bookshop, which is said to have caused Meyerbeer embarrassment—on account of his "bad conscience," Wagner asserted in a report to his wife—put the stamp of finality on the break between the two.[44] The insinuations against Meyerbeer were repeated in Wagner's letters to his friends: Meyerbeer's moneybags ruled the musical market in Paris, he asserted, and whoever wished to succeed had to be his serf.

The way in which Wagner sought to blacken the name of his former patron in the eyes of his new mentor, Liszt, is particularly instructive: "Oh dearest Liszt, you still need to acquire a clear view of this man. Shouldn't you have known long ago that natures like that of Meyerbeer are diametrically opposed to those like yours and mine?" Liszt's actions were dictated by magnanimity, Meyerbeer's by cleverness, argued Wagner. Relations between Liszt and Meyerbeer could be based only on misunderstandings or on unwarranted indulgence on the part of Liszt.[45] Wagner's intention of alienating Liszt from Meyerbeer is obvious, and to achieve it he did not refrain from alluding to Meyerbeer's origin. He condemned Meyerbeer not simply on the basis of his individual character; rather, he said, "natures like Meyerbeer's" were different from the natures of Wagner's and his correspondent. The only thing missing was a quest for the origins of this difference, an inquiry that was for the moment omitted but that apparently was already present in the mind of the writer. Very soon the quest and its answer would be presented in great detail in *Judaism in Music*.

It is obvious that Wagner's opinion of Mendelssohn and Meyerbeer had been fixed before the publication of *Judaism in Music*. It is just as certain, however, that his negative image of both Mendelssohn and Meyerbeer was formed independently of their Jewish origin and was not at first connected with it. The composition of the anti-Jewish essay, therefore, marked the establishment of a quasi-factual foundation for his subjective judgment. The artistic inadequacy of the two composers was no longer regarded as accidental, since it followed inevitably from their Jewish descent. To be sure, this line of thought implied the adoption of an anti-Jewish attitude, which was doubtless shared by some of Wagner's contemporaries but which he himself had not yet displayed. It is reasonable to assume, therefore, not that his condemnation of his rivals was due to his anti-Jewish sentiments, but quite the contrary, that his anti-Jewish sentiments flowed from his rivalry with the two Jews. If we wish to examine the validity of this supposition, we must analyze those anti-Jewish sentiments, as they find expression in *Judaism in Music*, with regard to their sources and their composition.

# 4    *Judaism in Music*

Wagner's declared intention in *Judaism in Music* was to demonstrate the destructive effect of Jewish participation in artistic endeavors, especially in the composition of music—in short, "the Judaization of modern art."[1] The word *Judaization* (*Verjüdung*) is by all appearances a Wagnerian neologism.[2] Because of the negative connotations of the word *Jew*, it clearly indicates that its originator thought that this process represented a pernicious development. Wagner repeated this opinion in many different ways: modern conditions had "brought the public art-taste of our time between the busy fingers of the Jew." What the great artists of past centuries "had wrought with all-consuming efforts, today the Jew converts into an art-commodity-exchange [*Kunstwarenwechsel*]."[3]

In these formulations as well as in the application of other concepts, Wagner relied on the stereotype already fabricated by his anti-Semitic predecessors such as Bruno Bauer and Karl Marx. The word *Jew* used in the singular as a representative of the whole of Jewry was an abstraction employed by Bauer and Marx, who projected the qualities supposedly characterizing the Jews onto a suprapersonal reification.[4] Wagner adopted this usage. The terms *Jew* and *Judaism* were for him almost always synonymous, and only rarely did he concretize the word *Jew* by means of an adjective such as *educated*.[5] This process of abstraction was in tune with Wagner's intention. He wished to underline his belief that the Jewish character traits of the individual Jew were rooted in his collective, cultural background and were independent of his intentions and abilities.

The notion of an art-commodity-exchange follows the Marxist critique of Judaism. Marx said, "The bill of exchange is the actual god of the Jew. His god is only an illusory bill of exchange." In addition, Marx had much to say about the way in which capitalism conditioned the occupation of the Jew as a merchant and as a usurer: "Money is the jealous God of Israel. . . . Money degrades all the

gods of mankind and converts them into commodities."⁶ Wagner
used the term *art-commodity-exchange* to suggest that the relation
of the Jews to art was identical to their relation to wares and commerce. He then asked who would suspect "in the mannered bric-
a-brac what is glued together by the hallowed brow-sweat of the
Genius of two thousand years?"⁷ The art produced by the Jews was
therefore not worthy of the name; it was merely "bric-a-brac,"
which owed its origin to the Jews' appropriating a foreign, non-
Jewish tradition.

In the course of our investigation we will encounter still other
concepts and turns of phrase reminiscent of Wagner's anti-Jewish
predecessors. At the very beginning of *Judaism in Music* Wagner in-
vokes "criticism" as the obvious method for penetrating a given historical object.⁸ But it was Bruno Bauer who conferred this methodological capacity on the concept of criticism.⁹ Traces of Wagner's
predecessors are discernible, then, in his store of ideas. That he read
or even studied these works is indeed probable, though it cannot be
proved. These ideas and concepts could also have come to him
through the *Zeitgeist*—concretely, the periodicals, newspapers and
journals.

In any case, Wagner took his place in a succession of anti-Jewish
figures. Like his predecessors, he analyzed the Jewish question, declaring some aspects of it to have been settled, others still of immediate interest. He thus marked off the area requiring further critical
treatment. Religion and politics he eliminated as zones of conflict.
Religion was no longer a divisive factor since "in religion the Jews
have long ceased to be our hated foes." Though others attributed
this change to the spread of enlightenment and tolerance, Wagner
referred to the decline of the Christian religion, whose representatives had "drawn upon themselves the people's hatred." Religiously
conditioned hatred had therefore been deflected from the Jews. Politics, strictly speaking, was not a source of conflict, since the Jews had
renounced the establishment of a polity of their own. Wagner noted
this renunciation with a malicious allusion to Rothschild, who instead "of wishing to be the king of the Jews . . . preferred to remain
the Jew of the kings."¹⁰

In the sociopolitical sense, that is, in relation to the granting of
civil equality to the Jews, conflict could have arisen, had not the
question of emancipation long since been decided in favor of the

Jews. The struggle for the emancipation of the Jews, said Wagner, was "extremely naive . . . seeing that it is much rather we who are put into the necessity of having to fight for emancipation from the Jews. The Jew is . . . already more than emancipated; he rules, and will rule for as long as money remains the power before which all our actions lose their power." [11] This statement sounds original and radical, and in reality the attack on the power of money represents a remnant of Wagner's prerevolutionary, extreme socialist enthusiasm. In his anti-Jewish incarnation, however, Wagner followed his predecessors. Bruno Bauer had already declared that even in Vienna, where the Jew "is only tolerated, he determines the fate of the entire realm with his monetary power." [12] Marx varied the idea in the concluding sentence of *On the Jewish Question* and lent it a deeper philosophical meaning: "The social emancipation of the Jews is the emancipation of society from Judaism." [13] In this passage Judaism probably stands as a substitute for the capitalistic world order.

Wagner adopted this dialectical formulation: it is not the Jews who require emancipation but the society ruled by them. Yet in contrast to Marx he focused his attention exclusively on the Jews. Wagner's remarks concerning their economic role and the predominance of money are book-learned ideas, which are presented as a prelude to his real subject. No challenge followed his statements. He noted with resignation the predominance of capitalism and did not contest the emancipation of the Jews. He did, however, offer a new explanation of the political support for emancipation, a cause with which he claimed to have sympathized in his liberal phase: "When we fought for the emancipation of the Jews we really were more the champions of an abstract principle than of a concrete case." Even the liberals' struggle for the people's freedom proceeded without knowledge of the people: "Thus our zeal for the Jews' acquisition of equal rights also sprang much more from the stimulus of a general idea than from a real sympathy." Then came the foundation for the main thesis of the tract: "For with all our speaking and writing in favor of Jewish emancipation, we always felt instinctively repelled by any real, active contact with Jews." [14] Between the Jews and their neighbors there was never any genuine emotional rapport, which could also have given them access to the artistic and especially the musical world of their environment. Such a relationship never could have existed, in view of the deep gulf between the different cultural traditions. In this analysis Wagner referred to "the unconscious feeling, which among the people takes the form of the most profound repugnance for the Jewish nature." He also spoke of an "instinctive antipathy" and of "a natural aversion to the Jewish nature"—feelings that were concealed or repressed for the sake of the ideology of emancipation but that had better be unleashed after the abandonment of liberal illusions.[15]

Wagner's declaration that the Jews seemed foreign was certainly not pulled out of thin air. Wagner, as well as others among his contemporaries, may have had such feelings upon meeting older Jews, especially those who spoke Yiddish and were outwardly recognizable as Jews. Such Jews were still to be found in Leipzig and Dresden and must have been an everyday sight in Königsberg and Riga, where Wagner lived in the 1830s. Wagner's description of the "purely sensual manifestation of Jewish speech" is "a creaking, squeaking, buzzing snuffle" and his characterization of traditional Jewish worship as a "gurgle, yodel and cackle" were of course conscious caricatures and exaggerations.[16] But they were certainly rooted in his own experiences, the hearing of Yiddish and the observation of the proceedings in the synagogue. When he pretended, however, to have felt "irresistible repulsion" and "an instinctive antipathy" also with regard to Jews who were of the same class and who had had the same education as himself,[17] this assertion is refuted by the record of his free and easy dealings with them.

Wagner did not restrict himself to a repetition of his observations and feelings, but rather erected an ideological superstructure over them. Thus he fabricated the theory that the Jew (i.e., all Jews) spoke "the modern European languages only as acquired, not as mother tongues," a circumstance that excluded "him from any capacity to express his nature in them in a suitable, authentic and independent manner." In support of this thesis Wagner argued that "a language, its expression and its evolution . . . [was] the work not of individual persons, but of a historical community" and only "he who has grown up in this community also has a share in its creativity."[18] Jews were excluded from the community of the European peoples, whose languages, therefore, could not serve as the medium of Jewish intellectual and artistic creativity.

In propounding this theory Wagner was apparently guided by Johann Gottlieb Fichte's well-known thesis, which the philosopher developed in his *Speeches to the German Nation*, in defense of the purported cultural superiority of the Germans. The German national language, Fichte maintained, had been transmitted in its unbroken purity from generation to generation, and that was the source of its fertilizing, generative power. With their acceptance of the foreign, Latin linguistic heritage, the French had forfeited their cultural originality. The same thing happened, according to Wagner, to all the European Jews, through their appropriation of means of expression essentially foreign to them.[19] Fichte's theory must be regarded as indemonstrable in relation to an entire national culture. Similarly, its application to the individual Jew, who supposedly can never appropriate the language in which he grew up, must be seen as having been pulled out of thin air.

The Jew's supposed foreignness in the language he speaks is, however, only a preliminary step in the development of Wagner's argument. His principal thesis is that the whole of European culture, in particular its musical creativity, remains a world inaccessible to the Jew. For that reason the Jew is in no position to make any genuine contribution to its further development. Cultural creativity, even in its most refined form, springs from "its natural soil, the true folk soul [*Volksgeist*]." In order to draw upon this spirit, the artist must have a living connection with the common people who embody it. "Now where does the educated Jew find this people?" asks Wagner. The Jew does not belong to it, and his attempt to approach it fails because of the Jew's incomprehension and the reluctance of the people. The Jew finds access only to the "richer classes," which share common interests with him but which are themselves alienated from the national culture and thus cannot possibly serve the Jew as a source of inspiration.[20]

The Jew can receive a stimulus corresponding to his nature only from his own tradition, the synagogal music. But it is from his own national tradition that the assimilated, baptized or unbaptized Jew has distanced himself.[21] In spite of this, traces of this tradition, which insult the ears of a European, are discernible in the musical works of Jewish composers, claims Wagner. They are "outlandish, odd, indifferent, cold, unnatural and twisted to us . . . so that Jewish works of music often produce on us the impression as though, for instance, one of Goethe's poems were being rendered in the Jewish jargon."[22]

In reality, during the years of the first reaction against the cultural absorption of the Jews, the then-famous actor Albert A. Ferdinand Wurm recited Goethe's poems in Berlin in Jewish-German dialect for the amusement of his audience and at the expense of the Jews.[23] Wagner may have heard or read of that performance. In any case, he suggested through this comparison that discordant, Jewish notes could be heard in the compositions of his Jewish competitors, Mendelssohn and Meyerbeer.

In his description of the social position of the Jewish artist as well as in the question of the appropriation of language, Wagner proceeded on the basis of observable facts. It is correct that the Jews found entry only into the middle class, into the educated bourgeoisie, and not into the more popular strata (or into aristocratic circles). It is likewise true that the Jewish artists avoided any connection with their own people's tradition and thus renounced a possible source of artistic inspiration. Yet the contention that the attachment of the Jews to the European cultural tradition was from the beginning condemned to failure on account of an insurmountable difference in nature is just as arbitrary as the supposition that even the educated Jew can speak a European language only as a foreign language. The purpose of this theory of Wagner's was to attribute the imaginary or real weaknesses of the artistic endeavors of Mendelssohn and Meyerbeer—the objects of his criticism—to an objective cause, their Jewish origin. The allusion to these weaknesses is not new. Wagner's assessment of them in *Judaism in Music* corresponds precisely to the occasional statements that we found in his correspondence of the previous years. What is new is only the supposed linkage of these artistic weaknesses to the Jewishness of the two men.

In Wagner's opinion, Mendelssohn recognized the limits of his artistic gift, namely, that in the creation of new musical forms he could not go beyond Beethoven. He had already made this observation in his first remarks about Mendelssohn, as we saw in chapter 3. At that time he had intended it as praise, and he had accepted the conclusions that followed from it as binding on himself as well.[24] According to the first version, Mendelssohn had restricted himself to the production of "small orchestral compositions" in obedience to a correct self-understanding. In *Judaism in Music*, Mendelssohn's recourse to pre-Beethovenian, mainly Bachian, styles is represented as the result of his limitations. Wagner, as we have noted, accepted in his youth the position he ascribed to Mendelssohn. He had believed that in the area of musical creation only bypaths remained open to post-Beethovenian musicians. Now, when he was bursting with the idea of presenting the world with an unprecedented artistic genre, the *Gesamtkunstwerk*, what Mendelssohn in his modesty was capable of producing seemed to him to be of secondary rank.

This classification of Mendelssohn's music is, at bottom, the sole critical objection Wagner makes against the Jewish composer. Neither in *Judaism in Music* nor, for that matter, in his later remarks, does Wagner deny the significance of Mendelssohn within the bounds that composer set for himself. The analysis of Mendelssohn's achievement in the essay oscillates between the positive impression that his music had made on Wagner since his youth and the reflective critique, which cannot admit the possibility of any complete artistic satisfaction on the part of the audience. One would be enthralled by Mendelssohn's music if it were meant to satisfy the "entertainment-seeking fancy" but not the "deep and genuine feelings of the human heart," wrote Wagner. Our whimsical imaginative powers are entranced by Mendelssohn, "but our purely human inner yearnings for a clear artistic vision are scarcely touched." In the end, however, Wagner cannot deny the master he once revered the capacity to have occasionally found the "expression of mellow and melancholy resignation," a compliment that is immediately weakened by the contention that this tragic characteristic stems from "his oppressive sense of this incapacity" to go beyond his own limits.[25]

The soundness of Wagner's analysis is a question for researchers in the field of music. Once it is assumed, however, that Mendelssohn's limited creativity is a demonstrable fact, how can it be derived from his Jewish origin? Wagner explains at the outset that the example of Mendelssohn proves that a Jew can possess the most outstanding qualifications, "a fullness of talent . . . the finest and most varied education . . . a delicate sense of honor" for artistic creation, "without being able to bring about "heart- and soul-stirring effects" in his art.[26] In the subsequent analysis of his works, Wagner makes no attempt to trace the supposed weaknesses of Mendelssohn's art to his Jewishness. Wagner's concluding judgment of Mendelssohn is restricted to the assertion that the "tragedy of his situation"—that is, his inadequacy, conditioned by Judaism—"rather hung over him than came to actual, sore and cleansing consciousness."[27] Mendelssohn, therefore, did not know what was happening to him, and only Wagner discovered that Judaism was his tragic fate, barring his way to artistic perfection. The forced character of this conception is plain. It is probably due to Wagner's intention of preventing the subsequent critique of Meyerbeer, in which the Jewish background plays a decisive role, from appearing to be an isolated instance.

If, in the end, Wagner held it to Mendelssohn's credit that he was not entirely conscious of being torn between his wishes and his ability, he said of the other, unnamed composer "that he wants to create works of art, yet at the same time knows that he cannot create them." Though this composer is not identified, no contemporary could misunderstand the allusion: "In order to extricate himself from this painful conflict between Will and Can, he writes operas for Paris, and sends them touring round the world." Mendelssohn was no longer alive, and in the end Wagner said may good things about him. His critique of his unnamed contemporary was, on the other hand, withering. As we already know from Wagner's correspondence, Wagner denied that Meyerbeer had any capacity for original artistic work. He could only drive away the boredom of the public by providing it with diversions through the piquant and indiscriminate accumulation of musical motifs already known to the public, heightened by "the effective weaving of emotional catastrophes." In his efforts to deceive the public, Wagner said, the composer deceived himself with regard to the artistic merit of his works. The weakness of character thus revealed, in contrast to the tragic situation of Mendelssohn, lent a tragicomic aspect to the tension between "Will and Can."[28]

This tragicomic aspect, like everything negative about Meyerbeer, Wagner readily ascribed to his Jewish background. In his description of the eclectic composition of Meyerbeer's operas, Wagner used the word *jargon*, which suggests Yiddish. He spoke in a footnote of a "Jewish operatic composer" who was not bothered by the absentmindedness and apathy of the theater public—Wagner was thinking of the disturbances and interruptions he could observe at performances in Paris—because he was used to similar occurrences in every "Jewish congregation, throughout the musical performance of divine service in the synagogue." From diagnosing the tragicomic aspect of the Meyerbeerian phenomenon Wagner proceeded to a comparative characterization of everything Jewish, "as in general the uninspiring . . . is the mark whereby this famed composer shows his Jewishness in his music." [29]

Mendelssohn and Meyerbeer are presented to us, with different emphases and arguments, as representatives of Jewish existence and the Jewish nature. Astonishingly, Wagner simultaneously presents them as symptoms and symbols of contemporary conditions. The limited creative power of Mendelssohn, "the uncommonly gifted specific musician," demonstrates "the ineptitude of the present musical epoch" in general, whereas the success of the fundamentally barren Meyerbeer testifies to the "unartistic nature and desires" of the public. [30] But if Wagner asserts that the characteristics represented by the two Jews are typical of the entire age, then they cannot be derived from their Jewish origin.

This obvious contradiction in his argumentation did not escape Wagner. He met it with an answer that does credit to his ideological ingenuity but hardly to his inner quest for truth. Neither the stagnation of artistic creativity, as displayed in Mendelssohn, nor the decline of musical taste, which made possible the ascent of Meyerbeer, is the work of Jews, said Wagner. Both are determined by the general enervation in the "musical epoch" following Mozart and Beethoven.

Nonetheless, there is good reason to connect the poor state of affairs in the world of art with the Jews' entry into it. Their entry became possible only when this world lost its "organic life-need." "Down to the epochs of Mozart and Beethoven, a Jewish composer was not to be found anywhere: it was impossible for an element entirely foreign to that living organism to take part in the formative stages of that life." [31] There was, of course, a simple explanation for the absence of Jewish musicians prior to that time, namely, that the Jews had lived until then in the isolation of the ghetto. But this fact disturbed Wagner just as little as the obvious contradictions of his theory mentioned above. The belief in the foreignness of the Jewish nature as the key to explaining deplorable phenomena in musical life had become a necessity for him.

How deeply he felt the necessity to distance himself from things Jewish can be seen in the picture he sketched of an organism analogous to musical life. After its death the organism lends "foreign elements the power to take possession of it—yet merely to destroy it. Then that body's flesh dissolves into a swarming colony of worms; but who, in looking at that body, would hold it for still living?" [32] The decomposition of the already deceased body of German music is therefore ascribed to Judaism—a division of roles dictated by the idea of the corruptive powers inherent in Judaism.

There can be no doubt about the historical source of this conception. It is a residue of the centuries-old demonization of the Jews and Judaism in their conflict with Christianity. Traces of this demonization can also be discerned among persons who, like Wagner, declared that the religious tension between Jews and their environment had been overcome. They could not connect the ideas they had absorbed about Jews with their religious origin, and they therefore had to summon new, secular grounds for these ideas. [33] Wagner, too, must have been searching for such a justification, even if he did not develop it systematically or clarify it conceptually.

The concept of race, which Wagner later utilized, did not serve in *Judaism in Music* as a distinctive feature for characterizing the Jews. Once, in passing, Wagner stated that the "Jewish way of speaking," supposedly found also among educated Jews, was "to be explained purely on the basis of physiology." Elsewhere, he explained the same phenomenon by referring to the "peculiar obstinacy of the Jewish nature" [34]—an expression that likewise pointed to a hereditary characteristic. But the use of these expressions in no way implied the idea of a biological basis for Jewish characteristics. Wagner attributed the linguistic peculiarities of Jews rather to their historical fate of living outside the language-forming community, "isolated . . . in a dispersed, uprooted tribe." [35] The concept of tribe (*Stamm*) was repeatedly used to designate the peculiarity of the Jews. [36] The isolation of the Jew, even the educated one, did not cease with his formal entry into modern society. As before, the Jew was shut off from access to the popular strata, the bearers of the "folk soul" (*Volksgeist*).

If there is a fundamental concept underlying Wagner's theory of the incompatibility of Jewish artistic creation with that of the Germans, then it is that of the folk soul. The Jews too had their "folk sources," which, because they were different from, and inferior to, the German or the European, permitted them to exist as a foreign peculiarity.[37] Wagner repeatedly stressed and referred, with an undertone of denigration, to the foreignness of the Jew, in order to explain the German's supposed "involuntary repugnance" for and "instinctive antipathy" toward the Jew.[38] In any case, these explanations represent a cultural-historical, perhaps a sociological, interpretation, but by no means one that is biologically based.

Whether or not it is explained biologically, the permanence of the Jewish character is presupposed. Thus the question arises whether there are means by which the Jew can somehow shed his odious "nature." We receive the answer in the last paragraphs of the tract, which sound like a surprising final chord. Here Wagner refers back to his own statement that the Jews of modern times had indeed produced thinkers—he certainly meant Spinoza and Moses Mendelssohn—but no poets.[39] Thinking is an activity that can be engaged in by the isolated individual. Composing poetry, however, requires rootedness in a community. Glancing back at his arguments, Wagner seems to have realized that his assertion was called into question by the familiar figure of Heinrich Heine. The effort to solve the problem posed by Heine compelled Wagner to make statements full of ambiguity: "At the time when Goethe and Schiller sang among us, we certainly know nothing of a poetry-writing Jew." This line of thought runs parallel to the one concerning the absence of Jewish composers during Beethoven's time. Thus the postclassical period in poetry is characterized as devoid of any originality, and as a time "when our poetry became a lie, when every possible thing might flourish from the wholly unpoetic element of our life, but no true poet."[40] Whether this devastating judgment would be validated by literary historians, in particular students of the romantic period, may well be doubted.

At any rate, since the situation in poetry appears to run parallel to that in music, we must now expect to encounter a mendacious rhymester à la Meyerbeer. Instead of that we meet Heine, the "highly gifted poetical Jew," who exposed "with fascinating taunts that lie, that bottomless aridity and jesuitical hypocrisy of our versifying

which still would give itself the airs of true poetry." Heine also castigated "his famous musical fellow tribesmen . . . for their pretense
to pass as artists." For that, Wagner had to give him credit. Yet
Wagner, in accordance with his scheme, could not possibly stop at
simple praise of Heine, and thus he wrote of the "remorseless demon of denial" that "drove [Heine] on without a rest, through all
the mirage of our modern self-deception, till he reached the point
where he in turn duped himself into thinking he was a poet." At the
outset Heine is designated as an uncommonly gifted poetical Jew. In
the end, however, he is placed in the category of self-deceivers like
Meyerbeer. As proof of this spiritual affinity Wagner mentions that
Heine "also, for that reason, had his versified lies put to music
by our composers."[41] This argument would be very convincing if
one did not know that Wagner had been one of the first to set *Two
Grenadiers* to music.[42]

The entire passage on Heine abounds in ambivalent statements,
since Wagner's thesis of the artistic barrenness of Judaism meshes
poorly with his high opinion of Heine's poetic talent. The concluding sentence is almost incomprehensible: "Heine was the conscience of Judaism, just as Judaism is the bad conscience of our
modern civilization."[43] Neither the first nor the second part of this
antithesis can be derived from what preceded it or can be compre-
hended on that basis, and it probably has to be seen as an attempt to
elude embarrassing difficulties with a rhetorical flourish.

Without a proper transition, and apparently only because Heine
and Börne had already become an inseparable pair in people's minds
at that time, Wagner began the next section, the last of the essay,
with this sentence: "Yet another Jew have we to name, who appeared
among us as a writer." "Seeking redemption," Börne emerged from
his "isolation as a Jew" and decided to find his own redemption
"with ours as genuine human beings." Though Wagner does not say
how others will become genuine human beings, for the Jew the
recipe is ready: "To become a human being together with us means
for the Jew as much as first of all ceasing to be a Jew." Börne
achieved that goal; he ceased to be a Jew. At the same time, however,
his example teaches a lesson: "This redemption cannot be reached
in ease and cold, indifferent complacency, but costs—as cost it must
for us—sweat, anguish, want, and all the dregs of sufferings and

sorrow."[44] Wagner probably had in mind Börne's selfless battle for a free and better society in a democratic state. At one time Wagner had identified himself with this sociopolitical ideal, and he remembered the idealized image of Börne, whom he had never met personally, as the champion. Thus the figure of Börne was set up as a positive counterpart to the other Jews. What was positive about him was his supposedly absolute renunciation of Judaism and his attachment to the new mankind that was coming into being. Wagner held this road open to other Jews as well and ended his tirade with a call to all of Jewry to take part in the still ongoing struggle for the redemption of humanity. But at the same time he warned the Jews that their participation in that struggle depended on their complete abandonment of Judaism: "But remember that only one thing can redeem you from the burden of your curse: the redemption of Ahasuerus—going under."[45]

Here Wagner is clearly referring to the Christian concept of redemption, to the idea of a curse burdening the Jew and the image of the eternal Jew symbolizing Judaism. Thus our attention is unintentionally directed to the source from which the animus to Jewish existence appears to flow. In Wagner's own world of ideas the Christian concepts appear in a secularized form, which is clearly recognizable in the way in which he imagines the redemption of the Jews. Wagner does not have in mind individual baptism or collective conversion to Christianity, as the Ahasuerus myth foresees. For him, baptism has lost its sacramental significance and therewith also its capacity to transform the basic nature of the Jew. The fact that the three Jews mentioned by name—Mendelssohn, Heine, and Börne— were baptized does not differentiate them in Wagner's opinion from the unbaptized Meyerbeer. Liberation from Judaism is possible not through the solitary act of baptism, but as a consequence of a self-negating process, one that is scarcely subject to external verification. Therefore self-liberation from Judaism remained open to all Jews in theory, but the decision as to whether it had taken place in an individual instance lay in the eye of the beholder, as we shall see when we examine Wagner's relations with his Jewish admirers and acquaintances.

For the rest, the idea of the limited role of baptism, as it is reflected in Wagner's theory, corresponds to the concrete social relations of the time. Baptism was no longer capable of uprooting the Jew from the social structure of his community and transplanting him into that of the Christians. Jews and Christians continued to oppose each other as two separate social units, only the transitional zone was blurred. There was a neutral region in which members of both groups could meet and in which baptized Jews could settle. In view of this disarray in the social reality, it is no wonder that theories like those of Wagner give evidence of conceptual confusion.

# 5 Consequences of Publication

What moved Wagner to make public his opinion of Meyerbeer and his theory of the harmfulness of Jewish participation in German cultural life? At the beginning of *Judaism in Music*, which was first published on 3 and 6 September 1850 in the *Neue Zeitschrift für Musik* (numbers 19 and 20) in Leipzig, Wagner referred to the expression "Hebrew artistic taste," which had been mentioned in the periodical and which then gave rise to an "attack and a defense."[1] The originator of the expression was Wagner's friend and admirer Theodor Uhlig, who had used it in a critical review of Meyerbeer's latest opera, *Le Prophète*, which had recently been brought to the German stage. Uhlig's critique culminated in an unmistakable allusion to the opposition between Christian and Jewish artistic trends and concluded that "such kinds of songs seem to a good Christian at best artificial, exaggerated, and unnaturally delicate. Moreover, it is not likely that this kind of propaganda for the Hebrew taste in art will enjoy any success."[2]

A protest against this Christian-Jewish contrast appeared in the first number of the *Rheinische Musik-Zeitung für Kunstfreunde und Künstler*, a paper that had just been launched in Cologne. Uhlig's observation was there characterized as "an unjustified attack on the people of Israel." Uhlig supposed that the author of this reply was a Jew,[3] but the article probably came from the pen of the editor of the newspaper, Professor L. Bischof.[4] In any case, Uhlig felt obliged to define his anti-Jewish arguments more precisely. He was, he said, referring only to the Jewish musicians, for "in the music of many Jewish composers there are passages which almost all non-Jewish musicians call Jewish music, Jew-jabber [*Gemauschele*] or something like that . . . with reference to the familiar, ordinary Jewish manner of speaking." The traces of "Jew-jabber" are not discernible in the same measure in all Jewish composers; they emerge "here only slightly, there quite strikingly, in Mendelssohn, for example, very mildly, in Meyerbeer, on the other hand, most sharply, namely in his *Les Huguenots*, but no less in his *Le Prophete*."⁵ Uhlig thus anticipated Wagner's central thesis concerning the influence of the Jewish manner of speaking on the music of the Jewish artist and even the related ranking of Mendelssohn and Meyerbeer.

Uhlig was not the only one to connect the criticized features of Meyerbeer's operas with his Judaism. Dr. Eduard Krüger likewise declared in the *Neue Zeitschrift für Musik* that the operas of Meyerbeer were a "cold fluttering of declamations, wishy-washy, without melody, without beauty." The acclaim these operas received was due to their external features, the "ballet, scenery, tubas and harp-playing." The public was not interested in the actual singing of the operas, for Krüger observed in Berlin, Hannover, Hamburg, and Kassel that there was "chatter, winking and yawning" when it was going on. No wonder, for the songs did not spring from the soil of the German folk song, nor were the melodies of the opera "being hummed by the people." That these weaknesses were to be attributed to Meyerbeer's Jewish origin was made evident by the insistent use of the name Jacob Meyerbeer, or simply Beer, "called Giacomo in the bookstore."⁶ Wagner took up this observation of Krüger's as well.

With the reference to this discussion at the beginning of his essay in the *Neue Zeitschrift für Musik*, Wagner could thus take his place in an anti-Jewish polemic that had already gone quite far. Years later in his autobiography he explained his intervention in the debate as resulting from his intention not to leave the matter at the "meaningless provocations" of his predecessors. They stimulated him "to consider more closely the subject of the modern Jews' meddling in music and their influence on it, and to point out the characteristic features of the phenomenon."⁷

Though Wagner's own information about what inspired him to write *Judaism in Music* is well substantiated, it conceals his deeper motive for joining the debate. We learn what he was really thinking from his letter to Franz Liszt some time after the appearance of the essay. Wagner had it published under the pseudonym of K. Freigedank, but interested circles quickly learned who was hiding behind that name. Liszt therefore asked Wagner whether it was true that he was the author. Wagner reacted with irritation: "Surely you know that I wrote the article. Why are you asking me now?"[8] He proceeded to give a detailed explanation of his reasons, which give the impression of release from an almost unbearable burden.

Wagner wrote that he nourished "a long-suppressed anger against this Jew-business, and this anger is as necessary to my nature as bile is to the blood." The occasion for the explosion of this anger was "their accursed words," which annoyed him. After this general statement, which was embellished by the observation that an attack on the Jews was useless, since "now it is not our princes but the bankers and the philistines who are the rulers," Wagner arrived at the personal aspect of the matter, namely, his relations with Meyerbeer. Here his utterances took on the character of a confession. He did not hate Meyerbeer, but he found him "infinitely repugnant." Meyerbeer reminded him of the days of his "vicious period," when he wanted to make his way as a musician under the protection of patrons of Meyerbeer's ilk. It was in the end a good thing that Meyerbeer had not helped him, for Wagner was thereby not as deeply indebted to him as some others were. The relations between them were never honest; both acted for selfish reasons as long as it appeared to be to their advantage. But to Wagner the connection with Meyerbeer brought the misfortune that many people, friends included, had received the impression that he had something in common with Meyerbeer artistically. That notion had brought Wagner to despair and caused him to demonstrate publicly his distance from his former patron. Why, then, did the article not appear under his own name? "Not out of fear, but in order to prevent the question from being dragged by the Jew into the purely personal, did I resort to using a pseudonym."[9]

We have every reason to take very seriously this confession to an intimate friend, though it must be subjected to a critical examination. According to this letter, *Judaism in Music* owes its origin to Wagner's need to come to grips with his relationship with Meyerbeer. Wagner makes no reference to the other Jewish figures mentioned in the essay—Mendelssohn, Heine, and Börne. These men apparently played no role in stimulating his writing. Wagner brought them in, as the analysis of the pamphlet's contents also shows, only to provide a broader justification for his dissociation from Meyerbeer on account of his Jewishness.

Wagner's relationship with Meyerbeer was the source of the uneasiness that prompted him to act. The gradual growth of Wagner's antipathy can be observed in his correspondence. We saw how his sycophancy to Meyerbeer, which did not even yield any results, became a burden to him. That his feigned admiration for the master made insincerity unavoidable may have weighed lightly on him. Wagner was anything but prim in his attempts to approach persons from whom he could expect an advancement of his career. Meyerbeer, however, was an artistically controversial personality, and a connection with him could easily be interpreted as approval of his art. To be lumped together with Meyerbeer, or even just to come under the suspicion of having been under the musical influence of Meyerbeer, was Wagner's paramount anxiety. We have already seen, in chapter 3, how passionately he protested against such a suspicion on the part of Schumann. But Schumann was not the only one who believed—in full recognition of the originality of Wagner's creation—that he had discovered Meyerbeerian elements in it. In the course of a critique of Meyerbeer's *Le Prophete*, an anonymous admirer of Wagner came to speak of his *Rienzi* and *Tannhäuser*. He insisted that they deserved an artistic evaluation as a unique category, and he also saw as one aspect of Wagner's work the "combination of Weber and Meyerbeer." [10] This insight with regard to Wagner's more or less substantial dependence on Meyerbeer's example is shared by modern historians of music. [11]

Whether Wagner was conscious of this burden of debt and wished to repress it or whether his sense of his own originality rejected from the start the idea of his having been influenced by his immediate predecessors may remain undecided. In any case, *Judaism in Music* is a clear and unequivocal protest against such a supposition. In his letter to Liszt, Wagner makes clear that the publication of his essay was tied up with this intention. It drove him, he wrote, "to true despair when I ran into the erroneous view even of many of my friends that I have anything at all in common with Meyerbeer." [12] In Wagner's opinion, this view represented a fatal misunderstanding of his art, and he must have encountered it among others as well. To come upon it in a public defender of his art was probably enough to induce him to confront it energetically.

The simplest way for him to distance himself from Meyerbeer's work, of course, would have been to come forward with a direct critique of it. Wagner, however, shied away from such an open rejection of his former mentor. To himself and to his trusted friend Liszt, Wagner apologized for his change of opinion, which was apt to give rise to the accusation of disloyalty. He asserted that his relations with Meyerbeer had always been marked by reciprocal dishonesty,[13] a confession that also implied a scathing moral judgment of Wagner himself. One could make such a confession in confidential correspondence but by no means in a public reckoning.

Wagner chose two other means to avoid leaving an impression of disloyalty: he had the article appear pseudonymously and he gave his dissociation from Meyerbeer a seemingly concrete foundation—the rejection of Jewish influence on German art. Wagner justified the pseudonymity of the publication, as we have seen, with the alleged fear that the matter could be interpreted as a personal attack. To this argument he continued to adhere at a later date in his autobiography. He wished to avoid a situation in which "a matter that I took very seriously would be dragged right away onto the purely personal level and its true significance would thereby be concealed."[14] Thus his attack on Judaism appeared as the actual goal of his article and the unnamed Meyerbeer only as an example. In reality, it was the reverse. The complicated and oppressive relationship with Meyerbeer, and the wish to be free of it, caused Wagner to venture into an area which, as far as was known at the time, appeared to lie outside his interests—the critique of Judaism.

Because of Wagner's own confession to Liszt that he nourished "a long-suppressed anger against this Jew-business," we are obliged to believe him when he states that his objections against the Jews and Judaism began to accumulate before his altercation with Meyerbeer. That he was familiar with the problems of modern Judaism and especially with the anti-Jewish writings of the previous decades emerges, as we have seen, from an analysis of his essay. As a source for his information concerning the modern Jewish problem, he cited his association with Berthold Auerbach in Dresden, in whom, he wrote in his autobiography, he "met with the first Jew with whom I could speak even about Judaism with cordial impartiality."[15] From Auerbach he may have heard critical opinions of modern Jewish conditions, but certainly not with an undertone of hatred and sarcasm. Such a tone was altogether uncharacteristic of Auerbach,[16] whereas it predominates in Wagner's account. Wagner's statement that he was among those who "fought for the emancipation of the

Jews" probably refers to his Dresden period.[17] If he was not an active participant—and there is no evidence that he was—he at least followed the struggle sympathetically. When, therefore, did his "anger against this Jew-business" begin?

In the outline of a letter of Minna Wagner's dating from 1850, in which she recapitulates the history of her stressful marriage in order to bring Richard—then staying in Paris—back to her, she gives the reason why he ceased to allow her to participate in his creative life: "And again, since two years ago, when you wanted me to read that essay in which you defame an entire race, which actually did you many favors—since that time you have been so resentful of me and punished me with that so severely that you never let me hear any of your works any more." [18] If the reference here is to Wagner's anti-Jewish pamphlet—we know nothing of another "defamatory writing"—then it must be, as one of Wagner's biographers supposed, an earlier version already composed at the end of his Dresden period.[19] In any case, the final formulation bears the mark of the period of its publication. It is connected with Wagner's other writings originating in Zurich (see chapter 3), in which Wagner asserted the depravity of the artistic production of the present, which he associated in *Judaism in Music* with the Jews. Even this published version underwent changes. To the young Karl Ritter, an intimate friend of Wagner's around this time, who had the task of transmitting the manuscript to the *Neue Zeitschrift für Musik*, Wagner wrote: "Here you have the manuscript. . . . I touched it up in many ways—as you shall see—when I had it copied." [20]

Wagner must have carried the idea of the pamphlet around with him for some time. It is unlikely that the many anti-Jewish associations, which go back to earlier sources, entered his mind in the process of writing, though they were familiar to him from earlier reading and were certainly latent in his mind. The good taste reigning in liberal circles led Wagner to avoid the "subject of Jew" when mentioning persons of Jewish origin. He himself confirms this in his report of an episode in Paris, in which Maurice Schlesinger was asked whether he was Jewish: "I was pleasantly astonished by this unembarrassed conversation about a point which in similar cases among Germans we anxiously avoid as insulting to the person concerned." [21] He held fast to this reserve until he broke the taboo in order to condemn the Jewish influence on contemporary art and thereby to demonstrate his particular position.

Wagner does not provide any satisfactory information concerning the reason for this decision in the fall of 1850. His annoyance over the widespread misjudgment that he owed some of his musical inspiration to Meyerbeer was not new. His remarks on that subject in a letter to Robert Schumann in 1843 are of almost the same tenor as what he wrote eight years later to Liszt.[22] Wagner's statement to Liszt that the Jews' "accursed writing" angered him, "and so all at once I broke loose,"[23] may have been occasioned by Uhlig's supposition that the protest against the concept of the "Hebrew taste in art" originated from a Jew. Even then the literary feud could only have stimulated the crystallization of feelings he had nourished for a long time. That he yielded this time to the temptation must have been due to his awareness of standing at a turning point in his life and work, and the wish to place a visible capstone on his past.

This inner drive may, however, have been strengthened by an external circumstance. After his return from Paris (and this affair with Jessie Laussot in Bordeaux), the Ritter family promised Wagner a permanent grant.[24] He could therefore feel himself economically secure, without having to trouble himself over the consequences of his semipublic declaration of war against an influential circle. Wagner, to be sure, declared to Liszt that "from inner motives it became necessary for me to abandon all regard for ordinary prudence in relation to him [Meyerbeer]."[25] As long as Wagner had hoped for help from Meyerbeer, he had strictly adhered to the rules of prudence at the expense of sincerity. Now, when he no longer expected any help from these quarters and found his situation secured by assistance from elsewhere, he could toss all fears to the winds.

The attack issued under the name of Freigedank was sharp by any standard, and its reference to Jews was highly unusual. As was to be expected, it aroused considerable attention, at least in interested circles. "It seems to have struck a frightful blow," noted Wagner with satisfaction, "for I really wanted to give them just such a fright."[26] Franz Brendel, the editor of the newspaper, confirmed this impression: the essay had "called forth a real storm"; friendly and hostile discussions had "appeared in a host of other papers."[27] Brendel received numerous letters, of which he published only one that was commendatory, by Eduard Krüger, and one that was disapproving, by Eduard Bernsdorf. Half a year later, when the "agitated passions" had died down, he himself offered a "conciliatory" conclusion, which in reality sought to render Wagner's opinions harmless. Brendel had every reason to do so. Since the author was protected against personal attacks by his pseudonym, the indignation over the sharpness and tactlessness of the anti-Jewish charges was directed against the editor in charge. Brendel was threatened by a still more palpable unpleasantness. He was at the time a professor at the Leipzig conservatory, where five of his colleagues were Jews or friends of Jews who, incensed over the publication, demanded his dismissal—without success.[28]

Eduard Krüger, whose anti-Jewish banalities had been among the stimuli that motivated Wagner to compose his essay, greeted the pamphlet as a congenial statement. He repeated in a coarsened form many of Wagner's accusations and named Meyerbeer as the Jewish musician against whom Wagner's writing was directed. Only in the critique of Mendelssohn did Krüger find something to which he objected. Wagner went too far in his repudiation of every Jewish cultural production: "The Jewish nation, like the whole tribe of the Semites to which it belongs, was never artistically gifted. . . . But that is not to say that Jews cannot achieve this or that lucky success, especially when they have lived for a long time in close contact with deeply gifted peoples who possess a highly developed culture."[29] To this category of fortuitous, adopted talents Mendelssohn belongs.

Even if Krüger was a more dispassionate judge with regard to Mendelssohn, he subsumed the Jews among the supposedly culturally barren Semites more openly and more explicitly than did Wagner. In any case, Wagner could be satisfied with the support his main thesis received from Krüger. The opposition of Bernsdorf, however, put him in a rage, to which he gave free rein in a short, abundantly rude letter to the author. Wagner accused Bernsdorf of distorting his basic thesis; he did not attribute the decay of art to Jewish influence but only maintained *"that the Jews could only interfere in our art when it had become organically incapable of living."*[30] Bernsdorf did in fact fall victim to this misunderstanding, as did many of Wagner's later readers and critics, but this error makes no difference with regard to the defamation of the Jewish character. In any case, Bernsdorf's main intention was to protest against this defamation, which went beyond the denial of Jewish capacity for art to include disparaging remarks about the way Jews conducted themselves in business and the like. Bernsdorf pointed out that the arbitrary connection between the supposed or real weaknesses of the Jewish musician and his Jewish origin, particularly in the case of Mendelssohn, was asserted without proof as self-evident. The reason for Wagner's mistakes, he maintained, was that Wagner allowed his image of the Jew to be determined by "the Polish Jewish second-hand dealer," as was shown by his example of the Jewish way of speaking. Yet such outward characteristics could be overcome, and the creative artists whom modern Judaism had produced testified to the "quest for culture and the capacity for culture" of the Jews. The Jew was ceasing "to be a foreigner in art, which pours out its rays over everyone, transfiguring all of humanity." [31]

The insistence on the human dignity of the Jew, the highest principle of the emancipatory endeavors, is the decisive point in the argument of this opponent of Wagner. But since Wagner had turned his back on these endeavors, he could only reply disdainfully, "Thus I have nothing to say in reply but the words of Pontius Pilate: *I wrote what I wrote*" (emphasis in the original), and signed it "K. Freigedank." [32]

The people involved knew, of course, who was hiding behind this name, but Wagner's anonymity was not lifted. Brendel wrote in defense of the author that his judgment concerning the Jews would lose some of its harshness "if one were acquainted with the views of Freigedank on a larger scale. What appears here to be imputed to the Jews in particular is actually only a result of his overall conception of the nature of modern art." [33] Thus the reader was referred to Wagner's writings, without his name having been mentioned.

Otherwise, however, Brendel's apology scarcely allowed Wagner's anti-Jewish conception to appear in a milder light. First, Brendel maintained that the contemptuous characterization in *Judaism in Music* applied only to the "common Jew": the excellent men who "stripped off" the unlovely Jewish nature that was a general characteristic of the tribe were by no means barred from "the path to higher things." But then he said that "the cultured Jew has not entered in a truly inward manner into our spiritual life, into our morals." Those who attempted to do so "deceive themselves in the undertaking, wishing to unite incompatible things." Is the Jews' integration into their environment therefore impossible? Not entirely. "The Jews are welcome if they truly, sincerely, and inwardly wish to belong to us. They then cease to be Jews. But to exploit our culture, without having inwardly achieved this . . . is pernicious." [34] This movement back and forth between the rejection of everything Jewish and the wish nevertheless to hold the door open to the select Jews was expressed even more crassly in this version than in Wagner's original.

Since the name Wagner was not mentioned in the discussion of *Judaism in Music*, the knowledge of his authorship remained restricted to the initiated circles. In the public mind he was identified with the venomous anti-Jewish pamphlet only after its republication in 1869 under his full name. The initial publication had a direct impact, however, on the author himself. His semipublic reckoning with Meyerbeer did not free him from his Meyerbeer complex, but deepened and fixed it still more. Wagner ascribed difficulties that beset him to the intrigues of Meyerbeer. When an unfriendly discussion of Wagner's works appeared in Paris, the composer remarked in a letter to Theodor Uhlig, "Meyerbeer is endlessly active, he fears my propaganda directed toward Paris—the ass." [35] Wagner obviously expected a reaction from Meyerbeer to his attacks and believed he had found it here. At the Prussian court the performance of *Tannhäuser* ran into resistance; something like that "does not come about by chance; it is the work of Meyerbeer." [36] Wagner was now fixated on the idea of a regular "movement brought into a well-planned system by a great expert in such things, Mr. Meyerbeer, which he will put into practice with a sure hand from now until his blessed end." [37]

With his renewed attempt to attain a success through the performance of *Tannhäuser* in Paris, Wagner attributed every setback as well as the final fiasco to the cunning machinations of Meyerbeer. [38] The conspiracy was universal-Jewish and international. In early 1855, when Wagner failed to attain a hoped-for success in London, he wrote to his intimate friend Ernst Benedikt Kietz in Paris: "I am for the most part torn down in the press on account of Mendelssohn and the other Jews, who wish me eternal life." [39] Around this time Meyerbeer likewise found himself in London, and chance had it that the two of them met—for the last time in their lives. In view of their strained relations, it was no wonder that, as Wagner reported, not a word passed their lips.[40]

How elementally, indeed almost metaphysically, Wagner experienced his opposition to Meyerbeer can be seen from his reaction to the report of Meyerbeer's death. This news reached him on 3 May 1864, just as he was celebrating with his friends the surprising message of support from King Ludwig II, which must have seemed to him a heaven-sent salvation from the direst need and a turning point in his destiny. Wagner wrote, "At dinner we received the telegraphic report of Meyerbeer's death, which had just occurred in Paris: Weinheimer [one of his friends] burst into rustic laughter at this wonderful coincidence, that the opera master who had become so harmful to me should not live to see precisely this day."[41] According to Wagner's report, to be sure, the symbolic connection of the events stems from the mouth of a friend, but it obviously comes also from the heart of the reporter.[42] The triumph over the foe who has now been swept out of the way breaks through here with—one is inclined to say—Old Testament-like vehemence. In his reaction to Mendelssohn's death we have already caught Wagner evincing similar, though more disguised, feelings.

It is true that Wagner's anti-Jewish ardor was inflamed by his conflict with Meyerbeer, but once kindled it was directed against Jews in general. His rejection of the musical works of Jewish composers became a rejection of all areas of cultural creation by Jews, and like a common Jew-baiter, he habitually found fault with the Jewish character. While the article was still in press in 1850, he wrote to Theodor Uhlig, who lived in Dresden (from which Wagner was barred) and who maintained contact with the editor, Brendel: "Will he pay me for Judaism? Forgive me this Jewish question, but it is the Jews' fault that I have to count every farthing."[43] Remarks of this kind are not found in his statements dating from earlier decades, whereas from now on they are part of his agenda.

This change is likewise reflected in his retrospective view of past events and encounters, as the example of Berthold Auerbach makes clear. The encounter between the two men was marked by mutual enthusiasm. In *My Life*, dictated in the middle of the 1860s, Wagner had to admit that he had been keenly interested in Auerbach's literary work, the famous *Village Tales from the Black Forest*, as well as in its author: "The short, burly Jewish farm boy, as he greatly liked to style himself, made an altogether agreeable impression." Even more instructive is Wagner's statement concerning the role that Judaism played in his conversations with Auerbach: "What attracted me in particular was that I met in him the first Jew with whom I could talk even about Judaism with cordial impartiality. He even seemed to be set on destroying all prejudices against that characteristic in a genial manner." Auerbach told him about insults that he had had to suffer as a Jewish schoolboy, experiences that "left him melancholy and reflective, but not embittered. These were now traits which very much won my heart." The only thing that Wagner found objectionable in Auerbach's conduct at that time was his excessive preoccupation with Jewish matters: "The whole world and its history contain for him merely the problem of the transfiguration of Judaism," a characterization also supported by other sources.[44]

In Wagner's rendition his initially positive impressions of Auerbach were interspersed with revised opinions dating from the later period. Wagner was advised by Gottfried Keller that Auerbach's outward manner should by no means be taken as a naive self-presentation of a "Jewish farm boy." It was rather a calculated means with which "one best brings one's literary opus before the public and turns it into gold."[45] Rumors concerning Auerbach's dubious character reached Wagner's ears from other sources as well. There was, for intance, the report that Auerbach "had in the course of time married numerous Jewish women [and] thereby become wealthy"—a rumor of whose falseness Wagner could easily have convinced himself.[46] As anti-Jewish prejudices became entrenched in Wagner's mind, his original image of Auerbach was displaced: "When I saw him again in Zurich after many years, I was sorry to note that even his physical appearance had altered in disquieting ways: he looked really extraordinarily common and dirty. The earlier fresh liveliness had turned into the ordinary Jewish restlessness; he phrased everything in such a fashion that one could see that it grieved him not rather to have used what he had said for the newspaper,"[47] an observation that appears rather to have lain in the eyes of the beholder.

Had Wagner consistently distanced himself from all the Jews in his circle of acquaintances, we could give more weight to his confession that his recently awakened anger against the "Jew-business" was as necessary to his nature "as bile is to blood." In reality, his rejection of Jews was selective as well as vacillating and very often dictated by transparent motives. A striking example is his relationship with Ferdinand Hiller. As we have seen, Wagner was friendly with him in Dresden. That the musician, stemming from a Frankfurt banking family, and his Polish wife were baptized Jews did not hinder them from making their house the center of social and, to a large extent, artistic life in Dresden. Nor did it hinder Wagner from taking part in that life. Only in his memoirs, after his anti-Jewish turn, did Wagner find the origin of the Hillers at all worthy of mention. Here, too, Wagner admitted that he very soon became convinced that Hiller was insufficiently original, and that it became clear to him that Hiller's artistic ambition found occasional satisfaction only through his social position.[48] It was therefore, in Wagner's opinion, a phenomenon similar to the case of Meyerbeer. As the passionate protest against Meyerbeer in *Judaism in Music* unfolded, one might have expected a similar reaction against Hiller as well. Yet Wagner's relations with Hiller remained completely unaffected by his awakened aversion to the Jews, which had become as necessary to Wagner as "bile is to blood." The two men's paths separated in 1847, when Hiller was called to Düsseldorf as a conductor. In 1848 Wagner left one of Hiller's letters unanswered. In August 1850, precisely at the time of the publication of his essay, Wagner used the report of the birth of a daughter to Hiller as an occasion for the resumption of friendly ties: "You have probably been informed of late about my sentiments in general. That you completely share them I do not believe. But it does not occur to me to hold you less dear than I did on that account."[49] Was this a sudden fit of sentimentality? Probably not. Wagner's letter was addressed to Cologne, where Hiller had established himself a short time earlier as the director of the newly founded musical conservatory. In his letter Wagner made a witty reference to Hiller's assumption of the leadership of the new institute, and he would not at the same time have overlooked the fact that the *Rheinische Musik-Zeitung für Kunstfreunde und Künstler* was published under the aegis of the institute and that Hiller had thus obtained a very significant influence on the public opinion of the circles interested in art. Wagner's hope of being surrounded by the new organ was immediately disappointed. The Cologne school resolutely took the side of Wagner's opponents in the argument that developed around this time concerning his artistic direction.⁵⁰ Wagner now numbered Hiller among the members of the Jewish conspiracy who, he was convinced, wanted to take revenge for *Judaism in Music*.⁵¹ This idea, which operated almost like a persecution mania, was the tangible personal result of Wagner's anti-Jewish essay.

To be sure, from this time on Wagner was no longer likely to overlook the Jewishness of any of his acquaintances. Whether he drew any consequences from it or merely alluded to it depended on how the particular person related to Wagner and to his music. Of course, there was no question of his avoiding social or professional intercourse with Jews. On a visit to Russia in 1863 Wagner received with thanks the compliments of the brothers Anton and Nikolai Rubinstein, the pianist and the director of the musical society, and around this time Heinrich Porges in Prague helped him to arrange concerts.⁵² In Vienna, during an illness, he allowed himself to be attended by Porges's brother Fritz, a future doctor.⁵³ With his renewed attempt at the beginning of the 1860s to conquer Paris with *Tannhäuser*, Wagner received financial assistance from a Mrs. Schwabe.⁵⁴ At the same time the banker Emil Erlanger offered to pay him advances for the preparation of the planned performance of the opera.⁵⁵ Not only was Wagner ready to accept the urgently needed assistance from Jewish hands, but there is no sign that he had to overcome any internal resistance to doing so.

Erlanger continued to assist Wagner's undertakings during his Bayreuth days. In Cosima's diaries he is always praised or blamed according to his performance. If blame appears to be in order, not only Erlanger but his tribe as well receives it.⁵⁶

The variability of Wagner's attitude toward Jews is particularly clear in his fluctuating relations with Joseph Joachim, the great violinist of Jewish origin and one of the most significant virtuosos and productive composers of his time. Joachim belonged to a group of musicians which, assisted by Franz Liszt and Hans von Bülow, had given a festive reception following Wagner's return from Italy to Basel in 1853. In the general liveliness of the gathering Wagner was struck by Joachim's reserve, whereupon Bülow explained to him that Joachim was self-conscious on account of his "opinions expressed in that famous article about Judaism." Joachim had asked Bülow, Wagner wrote, "at the presentation of one of his compositions . . . with a certain friendly anxiety, whether I [Wagner] would be able to note anything Jewish in that work."[57] Joachim was one of the Leipzig professors who had protested the publication of Wagner's article. What we otherwise know about Joachim's life permits us to assume that his question to Bülow was meant ironically.[58] Wagner for his part found in Joachim's supposed embarrassment a "touching, indeed moving characteristic," and condescended to placate Joachim with "particularly sympathetic parting words and a hearty embrace."[59] At this time Joachim, as an adherent of the Wagnerian artistic trend, was numbered among Wagner's "exceptional Jews," a position that he completely forfeited with his later change of mind, as we shall see.

Wagner's capacity to depart from his own ideology is most clearly illustrated in the case of Karl Tausig. The seventeen-year-old Tausig came to Wagner in Zurich in May 1858, just when Wagner had put the crisis with Mathilde Wesendonck behind him. The master recognized the great musical gift of the radiant, precocious youngster and kept him in his company. There developed between the two of them a father-son relationship, in which the "father" profited no less than the "son" from the connection.[60] The appearance of this son, worthy of adoption, among the contemptible tribe of the Jews threatened to overthrow the theory of its artistic inferiority. Consequently violence had to be done to the facts. Wagner explained in a letter to his wife that Tausig's father was "an honest Bohemian, thoroughly Christian."[61]

Tausig himself was not hindered by his Jewishness in his friendship with Wagner. In contrast to Joseph Rubinstein, of whom we shall speak later and who precisely out of despair at being Jewish sought a cure from Wagner, Tausig apparently felt that his Jewish origin was not a burden. This difference may be due not merely to the different personality structures of the two men. Rubinstein presented himself to Wagner early in 1872, three years after the republication of *Judaism in Music*, which undoubtedly played a role in his mental crisis as well as in his search for salvation at Wagner's side. Tausig, who was nine years old when the article appeared pseudonymously and who came to Wagner before its republication, may not have known of its existence.

As we have already mentioned, Wagner's anti-Jewish sentiments had not made their way to the public consciousness prior to the republication of his article. Upon its first publication the essay was not discussed in the Jewish press. In any case, to the extent that the Jewish public took pleasure in Wagner's music, it was not hindered from acclaiming that music by anything Wagner had written. That the Jews actually did hail him is attested by Wagner himself in his report on a concert in Breslau in 1863: "To my horror I saw almost the whole place, namely the front of it, occupied solely by Jews." The next day, when he attended a luncheon arranged in his honor, in "which only Jews took part," he saw that he did in fact owe his success in Breslau "on the whole only to the excited sympathies of this part of the population." [62] Wagner's horror at the sight of the Jewish physiognomy of his public reveals the fixation of his phobia about Jews. He was quite ready and able to conceal or suppress it when dealing with an individual Jew, but upon his surprising encounter with the Jews en masse, his aversion broke through with elemental force.

We therefore have confirmation of our assertion that the lasting consequences of the first publication of the essay actually occurred only in the consciousness of its author. While others had long since forgotten the essay or had never heard of it, Wagner believed that the enmity he projected between himself and the Jews was an ever-present factor that helped determine his fate. This idea then served him as an explanation for setbacks and failures in his private and artistic career. Behind every obstacle, he believed, a conspiratorial Jew was hiding, the Anti-Wagner incarnate. In this way Wagner was spared the task of examining his own deeds and convictions. However, in order to be entirely protected from self-criticism, he had to go one step further and reverse the equation Jew = opponent to opponent = Jew.

The music critic of the *Times* of London, Davidson, who was known as a merciless critic, energetically rejected Wagner's music. "Above all, the music reviewer of the 'Times,' Mr. Davidson, declared himself against me in the most hostile manner. On account of this man I definitely and clearly suffered for the first time the effect of my earlier essay on Judaism in music." [63] The Jewishness of the critic (a Scot) and his familiarity with the essay written five years earlier in German were taken for granted. Similar was the case of Eduard Hanslick, the Vienna critic, who followed Wagner's musical development for some time with sympathy and understanding and who also had occasional personal contacts with Wagner.[64] Later, because of Wagner's particular musical style, Hanslick, like many others, turned his back on him. As a result, and probably through the fault of both men, the opposition became a bitter feud, for which Wagner was able to state no other cause than the alleged Jewish background of his critic. When Hanslick asserted that his father was of rural origin, Wagner procured the information that Hanslick's mother was a Jewess, which sufficed for him as an explanation of his critic's conduct.

Wagner's intellectual development reflects a series of processes of adoption. The teaching of Ludwig Feuerbach, the worldview of Arthur Schopenhauer, the racial theory of Count Gobineau, and finally the belief in the regenerative effect of vegetarianism became for him lasting creeds, which he defended with some degree of passion. His consciousness of his brilliant originality in music seems to have given him a sense of confidence in his own judgment, even in areas in which he had very little knowledge at his disposal. Hence the self-reliance that enabled him to serve as a political adviser to King Ludwig II of Bavaria. His counsel contained, by the way, elements of his anti-Jewish sentiments, which fit in easily with the royalist picture of the world and which Wagner found appropriate to his situation. Denying his former democratic leanings, he now viewed the political as well as the spiritual leadership of the German people as having been bestowed by destiny on the princes. Revolution and democracy, he maintained, were foreign to the German folk spirit; wherever they appeared they were to be accounted for by foreign "French, German-Jewish" influence.[65] The fundamental concept with which Wagner operated—here as in *Judaism in Music*—was that of the folk spirit that all the European peoples possessed; the Jews, as a "peculiar race of men," could simply have no part in it. If the Jews had succeeded in taking the place of the missing middle class in Hungary and Poland, and in placing themselves at the side of the bourgeoisie in Germany, this process was unnatural, injurious. The worst thing was that the interlopers had become the sole rulers in the sphere of "the public intellectual life [*Geistesleben*] . . . politics, literature, public art, namely, music and the theater." The German princes, who had neglected their task as the protectors of the national spirit, were responsible for this situation. The cultural vacuum that thus came into being was an enticement to the alien Jew. Here Wagner resorted once again to the image known to us from his essay: "A dying body was immediately found by the worms who fully destroyed it and assimilated it." [66]

This presentation was meant to induce Ludwig to remember his task as ruler and guide of the history of his people and to take charge of the renewal of the German spirit by means of Wagnerian art. Wagner's belief that he could convince the king not only of German culture's need for regeneration, but also of the Jews' responsibility for it, shows how deep-seated was his phobia of Jews at this time.

# 6 The Republication

In 1867 Franz Brendel planned to publish some of Wagner's lesser works. Hans von Bülow reported that Wagner directed Brendel "by all means to refrain from . . . reprinting the article on the Jews, either under a pseudonym or signed. He fears the renewal at this time of a perhaps uselessly injurious scandal. He also has the intention of . . . publishing . . . his scattered essays . . . together in a small volume at a later date."[1] A republication was therefore considered but was not then undertaken. Scarcely a year and a half later Wagner overcame his misgivings. Brendel had in the meantime died, and Wagner himself published the essay, signed and enlarged by a preface and an afterword, additions that were by no means apt to soften the scandalous tendencies of the writing. Before we examine the decision to republish the essay, it is advisable to consider the contents of the supplements.

Wagner dedicated the brochure, into which the essay had now grown, to Madame Marie Muchanoff, née Countess Nesselrode, and placed a letter to her at the beginning of it. In a conversation that had taken place not long before, Madame Muchanoff, full of astonishment, had asked "the reason for what was to her the seemingly incomprehensible enmity, so visibly tending toward disparagement . . . which every one of my artistic achievements encounters in the daily press not only in Germany, but also in France and England."[2] The countess was not the only one who was amazed by this spectacle. The author therefore felt himself bound to respond publicly to this question posed in public. The answer was contained in the essay or rather in its lasting effect. Since Wagner's article threw a critical light on the part played by the Jews in the development of modern music, he stated, Jewry, which of course ruled public opinion, revenged itself on the author. Wherever one of Wagner's pieces was presented—in Berlin, Vienna, Paris, or London—it was rejected out of hand, condemned, and made a laughingstock by the press on account of the author's article on the Jews. The rejection had the appearance of being spontaneous, but its uniformity entitled one to assume that it was the work of "an energetic organization and leadership."[3] "Of that article on 'Judaism in Music' . . . not the least bit ever comes up,"[4] but the very silence about it was a sign of the conscious concern with it and the mutual understanding. The Jews wished to evade an argument with the critique directed against them in the essay and feigned other motives for their rejection of the Wagnerian direction in art. The republication of the hushed-up essay was meant to make clear to Wagner's adherents the origin of the otherwise inexplicable opposition to his art. At the same time it was meant to force the Jews to give up their game of hide-and-seek and to face up to the critique directed against them in the essay.

The preface and the afterword of the essay therefore purport to serve only as an introduction and justification for the new publication. But it did not escape the reader's attention that they represented at the same time a continuation of Wagner's anti-Jewish campaign and gave him a new opportunity to settle accounts with his Jewish opponents, or those whom he declared to be Jewish. These opponents were no longer predecessors or rivals, like Mendelssohn and Meyerbeer, but critics and colleagues, who aroused Wagner's ire, above all, by numbering themselves at first among his admirers or collaborators but then deserting him for reasons he found incomprehensible. What could have motivated them except a connection with the conspiracy directed against him? There was the influential critic of the Vienna music world—unnamed but identified as Eduard Hanslick by the mention of his "opuscule on the 'Musikalisch-Schöne'"—who "in the beginning declared himself for me almost enthusiastically," but then allowed himself to be recruited "for the general purpose of music-Jewry." He was "particularly amenable" to that, "on account of his prettily concealed Jewish origin"—an allusion to Hanslick's supposedly Jewish mother.[5] Now a "thoroughly blond German aesthetician," Professor Friedrich Theodor Vischer of Vienna, had associated himself with Dr. Hanslick and had incorporated Hanslick's theory in his "large work." Thus "the musical Jew-beauty" had found a place "in the heart of a full-blooded German system of aesthetics." This was the work "of Jews and Christians who had been taken in."[6]

In the same way, Wagner explained the connection between Professor Ludwig Bischof and Ferdinand Hiller. Wagner held Bischof to be the inventor of the expression "future-music" [*Zukunftmusik*], with which Bischof wished to parody Wagner's idea of the "artwork of the future."[7] Bischof's conduct was also said to be a reaction against *Judaism in Music*, which he did not mention at all. On the contrary, he preened himself on being a Christian and the offspring of a superintendent. But wasn't Bischof "a friend and admirer of Mr. Ferdinand Hiller?" asked Wagner. Although Wagner had not earlier held Hiller in high esteem, the composer had applied to him for assistance. Yet Hiller had in the meantime gone over to Wagner's opponents. What other reason would he have had for doing so than retaliation for *Judaism in Music*?[8]

The third person whose defection from Wagner was attributed to his Jewish origin was Joachim, whose Jewishness had been quite condescendingly forgiven as long as he had been one of Wagner's adherents. Joachim's name was not mentioned in the afterword to *Judaism in Music*, but every reader had to know who was meant by "the falling-away of a hitherto warmly devoted friend, a great violin virtuoso" who had renounced his discipleship with the development of the late Wagnerian music.[9]

Particularly instructive, finally, is the case of Berthold Auerbach. Auerbach was, to be sure, not a musician, but in Wagner's opinion he could have helped him as a writer. The name of Auerbach was also avoided in the afterword, but for the contemporary reader the description was unmistakable: "an undoubtedly very gifted, truly talented and ingenious writer of Jewish origin, who seems to have almost grown into the most distinctive traits of German folk-life." Who else could that mean but the author of the famous *Village Tales from the Black Forest*, who in the 1860s had expressed himself with "appreciative warmth and . . . clear understanding" about the poems *Der Ring des Nibelungen* and *Tristan und Isolde*. Asked by Wagner's friends "to publish openly his views about these poems that had been so astonishingly ignored by our own literary circles," he had evaded that task. Why? Wagner had his answer ready: since Wagner was proscribed by Auerbach's tribe, it would have counted as "capital crime" to come to his rescue.[10] We recall that Wagner reported a later meeting with Auerbach in which, in contrast to the Dresden period, he found the writer physically repulsive as well.

It is probably not incorrect to connect this change in taste with Auerbach's refusal to perform the favor that was asked of him.

Wagner was well aware that his theory of a general Jewish conspiracy against him was hard to reconcile with "the undeniable successes I have enjoyed."[11] But it was not beyond him to solve the difficulty. He distinguished between the press and the general public, "whose favorable reception of my work the Jews were nowhere able to spoil,"[12] as if the Jews were not included in that public. In fact, as he must have known from his experience in Breslau, they were very often represented in large and even overwhelming numbers. The broad participation of the Jews in the theater and musical life was common knowledge. It was admitted by Hans von Bülow, who shared Wagner's opinion of the Jews but who was not led by ideology to do violence to the facts.[13] But Wagner's capacity not only to interpret the facts in accordance with his theory but also to perceive them selectively knew no bounds.

There was, however, one fact that Wagner could not overlook. Jews were included in the foremost ranks of his followers in the battle over his direction in art. Here something had changed fundamentally since the first publication of the essay. At that time he had had Jews like Hiller and Auerbach as companions; now, when those men had deserted the ranks of his admirers, their place was taken by active collaborators like Karl Tausig and Hermann Levi and zealous propagandists like Heinrich Porges and some others. We have already seen how Tausig came to Wagner. Levi, the unbaptized son of a rabbi, was a conductor in Karlsruhe, where he happily and successfully directed Wagner's works. Porges had helped Wagner to attain artistic and financial success in 1863 in his hometown of Prague, and since then his enthusiasm for the master and his readiness to assist him had continued to grow.[14] How was this support to be reconciled with the existence of a general conspiracy?

Here Wagner had the help of a theory that was already present in the first version of the article and that was illustrated by the case of Börne. An individual can overcome his Jewish nature by means of a change reaching down into the depths of his personality. This assertion no longer appears, as it did in the first version, as a kind of afterthought, but rather is discussed in detail in the covering letter at the beginning of the new edition as well as at the end of the afterword. It therefore represents the intellectual framework of the new edition of the essay. Wagner speaks of "truly sympathetic friends, delivered to me by fate from their tribal kinship [with the Jews]." Yet the essay says that they have to be disciplined because of their "characteristics which are so difficult to extirpate and so disadvantageous to our culture." These friends, however, would not feel hurt by his statement, for, thanks to a "truly human development," they were able to strip themselves of such characteristics. These friends stood "on exactly the same ground" as Wagner did, and they had to "suffer more acutely, even more ignominiously" under the same pressure.[15]

This liberating act of de-Judaization was by no means restricted to the few who had already tried it. It was rather to be recommended for Jewry in general, as Wagner argued at the end of his considerations. There he attempted to remove the personal reference from his statements and to advance a general analysis. In view of the "influence over our intellectual life which the Jews have acquired," which found expression in the "decay of our culture," only two paths were open, he argued. One was "the violent ejection of the destructive foreign element"; the other was the assimilation of this element "in such a way that, in common with us, it shall ripen toward a higher evolution of our nobler human qualities." The author did not allow himself to judge whether the first alternative was practicable, "for this would require forces whose presence is unknown to me." The forcible removal of the Jews was therefore a question of practicality. In Wagner's opinion, there were no moral objections to it. Still, since this solution could not be put into effect, the path of assimilation was the only applicable one. If this was the case, "then it is obvious that not the concealment of the difficulties of this assimilation, but only the clearest exposure of them can be of use here."[16] Wagner's libelous work therefore ultimately served the praiseworthy purpose of showing the Jews the thorny road to assimilation, and Wagner consequently believed himself entitled to the gratitude of his Jewish as well as non-Jewish contemporaries.

We have every right to doubt whether Wagner seriously expected his highly subjective analyses of the Jewish question to be regarded as a public service. A year earlier he had recoiled from the idea of republishing the original text, fearing the scandal that would ensue. Yet the later version was more insulting, since it repeated the critique of Jewish artistic activity and added attacks on a series of personalities still living. The author could hardly have deceived himself with regard to the likely reaction. What, therefore, induced him to take the risk?

In the Wagner research this question is answered only with conjectures. One paradoxical assumption is that the republication was a tactical move, and that Wagner counted on the anticipated scandal to heighten public interest in his works. Since the polemics surrounding Wagner's new creations had begun to die down, and since the press had even taken a turn in Wagner's favor following the premier of *Die Meistersinger* in the summer of 1868, Wagner needed opposition. The publication of the brochure on the Jews was supposed to have provided it. This explanation was suggested decades after the events by a contemporary, Wendelin Weissheimer, in his memoirs (1898), and was accepted by later researchers for lack of a better one. [17] It is, however, unequivocally refuted by Wagner's own statements.

His first confidential remarks concerning the republication of the brochure are found in a letter to Hans von Bülow of 27 December 1868. There Wagner referred to Madame Muchanoff, "who asked in such amazement about the source of the unrelenting hostility of the press, etc. toward me. This amazement, which also slips in from time to time among some innocent reporters about me, should be put to an end." [18] From an objective point of view, the resistance to Wagnerian music may have diminished around this time. Subjectively, however, Wagner still regarded himself as being persecuted by the press. "The unheard-of insolence of the Viennese press on the occasion of the 'Meistersinger,' the constant spinning of lies about me . . . finally induced me to take my reckless step," [19] Wagner wrote to Karl Tausig in April 1869, when the storm over the recently published brochure was in full swing. In February he had notified Julius Lang in a letter of the impending appearance of the brochure: "I have now decided to confront the effronteries even where my own person is concerned." He added, in a self-pitying tone, "I have now suffered enough to think finally about . . . protecting . . . my life's work from these effronteries." [20]

Any doubts one might have about the sincerity of Wagner's remarks in these letters are dispelled by Cosima Wagner's diaries. Beginning on 1 January 1869, while the brochure was being prepared, they contain the most intimate statements. There appears to have been a discussion concerning the "opportunity for immediate publication of the essay on the Jews." Cosima raised the question of whether that would "bring Wagner the greatest unpleasantness," have "a good effect," or perhaps be "completely ignored." She undoubtedly inclined toward the first possibility, as one can see from her entry of 11 January: "He sent off the essay on the Jews. That filled me with anxiety, but I did not wish to hinder it."[21] Wagner was conscious of his companions's doubts, and three years later he referred to them: "He said . . . he always has to do something that I cannot call completely good but about which, when it occurs, I never make accusations against him. . . . He reminded me of the publication of 'Judaism.'"[22] Cosima therefore had every right to smile at the report transmitted by Marie Muchanoff that "people blame me for the brochure on the Jews."[23]

Scruples about the publication of the essay also played a part in Wagner's decision not to include it in the 1871 edition of his collected works. A year later he changed his mind and allowed the essay to be printed in the fifth volume, without the afterword.[24] The decision to publish it was in any case Wagner's own. He was sure that the "good effect" of the brochure would outweigh the unpleasantness connected with it. As absurd as it may sound, he believed that the Jewish conspiracy was responsible for the continuing incomprehension of his work, much as one believes in a theory that suddenly explains otherwise unintelligible facts. Instructing the public about that conspiracy seemed to him to be nothing more than disclosing the truth. Every person of good will would have to be convinced that Wagner was correct. In the February letter to Lang he said: "I will soon publish a brochure, 'Judaism in Music,' which will provide you too with new and curious revelations."[25] Friends and foes should know what his sworn enemies had done to him.

At first it seemed as if Richard and not Cosima would prove to have been right. The negative and positive reactions to the brochure were more or less in balance. The first report came from Hans von Bülow, who did not allow his artistic dependence on Wagner to be disturbed by the domestic misfortune that had befallen him on account of Wagner. Himself hostile to the Jews, he joyfully awaited the spectacle, which, as he correctly foresaw, would have to follow the publication. "It will create a hullabaloo," he wrote to a friend upon receiving the brochure.[26] The acknowledgment he sent to Wagner probably did not have such a pert ring to it. "Hans is very charmed by the brochure," Cosima noted.[27] Many people privately expressed their agreement with what Wagner had written. The most important of them was perhaps the publicist Constantin Frantz, who observed that it was "the right word at the right time."[28] For years he had been critical of the emancipation of the Jews, and no other response could have been expected from him. With particular satisfaction Cosima noted the remarks of her family doctor in Luzern. He had "mentioned in passing that he had read the brochure on the Jews and had been very pleased to learn the source of the incessant hostility. A woman from Zurich brought the brochure with her to read on the train."[29] Wagner had therefore convinced these readers. No wonder Cosima added: "We like this." But not all expressions of agreement were welcome: "An ultramontane paper praised the brochure on the Jews and praised the young king who . . . loves and honors the composer of heroic music, R. Wagner." "Such is the world," Cosima commented.[30]

The personal statements were not all full of praise. There were also private protests and warnings. An anonymous letter from Breslau, where the Jewish public had acclaimed Wagner a few years earlier, included "abuse and threats . . . in the name of seven thousand Jews." From Berlin Julius Lang reported "that Jewry is . . . in great ferment." From other cities, such as Münster, Karlsruhe, and even Paris came reports indicating "that R[ichard] is harming himself and his cause." Particularly depressing were the newspapers sent to them by the publisher of the brochure. "They all storm, rage and jeer," observed Cosima, summarizing their contents. She saw her fears confirmed but did not grumble: "I will gladly submit to everything, as long as I am able to stand by his side."[31]

Wagner himself tried for a time to dismiss this hostility with irony. He read somewhere "that he wrote his book on the Jews out of envy of Mendelssohn's genius and Meyerbeer's success," and responded: "but not of Hiller's wife, for he could not envy him on account of his genius or his successes."[32] He certainly was not unimpressed by the growing rejection of his theory and criticism. When "a letter from the Berlin intendancy" reached him, he feared that it referred to the suspicions expressed in his brochure that the directors of the Berlin theater had obstructed the performance of *Die Meistersinger* in Berlin or elsewhere.³³ It cost him great effort to open the letter at all. Instead of the reprimand he had feared, it contained the information that *Meistersinger* would be performed in Berlin as well as in Hannover.³⁴

This episode showed how poorly Wagner understood his situation. The publication of the brochure coincided with the first performance of *Meistersinger* in Dresden and Karlsruhe and the efforts to arrange a performance in Berlin and Vienna. The performance of *Rienzi* was in preparation in Paris and that of *Lohengrin* in Berlin.³⁵ It is more than probable that the deliberations over whether the publication of the essay was at the moment opportune were related to these expectations. Wagner feared the criticism of the press and hoped to counteract it with his "disclosure." What actually happened shows that Wagner fell victim to a double misjudgment. First of all, the anti-Wagner mood diminished around this time. *Meistersinger* in particular enjoyed an enthusiastic reception in Dresden and Karlsruhe, where performances took place on 21 January and 5 February, respectively—prior to the appearance of the brochure in the beginning of March. The *Rienzi* performance in Paris followed its publication, and the translator of the opera thought that "it would probably harm 'Rienzi.'" Wagner and Cosima, for their part, remembering previous experiences in Paris, feared a repeated failure irrespective of the brochure and would have liked to prevent the performance. To their surprise, telegrams on 7 and 9 April reported the great success of the first and second performances. Their joy, however, was clouded by the news from Wagner's publisher that the brochure on the Jews was detracting from his success.³⁶

The reports from the German cities pointed in the same direction. The success of *Meistersinger* could not be undone through the appearance of the brochure—the acceptance of the opera in Berlin was connected with it—but was probably diminished by the reaction of the Jewish theater-going public. The anonymous letter from Breslau, which purported to speak in the name of the entire local Jewish community, may have indulged in exaggeration, but the protest was not insubstantial. In fact, the directors of the theater there felt compelled to postpone the planned performance of *Lohengrin* on account of the brochure. Hans von Bülow, who was at first so taken by the brochure, reported "concerning the broader effect of *Judaism*" that "the rich Jews in Munich . . . no longer attended Wagner's operas so dilligently."[37]

The situation was therefore completely different from what Wagner had imagined. He apparently did not have to look for special means to break the alleged ban against him. That would be taken care of by the jubilant public, which would finally succeed in overcoming the reservations of the critics as well. However, the means with which he had wished to combat the ban, the publication of the brochure on the Jews, proved to be a serious obstacle on the road to recognition. Despite his great success, many of his adherents were concerned about the effect of the brochure. Thus Tausig telegraphed on 7 April, a day after the first performance of *Lohengrin* in Berlin: "Colossal success of *Lohengrin*, all the Jews conciliated, your admiring Karl."[38] Tausig, too, evidently saw the brochure as a potential threat to the recognition of Wagner's art.

To be sure, Wagner's answer to Tausig, which apparently was intended from the start to be made public and was in fact very soon published by Julius Lang, showed no regret at his blunder. Still, Wagner at least conceded that he was impressed by what he had heard from Tausig. Yet he held fast to his belief that there was a constant plot against him and he described the history of that "unheard-of persecution" with unprecedented "objective calm."[39] He maintained that he had done a service by supplying in his pamphlet the necessary information for dealing with "our most important cultural concerns" and believed that it was up to the Jews themselves to pursue the matter courageously. He understood the telegram from Berlin to imply "that my brochure is seen as thoughtlessness and as such it is forgiven me." But with that he had not gained very much: "*I have already come to know good nature in abundance even among Jews. If one should be found to have courage, then I will rejoice*" (emphasis in the original).[40] In this somewhat conciliatory tone Wagner sought to put an end to the affair. That he privately judged it a failure can be seen from his much later remark, which we have already quoted, that the publication of *Judaism* belonged among those matters in which he should have relied on the cautionary instinct of his wife.

He had good reason to regret his overhasty step. Most of the responses to the brochure on the Jews could be dismissed as libelous pamphlets written by Wagner's opponents or as the sentimental effusions of Jewish devotées.[41] Yet in reply to Wagner's contention that the rejection of his music was to be understood as Jewish revenge for his essay on the Jews of two decades earlier, those in a position to know declared almost unanimously that they had never heard of the existence of the article.[42] In doing so they virtually demolished the factual foundations of Wagner's claim that he was unmasking his enemies and the related theory of the destructive role of the Jews in modern music. It was therefore an easy matter for Wagner's critical opponents to seek the basis of his theory in the psychological state of its author. Eduard Hanslick, for example, was able to parry the attack against him. After pointing out the audacity of Wagner's thesis, according to which not only his own fate but also that of Franz Liszt and of Robert Schumann was determined by his unknown article on the Jews,[43] he made the following analysis: "For the characterization of Wagner it [the brochure] really has only a psychiatric interest. The most boundless self-deification has here reached a peak on which a man with healthy brain functions can no longer breathe."[44] Similar allusions to Wagner's megalomania were repeated by other critics, who were forced by Wagner's obvious fantasies to resort to a psychological interpretation of the phenomenon.[45]

Similar conclusions were reached by the literary historian Julian Schmidt, who, as we shall see, believed that Wagner's misgivings about the Jewish influence on contemporary culture were not without foundation. As a one-time resident of Leipzig, Schmidt could well recall the first publication of the essay, but like the other critics who had never heard of it, he minimized its impact.[46] He understood Wagner's struggle for recognition as the natural consequence of his "vandalic onslaught against all the hitherto accepted canons of art." In the meantime Wagner's art had achieved substantial successes, and Wagner's attempt to attribute his difficulties to the effect of the essay was "the outbreak of a persecution complex, as if there were a universal Jewish plot against the fame of Richard Wagner." Schmidt therefore defined his diagnosis in nonmedical terms, believing rather that it was a culturally conditioned phenomenon, one that was also to be found in two other contemporaries, Karl Gutzkow and Friedrich Hebbel: "All three have something in common: they are not so absorbed in their work as to disregard the other movements of the *Zeitgeist*, but neither are they in a position objectively to enter into them. Instead, they only search out the aspects of those movements which they can somehow place in relation to their 'ego.' A mind that is anyway not firmly grounded in itself sometimes produces exaltation, sometimes depression. At one moment a man is convinced that he has in his hands the reins of all the strivings of the age, at the next moment he sees the whole public conspiring against him." [47]

Whether or not Julian Schmidt's characterization holds true for Gutzkow and Hebbel is a matter we must leave open; for Wagner it is exactly correct. The consciousness of his artistic superiority carried over to every area accessible to him. Thus he believed that he could issue universally valid judgments concerning all cultural, sociopolitical, and even scientific phenomena, including the role of Judaism in the modern world. As Julian Schmidt put it: "Judaism is only one of Wagner's various crotchets." [48] In order to substantiate this assertion Schmidt points to the contradictory phases of the composer's world-improving fanaticism: the dream of an art supported by a popular, democratic movement, and then the opposite, the harmonious collaboration of an ideal king with a brilliant artist standing at his side. And in the later years, we may add, there was his faith in bringing about the happiness of mankind through the prohibition of vivisection and the universal requirement of vegetarian nourishment.

As accurate as Julian Schmidt's observation may have been, hostility toward the Jews cannot be dismissed as one of Wagner's caprices. It by no means proved to be a passing whim, but rather remained a permanent characteristic of his mentality from the time of the publication of the essay on the Jews. The retreat Wagner made under the impact of the reaction to the publication proved to be of a tactical nature. Wagner gave up neither his belief in the existence of a Jewish conspiracy nor the thesis of the destructive influence of the Jews on German cultural life. Besides protests he also heard voices that strengthened him in his opinion. If at the time of the republication these voices were audible in private rather than in public, Wagner lived through the rise of the anti-Semitic current in the middle of the 1870s, when the view he represented gained more and more ground. His role in this development and its influence on his attitude will be our concern in a later chapter. Before we turn to that subject, however, it will be useful to describe the years when the larger public still felt the essay to be altogether out of step with the times. The contrast between this period and the following phase will enable us to see the extreme dialectic present in the historical development.

# 7    The Illusion of Emancipation

The year of the republication of Wagner's brochure on the Jews and the ensuing public controversy is also the date of the formal emancipation of most of the German Jews. The constitution of the Northern German Confederacy, dated 3 July 1869, which after two years became the law of Germany's Second Reich, severed a citizen's civil, political, and other rights from his religious affiliation.[1] Even before the publication of this legislation, the confederacy's decision on this matter was well known. In his *International Law and Politics*, which appeared at the beginning of the year, a professor of constitutional law, Robert von Mohl, described the emancipation of the Jews as a mistake, the product of political shortsightedness. Nevertheless, he treated it as a *fait accompli*, one that could not be tampered with under the existing circumstances.[2] German Jewry seemed to have reached the peak of its political ambitions, the recognition of the right to full civil equality. The significance of this achievement was only increased by the fact that it came into being without opposition, indeed without attracting the attention of the public. The only scruples about the final incorporation of the Jews in the political system were those expressed—in a tone of resignation—in the learned treatise of Robert von Mohl. This situation stood in stark contrast to the earlier phases of the struggle for emancipation, which, beginning with the proposals for reform of Christian Wilhelm von Dohm at the time of Moses Mendelssohn, were all accompanied by controversies in the press and polemical writings.[3] The public silence may have been connected with the fact that at this time no special legislation dealing with the Jewish question was under consideration. The granting of equal rights to the Jews followed from the definition of the state as a secular institution independent of the churches. From the Jewish point of view, the anchoring of emancipation in the general principles of the state must have been a source of satisfaction. Expressions of contentment were not lacking. Isidor Kaim, who used the event as an occasion to summarize the century-long struggle for emancipation, declared, "There is in fact no longer any Jewish question."[4]

Kaim's contemporaries would soon see how illusory that conclusion was. Scarcely five years later the missing public debate over emancipation was more than made up for. The year 1875 saw the beginning of a press campaign against the Jews, a campaign that culminated four years later in Adolf Stöcker's anti-Semitic movement.[5] Between the emancipation legislation and the public debate lay the onset of the economic crisis, beginning with the stock market crash of 1873. The collapse of the illusory prosperity of the empire's early years after the Franco-Prussian War created an atmosphere of depression, which led to political dislocations—the move away from liberalism—and to social tensions—the rise of the labor movement. One of the most striking signs of social strain was the growing consciousness of the contrarieties between those who had always been citizens of the state and those who had joined it only a short time earlier—the Jews. Despite their advances in cultural assimilation the Jews, because of their professional, familial, and religious concentration, represented a separate group and were perceived as such.

Today the growth of the anti-Jewish movement is often understood and interpreted as a mere by-product of the political dislocations, as if the anti-Jewish movement operated as an outlet for other frustrations and received no nourishment from the real field of tension between Jews and non-Jews. This is not the place to investigate the ideological motives underlying that mode of interpretation. It no doubt stems from the apologetic attitude of opposition to anti-Semitism, an attitude that, out of fear of entering into anti-Jewish arguments, locates the cause of anti-Semitism entirely outside the realm of Jewish affairs.[6] In reality, after they are cleansed of pathological exaggerations and distortions, the anti-Semitic accusations often provide information about the burdensome relations between Jews and non-Jews that continued to exist despite formal emancipation—or, in a certain sense, even because of emancipation. Closer observation reveals the existence of these burdensome relations even in the period not marked by anti-Semitism, that is, when the Jews' critics were not yet striving for the revision of emancipation but, on the contrary, purported to hope for the complete absorption of the

Jews into the non-Jewish population.[7] The tension between the two groups arose because the social reality of the Jewish minority was far from corresponding to this hope. Later, at the time of the economic and political crisis of the 1870s, this discrepancy between expectations and reality led to a turn in the opposite direction, namely, a call for the repeal of emancipation.[8] The Wagner controversy, which fell at the end of the first phase of these developments, offers us the opportunity to pursue this earlier critique of the Jews and Judaism and the Jewish reaction to it. This investigation may assist us in understanding the momentous turning point in the Jews' destiny that was about to follow.

The critique of the Jews and Judaism, before and after the rise of anti-Semitism, was connected, as we have said, with the discrepancy between the expectations linked with emancipation and its real consequences. It is also evident that there was a gap between the legal position occupied by the Jews after emancipation and their social reality. According to the law, the Jews were members of a religion recognized by the state. Their communities and their associations enjoyed rights similar if not identical to those of the Christian churches. The emancipatory legislation put an end to the long-standing status of the Jews in the Christian lands. Up to that time they had been tolerated as a religiously as well as ethnically foreign group. They had possessed particular rights that had served as the basis for their national-religious separation from the world around them.[9] Despite the sharp demarcation between the Jewish and the non-Jewish realms, it was entirely possible to pass from one to the other by means of a change in religion. Though the conversion of a Christian to Judaism was hindered by ecclesiastical as well as secular authorities, the journey in the opposite direction was supported and facilitated by them. Only rarely did Christians convert to the other religious-national community; Jews did so rather often. Once that move had taken place, the detachment from the original community and the absorption into the chosen group was unequivocal and radical.[10]

With the onset of the epoch of emancipation, the opposition between the Jewish and the non-Jewish realms diminished. It is true that even after generations of cultural assimilation to its environment Jewish society remained a separate group characterized by its familial ties and occupational proclivities. Nevertheless, the line dividing it from the world around it had lost its sharpness. Cultural commonality and occasional contact had shaped a common basis for the Jewish minority and the non-Jewish majority.[11] Under these conditions the change of religion was no leap over an abyss. To many Jews, especially in the higher social, intellectual, and artistic circles, the conversion to Christianity marked the completion of their incorporation into the dominant culture, in the shaping of which they took part.[12]

There was, however, another side to the facilitation of conversion. While the decision to convert was easy to make, its consequences were less conclusive. Conversion to Christianity did not ensure total transplantation into Christian society. The act of baptism, which was indeed often undergone without any religious experience, lost its transformative power and was simultaneously deprived of its social effect. Jews as well as non-Jews continued for the most part to regard the person who had been baptized as a Jew. Even if the state authorities freed the convert from the restrictions pertaining to the Jews and allowed him to become, for instance, an army officer or a university professor, public opinion was as little influenced by that as it was by the declarations of the Jewish authorities, the rabbis and the communal leaders, that they no longer had anything in common with those who had been baptized.[13] The spontaneous reaction of both communities contradicted the official attitude, a circumstance graphically illustrated by the Wagner controversy.

Wagner himself relied in his theory concerning the Judaization of music on the examples of the baptized Mendelssohn and the unbaptized Meyerbeer. For the parallel phenomenon in literature and journalistic writing he had Heine and Börne (both baptized) at his disposal. At the time of the republication, the baptized Hiller and Joachim served as targets of his suspicions, as did the proud Jew Auerbach and the alleged half-Jew Hanslick. All of these men, indeed the whole of Jewry, were, according to Wagner, participants in the plot against him. In order to explain the anti-Wagner attitudes of non-Jews, Wagner resorted to the notion of the "duped Christian."[14] The Jewish spirit could make a nest for itself even in the mind of Christians and was in any case not driven out by baptismal water.

It is characteristic of the times that even Wagner's adversaries did not oppose this blurring of boundaries. They contradicted, criticized, and ridiculed the Wagnerian thesis, but it did not occur to any critic to invalidate it by pointing out that the people Wagner was attacking were often, if not mostly, not Jews but converts to Christianity.

On the ideological plane, that is, in purposeful self-assertion, the Jewish participants in the discussion here and there held fast to the religious definition of Judaism. Emil Breslauer complained that Wagner's insolence "permitted him to fling . . . reckless insults . . . against an entire religious society." [15] E. Liéser apparently expressed the wishes of most Jews when he wrote: "We want nothing more and nothing less than all the other citizens of the state, from whom we are separated only by our religious faith." [16] Other writers also complained about the attack on the fundamental principles that served, in their opinion, as the basis for Jewish existence in the German world. "Is the Jew not a man created in the image of God, like other men?" wrote Joseph Engel, evoking the idea of humanity, which served as a presupposition of Jewish emancipation. [17] Similarly, Breslauer complained about Wagner's retreat into darker times, when "it was seriously debated whether the Jews were to be counted at all as human beings." [18] Though the apologists for the Jews conceded that the masses of Jews possessed character traits distinguishing them from the world around them, these differences, Liéser wrote, owed their existence "not to their blood, not to their race," but to their religiously conditioned separation and their long-standing oppression, as in general all "national characteristics of peoples" were to be attributed to the influence of external conditions. At the same time all of the apologists assumed that the Jewish character traits would disappear with the consistent implementation of political emancipation and social amalgamation. [19] What shocked them was the realization that Wagner and the defenders of his thesis insisted on the innate distinctiveness of the Jews and made it the basis of their protest against Jewish participation in German culture.

This indeed was the central idea of the opponents. An anonymous critic of Wagner who styled himself "nonpartisan" spoke of a "religio-national association" against which Wagner had directed his attacks. To be sure, the author distanced himself from Wagner and believed that the theory of a Jewish plot stemmed from Wagner's "blindness and self-deification," but he agreed with Wagner's assessment of the role of the Jews in the artistic life of the nations. "Precisely the work of art is like nothing else a product of the whole, most essential individuality, and bears its spiritual signature with inexorable necessity. The child of a Jew will always be a Jew, a Jew's artistic product will . . . always have a Jewish character." The author then attempted to point out the negative traits—"the lack of deep, heartfelt passion" and so forth—in the works of Mendelssohn and Meyerbeer. One could not deny that the Jewish artists possessed a certain aptitude and creativity, "but where deep, genuine feeling, true passion and warmth, and *ethical* depth are required to give the stamp of classicality to *great* forms, only the Germanic stock with its best inheritance which it has received from nature can create truly effectively, as it has already created the highest." [20] Here, therefore, the inferiority of the Jew vis-à-vis the German is clearly attributed to his extraction. Conversion to Christianity changes nothing, as the test case of Mendelssohn shows.

Similar views were also expressed by Julian Schmidt, who, as we saw in chapter 6, criticized Wagner's self-deification while at the same time accepting his critique of Judaism. The theme of Wagner's essay, Schmidt believed, ought not to be rejected out of hand. As a literary historian, he preferred to illustrate the problem with the example of the Jewish writer. Schmidt stressed the "colossal percentage of Jewish literati vis-à-vis the non-Jewish. It is necessary to investigate what presuppositions of German literature rendered this proportion possible, what characteristics of the Jewish spirit were set in motion by precisely these conditions, and what kind of influence they exercise on German literature." Schmidt mentioned Heine, Börne, and Auerbach, "all three . . . writers of great importance, and as widely as they appear to differ from one another, there is nevertheless one point on which they are related." [21] No literary documentation of this relationship was provided. It is doubtful whether Schmidt connected any concrete idea with this statement. It was enough to know that the three writers were Jews in order to presuppose their common spiritual orientation. Only one of the three, Auerbach, belonged to the Jewish religious community; Heine and Börne had been baptized at an early date. That fact, however, made no difference to Schmidt, since all three men nevertheless remained carriers of "the Jewish spirit."

Whether or not Wagner's supporters shared his assessment of some of his objects of hatred, they all held fast to his conception of the Jewish element as something essentially foreign to the German. Max Fuchs sought to soften the Wagnerian critique of Judaism and argued that Wagner understood "by Judaism' . . . really only the plutocracy unconcerned with confession." Since the Jews had a plutocracy, one had to blame them for not employing their wealth "more profitably for art." No wonder the Jew, apart from "welcome exceptions," had "only a desire to acquire, increase and maintain his power." The Jewish quest for money and power was, however, only one of the attributes that separated the Jew from his environment. As members of different tribes, Germans and Jews had an insurmountable antipathy toward each other: "They are so dissimilar in their characteristics that their union was never conceivable and will never take place."[22] The author's intention of weakening Wagner's critique of the Jews culminated, ultimately, in the complete denial of the possibility of a union of Jew and German, a possibility held open, at least theoretically, by Wagner and his defenders.

Chief among Wagner's advocates was Julius Lang, whose consciously apologetic intention was announced in the title of his pamphlet: *Toward the Reconciliation of Judaism with Richard Wagner*. Lang, who belonged to the close circle of Wagnerians in Berlin and who was friendly with the master, called himself "a true friend of Richard Wagner's and an enthusiastic admirer of his art for many years."[23] He had at his disposal private sources of information, including Wagner's conciliatory letter to Tausig, which he believed he could rely on in his role as intermediary.[24] In fact, his tortuous tract is nothing other than an elucidation of Wagner's basic thesis and a correction of individual points, particularly with regard to developments in the future, when the Jews should be able "to enter into our civil community—but fully, totally, frankly and without reservations." Although he was a practicing Catholic, Lang did not make the fusion of the Jews with their environment dependent on their baptism. In the past, he wrote, "it was less the religious than the national element that obstructed a rapprochement between Christian and Jew in Germany." If one wished to make this rapprochement possible in the future, all of the Jews' national characteristics had to be expunged: "The family that adopts a son can rightfully demand that he become completely merged with it, entirely at one with it."[25]

If Wagner's allusion to the theoretical capacity of Jews to transform themselves received a more concrete formulation here, Lang still did nothing more than point to a quasi-accessible way out of the situation. Lang quoted a statement of Heinrich Laube's: "There are only two ways of solving the Jewish question. One must either fully annihilate the Jews or completely emancipate them. As the former is not possible, the latter recommends itself." When he spoke of "emancipation," Laube himself probably meant more than the granting of equal rights. Lang went on to say that despite emancipation Jewry remained an "Ahasuerian phenomenon," which up to then, at least, was unable to live and unable to die, "which cannot die, as a foreign stock in many ways antipodal to us, and which cannot live with us as citizens, related to us in spirit and mentality, sharing our thoughts and feelings."[26]

Lang referred to his own experience even with baptized Jews— "at any rate, the so-called forcibly baptized"—who exchanged their religion for a career, and of whom there were many in his earlier homeland of Austria. With all their zeal for assimilation they "could not completely overcome their hostility—though repressed—to our culture, based on Christianity and its development, and the modern state which had emerged from it." How could they do so, when the events of history, such as Luther's liberating act of the Reformation, the background experience for the modern world, had rather negative connotations for them, because of Luther's and his followers' enmity to Judaism? Likewise, the modern Jew was deprived of experiential access to the visual arts that bore the impress of Christian motifs. Their approach to art was an intellectual one, if it was not simply artificial.[27]

Thus, in Lang's presentation, as in Wagner's, modern Jews stood ouside the German cultural community. Lang softened Wagner's judgment only in reference to the poetic achievements of Jews and their talent for representation. Wagner, he said, went too far in the rejection of that talent, in the light of the phenomena of Heine, Börne, Auerbach, the French Jewess Rachel (Félix), and the German-Jewish actor Ludwig Dessoir. Lang vacillated between his own observations and the stereotype he borrowed from Wagner. Wagner's statement that "the Jew speaks the modern European languages only as acquired, not as mother tongues" Lang declared to be "perfectly true," only to testify two pages later that among cultured Jews he had "only very rarely noticed the shrill, shadowy side of the Jewish-German manner of speaking."[28]

Stereotypes and prejudices also set the tone in Lang's pamphlet, although he claimed to have been free of them as a result of his friendly contacts with Jewish classmates in his Austrian gymnasium. He had had "abundant opportunity to learn the strengths and weaknesses of this nation." Of nine Jews, five had been "special favorites of the clerical professors from the highly educated Benedictine order," and his Jewish classmates in general had been "models of efficiency, industry and modesty." And then follows the surprising sentence: "Only in a single one of my classmates at that time . . . did the entire dark side and defect of the tribe come to light."[29] This naive confession, in which Lang represents the exceptional case as typical for all of Jewry, reveals the deep roots of his negative image of Jews.

Lang regarded himself as one "of those Catholics who had not broken with their church and who upheld its dogmas openly and unembarrassedly." It is significant for our study that even an author who described himself in this way developed his image of Jews not from the contrast between Judaism and Christianity but from the nature of the Jewish tribe. To be sure, Lang, as we have seen, based the Jew's alleged lack of understanding of modern culture on his alienation from the Christian world. But, Lang maintained, the gulf between Jews and Christians lay no longer in the "religious difference" but in the different characteristics of the stock, "in the ongoing struggle between Jewish-oriental and Christian-Germanic elements."[30] The elimination of that gulf in the future was tied no longer to a conversion of the Jews but, as Wagner had also stipulated, to a basically indefinable transformation of their nature.

The Wagner controversy gave those who were interested in the Jewish problem the opportunity to take stock of developments up to that point. Gustav Freytag, the famous novelist and liberal journalist, had played his part in the formation of a negative image of Jews, as can be seen from his widely read novel of the 1850s, *Debit and Credit*.[31] In 1869, however, he found "an attack on the Jewish nature among us to be in no respect in tune with the times, not in politics, not in society, not in science and art." The Jews, he argued, had succeeded in making strides toward assimilation to the desired model of the future—respectable citizenship. "In all these areas our fellow citizens of Israelite faith are worthy allies in the pursuit of proper goals. . . . Only the last remains of old traditions and intolerance must be overcome . . . in order fully to include the hearts and minds of the German Jews in our nationhood." Freytag sought to characterize the still-disturbing Jewish qualities as "excessive pleasure in word-play and sophistical arguments," inadequacy in "expressing inner and aesthetic [schöngewogener] perceptions in word and tone," a lack of "genuine cheerfulness and liberating humor," and other more or less noticeable character traits. However, Freytag warned against "conceiving of these as peculiarly Jewish as opposed to German." The characteristics of the Jews were to be attributed to their uncertain political and social existence and would disappear with a change in the conditions under which they lived. The present was to be seen as a transitional period, one in which "weaknesses and perversities . . . are occasionally . . . criticized as Jewish qualities."[32] One should not take such attacks too much to heart. Freytag was doubtless of the opinion that the quiet process of reconciliation would be better off without them.

The analysis presented by Freytag amounted to a declaration that there were on the non-Jewish side no serious reservations against a complete incorporation of the Jewish minority into the social structure. That was also the hope of the Jewish ideologues of emancipation. However, the Wagner controversy dealt a heavy blow to this optimistic conception. The Jewish participants in this discussion found themselves face to face with opponents who made no secret of their scruples and their antipathy to Jews, even if they also held the gap between Jews and non-Jews to be bridgeable. The Jewish apologists could not avoid responding to the views of their opponents and thereby more or less consciously surrendering their own conception of the particularity of the Jews as being exclusively conditioned by religion.

M. Gutmann stated that Wagner's real motive was to get even with his rivals Mendelssohn and Meyerbeer, and in doing so "his personal antipathy to everything of a Jewish nature came admirably to his assistance." Gutmann noted, "The Christian-German nature of the man recoiled from assimilation with the Jews."[33] The attitude of the "Christian-Germanic" circles of the Restoration period is indeed sufficiently well known. The fact that Wagner, as a democrat, had previously been numbered among their opponents but had now joined them stamped him as a renegade and made him the target of the ridicule and the contempt of the Jews under attack. They would not in any case expect their salvation to come from those who shared Wagner's views. Thus, at the end of *Judaism in Music*, the "climax of the masterpiece," the call to the Jews to seek their redemption through a transformation of their nature, as Börne had done, was to be regarded as double-dealing, according to Gutmann. The Jews were to be redeemed and to perish at the same time. "A son of Jacob can scarcely be motivated to participate by such tempting prospects." [34]

Edmund Friedmann wrote, "It is not the Christian's hatred of the Jew but the antipathy of the Indo-Germanic stock to the Semitic." [35] The antipathy of the simple people to the Jews was one of the pillars of Wagner's theory, and here it was accepted as a fact by one of his sharpest critics. Though Emil Breslauer also accepted Wagner's assertion, he blamed Wagner for not resisting the prevailing opinion, as he had done on other occasions, but allowing himself to be swayed by the *vox populi*.[36] The only one who denied the existence of a popular antipathy to the Jews was Joseph Engel, who said that it is "no longer present today, or is to be found only in extremely rare instances," and is "therefore merely of a subjective nature" in the case of Wagner and his followers.[37]

The Jewish authors named up to now were independent writers who set forth their own personal views. The abandonment of religious differentiation between Jews and non-Jews can be seen, however, even among the quasi-official representatives of the two religious divisions in Judaism, Orthodoxy and Reform. The Orthodox newspaper *Der Israelit* wrote half ironically that Wagner's assertion that "Jews and Judaism exercised a never-suspected, immense, irresistible influence over every branch of human knowledge and endeavor" can only confirm that the "human stock [*Menschenstamm*] of the Jews occupied a special place in the human universe." [38] It apparently did not bother the Orthodox correspondent that many of those who were, in Wagner's opinion, responsible for "Judaization" had been disloyal to Judaism. In this polemic one fell willy-nilly into the streams of thought based on extraction and not on religion.

The organ of liberal Jewry, the *Allgemeine Zeitung des Judentums*, edited by Rabbi Dr. Ludwig Philippson, who doubtless wrote the article on Wagner, deliberately entered into the conceptual world of the opponent and asked: "What kind of a German and a Latin race must this be, to let itself be thrown to the ground by these scattered, isolated, despised and hated offspring of a superannuated little Semitic clan?"[39] The concept of race tacitly included all the Jews, baptized or unbaptized. Philippson himself made the observation that the more recent attacks—such as those of Wagner and von Mohl—were aimed not only at the Jews' religion but also at their tribe. He also noted that they did not distinguish between baptized and unbaptized Jews, and "now called on the latter to come to the defense of their fellow tribesmen."[40] There were, in fact, among the critics of the brochure two converts, who took positions in favor of the Jews.[41] Understandably, Philippson saw such a change of positions as an unwelcome blurring of the boundaries between the adherents of the Christian and the Jewish religions. It likewise seemed paradoxical to him that Mendelssohn, who, in Heine's words, had made himself "the hod carrier of the Protestant Pietists," had now "to be delivered back to his high-minded grandfather."[42] But even Philippson succumbed to the temptation to refer to baptized Jews as evidence of Jewish capabilities. In connection with the Wagner polemic, to refute the thesis of the Jewish musicians' inadequacy, Philippson reported on a concert in Cologne where two artists took the floor "with complete mastery." "Both were Jews," noted Philippson[43]—their names were Ferdinand Hiller and Joseph Joachim. Both had long since been baptized, a fact that Philippson either forgot or repressed on this occasion.

Drawing boundaries between Jews and non-Jews on the basis of their religious affiliation had become hopelessly difficult. Too many had settled in the no-man's-land between the two groups: the radically secularized members of both societies, who wished to have nothing to do with any religion, and especially the newly baptized Jews, who, though they formally belonged to a church, had neither spiritually nor socially completed the transformation from Jew to Christian. If one spoke of Jews, particularly in a secular context, these people were by no means excluded. What therefore determined their inclusion in the category "Jew"?

Contemporaries sought an answer to this question, and in the course of doing so they employed new terms to designate the whole of Jewry. These terms were based on the extraction of the individual and ignored his religious confession or other spiritual attitude. The concept that arose in this situation, and that we often encounter in the Wagner controversy, was that of tribe or stock (*Stamm*). Again and again reference is made to the artistic or general cultural capabilities of the Jewish tribe, often even in connection with biblical antiquity. Here and there the concept of race also surfaces, without attaining any more far-reaching significance than its synonyms, tribe or stock. This casual application of the term provides us with an insight into the rise of modern anti-Semitism, which was later to be fatefully associated with the concept of race.

If we collect the anti-Jewish statements uttered by Wagner himself and by others in the course of the Wagner controversy, we have before us the fundamental elements of the anti-Semitic ideology. The Jews are foreign to the European peoples, especially the Germans, and are at bottom a culturally and morally inferior breed. Because the determination of foreignness and inferiority is based on observation, it is upheld whether or not a plausible historical or other explanation can be offered for it. Rudimentary attempts to explain the observed "facts" turn up sporadically—for example, when Wagner let slip in a subordinate clause the remark that "the Jew . . . , as is well known, has a God all to himself,"[44] or when Lang spoke of the "subjective exclusivity which impedes the process of their amalgamation with other nations."[45] Both point to an original, almost metaphysical quality of the Jewish nature.

No matter how deeply rooted the Jewish mentality was considered to be, and no matter how acutely the foreignness of the Jew was perceived, the Jews' opponents did not hold their characteristics to be ineradicable. They held open, in principle, the road to assimilation, designated at the time as "amalgamation." The condition for attaining that goal was the complete abandonment of Jewish character traits—an indefinable process, which now took the place of the institutionally fixed act of baptism. It was only one more step to a complete negation of the possibility of a transformation of the Jews. In the interest of historical accuracy, it must be established that neither Wagner nor his defenders (with the exception of Fuchs) took that step during the Wagner controversy.

# 8  Private Jewish Phobias

The reaction to the republication of his anti-Jewish brochure may have given Wagner cause for reflection. It did not cure him of his Jewish phobia, but rather strengthened it.

As we have already noted, Cosima (at the time still the wife of Hans von Bülow, but already living with Wagner in the refuge of Triebschen near Luzern) began writing her diary while the preparations for the republication were underway. The entries give us a glimpse of the daily thoughts of the intellectually symbiotic couple. For the most part they reveal Wagner's reflections, which Cosima repeated uncensored. Insofar as the Jews were concerned, she lacked any motivation to correct Wagner's judgments. Her Catholic education had left her with a good measure of anti-Jewish prejudices. Nor had her roughly ten years of living with Bülow given her any cause to rethink matters, since Bülow himself, as we have seen, had a strongly anti-Jewish attitude.[1]

After the publication of the diaries critics were reminded of the confidential nature of their entries.[2] They do in fact contain many spontaneous remarks that Wagner cannot have meant to be taken seriously. On hearing a report of the numerous Jewish casualties in a fire in a Vienna theater, Wagner, according to Cosima, said that one should burn all the Jews at a performance of *Nathan the Wise*. And during the siege of Paris in the Franco-Prussian War Wagner hoped that this "*Femme entretenue* of the world" would be burned.[3] But does that mean that he would have had the heart to order it to be done? Strong language of this sort can slip out in an intimate conversation. It was Wagner's misfortune that his intemperate remarks were recorded by an infinitely devoted companion.

Even if one overlooks these utterances, sufficient evidence of Wagner's Jewish phobia remains. In the thirteen years covered by the diary, a period that began with the scandal over *Judaism in Music*, Cosima and Wagner by no means avoided contact with Jews.

Yet their judgment of the Jews did not soften and they remained as sensitive as ever to their presence. Cosima twice mentioned a Mr. Seligsberg, apparently an art collector or an art dealer, to whom she owed thanks for the delivery of some art objects: "In the evening we look at old etchings sent to us by the Jew Seligsberg" and "I have captured an Apostle tankard with the help of the indispensable Jew Seligsberg, for R[ichard] longed for one!"⁴ It was a matter of course in the period before emancipation to designate a person as a Jew when mentioning his name, doubtless as a means of hinting at the social barriers.⁵ This method of preserving a certain social distance persisted here. It was certainly not uncommon in private conversation even in less anti-Jewish circles. With the Wagners, to be sure, the tendency to pay attention to the Jewish origins of their acquaintances operated almost like an obsession and often led to grotesque scenes. The patriotic Wagners followed with enthusiasm the triumphant advance of the Germans in the Franco-Prussian War of 1870–71. In June 1871 Cosima reported: "In the newspaper the entry of the troops into Berlin . . . moved us indescribably." Then the addendum: "Unfortunately the description is by a Jew [J. Rodenberg]."⁶ Thus the Jewish origin of the article spoiled their pleasure.

Only rarely did the Wagners pass in silence over the Jewish origin of their acquaintances. In April 1876 they received a visit from Professor Michael Bernays, the baptized son of a noted rabbi from Hamburg, whose brother, the famous classical philologist Jacob Bernays, had remained a strictly traditional Jew and had consequently never become a full professor.⁷ Michael too was a scholar of rank. Cosima called him "the greatest living authority on Goethe." The Wagners studied Bernays's introduction to Goethe's correspondence with pleasure. He himself was a welcome guest in their house, since the "well-educated, fiery, curious man seems really to understand R[ichard]." That Bernays belonged to the Wagner society in Munich, where he was a professor of German literature, and had cosigned the society's appeal to join it, the Wagners noted with satisfaction. Very soon, however, they were disappointed with Bernays. A friend of theirs reported: "He doesn't dare to write about MS [*Meistersinger*]." When the name of Bernays came up again somewhat later, it led to a discussion of "the peculiar nature of the Jew," which ended with Wagner's words: "a strange, foreign element has come among us." Visibly annoyed, the Wagners nevertheless maintained their relations with Bernays. Cosima indemnified herself for this inconvenience with a remark about Bernays's "ridiculousness (always as if charged to hold forth on everything sublime)."[8]

Only rarely was someone identified as a Jew without being simultaneously disparaged. Wagner found a true benefactor and admirer in Bernhard Löser, a banker in Berlin. In the diary he is condescendingly mentioned as "the touching Jew Löser." Wagner visited him in Berlin, "gave him cigars and thankfully sent him brochures." On his next visit to Berlin Wagner was annoyed by the bad hotel to which Löser had sent him. Löser had also had his rooms there "filled with plants and trees whose odor made me sick." What was even worse, however, for Wagner, was to learn that the Wagner society founded by Löser had not enjoyed the hoped-for success, "whereupon the Wagneriana disintegrated for me in the usual Jewish aroma." From then on the Jewish banker from Berlin was mentioned either with praise or disparagingly, depending on the level of his accomplishments.[9]

Wagner's ambitious, mostly very costly, artistic plans made disappointments unavoidable. He was extremely resentful of those of his contemporaries who failed to understand the significance of his works and as a result did not support him sufficiently. If Jews were involved in the matter, the guilt was immediately transferred to their entire "clan." When a money order from the banker Erlanger did not arrive at the proper time, Wagner said: "Like his entire tribe, this fellow seeks and finds excuses, deep annoyance and disgrace; Judea will always remain the same."[10]

There was nothing for which the Jews could not be made responsible. When a proposal came from London in 1871 to perform the *Tannhäuser* march there, and the trifling sum of twenty pounds was offered, Cosima quoted Richard as saying: "That too the Jews have on their conscience, that one pays so poorly for everything." Mendelssohn, Meyerbeer, and Hiller were prepared to lend "their names for nothing," while Hayden and Jommelli allowed themselves to be well paid.[11] Elsewhere Wagner always spoke of the Jews engaging in art only as a business. In *Judaism in Music* he had already spoken of the Jewish "art-commodity-exchange."[12] Here the frequently observable fact that anti-Semites contradict themselves in their accusations against the Jews reaches the level of absurdity.

Wagner's tendency to evaluate men according to whether they were on his side or not is well known. He himself once enumerated the people who "had deserted him, such as Brockhausens, Karl Ritter, Willes, Laube, an immense number." Whereas the accusation of disloyalty here affected only the persons concerned, the defection of Hiller and Joachim was connected with their Jewish origins: "I am nevertheless glad that of the German musicians two Jews are the most repugnant to me: Hiller and Joachim. What was done to the latter, for example, that he should change from a rapturous enthusiast into a spiteful opponent?" If Wagner encountered anything unpleasant in a Jew, he unhesitatingly attributed it to his ethnic peculiarity. On one occasion the master took his dog Rus with him when he went to a public house to drink beer. The local piano teacher, a Jew, stumbled over the animal. Wagner apologized, whereupon Mr. Karpeles answered, "Oh, for me these are sacred beings, your dogs. I know Pips and Peps." The house pets of the famous inhabitant of the city of Bayreuth were probably subjects of local gossip, and the master could have put the remark down as a compliment. The lesson that the Wagners drew from this episode was, however: "We are astonished by this characteristic of the Jews, who, like the Jesuits, are able to keep track of everything."[13]

Again and again Wagner mentions Jews and Jesuits in the same breath. With Jesuits, however, Wagner had no personal contact, and his statements consequently lacked an address. Not so Jews, who were part of Wagner's immediate surroundings, and this fact created some highly ambiguous situations. Apologists for Wagner have repeatedly pointed to his uninterrupted dealings with Jews, especially with Karl Tausig, Joseph Rubinstein, and Hermann Levi, in the hope of thereby demonstrating the relative harmlessness of Wagner's hostility toward Jews.[14] In fact, in this phase of the relations between Jews and non-Jews, even the sharpest critique of Judaism and the Jewish nature did not rule out social or even friendly contact with individual Jews. Indeed, the negative assessment of everything Jewish was still connected here with the idea that Jewishness was something that could be given up. The social ostracism of the Jews resulted only from the anti-Semitic movement of the 1880s and

1890s.[15] On the ideological plane, Wagner acknowledged the possibility of the de-Judaization of individual Jews or even of all of Jewry. In particular cases, such as that of Joseph Rubinstein, his conduct may have been influenced by this possibility. In Rubinstein he encountered someone who took the matter personally and who declared himself ready for the process of de-Judaization. In a letter from the Russian city of Kharkov in February 1872 introducing himself to Wagner, Rubinstein wrote: "I am a Jew—For you, that says everything. All those characteristics noticeable in the present-day Jews I too possessed." He reported how he was once saved for a time from "complete despair and almost shameful weakness" by his occupation with Wagner's works. By 1872, however, he had once again fallen into that "wretched condition." "My condition constantly worsens, for I recognize that the Jews must go under; so how can I keep from going under, since I myself am a Jew?" he wrote. Rubinstein unmistakably diagnosed his spiritual instability with concepts borrowed from *Judaism in Music*. His object was to seek a cure through collaboration with Wagner: "From you, therefore, I await help which is urgently necessary. My parents are rich. The means to travel to you I would have immediately."[16]

Rubinstein appeared in April of the same year in Triebschen in the company of his guardian, a Dr. Cohen, who called Wagner's attention, behind the young man's back, to the fact that his ward required "very careful treatment." Cosima described Rubinstein as a "rare phenomenon and experience," and added: "R[ichard] is infinitely good to the young man, counsels him to keep calm, and offers him his company in Bayreuth."[17] Wagner apparently took a fancy to the musically highly gifted young man. From the moment of his arrival on the scene shortly before the Wagners moved to Bayreuth, Rubinstein was, with brief interruptions, a constant attendant to their household. With the financial assistance from his father, he could always afford to live in the vicinity of the Wagners. An almost daily guest in their house, he enjoyed the musical instruction of the master and, for his part, entertained the occupants of the house and their guests with his music-making. Because he was psychologically disturbed, it was necessary for the Wagners to have regard for his irritability, which led, of course, to complaints, although Richard showed more patience with him than did Cosima.

On his first departure after being with them for six months, Cosima noted: "This evening the good Rubinstein left—R[ichard] accuses me of having dismissed him too coldly, which I greatly regret." After Rubinstein's return their relations improved. Cosima celebrated Rubinstein's birthday with the children and always referred to him as "friend Rubinstein." Wagner himself was prepared to write to Rubinstein's father in order to smooth over conflicts between father and son.[18]

Here, therefore, the prejudice against Jews seems to have been overcome, and one can speak without exaggeration of an intimate friendship between master and pupil. But appearances are deceiving. The prejudice receded as long as the relations remained unclouded. If, however, the slightest misunderstanding arose, or if the young man showed a lack of musical comprehension or ability, Wagner immediately dragged out his Jewish origin as an explanation. Jews could "not really hear or play any theme," could not "perceive . . . the popular [*Volkstümliche*]."[19]

Since Rubinstein preserved "the most deplorable characteristics of his tribe," an "unbridgeable gap" opened up for Wagner between "this nature and our own" on the occasion of even a "small argument with friend Rubinstein." Wagner, it is true, acknowledged that his pupil sought "to be redeemed by the German spirit"—presumably through Wagner's mediation. But that attempt was not fully successful. Wagner certainly discussed Jewish matters in a scathingly critical fashion in Rubinstein's presence, yet he had to show a certain restraint before the young man who was so conscious of his Jewish origin. When the Wagners received the report of the fire in the Viennese theater and displayed their malicious joy over the Jewish deaths, Cosima remarked: "We do not express our feelings about the Jews in the theater in front of Rubinstein." On another occasion Rubinstein appears to have dared to contradict Wagner's judgment of the Jews, for Cosima reported: "R[ichard] had a bad night. The heated discussion concerning the Jews exhausted him. He praised Rubinstein's style and seriousness, but he should keep his mouth shut about the Jews."[20]

The maintenance of friendly relations with Jews simultaneously with the denial of their worth as human beings must have led to morally dubious dissimulation and dishonesty. In fact, the Wagners held an inner reservation, a *reservatio mentalis* toward all their Jewish acquaintances and supporters. Irrespective of the real or putative Jewish characteristics that they believed they could observe and that repelled them, the alleged difference of the Jewish nature became a dogma with them. The belief in the Jews' distinctiveness and therewith their inferiority barred the way to an honest, unreserved relationship with even the most highly valued companions. Wagner had been willing to close his eyes to Karl Tausig's Jewishness. Yet two days after his sudden death, which the Wagners perceived as a tragedy, Cosima said: "His death seems to us to be metaphysically founded; a poor nature, worn out early, lacking any faith in itself, which with everything that brought it close to us still felt an inner, deep foreignness [its Jewishness]." And two days later: "Reflections on Tausig's sad life; so precocious, already worked through Schopenhauer by the age of sixteen; he felt the curse of Judaism." Since there is otherwise no evidence that Tausig felt burdened by his Jewish origin, it is quite possible that we are dealing here with a projection of the reporter's own sentiments. But if Tausig in fact felt foreign and accursed by Judaism, this feeling, as also in the case of Rubinstein, may have resulted less from his own reflections than from the pressures emanating from Wagner. Oddly enough, Wagner said something extremely instructive about this phenomenon two days before his own death: "One really must not associate with the Israelites! They are either emotionally disturbed about it or it expresses itself through arrogance, as with J. Rub." [21]

Tausig and Rubinstein came under Wagner's influence as young men, whereas Hermann Levi first came into contact with him after Levi had made a name for himself as a successful court conductor in Rotterdam, Karlsruhe, and, after 1872, Munich. Levi was among the adherents of the artistic direction represented by Wagner, but he guarded his independence vis-à-vis the master. Cosima twice quoted Wagner's statement that he would respect the court conductor alone "because he really calls himself Levi, as in the Bible, not Löwe, Lewy etc." The biblical name, which the court conductor had inherited from his father, the rabbi of the Reform community in Giessen, was probably not the only reason for the esteem in which Wagner held Levi. With all his reverence for the master, Levi did not allow himself to be dominated by Wagner in his views and opinions.

Typically, on the occasion of one of Levi's first visits to Bayreuth (August 1872), the two men fell into an argument over Bismarck's expulsion of the Jesuits in the course of the *Kulturkampf*. Levi condemned the chancellor's measures, while Wagner raged at "the damage the Catholic Church did to Germany." Apparently, Levi also permitted himself to criticize the *Bayreuther Blätter*, which had been appearing since the beginning of 1878. He probably objected to the repeated attacks on the Jews, in Wagner's own articles as well as in the essays of the others. Cosima noted on 2 August 1878: "R[ichard] said to the conductor Levi with regard to the "Bayreuther Blätter": 'I seek conflict with no one, but I speak my opinion in disregard of all.'"[22]

Levi, though the son of a rabbi, probably did not retain any positive religious ties to Judaism, but his attitude toward it was nevertheless not one of indifference. In a conversation with Wagner in 1878 he designated his Judaism as "*a walking anachronism*" (emphasis in the original), a phrase that was probably meant to suggest the difficulty he had in finding an ideological justification for his continued adherence to Judaism. This statement elicited from Wagner one of his few appreciative remarks about Jews and Judaism. Moved by Levi's problematic avowal of Judaism, Wagner said to him "that if the Catholics consider themselves to be of a higher rank than we, the Protestants, then the Jews are of the highest rank, the oldest."[23]

At this time the agitation that finally led to the anti-Semitic movement directed by Adolf Stöcker was in full swing.[24] The Jewish question had become an unavoidable object of public attention and private discussion, a circumstance that may have awakened an awareness of being Jewish even among those, like Hermann Levi, who were very much alienated from their origins. Levi apparently had no qualms about discussing his Jewish origin or the problem of being Jewish. In January 1879 he mentioned in a conversation with the Wagners that his father was a rabbi. Wagner thereupon explained to him an idea that he had developed shortly beforehand, one that he subsequently repeated on many occasions and that struck a somewhat more conciliatory tone with regard to Judaism: "If I ever again write about the Jews, I would say that there is no reason to object to them. The only problem is that they came to us Germans too soon. We were not strong enough to absorb this element." That was the original formulation. In conversation with Levi, Wagner even stated that if the encounter between Jews and Germans had come at a better time, "the universally human, which could have developed out of the German, could have come as a benefit to everything Jewish." The fault lay with "the premature intrusion into our affairs, before we knew who we were." The conversation then moved from the theoretical plane to the concrete. The court conductor reported the existence of a great movement against the Jews in every region; "in Munich one wishes to remove them from the municipal council—he [Levi] hopes that in twenty years they will be eliminated root and branch and that the audience of the 'Ring' will be a different people. We 'know otherwise.'"[25] If Levi's words are correctly rendered, he sought to connect the anti-Jewish movement with the hope that the conspicuous Jewish nature would disappear under the pressure of opposition, a hope which the Wagners did not share.[26]

That Wagner himself perceived his relations with his Jewish friends to be problematic emerges from Cosima's observation concerning this peculiar conversation: "When we were alone again, R[ichard] and I spoke of the curious attraction of individual Jews to him." In the light of Wagner's palpable anti-Jewish attitude, the attachment of the Jews to him had to seem incomprehensible, and his connection with them must have appeared to be full of contradictions. Wagner rid himself of the burdensome problem with these words: "We shall have in Wahnfried [the residence of the Wagners in Bayreuth] a synagogue." Cosima attested that he felt inhibited by his connection with Jews from making public anti-Jewish statements. Wagner complained that he could not write his articles against the Catholic church in the *Bayreuther Blätter* because he had to show consideration for the Bavarian king and for his own Catholic father-in-law, Franz Liszt. A collaborator on the paper asked "if he might attack Levi, which also did not go over well." Immediately afterward Cosima noted: "It annoys him that it is now awkward for him to name the Jews, on account of three or four fellows. Davidsohn [one of the Jewish Wagnerians from Berlin] sent me a cigarette-holder, he called out cheerfully, flitting from annoyance to jest in his habitual manner"[27]—and thereby pushing weighty moral problems aside with empty phrases, we must add.

In the case of Hermann Levi the collaboration with Jews threatened to become particularly embarrassing. Levi was being considered as director of *Parsifal* because of his outstanding abilities as well as his position as court conductor for the king of Bavaria. But *Parsifal* was not for Wagner an ordinary musical work. He called the opera a "staged consecration festival [*Bühnenweifestspiel*]" and thereby indicated its religious objective. In fact, *Parsifal* was deeply affected by the idea of redemption and made use of the central Christian symbols of the Crucifixion and the sacrificial death of the Son of God on Good Friday. As artificial as this superimposition of Christian symbols on the saga of the Holy Grail may seem to us, Wagner was serious about the revivification of the primordial Christian experience.[28] He had already expressed himself in this sense on the religious function of art—his art—in the essay "Religion and Art" in 1880.[29] Even if this essay is to be dismissed as the belated justification for an artistic inspiration, Cosima's diaries testify that during the last decade of his life, at any rate, Wagner held fast to the idea of Christ as intermediary—"the noblest that humanity has produced"—and the Christian mysteries such as baptism and communion. Wagner made such statements very often. That he meant them seriously is shown by the fact that despite his obvious contempt for the church and its representatives, he himself occasionally took part in religious ceremonies and also required that his relations do so.[30]

Before her confirmation he had a conversation with Cosima's daughter Blandine "about the meaning of confession and communion, and showed her that they represented the whole essence of Christianity, faith and redemption."[31] Typical of this period was the way he took to task the radically minded Malwida von Meysenbug, a friend of the family, "who did not baptize her pupil. This is improper. Everyone is not entitled to create his own religion at will . . . nor must one choose, but it must be possible for one to be told, 'You belong to Christ through baptism; unite yourself with him once again through communion.'"[32]

The negation of Judaism proceeded apace with the affirmation of the foundations of Christianity, and Wagner's anti-Jewish passion absorbed an undisguised Christian religious influence. But that influence by no means entailed a return to the church's doctrine that conversion to Christianity was the Jews' ultimate destiny. In another conversation with Malwida von Meysenbug, Wagner explicitly stated that baptism was obligatory only for those who were "born into this community." He conceded that "it would make no sense for those born outside of this community to have themselves accepted into it, since the church is in such a bad way."[33] In fact, it seems to have been far from Wagner's mind to lead any of his Jewish friends—with the exception of Hermann Levi—to Christianity.

The reason for this exception is apparent. On 28 April 1880, Wagner commented on a letter from Levi that apparently concerned the performance of *Parsifal*: "He must not direct Parsifal unbaptized; but I'll baptize both of them and we'll all take communion together."[34] Since *Parsifal* was intended to be not merely a musical drama but a Christian festival of consecration, it seemed highly inappropriate to allow someone who was not baptized to play a leading role in it. The collaboration of a Jew would have contradicted the whole tenor of the piece and undermined the effect of the Christian religious experience. The way out of this dilemma seemed to lie in Levi's baptism. Wagner was preoccupied with this idea, but he hesitated to suggest it to Levi. Of their next meeting in November Cosima reported: "Very excited, he said in a conversation with Levi that he—as a Jew—had now to learn how to die, which Levi understood quite well." That the Jews, since they are unredeemed, awaited death with anxiety and dread is an old Christian notion, and it was precisely the grace of redemption that *Parsifal* was supposed to bring before the eyes of its audience. Wagner's intention was to point out to Levi this drawback of his Jewish existence. A couple of days later Wagner spoke in Levi's presence "about the deplorable influence of the Jews on our situation" and warned Levi against associating with them. Levi should recognize the practical advantages of distancing himself from the Jewish community. A few weeks later, this time in the absence of the conductor, Wagner said, "It is still not possible to estimate what effect the third act of P[*arsifal*] will have." That comment was probably a reference to the anticipated religious effect of *Parsifal*. Immediately afterward he asked "whether the formula could be found . . . for baptizing such a poor man as Levi—I believe I can find it."[35] Wagner did not expect Levi to adopt the ecclesiastical, dogmatic, fixed form of Christianity that Wagner himself rejected and despised. But in his essay entitled "Religion and Art" Wagner had reduced Christianity "to faith, love, and hope." [36] This Wagnerian Christianity he now wished to bestow on the "poor man" Levi by means of an appropriate formula.

These preparations were merely mental. On 19 January 1881 Wagner finally informed Levi of his intention. Cosima reported: "Then he announced to the conductor, to his astonishment, that he would conduct 'Parsifal'; 'before that we must take up an act with you. I would like to find a formula that will enable you to feel among us as if you belong to us completely.' The veil covering our friend's face made Richard break up." After Levi had gone, Wagner referred to his last essay, where "he had given some idea of what that formula could be." [37] No doubt, Wagner deluded himself with the thought that he could somehow make baptism palatable to Levi as an expression of affiliation with a truncated Christianity. Levi, however, remained inaccessible to approaches of this kind as well.

There was a sequel to this matter. On 29 June, when Hermann Levi was once again in Bayreuth, Wagner received an anonymous letter that called upon him "to keep his work pure and not to allow it to be directed by a Jew." When this letter was shown to Levi—perhaps with the intention of inducing him to be baptized after all—"he could not master his feelings, such baseness seemed new to him." The following day Levi departed for Bamberg, and from there he requested in writing "his dismissal from the directorship." Clinging to the hope that he could still change Levi's mind, Wagner assured him: "But by all means—you are my 'Parsifal' director." After a two-day absence Levi returned to Bayreuth. Wagner sought to give the matter a humorous twist; at dinner he asked for "Hebrew wine." He gave Levi to understand "that he had thought of having him baptized and going with him to communion." [38] With that he probably meant to concede that he had finally renounced any intention of leading Levi to Christianity.

Wagner's missionary project and its failure were typical of the misunderstandings that plagued Christian-Jewish relations at this time. Christians who gave their tradition modern rendering and who were able to retain their Christianity thanks to this new interpretation believed that they would be able to offer their religion to the Jews as well. They thereby failed to bear in mind that their emotional ties to Christianity, conditioned mostly by childhood experiences, comprised the decisive factor for them. Their ideological reinterpretation of Christianity had nothing to say to Jews, who were emotionally rooted in other experiences. The attempt to win them for Christianity in this way was doomed to failure. Whatever else one has to say about Levi's submission or even self-abasement before Wagner, its limits were reached with the attempt to induce his pseudoconversion to Christianity.[39]

# 9    Public Anti-Semitism

Most of the anti-Jewish utterances quoted in the previous chapter
stemmed from the private sphere of the Wagner household. Many
of them, however, had to do with the public political and social
realms. As much as Wagner's resentment sprang from personal motives, stimuli stemming from public events were largely responsible
for the profuseness and intensity of his anti-Jewish statements. In
the fourteen years between the republication of *Judaism in Music*
and Wagner's death in 1883, the number and strength of these stimuli did not remain constant. As we have seen, the republication occurred during the most optimistic period in the history of German
Jews, who placed their hopes in the full political and social consequences of the emancipation legislation. The republication of *Judaism in Music* appeared at this time to be extremely untimely, and the
end of the short-lived scandal seemed to lay the matter to rest. As
stated above, Wagner himself wondered whether the decision to
publish the brochure had not been precipitate and inexpedient.

Nevertheless, *Judaism in Music* was not completely forgotten.
The apparent inattention and the period of relative calm by no
means signified that the Jews or the problems that had from the beginning accompanied their entry into the non-Jewish social sphere
were being ignored. The silence concerning these matters is rather
to be attributed to the feeling that the problematic side of the Jews'
existence—namely, their strikingly peculiar status within non-
Jewish society—was steadily declining in significance, and that a
public debate on this process would tend to obstruct it. In the private, unpolitical, aesthetic sphere, as revealed especially in the
comic papers, the Jewish type was portrayed more or less good-
humoredly.[1] The irritated reaction to the encounter with Jews and
Jewishness that we can observe in Wagner's conversation was certainly unusual in its sharpness and above all in its tone of condem-

nation. Yet special attention to things Jewish, wherever they appeared, were quite widespread during this period.

Public statements concerning the Jews were not entirely absent either. To begin with, the radical rightist groups around the newspaper *Kreuzzeitung* continuously attacked the legislation granting the Jews equal rights.[2] And even during the honeymoon of emancipation other writings that, from other motives, took a critical position vis-à-vis the Jews appeared. Constantin Frantz, an independent journalist, and Paul de Lagarde, a well-known biblical scholar and orientalist, repeatedly expressed their anti-Jewish views.[3] It is characteristic that these as well as other like-minded intellectuals sooner or later came into contact with Wagner. Wagner had carried on a correspondence with Frantz for a long time,[4] and Nietzsche brought Lagarde to his attention in April 1873.[5] Three years later Lagarde sent one of his writings to Cosima.[6] The Wagner home became a sort of magnet for anti-Jewish publications.

In May 1873 Ottomar Beta published in a Berlin newspaper a series of articles entitled "The Semitic and the German Race in the New German Empire," which later appeared as a brochure.[7] Around the same time a pamphlet translated from the French "The Conquest of the World by the Jews" was published under the pseudonym Osman-Bey.[8] Both essays were delivered to Wagner by their authors. Beta's was accompanied by the request that Wagner allowed him to dedicate it to him.[9] Two years earlier Wilhelm Marr had sent one of his books to Wagner,[10] who received it with the remark that "with much sharpness it showed me new points of view from which Judaism can be considered."[11] At this time Marr still pleaded in his publications for the full absorption of the Jews into their surroundings.[12] Subsequently, with the beginning of the anti-Semitic movement, he began pressing for the exclusion of the Jews from the life of the German people. He then sent his notorious book *The Victory of Judaism over Germanism* and later yet another brochure to Wagner.[13] Marr was not the only anti-Semitic agitator who made a habit of doing that. Otto Glagau sent three of his publications to Bayreuth,[14] as did the author of "a brochure about Jews, excerpts from a newspaper 'Deutsche Reichspost,'" which revealed "upsetting statistics" to Wagner.[15] All of these people obviously regarded Wagner as someone who would sympathize with their views, and we will soon see how the organizers of the anti-Semitic movement took for granted that the master would lend the weight of his name and his authority to their movement.

Privately, at least, Wagner was prepared to acknowledge his affinity with the new movement. As we have already observed, he was quite willing to learn from the agitators. Upon receipt of Glagau's second brochure ("National Liberalism and Reaction"), Cosima noted: "A horrifying picture of our present condition, R[ichard] said, but now he finally knows what became of the French billions." Particularly instructive is the commentary on Wilhelm Marr's *Victory of Judaism over Germanism*, which "contains views that ah! are very close to R[ichard]'s opinion." [16] As I have shown elsewhere, this writing from the winter of 1879 represented a high-point in the anti-Jewish agitation that had developed since the middle of the decade.[17] The years 1875–79 were an incubation period for the anti-Semitic movement, which was marked by the interaction of a literary agitation against the Jews and a positive reaction on the part of the public. The literary feud began with a relatively harmless series of articles by Otto Glagau in the popular periodical *Gartenlaube*. The anti-Jewish tendency of these articles mounted as their author discovered among his readers signs of consent and appreciation, especially for the Jewish aspect of his critique of the times. It was similar with other writers who engaged in a critique of existing conditions and those responsible for them during the years of economic distress following the stock market crash of 1873. Wherever Jewish activity in the economy and in other areas of public life was made responsible for the current distress, this point of the critique evoked a reverberating echo, which in turn made the critics concentrate on it even more. As we have noted, Marr's 1879 pamphlet, with whose analysis Wagner identified himself, marked a high-point of anti-Jewish agitation, insofar as it attributed all the ills of the time exclusively to the omnipotent influence of the Jews and recommended at the same time a struggle against Jewry as a cure for the defects of the present.

Moreover, Wagner himself was by no means merely a passive observer of this process of incubation. In the years 1878–79 he made his own contribution through the foundation of the *Bayreuther Blätter* and through his own publications in that periodical.[18] The direct purpose of the new journal was to create a central organ for the Wagner societies, newly organized in support of the Bayreuth festival. The contents of the journal were devoted to the interpretation and glorification of Wagner's works. Among those collaborating on it were also some of the Jews from Wagner's circle, namely, Heinrich Porges and Joseph Rubinstein. At the same time the journal opened its pages to writers of an outspokenly anti-Jewish tendency, and its editor, Hans von Wolzogen, proved to be a radical opponent of the Jews and in the course of time an active supporter of the anti-Semitic movement.[19]

Wagner himself felt obligated to collaborate on the journal. His first contribution was the essay "What Is German,"[20] which he had written in 1865 for the enlightenment of the young King Ludwig of Bavaria.[21] As Wagner remarked in his introductory words in the *Bayreuther Blätter*, he had intentionally excluded the article from his *Collected Writings and Poems*, which began to be published in 1872.[22] From Cosima's diaries we learn that even at this later date, toward the end of the 1870s, he had scruples about publishing it: "In the evening we take out 'What Is German' for some revision. . . . R[ichard] believes he can only speak the truth unreservedly, and I agree with him, since only truthfulness or silence becomes us." The essay, however, contains nothing risky, and the scruples can be related only to the anti-Jewish position at which the essay ultimately arrives. After his experience with the republication of *Judaism in Music* Wagner had resolved to be discreet, and Cosima also preferred—as she had at the time of the brochure on the Jews— to remain passive: "I consider silence best, no doubt R[ichard] does too, but the appointment of H.v.W. [Hans von Wolzogen] and thus the 'Blätter' compels one to speak."[23] The connection with Wolzogen plainly signifies a commitment to an anti-Jewish line. Thus, after nine years of caution with regard to the Jews, Wagner once again expressed himself publicly. But how different were the circumstances! In 1869 the broad public still regarded an anti-Jewish position as a lapse. By 1878 it signified nothing more than association with the ever-stronger current of anti-Jewish agitation.

As to its contents, the essay had recourse to Fichte's idea of the originality of the German spirit, which could remain purer than that of the French,[24] until it became—and this was Wagner's addition—a caricature of its pristine form as a result of the intrusion of the Jews. It was the Jews' talent to perceive otherwise unrecognized benefits in the life of the European peoples. In Poland and Hungary, industry and trade had fallen into their hands. Modern advances had made it possible for all peoples to derive benefits from the proper "relation of work to capital," yet these benefits had remained unused, and it was the Jews who were seizing them. It was a peculiarity of the German to ignore the advantages of "the sincerity and purity of his visions and perceptions" and the "poetry and music" that emerged from them, and not to make use of them, "especially for his public and political life." "The Jew corrected this clumsiness of the German in that he took the brain-work of the German into his hands." Originally tailored to the taste of the Bavarian king, the article also contained the political condemnation of the "translated French-Jewish German democracy," which was forced upon "the misunderstood and injured German *Volksgeist*" by the press.[25]

In his afterword Wagner expatiated on his vain attempts to represent the German spirit with his music at the victory celebrations following the Franco-Prussian War. He had gradually begun to feel strangely ill at ease in the new empire, and that unease subsequently hindered him from pondering once again the question "What Is German?" After allusions to the symptoms of Jewish influence on the public life of the empire, Wagner concluded with a call to Paul de Lagarde and Constantin Frantz, with whom he said he felt a spiritual kinship, to "take on the task of answering this fateful question."[26]

Whether Lagarde reacted to this suggestion is not known.[27] Frantz, however, perceived the opportunity to reiterate his views in the *Bayreuther Blätter*. In his reply of March 1878, his rejection of the new empire was even more radical and fundamental than Wagner's. In accordance with German tradition, he maintained, the German empire had to stand in the service of the universal idea of Christendom. The new state, however, had from its inception and in the formulation of its constitution renounced any Christian obligations, and it therefore was "rapidly on the way to reveal itself to be a *German empire of the Jewish nation*" (emphasis in the original). In its capital, "the communal life, like economic and intellectual life," already stood "entirely under Jewish influence." The new empire bore itself not in a Christian but in a German-national manner. He wrote, "If we insist by all means on becoming so completely German-national, let us first of all throw out the Jews, who have nested in our bodies like tape-worms." [28]

As Frantz's essay, rooted in positive Christian assumptions, illustrates, the *Bayreuther Blätter* became a meetingplace for anti-Semitic authors representing different variations. Wagner himself, once he had overcome his inhibitions, returned repeatedly in his contributions to the *Bayreuther Blätter* to the subject of the Jews. In one essay he took aim at the Jewish claim to originality in the leadership of the modern world. [29] In another essay he advocated the de-Judaization of Christianity and the rejection of any connection between "our Savior" and "the tribal God of Israel." He was not above making extremely demagogic statements: "We must witness the fact that the Christian God is banished to empty churches while ever prouder temples of Jehovah are constructed in our midst." [30]

Wagner's aversion to the sight of synagogues came to light during his visit to Nürnberg in July 1877. Trips to the city's churches had put Cosima and Richard in a "'Meistersinger' mood." But they were "unfortunately, on the H[ans] Sachs-Platz, very disturbed by the synagogue, insolently ostentatious." [31] The experience left traces, for in his essay "We Wish to Hope" Wagner reported an unsuccessful attempt to finance the erection of a Hans Sachs memorial from the proceeds of the performance of the *Meistersinger* and concluded: "Facing the memorial to Hans Sachs in Nürnberg stands, however, an imposing synagogue in the purest oriental style." [32] Later, when the anti-Semites proposed special laws against the Jews, Wagner thought that there was "nothing to be done now," except that "he would, however, forbid the Jewish holidays . . . and the ostentatious synagogues." [33]

In view of this attitude, the *Bayreuther Blätter* must be counted among the factors that paved the way for the anti-Semitic movement, even though Wagner, in order to placate his patrons, occasionally acknowledged that there were exceptional Jews: "But these have completely turned away from the modern struggle for world conquest of their former coreligionists. Indeed, they have very earnestly befriended me, for example." [34]

The four- to five-year incubation period finally produced the so-called Berlin movement under the leadership of the court preacher Adolph Stöcker. As is well known, Stöcker's anti-Semitic activity began with a speech in Berlin on 19 September, in which his demagogically honed invective against Jewish impudence won over his audience.[35] This enthusiasm stood in stark contrast to the cool reception of his earlier addresses, which dealt only with the Christian-social idea with which he wished to attract the Berlin working class to his newly founded party. On the basis of this experience Stöcker altered the course of his political agitation, gave up his competition with the Social Democratic party, and gathered around himself elements that, under the newly coined slogan of anti-Semitism, declared the struggle against Jewry to be their goal.

The report on events in Berlin did not fail to have its effect on the couple in Bayreuth. On 11 October Cosima noted: "I read a very good speech of Pastor Stöcker on Judaism. R[ichard] is for total expulsion. We laugh over the fact that really, it seems, his essay on the Jews marked the beginning of this struggle."[36] The fact that Wagner was immediately ready to make a practical proposal—the total expulsion of the Jews—shows that he correctly interpreted the appearance of Stöcker as the transition from mere agitation to political action. Pleased by this development, he was prepared to register it as the success of his anti-Jewish brochure. Two months later he said: "From 'What Is German' and the essay of Constantin Frantz much has resulted in the Jewish question,"[37] thereby claiming a place of honor for himself among the anti-Semites. There is hardly any historic justification for either claim, no matter how much Wagner's sentiments would have accredited him with this "honor." *Judaism in Music* played a certain role in stimulating the thoughts of like-minded people, but it failed to have any broader impact at the time. The agitation against the Jews that flared up five years later was fed by completely different sources. When the essay "What Is German" appeared, the anti-Jewish current was already swelling. A contribution in the publication aimed at the restricted circle of the Wagnerians could therefore not have had any decisive impact. The anti-Semitic movement would no doubt have gone its route without the collaboration of the *Bayreuther Blätter*.

After the consolidation of the movement in the years 1879–81, when its leader wanted to proceed to concrete political actions, people remembered Richard Wagner's anti-Jewish statements and sought to gain his support for the movement as a particularly important personage. The irony of the situation was that Wagner—despite his claims to authorship—refused to collaborate on that occasion—a fact that may matter more for the assessment of his character than his ambivalence toward his Jewish patrons.

Wagner had an opportunity to show his credentials as an anti-Semite when Dr. Bernhard Förster, known to him as a collaborator on the *Bayreuther Blätter*, asked him to sign the so-called Jew- or anti-Semite-petition.[38] The petition called for the revision of Jewish emancipation—not abolition but a restriction of the Jews' civil rights—and was supposed to be delivered to the chancellor. It contained more than two hundred thousand signatures but was endorsed by only a few important figures. It was regarded as a great achievement when Hans von Bülow, at the request of Dr. Förster and under pressure from Hans von Wolzogen, lent his name to the cause.[39] Close collaborators of the Bayreuth circle were therefore numbered among the initiators of the petition. The call to Wagner, the idol of the circle, was thus a matter of course. It reached him on 16 June 1880. Here is Cosima's note on the matter: "He was called upon to sign a petition to the Chancellor in behalf of exceptional laws against the Jews. He didn't sign it because 1) he had already done his part, 2) he did not like to turn to Bismarck, whom he knew to be frivolous and subject only to his caprices, 3) there was nothing more to be done in this matter."[40]

These were the considerations in the Wagner household. How Wagner responded to the petitioners we do not know. It is possible that on this occasion the request was put to him only orally. A few weeks later a "renewed request," including the wording of the planned petition, reached him from Dr. Förster. Wagner was revolted by the "humble expressions" in the address to the chancellor. In his response to Dr. Förster he resorted to an excuse: the fate of the petition dealing with vivisection had taught him never to sign another one.[41]

An indirect judgment of Wagner's behavior in this matter came from Hans von Bülow and was faithfully transmitted by Cosima. Bülow saw the request to sign the petition as an "appeal to my civil courage" and appended to his letter to Hans von Wolzogen: "since it will become notorious—that is, after all, really the purpose—I must count on a certain amount of defamation in the press as well as a reduction of my concert income of at least fifty percent. It is a fact confirmed on all of my trips that Shem and Hebron supply the most receptive and the most generous concert-goers, and what is more, the participation of the non-Semites is completely dependent on theirs."[42] If this statement reveals the firmness of Bülow's character and his sincerity, it also provides at the same time information concerning the decisive role that the Jewish minority played in the musical life of the period. And that, in turn, explains why Richard Wagner took care not to step forward ostentatiously as an anti-Semite. When Bülow heard that Wagner had refused to sign the petition, he reacted "with a flood of remarks against Bayreuth . . . namely, against Wolz., who had misled him into signing the Jew-petition, while he saw that R[ichard] held back, was in a fair way with the Jews."[43]

Bülow's disappointment was probably not the only sign that could have indicated to Wagner that his reservations vis-à-vis the new movement must have appeared incomprehensible and full of contradictions.[44] In any case, he decided to clarify his attitude and attempted to do so in an essay written in the first months of 1881 entitled "Know Yourself." The title addressed the German people, who, summoned to reflect on their own history, ought to recognize the deeper meaning of "the current movement against the Jews . . . the late reawakening of an instinct." Thirty years earlier he himself had indeed reflected on "the incapacity of the Jew to take a productive part in our art," and in doing so he had encountered stiff resistance. Now, however, protests "in a popular, rough style are being heard in the realm of civil affairs and state politics."[45]

Wagner wrote that the instinct of the people rebelled therefore against "granting the Jews full rights to see themselves as Germans in every conceivable respect—roughly the way the blacks in Mexico were authorized by a blank form to regard themselves as whites."[46] With this comparison he declared Jewish emancipation to be contrary to nature and thereby affirmed the fundamental direction of the anti-Semitic movement, which was the revision of the emancipation legislation. Why, then, did he remain passive vis-à-vis the movement? The answer to this question follows from Wagner's call to reflect on the deeper causes that made the admission of the Jews possible. Instead of assailing Jewish emancipation, the real task consisted in removing its foundations, and there, Wagner declared, he was doing his part. Two factors had paved the way for the Jews. First, the connection of Christianity with the Old Testament tradition had conceded the Jews rights equal to those of the adherents of other religions. After the church had lent religious legitimacy to the Jews, the modern state had accepted the role of guarantor of property, money, and credit, and the greatest beneficiary of that guarantee was of necessity the possessor of all those things, the Jew. Second, all of that had become possible through the self-alienation of the German spirit, whose renewal was nevertheless already being worked on—namely, by the artistic life-work of the author. With the rise of the German spirit through the fulfillment of the commandment to know itself, all the abuses of the current system would disappear like a bad dream. But then "there will be no more Jews." [47]

This recipe for the handling of the Jewish question bears a formal resemblance to that of Karl Marx and may actually have been influenced by him. Marx too rejected a direct tackling of the Jewish problem and expected its solution to come through an alteration in the system from which Jewish existence had sprung. It should be noted, however, that with Marx the disappearance of the Jew concerned only his special Jewish function and mentality, while the Jew as a human being remained a part of the transformed human society. With Wagner, though, the fate of the Jew was cloaked in darkness. Indeed, with Wagner we are by no means dealing with a consistently conceived solution to the Jewish problem. In reality, he lacked a clear idea of what should be done with the Jews. Thus he became enmeshed in contradictions and his remarks in "Know Yourself" were intended only to rescue him from the accusation that he, who had helped to lay the groundwork for the anti-Semitic movement, shrank from its consequences when the time came to take the first practical step. His alibi was therefore that he was laboring in a higher sphere to bring about a much more far-reaching solution to the problem, one that would, for the time being, hurt no one, not even his Jewish patrons.

Very soon Wagner would have an opportunity to make use of his essay's apologetic purpose. His newest Jewish admirer, Angelo Neumann, had been trying for some time to have *Der Ring der Nibelungen* performed in Berlin. In February 1881 Neumann received a warning from Georg Davidsohn, "the worthy journalist, whose friendly relations with Bayreuth were well known," that the anti-Semites were endeavoring to proclaim Richard Wagner as their chief apostle. If there were proof that Wagner was participating in the anti-Semitic agitation, or even if people believed that he was doing so, one would have to fear "serious danger to the Berlin enterprise." The days had passed in which one could take for granted a conciliatory attitude on the part of the Jews of Berlin, despite *Judaism in Music*. One could pardon the great artist for literary skirmishes. But the anti-Semites, as their petition showed, sought the direct curtailment of Jewish rights. Wagner's participation in their efforts would cost him the support of his Jewish patrons and the goodwill of the Jewish public. Neumann therefore requested in a letter to Cosima an appropriate clarification from the mouth of the master. Before much time had passed he received one, which read as follows: "I stand completely apart from the current 'anti-Semitic' movement; a forthcoming article by me in the 'Bayreuther Blätter' will demonstrate this in such a way that it will be quite impossible for any *intelligent* man to connect me with that movement." Wagner obviously counted on his confession in "Know Yourself" to demonstrate his distance from the movement. Cosima added that she and her husband wished to attempt "to drop the hint you wish for." That is, to indicate to the anti-Semites that they should avoid invoking Wagner's name. Wagner's anti-Semitism was therefore restricted to household use and ideological pronouncements.[48]

In the Wagner literature, Wagner's negative reply to the anti-Semites is often interpreted in his favor and in any case is attributed to a respectable motive, for example, his antipathy to the party apparatus of the movement.[49] One could perhaps hold this view as long as one was not familiar with Wagner's thoughts accompanying the rise of the movement. Since we know, thanks to the diaries, of his joy over the impact of the movement and even his pride concerning his own contribution to its formation, our judgment can be no different from that of Hans von Bülow. The master did indeed poke the fire, but he let others burn their fingers in it.

Wagner's conduct was determined by the fact that he did not want to do without the assistance of his Jewish adherents and admirers. This caution contradicted not only what Wagner held to be in the public interest, but also the feelings he had for his loyal assistants. How conscious he was of this contradiction precisely at this time of heightened antagonism can be seen from his confession in a letter to King Ludwig II, who was far from sharing Wagner's views on the Jews and whom Wagner sought to make understand his own attitude. According to Wagner, the king's benevolence toward the Jews was based on the fact that "these people never touch his royal sphere." They were for the king merely a concept. But for Wagner the Jews were "an experience" imposed on him by fate: "The director Angelo Neumann regards it as his calling to make the whole world appreciate me. I have no say concerning it and must put up with the energy of Jewish protection, as awkward as I may feel about it." It seemed awkward because he had to confess at the same time "that I hold the Jewish race to be the born enemy of pure humanity and everything noble in it. It is certain that it is running us Germans to the ground, and I am perhaps the last German who knows how to hold himself upright as an artist in the face of Judaism, which already rules everything."[50] Here the capacity to disguise existential tensions and cleavages with an ideological cloak has reached the level of intellectual perversity.

Throughout his life Wagner was unconcerned about the logical consistency of the arguments with which he expounded his worldview. This unconcern was particularly clear during the last phase of his development, when he adopted two disparate motifs in his opposition to the Jews: the unbridgeable gulf because of the fundamental, essential difference between Judaism and Christianity, and the connection of the collective characteristics of the Jews with the concept of race.

To be sure, Wagner had already asserted in *Judaism in Music* that the Jew, as everybody knew, had "a God all to himself." There, however, he drew no consequences from that religious peculiarity. On the contrary, he made light of the religious opposition between Judaism and Christianity ("in religion the Jews have long ceased to be our hated foes"), since in that phase he had been under the influence of Feuerbach and had ascribed no formative power to religion.[51] That position changed in the 1870s, when he glorified the nonecclesiastical Christianity but lamented that it was "grafted upon Judaism." "Christian doctrine rests on the Jewish religion and that is what ruins it." The task was "to purify the revelation from the Old Testament," which never should have been accepted. The historical connection of the two religions was of a purely external nature. Jesus' membership in the Jewish tribe was not proved, and to designate Jesus as a Jew was "roughly as if one were to say that Mozart stood the Salzburgers in good stead." The Jews' doctrine of sin was pitiful and barred their way "to mystical things"; whether they could be saved at all was questionable, since "their nature condemns them to the reality of the world."[52]

These words, spoken in the privacy of Wagner's household, are also reflected in his publications. In the essay "Public and Popularity," published in 1878, he said: "Explaining the God of our Savior to us through the tribal God of Israel is one of the most frightful aberrations of world history." In "Know Yourself," which was supposed to demonstrate that Wagner had distanced himself from the anti-Semites, he wrote: "In truth, he [the Jew] has no religion, but only the belief in certain promises of God, which by no means extend, as in every true religion, to an otherworldly life beyond this, his real life, but refer solely to his present life on the earth, on which his tribe remains in any case assured of rule over all animate and inanimate beings."[53] While in Wagner's first anti-Jewish phase the traditional critique of Judaism hid behind a quasi-secular worldview, after his admittedly nonecclesiastical yet Christian transformation it appeared in its original context, as the expression of the traditional antagonism between Judaism and Christianity.

Paradoxically, it was at this moment that the concept of race entered into Wagner's world of ideas. He thus had at his disposal a purely secular means of rendering the religious justification for his anti-Judaism superfluous. The term *race* was, of course, not foreign to Wagner even earlier. He, like all his contemporaries, had used it as a synonym for tribe, people, humanity, and so forth, and by no means in reference to the Jews in particular. Wagner encountered it as a concept consciously employed for the interpretation of historical events only after making the acquaintance of Count Gobineau in December 1876 in Italy. A real association between the two men and Wagner's intensive occupation with Gobineau's writings began only toward the end of 1880. From then on, there were frequent discussions of the "theory of the races" in Wagner's house, but the idea was by no means uncritically absorbed.[54] Cosima wrote: "At dinner he regularly exploded in favor of the Christian as opposed to the racial view."[55] In the essay "Heroism and Christianity," devoted to Gobineau's theory, he wrote: "The blood of the Savior flowing from his head, from his wounds on the cross—who wishes to commit the outrage of asking whether it belonged to the white, or whichever other race?"[56]

Wagner accepted Gobineau's theory of the decline of the human race through the mixing of the races—the corruption of mankind was in any case one of his favorite ideas—but corrected it, so to speak, through the doctrine of Christian salvation, to which he had adhered for a long time. Parallel to that belief, which referred to the entire history of mankind, he denied in the essay "Know Yourself" the racial purity of the German people. The rape of German women by the foreign hordes of the Thirty Years' War alone would have damaged the purity of the race. What remained was the "spirit of its humanity," which, borne by the unimpaired "language of its forefathers," left open the possibility of "drawing from the wells of our own nature." If this possibility were noticed, Germans might perceive themselves "no longer as a race, as a variety of mankind, but as a primordial tribe of mankind." [57] This work was imposed on the "great men and spiritual heroes," among whom, it was understood, Richard Wagner occupied the foremost position. Parallel to the Christian Savior of antiquity, the renewer of the present now appeared, and his work too transcended the race and embraced all of mankind.

Only one branch of mankind, that of the Jews, remained unaffected by this regeneration, just as it had been left untouched by the redemption in ancient times. This "astonishing example of race-consistency" showed "the sure instinct of an absolute and inextinguishable peculiarity." Unredeemed and unregenerated, the Jews represented the "plastic demon of the decline of mankind in triumphant certainty." [58] Only in reference to the Jews did Wagner employ the newly acquired concept of race, in order to explain the persistency of their depravity. It was the belief in the corruptness of the Jews that led to the concept of race, and not the concept of race that led to that of their depravity—as the widespread view concerning racial anti-Semitism in general and Wagner's Jew-hatred in particular would have it. [59] It is precisely the case of Wagner that proves that anti-Semitism must have its historical causes and its psychological and sociological preconditions in order to summon the conceptual means for its justification. The link between the concept of race and anti-Semitism may harden and, in extreme cases, lend moral support to the annihilation of the incorrigible tribe of the Jews. That extreme is what happened at the end of the process that began when the idea of race was connected with anti-Semitism in the nineteenth century. This outcome was not inevitable. There are many intermediate stages that do not call into question the Jews' right to exist, despite the use of the concept of race for the justification of anti-Semitism.[60]

There is no sign that the adoption of the concept of race had any influence on Richard Wagner's constantly fluctuating idea of what should be done with the Jews. If he spoke in "Know Yourself" of "blood-mixing" ("if male or female blood is mixed with the foreign races, a Jew always emerges"),[61] there is evidence of his rejection of mixed marriage as early as 1873. He had had a dispute on that subject with a visitor, the deacon of the Bayreuth church, "who thought that mixed marriages are the solution to the problem. R[ichard] asserted: then there will be no more Germans. German blood is not strong enough to resist this 'lye.' We see how the Normans and the Franks became Frenchmen, and Jewish blood is much more corrosive than the Romance."[62] This rejection of biological interbreeding contradicts the concession made on the ideological plane, that is, that Jews who have completely given up the Jewish mentality can enter into the non-Jewish community.

Wagner did not retract this concession even in the final phase of his development. In January 1879, at a time when the public denunciation of the Jews was increasing, he developed in a conversation with Hermann Levi his thesis concerning the obstacles on the path to the general absorption of the Jews. These obstacles resulted from the fact "that they [the Jews] interfered too early in our cultural concerns; that the universally human, which should have developed out of the German, in order then to benefit the Jewish as well, was arrested in its development by their premature meddling in our affairs, before we knew who we were." This was no chance remark, for Wagner had said a few weeks earlier that personally he had had "his best friends among the Jews, but their emancipation and attainment of equality, before something had come of us Germans, was destructive."[63] However, this at least theoretical readiness to accept the Jews was opposed to his strong sense of distance from them. His relations with his friend Levi provide a truly grotesque example of that.

After the failed attempt to induce Levi to undergo baptism, the Wagners discussed what had happened and, Cosima wrote, "agreed that this foreign race can never be completely merged with us. R[ichard] told me (and I write it down here, since he said it to me without any scorn and with the utmost seriousness on repeated occasions) how, when our friend modestly approached him and kissed his hand, he, R[ichard], very intimately and warmly embraced him, and the emanation made him aware, with the most monstrous preciseness, of the nature of racial difference and division." Cosima concluded: "And thus the good Jew among us is always allotted a melancholy fate."[64] And this especially after the unsuccessful attempt to tie Levi, through the sacrament of baptism, to the Wagner community even more strongly.

The concept of race put an intellectual edge to Wagner's sense of foreignness vis-à-vis Jews, a feeling to which he had always referred. It did not, however, induce him to act in either the public or the private sphere in a manner free of contradictions. When it was a question of what was to be done with the Jews, he never, as we have already seen, went beyond occasional notions like burning, expulsion, or the prohibition of public manifestations of the Jewish religion.[65] Sometimes, too, he resignedly acknowledged that there was nothing more to do with regard to the Jews and that the Germans would go to ruin on account of them and perhaps would also deserve to do so.[66] Still, fleeting notions concerning possible action against the Jews are indication enough of the consequences that can follow from the passionate negation of Jewish existence. In this sense Wagner's mentality and way of thinking are indeed an anticipation of future horrors.

# 10    Retrospect

By using a developmental methodology, we have reached the conclusion that Wagner's attitude to Jews and Judaism was not a uniform phenomenon, but went through various phases in the course of time. These alterations were then connected, on the one hand, with other biographical data and, on the other hand, with the shifts in the Jews' position in public life, especially in the wake of the anti-Semitic movement that began in the 1870s. In this way we have avoided the tendency prevalent in the Wagner literature to proceed from a fixed conception of anti-Semitism and to presuppose or to discover traces of this undifferentiated hatred of Jews throughout his life.

If one does not follow the biographical and historical course of events as completely and consistently as possible, one can easily make the mistake of deriving Wagner's anti-Semitism from episodes of his life or from arbitrarily assumed, psychologically conditioned complexes. We have already encountered explanations that seek to attribute Wagner's resentment to the supposed destruction of his first works by Mendelssohn or his exploitation by his Jewish benefactor in Paris.[1] Worse is the apparently ineradicable supposition that Wagner was of Jewish extraction and that Jewish self-hatred makes his irrational reaction to everything Jewish understandable. It is worthwhile to pursue the history of the formation of this hypothesis, in order to do away with it once and for all.

As the American musicologist O. G. T. Sonneck showed many years ago, the legend of Wagner's Jewish origin goes back to the alleged paternity of his stepfather Ludwig Geyer.[2] This connection was also established by Friedrich Nietzsche. In a marginal note to *The Case of Wagner*, his final reckoning with his formerly revered master, Nietzsche asked: "Was Wagner a German at all? His father was an actor named Geyer. A *Geyer* [vulture] is almost an *Adler* [eagle]."[3] Geyer was a friend of the Wagner family and married

Wagner's mother barely a year after the death of her husband and fifteen months after the birth of her seventh child, Richard. Geyer's readiness to marry the widow of his deceased friend, the mother of many children, could easily lead people to conclude that intimate relations existed between the two at an early date.[4] Wagner himself, as we will soon see, considered this possibility. Nietzsche assumed Geyer's paternity to be a fact and his thoughts immediately leapt from the name of Geyer to Adler, a familiar Jewish surname. This leap was completely arbitrary, since the name Geyer, unlike Adler, scarcely ever appears among Jews.[5]

Nietzsche's assumption of Wagner's Jewish self-hatred and the theory connected with it never had any foundation. With the publication of Cosima's diaries all doubts are removed. Cosima made note of a conversation with Wagner concerning his alleged descent from Geyer. She observed the resemblance of her son Fidi to Wagner's stepfather and said, "Father Geyer was certainly your father." Wagner replied, "I don't believe so." "Then where does the resemblance come from?" asked Cosima. Wagner answered, "My mother loved him then, elective affinities."[6] They could therefore consider quite calmly the possibility of Wagner's descent from Geyer. There is no trace of any emotional reaction on the part of Wagner to the possibility of a Jewish origin.

The legend must therefore have arisen from the association of ideas attested in Nietzsche's words or simply as a defense against Wagner's anti-Semitism. The philosopher did not invent it, for as Ernest Newman shows in the classic biography of Wagner, it was already common ten years earlier for Wagner to be branded as a Jew in writings and in caricatures.[7] The legend, like many anecdotes about Wagner, spread. It was especially piquant, in view of his notorious ambivalence toward Jews, and it was at the same time well suited to make his anti-Semitism look ridiculous. Indeed, ridicule seemed for a long time the best means to neutralize the anti-Jewish current, which was believed to be relatively harmless. It is, however, more than curious that scholars of our own day, like Peter Burbidge and Hartmut Zelinsky, are unable to free themselves from this legend.

Burbidge does not appear to have any doubts at all concerning the Jewishness of Wagner's stepfather.[8] Zelinsky, however, is aware of the doubtful background of the legend; it is all the more astonishing that he is nonetheless inclined to derive Wagner's anti-Jewish complex from it. It was "the painful consciousness . . . of being a Jew or like a Jew" that nurtured Wagner's anti-Jewish passion, he argued. But since this explanation presupposes the Jewish origin of Wagner's stepfather and Zelinsky is aware of the uncertainty of that conjecture, he simultaneously offers a weaker alternative. Even if Wagner was not afraid of being a Jew, he may have felt "like a Jew." These two variants are, however, completely different. If Wagner's anxiety about his Jewish descent could be proven, one would have a tangible psychological basis for the theory of his self-hatred. The substitute suggestion—that Wagner had a sense of being like a Jew—is purely speculative. To substantiate it Zelinsky can in fact observe only that in his description of his spiritual make-up as an artist suffering in isolation Wagner employs expressions similar to those he used in the characterization of the Jewish artist as a culturally alien intruder who remained isolated from German society. This similarity sufficed for him to interpret *Judaism in Music* as Wagner's central autobiographical, self-revealing work and to divest it of its polemical character.[9] Here, it is obvious, a self-assured reliance on one's own associations, unconcerned with textual evidence, takes the place of critical biographical research, rooted in the sources.

Where this method can lead becomes clear when Zelinsky claims to have found the reason for Wagner's astonishing decision in 1869 to republish the brochure on the Jews under his own name. The hidden meaning of the brochure, he maintains, corresponded to Wagner's state of mind at that time as it was disclosed in his plans and in his artistic creation of *Siegfried*.[10] Zelinsky ignores the statements Wagner made in his letters and the entries in Cosima's diaries, which we quoted in chapter 6, that unequivocally characterized the brochure, precisely at the time of its republication, as a polemic and by no means as a veiled confession.

Insofar as Wagner's writings are concerned, our methodology enables us to rule out subjective, imaginative interpretations. Other interpretations see his artworks as reflecting aspects of his biographical development and themes of his social and political thought—including, therefore, his hostility toward the Jews. Zelinsky is not the only one who has attempted such an explanation,[11] although he has carried it to extremes, particularly with his central conception of the finale of *Parsifal*, "The Salvation of the Savior," which is supposed to signify the purification of the Jesus-figure of any Jewish reference. The question of whether such interpretations deepen our understanding of the artworks may be left to the historians of literature and music.[12] From the point of view of biographical research, such interpretations offer no rewards. They either repeat what is known from other sources or offer unprovable suppositions. On the basis of his consideration, I have in my work avoided relying upon evidence from Wagner's artworks and have restricted myself to the artist's direct statements along with other testimony. This restriction was, beside the developmental principle mentioned earlier, my second methodological guideline.

A third guideline follows from the observation that very many of the interpretations alluded to here were formulated under the impact of the later reception of Wagner's works, especially by Hitler and the national socialists. The adoption of Wagner as a kind of tutelary genius and herald of the national socialist worldview is certainly not incidental.[13] In their efforts to find a historically legitimizing forerunner in the German past, the national socialists could not pass by the phenomenon of Wagner. Wagner's themes, stemming from the world of German mythology, must have enticed the Nazis, who conjured up pre-Christian Teutonic sources of the nation's power, to identify with them. In his attitude toward the Jews, Wagner was especially well suited to serve as a model. Here the national socialists saw themselves as the heirs of the anti-Semitic movement of the imperial period. Even if Wagner, as we have seen, kept his distance from the movement, it was obvious that his sentiments were in accord with it.

Two paths of development appear then to be continuations of the road marked out by Wagner. The resumption of the Bayreuth festival under Cosima's leadership and with the help of the "Bayreuth circle" stood under the banner of a strongly German-national tendency, which excluded Jews. It is true, as the historian of the Bayreuth circle, Winfried Schüler, has shown, that the anti-Semitism of the Wagner epigones remained under the sway of the nebulous idea that the injurious Jewish element in German culture could be removed without direct action through the regeneration of the German spirit.[14] Nevertheless, this theory signified the fundamental rejection of Jewish participation in the hoped-for German renewal, a postulate to which the national socialists could append their numerous concrete anti-Jewish programs.

A second line of filiation that connected Wagner and the Nazis led through his son-in-law, Houston Stewart Chamberlain, and his doctrine. To be sure, Chamberlain deviated in many elements of his doctrine from the Wagnerian inheritance, especially in the importance that he assigned to racial theory. Nevertheless, these differences were concealed by the admiration and glorification he showered on the master as the highest development of German creative power. His uncommonly influential treatise, *Foundations of the Nineteenth Century*, could be read entirely as a continuation of the German efforts at regeneration and thus incorporated into the radical ideology of the national socialists.[15]

The course of history therefore offered the Nazis a convenient handle for presenting themselves as the heirs and executors of Wagner's ideas. Once this identification was achieved, Wagner's position on the Jews and Judaism appeared in sharper relief. What this connection meant for the future reception of Wagner we shall soon see. But first we must consider the possible sources of error even for interpreters of his works who seek to restrict themselves to the facts. Is it an accident that the location of anti-Jewish symbolism in Wagner's works took place only after Wagner himself was appropriated by the Nazis? Such belated illuminations are to be found even in relation to Wagner's ideological conceptions, which easily lend themselves to control. We have already noted the supposition that Wagner's anti-Jewish attitude had a racial basis. Just how incorrect that supposition is was demonstrated in chapter 4 by our chronological observation of his intellectual development. This supposition is undoubtedly an attempt at backdating—a reading of the continuation and modification of Wagner's ideas by Chamberlain and Hitler into the statements made by Wagner himself.

Other mistaken interpretations are easy to demonstrate. One striking example is found in the reading of the final passage of *Judaism in Music*. Wagner there calls upon the Jews to choose the path of "redemption as genuine human beings" through "self-annihilation" and concludes with a sentence laden with pathos: "But remember that only one thing can redeem you from the burden of your curse: the redemption of Ahasuerus—going under."[16]

The use of notions like "self-annihilation" and "going under" in reference to the Jews compels the post-national-socialist reader to think of the Holocaust,[17] unless, as a critically trained historian, he frees himself of such associations and considers the text in its original context and endeavors to understand it in the light of contemporary ideas.

What Wagner meant by the Jews "going under" in this passage is explicitly stated there: "To become a human being together with us means for the Jew first of all as much as ceasing to be a Jew." What is therefore desired of the Jews is their de-Judaization—a process of radical assimilation, not indeed to the existing bourgeois world but to the new social and political creation that Wagner anticipated and imagined as a revolutionary utopia. That he by no means intended physical "going under" here is made unmistakably clear by the example of Ludwig Börne, who had already succeeded in becoming "a human being together with us." Börne had achieved his redemption "not in ease and cold, indifferent complacency"; it had cost him, "as cost it must for us, sweat, anguish, want and all the other dregs of suffering and sorrow."[18]

As we have already noted, Wagner's line of thought ran parallel to those of two of his contemporaries, Bruno Bauer and Karl Marx. They too were prepared to assure the Jews of an honorable place in the world, provided that the Jews were ready to collaborate in the formation of the utopia that both thinkers had in mind. Bauer's utopia was that of the democratic state free of all religion, Marx's that of a self-reliant human society, freed of the capitalistic state.[19] Wagner's utopia is much less sharply definable, and ultimately amounts to a society where all social and political obstacles to the free development of redemptive (Wagnerian) art have been abolished. In this imaginary world the Jews too could participate, insofar as they wished to collaborate in its preparation.

Almost all the contemporary critics of the Jews, and even those who did not regard themselves as opponents of Jews, held a negative image of Judaism and placed it in the service of the hoped-for process of de-Judaization. Among the liberals, the pillars of the growing bourgeois society, the negative image served as a spur to the hoped-for adoption by the Jew of the model of the respectable citizen.[20] The utopians used it as a call to join the battle for the society of the future.

In fact other consequences could be drawn and later were drawn from this rejection of Judaism. In the empire these consequences included the political-economic repression and social ostracism of the Jews; in the Weimar period they included complete exclusion of the Jews from state and society and even their physical annihilation. The possibility of such a conclusion was considered even in the first phase. We remember the alternative set up by Heinrich Laube: "We must either be barbarians and expel the Jews to the last man or we have to incorporate them." [21] Wagner followed Laube when he too raised the possibility of a "forcible ejection of the destructive, foreign element." [22] Wagner, however, was discussing theoretical considerations, while he as well as Laube saw the alternative of complete incorporation as being in tune with the times. It is true that Wagner later called for radical measures such as limitations on freedom, expulsion, and burning to be taken against the Jews. But apart from the fact that he made these statements casually in private conversation, one should remember that he uttered them during the second phase of the rejection of the Jews, which was a result of the historical change in the relations between German society and the Jews in the 1870s. It would be an inadmissable procedure to interpret remarks about the downfall of the Jews in a work written a quarter of a century earlier in the light of these later statements or on the basis of the convictions and deeds of later figures who identified with Wagner.

Even more dubious is the attempt to derive Wagner's views from the language he had in common with Hitler, namely, the statements about annihilation. We can in fact find Wagner employing such turns of phrase. What they mean can be determined, paradoxically enough, precisely from the final passage of the brochure on the Jews, where self-annihilation is recommended to the Jews, so that they can take part in the "renascent work of redemption." [23] Wagner may have seen the downfall of the bourgeois world as the precondition (as Thomas Mann put it) for the formation of "a classless society, free of luxury and the curse of money and based on love, as he had imagined it as the ideal public for his art." [24] That Wagner occasionally called himself the "plenipotentiary of downfall" is entirely consistent with this view. [25] Cosima added in parenthesis: "he sees this as irresistible." That is to say, the decline in the world was preordained; Wagner was simply the herald of the inescapable. In any case, this foreboding of ruin referred to all of mankind. To refer it specifically to the Jews, and thereby to connect it with Hitler's program of annihilation, is arbitrary and anachronistic.

It should be borne in mind that Thomas Mann's statement comes from his famous appreciation of Wagner delivered in February 1933, at the beginning of the political rape of Germany by the Nazis. Already, on the fiftieth anniversary of Wagner's death, it seemed to Mann that an unbridgeable gulf lay between Wagner's time and his own, and Mann felt bound to warn against ignoring that gulf: "It is absolutely impermissible to give to Wagner's nationalistic gestures and addresses a contemporary meaning—the one which they would have today. That would be to falsify and misuse them, to sully their romantic purity."[26] As we know, this warning accomplished nothing. The Nazi adoption of Wagner was already in full swing. It began with Hitler's ostentatious visits to the Bayreuth festival in his years of struggle and was crowned, after his assumption of power, by the state support granted to Bayreuth. Thomas Mann's untimely warning unleashed the protest of the Nazi cultural spokesmen and their hangers-on and marked the beginning of his exclusion from the German cultural sphere.[27]

Wagner did not fall by chance into the conflict of opinions generated by the different currents of the day. Thomas Mann's attempt to salvage Wagner—it was not the only such attempt[28]—if not for a liberal then at least for a romantic-humanistic worldview, bears traces of its dependence on the time when it was voiced. The contemporary reader must be astonished to learn that Mann's long essay, which is not restricted to an interpretation of Wagner's art but also enters into the attitude of the artist to the social and political principles of his time, does not mention Wagner's anti-Semitism at all. Did this dark side of the man he was celebrating seem inessential to the liberal orator or did Mann consciously avoid the painful subject because of the public Jew-baiting that had already grown fierce at that time? It required the experience of Nazi rule and the war years for Mann to accuse another of Wagner's eulogists, Emil Pretorius, of leaving unmentioned such characteristics of Wagner's as his "wish to be the sole speaker, to have a say on any and everything, an unspeakable immodesty, which prefigured Hitler." On another occasion he wrote: "We have this Wagner before our eyes again, and we see too much that is repulsive, too much actual 'Hitler,' too much latent and forthwith also manifest Nazism, for it to appear possible to proper confidence, admiration, good conscience and a love for which one would not need to be ashamed." [29]

The alteration of Mann's judgment clearly brings the highly complicated problem of historical attribution and moral responsibility before our eyes. In 1933 one could still, in obedience to the historical-critical imperative, evaluate Wagner's views in their temporal context. With the flowing of the Wagnerian inheritance into the stream of national socialism, if only as one of the sources by which that stream was nourished, its latent potential as an ideology ostracizing the Jews was realized, an occurence that forced contemporaries to revise their opinion of Wagner's nature and character. The rational argument that people acting in the historical present cannot be held responsible for the unforeseeable future, that a suprapersonal destiny can weave their actions into the fabric of historical development, breaks down in the face of this fact. At the very least, it was Wagner's misfortune that tendencies potentially present in his way of thinking—and, in the opinion of others, also in his work—became reality under later historical conditions and thus became connected with his name.

Up to this point we have been concerned with historical attribution. In order to clarify the question of moral responsibility we must give consideration to another matter. If Wagner's contribution to further developments had been at its inception morally neutral, if it were possible to compare him, say, to an inventor whose scientific or technical innovation was employed for warlike ends, it would be possible to exonerate him on the grounds that the unforeseen development amounted to a misfortune. However, that was by no means the case with Wagner's world of ideas. It was morally dubious even in its own time. It signified the condemnation of individuals on the basis of their collective affiliation and led to insoluble conflicts in his relations with people around him. Since Wagner's anti-Semitism was morally questionable even in his own lifetime, it is difficult to acquit him of responsibility for subsequent objectively unforeseeable consequences.

Signs of the moral condemnation that Wagner suffered at the

hands of posterity can be seen in two countries, the Federal Republic of Germany and Israel. In order to enable people to enjoy Wagner's art again without inhibitions or pangs of conscience, many attempts have been made in Germany to draw a line of demarcation between Wagner and the Nazis or between Wagner's artistic inheritance and his worldview.[30] Since some of these attempts looked like cover-ups, there was a reaction against them that led to the equation of Wagnerian and Nazi tendencies. It is true that people appear to have calmed down recently, but this heated dispute has certainly not been settled for good.

In Israel the identification of Wagner with national socialism is clearly demonstrated by the public resistance to the performance of his music. It is interesting to note how and when this boycott came into being—the process is not without historical irony.[31] In pre-state Palestine Wagner's music was constantly on the program of the Palestine (now Israeli) Philharmonic Orchestra founded by Bronislaw Hubermann. As late as the fall of 1938 Arturo Toscanini, who in protest against the mistreatment of Jewish musicians by the Nazis had long since turned his back on Bayreuth, planned the performance of a piece from the *Meistersinger*, with the intention of demonstrating the separation between politics and art. Then came the reports of the pogroms on *Kristallnacht* and the complete appropriation of Bayreuth by the Nazis, which left the Jewish population with a distaste for the Wagnerian compositions. As the reports of the horrors taking place in Europe increased and worsened, knowledge of the special role that Wagner's music played in Hitler's life and in the party ceremonies strengthened the negative associations, and the ban on public performances became a matter of course.

In the first years after the war Israeli society, which included hundreds of thousands of survivors of concentration and death camps, and still more relatives of those who had never returned from them, showed an unwillingness to have anything to do with products of German origin, whether they were of an industrial or a cultural nature. This reluctance has diminished in the course of time—political and economic necessity, the example of leading personalities like David Ben Gurion and Martin Buber, who strove for a reconciliation, and not least the slow passing of the older generation, have done their part. In Israel today there are hardly any traces left of the former avoidance of the products of German industry or artistic endeavor. The public performance of Wagner's music remains an exception. At the request of music lovers and specialists, the Philharmonic Orchestra has often sought to break the ban against Wagner, but these attempts have always met with successful protests. Apparently, a sector of the Israeli public has come to see his music, indeed even his name, as a symbol of the Hitler regime. Against this fixed idea, rational arguments are for the time being as ineffectual as complaints about the loss of artistic enjoyment and the damage to the musical education of the younger generation.[32]

The time will no doubt come when the historical background of Wagner's art will have faded to such an extent that it will be possible to present his works detached from their moorings and solely on the basis of their innate aesthetic value. For the time being this development is not in sight, at least in Germany and Israel, which feel themselves to be historically and existentially connected with Wagner, although in different ways.

From time to time debates about Wagner flare up in Germany too, proving that the dubious traits of his personality and worldview, and still more the burden of his historical impact, continue to cling to his art. Any conscious acceleration of the process of disentangling the man from his artistic creation and thereby rendering the subject innocuous is bound to have the opposite effect. If historians can assist this process at all, it is only by striving, in obedience to their professional ethic, to research matters accurately and to describe them in accordance with the facts. In doing so they must above all pay attention to the factor of time. They must not assume Wagner's attitude to be fixed once and for all, nor can they understand his effect without considering the changing historical circumstances. An investigation of the impact of the times on the formulation of ideas is called for even in the analysis of systematic structures of thought. Wagner was far from being bound to a system of thought or from aiming at one. His creative power was devoted to the realization of artistic plans, while his ideas were exhausted in occasional flights of thought which, as original as they might seem, lack disciplined composure and consistency. They were scarcely more than inspirations of the moment, often expressions of the transient

phases of his intellectual development, and sometimes emotional reactions to events and experiences.

These peculiarities also pertain to Wagner's hostility to the Jews.
It was by no means an inborn or psychoanalytically explicable characteristic, but rather the result of a personal experience at a biographical turning point that can be precisely fixed. Once adopted, it
indeed fulfilled certain functions in his mental economy. It facilitated the projection of his own feelings into the consciousness of
others and explained the otherwise incomprehensible absence of
recognition for his artistic achievement, particularly among the experts. It is also true that Wagner's hostility toward Jews was nourished by previous anti-Semitic theories and was thus the continuation of an unbroken anti-Jewish tradition. Yet in the context of the
increasingly liberal 1850s and 1860s, it appears bizarre, capricious,
and untimely. And so it would have remained, had not a new anti-
Jewish movement—soon to be known as anti-Semitism—arisen in
the mid 1870s.

Thus a certain interaction between public events and Wagner's
way of thinking came into being. Wagner felt strengthened by the
opinions and stimulated to develop ever-sharper formulations by
the assent of an ever-broader public. The representatives of the new
movement came to hope that they could claim the artist, at that
time already world-famous, as a herald of their doctrine. The fact
that Wagner shrank from the practical consequences of his way of
thinking is an indication of the morally dubious position in which
his rhetorical radicalism had placed him. It should hardly have surprised him when the very people who shared his views accused him
of acting in a way that contradicted his beliefs. These objections he
sought to meet with threadbare ideologies, and he may thus have
succeeded in calming his conscience. But he did not thereby elimi-
nate the potential for disaster embedded in his life-work. Even if
during his lifetime he was still able to prevent his name from being
employed for anti-Semitic actions, developments took their own
course after his death. The name Wagner became a central symbol
of the anti-Jewish movement and later the banner of the campaign
for annihilation of the Jews.

Even if Wagner had no such intention, he bears a share of the historical responsibility. If he had naively and consistently taken part in

the Jew-baiting of his time, one would have to allow him an exoneration, at least before his own conscience. Yet it is precisely his restraint, his shrinking from the practical consequences of his way of thinking, that shows that he was aware of the problematic aspect of the situation. Therefore, the historical condemnation of Wagner by no means rests on the belated insight of the historian, but results from the correct understanding of his own statements and actions. Wagner himself sits in judgment on Wagner and is unable to grant himself a historical acquittal.

# NOTES, ADDITIONAL READINGS, AND INDEX

# Notes

## Chapter 1. The Problem

1. The term *anti-Semitism* first surfaced during the autumn of 1879. It was apparently first employed by Wilhelm Marr. See Jacob Katz, *From Prejudice to Destruction: Anti-Semitism, 1700–1933* (Cambridge, Mass., 1980), 261–63; Reinhard Rürup, *Emanzipation und Antisemitismus* (Göttingen, 1975), 95–103; Alex Bein, *Die Judenfrage: Biographie eines Weltproblems* (Stuttgart, 1980), 2: 163–68.

## Chapter 2. Historical Background

1. See Katz, *Prejudice to Destruction.* For a methodological treatment of the problem see Jacob Katz, "Misreadings of Anti-Semitism," *Commentary* 76 (July 1983): 39–44.

2. Jacob Katz, *Exclusiveness and Tolerance: Studies in Jewish-Gentile Relations in Medieval and Modern Times* (Oxford, 1961; reprint, New York, 1975).

3. Bein, *Judenfrage* 1: 69–122.

4. Jacob Katz, *Out of the Ghetto: The Social Background of Jewish Emancipation 1770–1870* (Cambridge, Mass., 1973; reprint, New York, 1975).

5. See Katz, *Prejudice to Destruction,* chap. 2–6.

6. Ludwig Geiger, ed., *Frau Rath Goethe: Gesammelte Briefe* (Leipzig, n.d.), 534; Volkman Eichstädt, *Bibliographie zur Geschichte der Judenfrage* (Hamburg, 1938), 25, nos. 294, 294a, 294b; Jacob Katz, *Jews and Freemasons in Europe 1723–1939* (Cambridge, Mass., 1970), chap. 2, 4, 5.

7. See Jacob Katz, *Zur Assimilation und Emanzipation der Juden* (Darmstadt, 1982), 185–98.

8. The progress in admission to Freemason lodges is a good example. See Katz, *Jews and Freemasons,* chap. 6–7.

9. Katz, *Zur Assimilation,* 46–71; Katz, *Out of the Ghetto,* chap. 5, 10.

10. Katz, *Prejudice to Destruction,* chap. 4–7.

11. Ibid., chap. 12–13.

12. Ibid., chap. 15.

13. Ibid., 72–73.

14. Ibid., 155–58.

15. Presented in his *Die Judenfrage* (Braunschweig, 1843). For an analysis of this work and the literature on it see Katz, *Prejudice to Destruction*, 166–70.

16. Marx's *On the Jewish Question* (1844) is reprinted in Saul K. Padover, ed., *Karl Marx on Religion* (New York, 1974), 169–92. It is analyzed by Katz, *Prejudice to Destruction*, 170–74.

17. See below, chap. 3.

18. Katz, *Out of the Ghetto*, chap. 7.

19. See Jacob Katz, "German Culture and the Jews," *Commentary* 77 (February 1984): 54–59.

20. Franz Kobler, *Juden und Judentum in deutschen Briefen aus drei Jahrhunderten* (Vienna, 1935), 259.

21. Börne's and Heine's positions as Jews have often been discussed. See Solomon Liptzin, *Germany's Stepchildren* (Cleveland and New York, 1961), 27–44, 67–87.

22. The pamphlet was published in Altona in 1831.

23. Meyer, "Against L. Börne," 9–10. On Saphir see Lothat Kahn, "Moritz Gottlieb Saphir," *Leo Baeck Institute Year Book* 20 (1975): 247–57.

24. Meyer, "Against L. Börne," 13.

25. Ibid.

26. Ibid., 14.

27. On the Young Germans see Helmut Koopmann, *Das junge Deutschland: Analyse seines Selbstverständnisses* (Stuttgart, 1970).

28. Erwin Schuppe, *Der Burschenschaftler Wolfgang Menzel* (Frankfurt a/M, 1952), 108–9.

29. Anonymous, *Votum über das "junge Deutschland"* (Stuttgart, 1836), 30–31.

30. Anonymous, *Die Jeune Allemagne in Deutschland* (Stuttgart, 1836), especially 12–14, 19–21.

31. The Gutzkow scholar Heinrich H. Houben devotes an entire chapter to Gutzkow and Judaism in his book *Gutzkow-Funde* (Berlin, 1901), 144–280.

32. The citation is in Julius Lang, *Die Versöhnung des Judentums mit Richard Wagner* (Berlin, 1864), 13. There it is probably a free rendition of the sentence mentioned below, in the introduction from *Struensee*.

33. Heinrich Laube, *Struensee*, in *Gesammelte Werke* (Leipzig, 1909), 24: 123–226.

34. Ibid., 131.
35. Ibid., 130.

### Chapter 3. Wagner's "Philo-Semitism"

1. A detailed analysis of *Judaism in Music* follows in the next chapter.
2. On these developments see Jacob Toury, *Soziale und Politische Geschichte der Juden in Deutschland 1847–1871* (Düsseldorf, 1977).
3. Richard Wagner, *Das Judentum in der Musik* (Leipzig, 1869), 10.
4. Ibid.
5. See Wagner's letter to Lewald of November 1839 in Richard Wagner, *Sämtliche Briefe* (Leipzig, 1979), 1:334, 346, and later correspondence with him. His relations with Lewald are described in the foreword to the letters by Gertud Strobel and Werner Wolf (ibid., 61, 63, 71, 90).
6. Toury, *Geschichte der Juden*, 192.
7. *Sämtliche Briefe* 1:313.
8. Wagner's relations with Schlesinger are described in the foreword to *Sämtliche Briefe* 1.
9. Ibid. 2:116.
10. Ibid. 1:479.
11. Ibid. 2:230.
12. See, for example, Herman Killer in the introduction to *Judentum in der Musik* (Leipzig, 1934) and Karl Richard Ganger, *Richard Wagner und das Judentum* (Hamburg, 1938), 9–11.
13. Richard Wagner, *Mein Leben* (Munich, 1969), 431.
14. *Sämtliche Briefe* 1:576.
15. Ibid., 107.
16. Ibid. 1:501, 523; 2:75, 89, 101, 151, 211, 224, 227, 231f., 319, 408.
17. Carl Fr. Glasenapp, *Das Leben Richard Wagners in sechs Büchern* (Leipzig, 1905), 1:343f.
18. See *Briefe* 2:24, 327, 424.     19. Ibid., 419f.
20. Ibid., 438, 456–58.     21. Ibid., 524.
22. Hans Knudsen, "Berthold Auerbach in Dresden," *Neues Archiv für Sächsische Geschichte und Altertumskunde* (Dresden, 1919), 374.
23. *Mein Leben*, 383.
24. Introduction to *Briefe* 2:59, 76; *Autobiographische Skizze*, ibid. 1:107.
25. Dresdener *Abend-Zeitung*, 2 and 4 August 1841.
26. *Sämtliche Briefe* 1:226.
27. Ibid., 102.

28. Ibid., 259f.

29. Cosima Wagner, *Die Tagebücher*, ed. Martin Gregor-Dellin and Dietrich Mach (Munich and Zurich, 1976), 1:535, 815.

30. Martin Gregor-Dellin, *Richard Wagner: Sein Werk, sein Jahrhundert* (Munich, 1980), 117.

31. *Sämtliche Briefe* 2:92; see also 76.

32. Ibid., 234.                33. Ibid., 268, 277, 297.

34. Ibid., 354f.               35. Ibid., 425.

36. Ibid., 487.                37. Ibid., 582, 585f.

38. The relations between Wagner and Meyerbeer are described by Heinz Becker in "Giacomo Meyerbeer—On the Centenary of His Death," *Leo Baeck Institute Year Book* 9 (1964): 178–201.

39. *Sämtliche Briefe* 1:384, 388.     40. Becker, "Meyerbeer," 183–94.

41. *Sämtliche Briefe* 1:576.          42. Ibid., 2:222f.

43. Ibid., 566, 569, 573.              44. Ibid. 3:68.

45. Ibid., 73; see also 147, 171, 178, 239.

### Chapter 4. *Judaism in Music*

1. Quotations are from the republished version (Leipzig, 1869).

2. Christoph Cobet, *Der Worthschatz des Antisemitismus der Kaiserzeit* (Munich, 1973), 147. Cobet does not seem to have noticed that the text stems from 1850.

3. *Judentum*, 12.

4. See Bauer, *Judenfrage*, and Marx, *Jewish Question*.

5. *Judentum*, 18.

6. Karl Marx, *On the Jewish Question*, ed. Saul K. Padover (New York, 1974), 189. (cf. above chap. 2, note 16).

7. *Judentum*, 12.

8. "Criticism goes against its very nature if, in attack or defense, it tries for anything else," namely, to "explain . . . the antipathy to the Jewish nature." Ibid., 7.

9. See the introduction to Bauer's *Judenfrage*, 1–3.

10. *Judentum*, 10. The Jews in general and the Rothschilds in particular were called the "*rois de l'époque*" in the French anti-Jewish pamphlets of the 1840s. Wagner was alluding to that. See Katz, *Prejudice to Destruction*, 123–28.

11. *Judentum*, 11.

12. Bauer, *Judenfrage*, 114.

13. Marx, *On the Jewish Question*, 192.

14. *Judentum*, 10.               15. Ibid., 9–11.

16. Ibid., 15, 22.               17. Ibid., 10.

18. Ibid., 14f.

19. Winfried Schüler, *Der Bayreuther Kreis* (Münster, 1971), demonstrated Fichte's influence on the essay "Erkenne dich selbst." The conclusion also holds true for *Judentum in der Musik*.

20. *Judentum*, 20f.  21. Ibid., 18.

22. Ibid., 23.  23. Katz, *Out of the Ghetto*, 86.

24. Wagner's *Autobiographische Skizze* of 1842 appears in *Sämtliche Briefe* 1:101f.

25. *Judentum*, 25–27.  26. Ibid., 25.

27. Ibid., 28.  28. Ibid., 29.

29. Ibid.  30. Ibid., 30.

31. Ibid., 31.  32. Ibid.

33. For proof of this thesis see Katz, *Prejudice to Destruction*.

34. *Judentum*, 20, 15.  35. Ibid., 15.

36. Ibid., 18–22.  37. Ibid., 22.

38. Ibid., 10.  39. Ibid., 19.

40. Ibid., 31.  41. Ibid., 32.

42. See *Sämtliche Briefe* 2:225.  43. *Judentum*, 32.

44. Ibid.  45. Ibid.

## Chapter 5. Consequences of Publication

1. *Judentum*, 9.

2. Cited by Tibor Kneif, *Richard Wagner: Die Kunst und die Revolution, Das Judentum in der Musik, Was ist Deutsch* (Munich, 1975), 115.

3. Uhlig describes "the moral indignation of the anonymous writer, who is probably a coreligionist," in his response in the *Neue Zeitschrift für Musik*, 23 July 1850 (no. 7), 30. Uhlig may have been thinking of Ferdinand Hiller, who was involved in the publication of the Cologne newspaper.

4. See Kneif, *Wagner*, 115.

5. Uhlig, *Neue Zeitschrift*; ibid.

6. *Neue Zeitschrift für Musik*, 18 and 21 June 1850 (nos. 49 and 50), 254–55.

7. Wagner, *Mein Leben*, 479.

8. *Sämtliche Briefe*, 3:544.

9. Ibid., 544f.

10. *Neue Zeitschrift für Musik*, 26 February 1850 (no. 17), 82. The article is signed "vt." Wagner may have known who the author was.

11. Robert W. Gutman, *Richard Wagner: The Man, His Mind and His Music* (New York, 1968), 68f.

12. *Sämtliche Briefe* 3:545.  13. Ibid.

14. *Mein Leben*, 479.  15. *Mein Leben*, 338.

16. On Auerbach see Jacob Katz, "Berthold Auerbach's Anticipation of the German-Jewish Tragedy," *Hebrew Union College Annual* 53 (1982): 215–40.

17. *Judentum*, 10.

18. Richard Wagner, *Briefe, Die Sammlung Burrel*, ed. John N. Burk (Frankfurt, 1953), 391.

19. Gutman, *Wagner*, 130f.

20. *Sämtliche Briefe* 3:383.

21. *Mein Leben*, 219.

22. Cf. *Sämtliche Briefe* 2:223 and 3:544f.

23. Ibid. 3:545.

24. "Introduction," *Sämtliche Briefe* 4:7f.

25. Ibid. 3:545.

26. Ibid.

27. Franz Brendel, "Das Judentum in der Musik," *Neue Zeitschrift für Musik*, 4 July 1851 (no. 1), 4.

28. *Aus Moscheles' Leben, Briefe und Tagebücher*, edited by his wife (Leipzig, 1873), 216–18.

29. Eduard Krüger, "Judentümliches," *Neue Zeitschrift für Musik*, 1 October 1850 (no. 27), 146.

30. *Sämtliche Briefe* 3:462; emphasis in the original.

31. E. Bernsdorf, "K. Freigedank und das Judentum in der Musik," *Neue Zeitschrift für Musik*, 15 October 1850 (no. 31), 166f.

32. *Sämtliche Briefe* 3:463.

33. Brendel, "Judentum," 6.

34. Ibid., 4–6.

35. *Sämtliche Briefe* 4:397; see also 457.

36. Ibid., 468.

37. *Mein Leben*, 480.

38. Ibid., 612, 625, 643, 645. Cf. Becker, "Meyerbeer," 190–92. Becker also considers the reception of this accusation of Meyerbeer in the Wagner literature.

39. *Briefe, Sammlung Burrel*, 471.

40. *Mein Leben*, 535f.

41. Ibid., 755.

42. Cosima noted in 1873: "Today is May 3: nine years ago yesterday Meyerbeer died, nine years ago today Pfistermeister [the representative of the king of Bavaria] came to R[ichard], and the following day, the fourth, he went to the king." Thus the connection of the two dates made a permanent impression.

43. *Sämtliche Briefe* 3:427.

44. *Mein Leben*, 337f.; Katz, "Auerbach."

45. *Mein Leben*, 338. The statements concerning Auerbach transmitted by Wagner are entirely believable. Keller had a very ambivalent attitude toward Auerbach, as his correspondence with Auerbach and his remarks about him prove. See Gottfried Keller, *Gesammelte Briefe* (Bern, 1946–54), vols. 1–4.

46. *Mein Leben*, 338. Auerbach remarried after the death of his first wife, and that unhappy marriage lasted.

47. Ibid. A visit by Auerbach to Wagner in Zurich is mentioned in a letter of 23 August 1852 to Uhlig (*Sämtliche Briefe* 4:448).

48. *Mein Leben*, 307f.

49. *Sämtliche Briefe* 3:375.

50. Ernest Newman, *The Life of Richard Wagner* (Cambridge, 1937), 2:429.

51. *Mein Leben*, 530.

52. Ibid., 728–32, 736, 746. For a detailed description of Porges's activities on Wagner's behalf see Leo Brod, "Richard Wagners jüdische Propagandisten," *Nordbayrischer Kurier, Festspielnachrichten, Parsifal* (1976). In *Mein Leben* Porges's Jewish origin is not mentioned; in Cosima's diaries, however, it is referred to often and not exactly flatteringly (*Tagebücher* 1:203, 206).

53. *Mein Leben*, 738f.

54. Ibid., 621f., and 281 (the editor's note). It is not clear whether Madame Schwabe was Jewish, but Wagner appears to have assumed that she was.

55. Ibid., 637, 647, 655.

56. Erlanger's activity can be followed with the aid of the index to Cosima's diaries. His Judaism was mentioned (*Tagebücher* 1:769).

57. *Mein Leben*, 514.

58. On Joachim see Andreas Moser, *Joseph Joachim*, 2 vols. (Berlin, 1907–10).

59. *Mein Leben*, 514.    60. Gregor-Dellin, *Wagner*, 436.

61. *Briefe, Sammlung Burrel*, 436.    62. *Mein Leben*, 747.

63. Ibid., 529.

64. *Sämtliche Briefe* 2:535–38 (535: editor's note).

65. *König Ludwig II. und Richard Wagner, Briefwechsel*, ed. Otto Strobel (Karlsruhe, 1936–39), 4:28.

66. Ibid., 19f.

## Chapter 6. The Republication

1. Hans von Bülow, *Briefe* (Leipzig, 1936), 3:110f.

2. *Judentum*, 7.

3. Ibid., 42.

4. Ibid., 38.

5. Ibid., 37. Hanslick wrote the book *Vom Musikalisch-Schönen* (Vienna, 1854). In his reply, Hanslick noted that the assertion that he was a Jew was "an untruth" (*Wilhelm Lübke und Eduard Hanslick über Richard Wagner* [Berlin, 1864], 21). Wagner (*Tagebücher* 1:251), however, believed that he knew that Hanslick's mother was a Jewess, and that sufficed. The *Jüdische Lexikon* confirmed Wagner's assertion.

6. *Judentum*, 37. Vischer was the author of *Aesthetik oder Wissenschaft des Schönen* (Reutlingen, 1846–57).

7. *Judentum*, 36. This fact is denied by Gregor-Dellin, 875.

8. *Judentum*, 36.                    9. Ibid., 40.

10. Ibid., 55f.                    11. Ibid., 39.

12. Ibid., 43.

13. Hans von Bulöw, *Briefe und Schriften* (Leipzig, 1' 98), 3:30.

14. Brod, "Wagners jüdische Propagandisten."

15. *Judentum*, 8.

16. Ibid., 57.

17. Wendelin Weissheimer, *Erlebnisse mit Richard Wagner, Franz Liszt und vielen anderen Zeitgenossen* (Stuttgart and Leipzig, 1898), 318.

18. Richard Wagner, *Briefe an Hans von Bülow* (Jena, 1916), 270.

19. Julius Lang, *Zur Versöhnung des Judentums mit Richard Wagner* (Berlin, 1896), 3.

20. Ibid., 9.                    21. *Tagebücher* 1:29.

22. Ibid., 698.                    23. Ibid., 151.

24. Ibid., 394. Rumors that he wished not to publish the brochure reached the ears of Ottoman Beta; cf. Beta's letter to Wagner, *Bayreuther Blätter* (1908), 262. The afterword was published still later; cf. Richard Wagner, *Gesammelte Schriften und Dichtungen* (Leipzig, 1873), 8:299–323.

25. Lang, *Versöhnung*, 9.

26. Bülow, *Briefe und Schriften* 4 (1900): 275.

27. *Tagebücher* 1:64.                    28. Ibid., 86f.

29. Ibid., 75.                    30. Ibid., 81.

31. Ibid., 70, 72, 76f., 80; cf. also 129f.

32. Ibid., 78.

33. *Judentum*, 45.

34. *Tagebücher* 1:80.

35. For the dates of the performances see *Tagebücher* 1 : 1108n.
36. Ibid., 32, 35, 49, 80–83.   37. Ibid., 77.
38. Ibid., 82.   39. Lang, *Versöhnung*, 3.
40. Ibid.   41. *Tagebücher* 1 : 71, 73f., 77.
42. Thus Hanslick (note 5), 17; H. Ehrlich, "Recension," *Neue Berliner Musikzeitung*, 17 March 1869, 85; *Allgemeine Zeitung des Judentums*, 30 March 1869, 245; A. F., "Fanatismus eines Musikers," *Deutsche Blätter, Beilage der Gartenlaube* (1869), no. 11, 43.
43. Cf. the afterword to *Judentum*, 39f., 51f.
44. Hanslick (note 5), 24.
45. *Allgemeine Zeitung des Judentums*, 23 March 1869, 244; A. F., "Fanatismus eines Musikers"; *Richard Wagner und das Judentum . . . von einem Unparteiischen* (Elberfeld, 1869), 4.
46. Julian Schmidt, *Bilder aus dem Geistigen Leben* (Leipzig, 1871), 416. The article published there is from 25 March 1869. Schmidt had expressed himself on *Judentum in der Musik* on its first publication in the *Grenzboten*, vol. 9, part 2, 2 : 106f., which he coedited.
47. Ibid., 416–20.
48. Ibid., 420.

### Chapter 7. The Illusion of Emancipation

1. Ismar Freund, *Die Emanzipation der Juden in Preussen* (Berlin, 1912), 2 : 522.
2. Robert von Mohl, *Staatsrecht, Völkerrecht und Politik* (Tübingen, 1869), 3 : 673–79. The *Allgemeine Zeitung des Judentums* had already discussed Mohl's book, together with Wagner's brochure on the Jews, in March.
3. Katz, *Out of the Ghetto*, 80–103.
4. Isidor Kaim, *Ein Jahrhundert der Judenemancipation und deren christliche Verteidiger* (Leipzig, 1869), 1.
5. Katz, *Prejudice to Destruction*, 245–59.
6. See Katz, "Misreadings of Anti-Semitism," *Commentary* 73 (July 1983): 39–44.
7. See Katz, *Prejudice to Destruction*, chap. 12–17.
8. Ibid., chap. 21.
9. See Katz, *Out of the Ghetto*, chap. 2.
10. Ibid., 105f.
11. Jacob Katz, *Die Entstehung der Judenassimilation und deren Ideologie* (Frankfurt, 1935); reprinted in Katz, *Zur Assimilation und Emanzipation der Juden* (Darmstadt, 1982), 32–46 ("Die neutralisierte Gesellschaftsform"); Katz, *Out of the Ghetto*, chap. 4.

12. Katz, *Out of the Ghetto*, chap. 7.

13. See notes 38–40.

14. *Judentum*, 47.

15. [Emil] B[reslauer], *Herr Richard Wagner und seine neueste Schrift "Das Judentum in der Musik"* (Breslau, 1869), 5. The author is identified in the *Allgemeine Zeitung des Judentums* (1869), 266.

16. E. Liéser, *Die modernen Judenhasser und der Versuch von Julius Lang, Das Judentum mit Richard Wagner zu versöhnen* (Nackel, 1869), 5.

17. Joseph Engel, *Richard Wagners "Das Judentum in der Musik"* (Leipzig, 1869), 8; see also 25.

18. Breslauer, *Wagner*, 6.

19. Liéser, *Judenhasser*, 6f.

20. Anonymous, *Richard Wagner und das Judentum: Ein Beitrag zur Culturgeschichte unserer Zeit von einem Unparteiischen* (Elberfeld, 1869), 3, 4, 6, 11, 14.

21. Julian Schmidt, *Bilder aus dem geistigen Leben unserer Zeit* (Leipzig, 1871), 418–19. The article published there dates from March 1869.

22. Max Fuchs, *Noch ein Wort über Richard Wagners Judentum in der Musik* (Munich, 1869), 10, 12, 14f.

23. Julius Lang, *Zur Versöhnung des Judentums mit Richard Wagner . . . Ein unparteiisches Votum* (Munich, 1869), 6.

24. Ibid., 9.                                25. Ibid., 40, 11, 40.

26. Ibid., 13f.                              27. Ibid., 14–17.

28. Ibid., 22–24, 26.                        29. Ibid., 6.

30. Ibid., 5, 12.

31. See Katz, *Prejudice to Destruction*, 203–5, and the literature mentioned there.

32. Gustav Freytag, *Die Grenzboten* (1869), part 1, 2 : 333–34.

33. M. Gutmann, *Richard Wagner, der Judenfresser* (Dresden, 1869), 6.

34. Ibid., 12f.

35. Edmund Friedmann, *Das Judentum und Richard Wagner* (Berlin, 1869), 4.

36. Breslauer, *Wagner*, 11.

37. Engel, *Wagners "Das Judentum,"* 7.

38. *Der Israelit*, 21 April 1869 (no. 16), 298.

39. *Allgemeine Zeitung des Judentums*, 30 March 1869 (no. 13), 247.

40. Ibid., 6 April 1869 (no. 14), 308.

41. The two were E. M. Oettinger, *Offenes Billet doux an den Berühmten Hepp-Hepp Schreier und Juden-Fresser Herrn Wilhelm Richard Wagner* (Dresden, 1869) and H. Ehrlich, "Recension," 85–87.

42. *Allgemeine Zeitung des Judentums*, 328.

43. Ibid., 346f.
44. *Judentum*, 3.
45. Lang, *Versöhnung* (1869), 10.

### Chapter 8. Private Jewish Phobias

1. On Cosima's Catholic education see Richard Graf Du Moulin Eckart, *Cosima Wagner: Ein Lebens- und Charakterbild* (Munich and Berlin, 1929), 1:40–88. On Hans von Bülow see his *Briefe und Schriften* 4 (1900): 275.

2. In his foreword to part 2 the editor, Martin Gregor-Dellin, rightly emphasized the intimate character of the document (*Tagebücher* 2:9–10). See also Theodor Schieder, "Richard Wagner, das Reich und die Deutschen nach den Tagebüchern Cosima Wagners," *Historische Zeitschrift* 227 (1978): 571f., 585–87.

3. *Tagebücher* 2:852; on Paris, 1:272.

4. Ibid., 1:657, 879.

5. See Katz, *Prejudice to Destruction*, 233.

6. *Tagebücher* 1:404. Rodenberg is referred to earlier by the name of Julius *Cohen* Rodenberg (1:221). Rodenberg's original name was Levi. He was known as a writer and especially as editor of the *Deutsche Rundschau*.

7. Hans J. Bach, *Jacob Bernays: Ein Beitrag zur Emanzipationsgeschichte der Juden und zur Geschichte des deutschen Geistes im 19. Jahrhundert* (Tübingen, 1974).

8. *Tagebücher* 1:980, 984, 1077, 1081; 2:126, 578, 617.

9. Ibid., 1:386, 488f. See also the index to the diaries.

10. Ibid., 769. On other relations with Erlanger see index to diaries.

11. Ibid., 363.

12. *Judentum*, 12.

13. *Tagebücher* 1:786, 593, 856.

14. During the Wagner controversy Lang, *Versöhnung* (1869), had already referred, just as Wagner would have done, to the master's friendly relations with his patrons, in order to defend him against his critics. Paul Lawrence Rose, "The Noble Anti-Semitism of Richard Wagner," *Historical Journal* 25 (3) (1982): 755, has alluded to the modern variations of the argument, especially in the case of Curt von Westernhagen.

15. See Katz, *Prejudice to Destruction*, 270f.

16. Rubinstein's letter is in *Bayreuther Tageblatt*, 12 August 1952, 4.

17. *Tagebücher* 1:513.

18. Ibid. 1:577; 2:885f.; see also 2:891.

19. Ibid. 1:521, 560, 873, 994; 2:344.

20. Ibid. 2:273, 852.

21. Ibid. 1:415–17; 2:1111.

22. Ibid. 1:225 (similarly, 470), 562; 2:152.

23. Ibid. 2:129.

24. See Katz, *Prejudice to Destruction*, chap. 20.

25. *Tagebücher* 2:236, 290 (similarly, 273).

26. My doubts concerning the correctness of Cosima's rendition of the conversation are due to the incomprehensibility of the text as well as to the contradictory attitude on the part of Levi that it seems to reflect. I discussed this passage with Dr. Hartmut Zelinsky in Munich and follow his interpretation, but not without reservations. On Levi's position see below.

27. *Tagebücher* 2:290, 235, 258.

28. Friedrich Naumann was emphatically opposed to this mixing of motifs; see his essay in Hartmut Zelinsky, *Richard Wagner—ein Deutsches Thema* (Frankfurt, 1976), 93–96. See also Dagmar Ingenchag-Goch, *Richard Wagners neu erfundener Mythos* (Bonn, 1982), 110f.

29. It appeared in *Bayreuther Blätter* in 1880 and was reprinted in Wagner, *Gesammelte Schriften und Dichtungen* (Leipzig, 1883), 10:273–324.

30. *Tagebücher* 1:1073; 2:728.

31. Ibid. 2:117. On Wagner's use of Christian symbols see Hans Mayer, *Richard Wagner, Mitwelt und Nachwelt* (Stuttgart and Zurich, 1959), 172.

32. *Tagebücher* 1:762.

33. Ibid. 2:337.

34. Ibid., 526. Who is meant by "both of them" is not clear to me.

35. Ibid., 620, 622, 659.

36. "And he expanded on his ideas concerning faith, love, and hope, as he had set them forth in his most recent essay" (ibid.).

37. Ibid., 669.

38. Ibid., 754–55. Wagner's letter to Levi is in the editor's notes (ibid., 1256). As the editor, Gregor-Dellin, observes, this entire episode is tendentiously exaggerated and distorted in the Wagner literature, as if the anonymous letter alluded to an intimate relationship between Levi and Cosima. Not even the slightest hint of any such relationship is to be found in the diaries. The question is strictly one of the court conductor's Jewishness.

39. Peter Gay, in his essay "Hermann Levi: Study in Service and Self-Hatred," in his *Freud, Jews and Other Germans* (New York, 1978), 189–230, does Levi an injustice when he describes him as a self-hater.

## Chapter 9. Public Anti-Semitism

1. See the instructive article by Henry Wassermann, "The Fliegende Blätter," *Leo Baeck Institute Year Book* 28 (1983): 93–138.

2. See Katz, *Prejudice to Destruction*, chap. 17.

3. On Frantz see Johanna Philippson, "Constantin Frantz," *Leo Baeck Institute Year Book* 13 (1968): 102–19. On Lagarde see Fritz Stern, *The Politics of Cultural Despair* (Berkeley, 1961), 3–36.

4. Philippson, "Frantz," 105.

5. *Tagebücher* 1:668.

6. Ibid., 966.

7. According to Gregor-Dellin, the editor of the diaries (ibid., 1192), the essays appeared in Krämer's *Freie Zeitung*, though not in 1874 but, as the diaries show, in 1873 (ibid., 683, 698). The brochure was O. Beta, *Darwin, Deutschland und die Juden oder der Juden-Jesuitismus* (Berlin, 1876).

8. Osman Bey, *Die Eroberung der Welt durch die Juden* (Basel, 1873); the French original was published in the same place and year.

9. *Tagebücher* 1:683. Cosima called the author of the Eroberung the "Turkish colonel," and Wagner confused him with Osman Pasha (ibid., 710, 1064). The editor of the diaries seems to have been unable to identify the brochure. Beta's brochure finally appeared with a dedication to Prince Bismarck. The Wagners were rightly surprised by Bismarck's acceptance of the dedication (ibid., 739).

10. Ibid., 251.

11. The letter of 29 June 1870 is preserved in the literary bequest. I received a copy from Dr. Moshe Zimmerman, the Marr biographer. No book of Marr's is known to have been published in 1870; it must have been an earlier work, perhaps the *Judenspiegel* (Hamburg, 1862).

12. See Katz, *Prejudice to Destruction*, 207.

13. *Tagebücher* 2:309, 382. The second publication sent to him was probably *Vom Jüdischen Kriegschauplatz* (Bern, 1879).

14. *Tagebücher* 2:155, 376, 674.

15. Ibid., 50. It was *Die Juden im Deutschen Staats- und Volksleben* (Frankfurt); republished from the *Deutsche Reichspost* (Frankfurt, 1878).

16. *Tagebücher* 2:159, 309.

17. See Katz, *Prejudice to Destruction*, 260f.

18. On the *Bayreuther Blätter* see Winfried Schüler, *Der Bayreuther Kreis von seiner Entstehung bis zum Ausgang der Wilhelminischen Ära* (Münster, 1971), 67–70.

19. On Wolzogen, ibid., 86–93.

20. Published in Wagner, *Gesammelte Schriften*, vol. 10.

21. See *König Ludwig II.* 4:192.

22. *Gesammelte Schriften* 10:53.

23. *Tagebücher* 2:43.

24. Schüler, *Bayreuther Kreis*, 18–20, emphasizes Wagner's dependence on Fichte.

25. *Gesammelte Schriften* 10:61f., 69.

26. Ibid., 71–73.

27. See Schüler, *Bayreuther Kreis*, 5–6, n. 24.

28. *Bayreuther Blätter* (March 1878), 157, 161.

29. In "Modern," *Gesammelte Schriften* 10:77–84, he took as his point of departure a quotation from a "pamphlet sent to me not long ago"; he probably meant the anonymous *Die Juden im Deutschen Staats- und Volksleben.*

30. "Publikum und Popularität," *Gesammelte Schriften* 10:118.

31. *Tagebücher* 1:1062.         32. *Gesammelte Schriften* 10:161.

33. *Tagebücher* 2:627.          34. *Gesammelte Schriften* 10:82.

35. There are countless studies of Stöcker; see Katz, *Prejudice to Destruction*, 262–65 and the literature mentioned there. The newest contribution is Günter Brakelmann, Martin Greschat, and Werner Jochmann, *Protestantismus und Politik* (Hamburg, 1982).

36. *Tagebücher* 2:424.

37. Ibid., 461.

38. Ibid., 546.

39. Bülow, *Briefe und Schriften* 3 (1898): 30f.

40. *Tagebücher* 2:461.

41. Ibid., 564.

42. Bülow, *Briefe und Schriften* 3:30.

43. *Tagebücher* 2:643.

44. On 14 March 1881 Cosima reported "pressure from an anti-Jewish newspaper," to which Wagner reacted as he had to Förster's request: "I may have nothing to do with the matter" (ibid., 710).

45. *Gesammelte Schriften* 10:339.

46. Ibid.

47. Ibid., 342f., 350.

48. Angelo Neumann, *Erinnerungen an Richard Wagner* (Leipzig, 1907), 138–41.

49. See Schüler, *Bayreuther Kreis*, 246f., n. 65.

50. *König Ludwig II.* 3:229–30. The letter is from 22 November 1881.

51. *Judentum*, 13, 10.

52. *Tagebücher* 2:147; 1:744; 2:228, 242, 664 (similarly 399), 152, 281, 687.

53. *Gesammelte Schriften* 10:118, 347.

54. *Tagebücher* 2:690, 721, 743, 1024f. among others.

55. Ibid., 744.

56. *Gesammelte Schriften* 10:358.

57. Ibid., 345, 348.

58. Ibid., 346–47.

59. See Leon Stein, *The Racial Thinking of Richard Wagner* (New York,

1950); Otto Dov Kulka, "Richard Wagner und die Anfänge des Modernen Antisemitismus," *Bulletin des Leo Baeck Instituts* 4 (1961): 290–96.

60. See Schüler, *Bayreuther Kreis*, 245–52, on the Bayreuth circle.

61. *Gesammelte Schriften* 10:347.

62. *Tagebücher* 1:667.

63. Ibid. 2:290, 273.

64. Ibid., 669f.

65. See Ibid., 627, 424.

66. See *König Ludwig II.* 3:230. "All speeches and rules are useless, as long as the possession is there" (*Tagebücher* 2:644). "If our culture goes to ruin, it is no loss, but if it goes to ruin on account of the Jews, it is a disgrace" (ibid., 690).

### Chapter 10. Retrospect

1. See chap. 3, n. 12.

2. O. G. T. Sonneck, "Was Richard Wagner a Jew?" *Proceedings of the Music Teachers' National Association* (1911), 21ff.

3. Friedrich Nietzsche, *Der Fall Wagner* (Leipzig, 1888), 42.

4. The question of descent is treated in great detail in Ernest Newman, *The Life of Richard Wagner* (New York, 1933–37), 1:3–18; 2:608–13.

5. Sonneck was right to stress this fact. Newman, who remained unaware of Sonneck's essay, held Adler and Geyer to be typical Jewish names.

6. *Tagebücher* 2:272.

7. Newman, *Wagner* 2:612f. This fact escaped Sonneck, and he therefore believed that Nietzsche gave birth to the legend.

8. Peter Burbidge, "The Man and the Artist," in *The Wagner Companion*, ed. Peter Burbidge and Richard Sutter (New York, 1979), 15.

9. Hartmut Zelinsky, *Richard Wagner—ein Deutsches Thema* (Munich, 1976), 19. Zelinsky repeated his theory in his article "Richard Wagner, wie antisemitisch darf ein Künstler sein?" *Musik-Konzepte* 5 (Munich, 1978): 93.

10. Zelinsky, "Richard Wagner, wie antisemitisch darf ein Künstler sein?" 96.

11. Theodor W. Adorno, *Versuch über Wagner* (Frankfurt, 1974), 19f., writing in 1939, interpreted certain figures in the *Meistersinger* as "caricatures of Jews." Gutman, 423–26, regards *Parsifal* as a comdemnation of the Jews. Rose, "Noble Anti-Semitism," 751–63, likewise sees Wagner's anti-Semitism as the key to an understanding of his artistic work.

12. Zelinsky's conception was rejected from a musicological viewpoint by Carl Dahlhaus in the *Süddeutsche Zeitung*, 8 August 1982. My attention was drawn to this article by Professor Zelinsky.

**150**                                    **Notes**

13. The adoption is documented in detail in Zelinsky, *Wagner*. The process is systematically presented by the Swiss scholar Jean Matter, *Wagner et Hitler* (Lausanne, 1977).

14. Schüler, *Bayreuther Kreis*, 245–48.

15. Ibid., 252–67. Geoffrey G. Field, *Evangelist of Race: The Germanic Vision of Houston Stewart Chamberlain* (New York, 1981).

16. *Judentum*, 32.

17. Thus already in Kulka, "Richard Wagner und die Anfänge des Modernen Antisemitismus," 291. In a later Hebrew essay, Kulka, "Richard Wagner: From Democratic Radicalism to Racial Anti-Semitism," in *Who Is Afraid of Richard Wagner: Aspects of a Controversial Personality*, ed. Riva Litvin (Jerusalem, 1984), 241, qualified his interpretation somewhat, but in any case ruled out the possibility that "going under" could mean assimilation. Similar views are also expressed by Zvi Bacharach, "Richard Wagner: The Anti-Human Humanist" (ibid., 223f.). Adorno, *Versuch*, 22, calls the final passage "ambiguous," since it supposedly "equates annihilation with salvation." These words, like many others written by Adorno, lead to the obfuscation rather than the clarification of the text being interpreted. Zelinsky, *Wagner*, 20, turns this idea around, since he interprets the "conclusion of Judaism in Music . . . as a concealed autobiographical confession." By the Jews "going under" Wagner in reality meant self-annihilation. Hitler's invocation of Wagner must therefore have rested on a misunderstanding.

18. *Judentum*, 32. Correctly viewed by Schüler, *Bayreuther Kreis*, 234f., and Matter, *Wagner et Hitler*, 117–18.

19. On Bauer and Marx see Katz, *Prejudice to Destruction*, 165–74.

20. Ibid., 147–58.

21. Laube, *Gesammelte Werke* 24:131.

22. *Judentum*, 57.

23. Ibid., 32.

24. Thomas Mann, "Leiden und Grösse Richard Wagners," *Gesammelte Werke* (Frankfurt, 1974), 9:418.

25. *Tagebücher* 2:624. Zelinsky, *Musik-Konzepte*, 81, took up this expression, and others (such as Bacharach, "Richard Wagner," 224) followed him. Cf. L. J. Rather, *The Dream of Self-Destruction: Wagner's Ring and the Modern World* (Baton Rouge and London, 1979). Rather entered into the history of the idea of self-annihilation.

26. Mann, "Leiden und Grösse," 9:417.

27. Documented in Zelinsky, *Wagner*, 195–99.

28. Bernhard Diebold had already attempted such a rescue in 1928; see his *Der Fall Wagner: Eine Revision* (Frankfurt, 1928).

29. Mann, *Gesammelte Werke* 10:926, 797.

30. For details see Zelinsky, *Wagner*, and Matter, *Wagner et Hitler*.

31. I follow the report of Yehudah Cohen in his Hebrew article "Wagner, Despite All Else," in *Who Is Afraid*, ed. Kiva Litvin, 289–90.

32. Cohen (ibid.) represents the view of a music lover. Haim Ganz "Who Is Afraid of Richard Wagner?" (ibid., 297–319), as a moral philosopher, discusses the problem as a conflict between value systems.

# Additional Readings

Adorno, Theodor W. *Versuch über Wagner.* Frankfurt, 1952.

Becker, Heinz. "Giacomo Meyerbeer—On the Centenary of His Death." *Leo Baeck Institute Year Book* 9 (1964): 178–201.

Burbidge, Peter, and Richard Sutter, eds. *The Wagner Companion.* New York, 1979.

Diebold, Bernard. *Der Fall Wagner: eine Revision.* Frankfurt, 1928.

Du Moulin-Eckart, Richard. *Cosima Wagner.* 2 vols. Munich, 1929.

Field, Geoffrey G. *Evangelist of Race: The German Vision of Houston Stewart Chamberlain.* New York, 1981.

Gay, Peter. "Herman Levi: Study in Service and Self-Hatred." In *Freud, Jews and Other Germans,* 189–230. New York, 1978.

Glasenapp, Carl Fr. *Das Leben Richard Wagners in sechs Büchern.* Leipzig, 1905.

Gregor-Dellin, Martin. *Richard Wagner: Sein Werk, sein Jahrhundert.* Munich, 1980.

Gutman, Robert W. *Richard Wagner: The Man, His Mind and His Music.* New York, 1968.

Ingenchag-Goch, Dagmar. *Richard Wagners neu erfundener Mythos.* Bonn, 1982.

Katz, Jacob. "Berthold Auerbach's Anticipation of the German-Jewish Tragedy." *Hebrew Union College Annual* 53 (1982): 215–40.

———. *From Prejudice to Destruction: Anti-Semitism 1700–1933.* Cambridge, Mass., 1980.

———. *Out of the Ghetto: The Social Background of Jewish Emancipation.* Cambridge, Mass., 1973. Reprint. New York, 1975.

Liptzin, Solomon. *Germany's Stepchildren.* Cleveland and New York, 1961.

Mann, Thomas. "Leiden und Grösse Richard Wagners." *Gesammelte Werke,* vol. 9. Frankfurt, 1974.

Marx, Karl. "Zur Judenfrage." In *Frühschriften,* edited by Siegfried Landshut Stuttgart, 1953. English version, "On the Jewish Question," in *Karl Marx on Religion,* edited by Saul K. Padover, 169–92. New York, 1974.

Neumann, Angelo. *Erinnerungen an Richard Wagner.* Leipzig, 1907.

Newman, Ernest. *The Life of Richard Wagner.* 4 vols. New York, 1933–46.

Philippson, Johanna. "Constantin Frantz." *Leo Baeck Institute Year Book* 13 (1968): 101–19.

Rather, L. J. *The Dream of Self-Destruction: Wagner's Ring and the Modern World.* London, 1979.

Rose, Paul Lawrence. "The Noble Anti-Semitism of Richard Wagner." *Historical Journal* 25 (3) (1981): 751–63.

Schüler, Winfried. *Der Bayreuther Kreis von seiner Entstehung bis zum Ausgang der Wilthelminischen Ära.* Munich, 1971.

Stein, Leon. *The Racial Thinking of Richard Wagner.* New York, 1950.

Stern, Fritz. *The Politics of Cultural Despair.* Berkeley, 1961.

Wagner, Cosima. *Die Tagebücher.* Edited by Martin Gregor-Dellin and Dietrich Mach. 2 vols. Munich and Zurich, 1976. English translation, *Diaries.* New York, 1979.

Wagner, Richard. *Briefe, Die Sammlung Burrel.* Edited by John N. Burk. Frankfurt, 1953.

———. *Das Judentum in der Musik.* Leipzig, 1869.

———. *Gesammelte Schriften und Dichtungen.* 10 vols. Leipzig, 1883.

———. *Sämtliche Briefe.* 4 vols. Leipzig, 1979.

Zelinsky, Hartmut. *Richard Wagner—ein deutsches Thema.* Frankfurt, 1976.

# Index